Cleveland
Family
FUN

3RD EDITION

Jennifer
Stoffel

GRAY & COMPANY, PUBLISHERS
CLEVELAND

Gray & Company, Publishers
1588 E. 40th Street
Cleveland, Ohio 44103
www.grayco.com

Library of Congress Cataloging-in-Publication Data
Stoffel, Jennifer
Cleveland family fun guide / Jennifer Stoffel
3rd ed.
Previously published: Cleveland discovery guide. 1997.
Includes index.
1. Cleveland (Ohio) Guidebooks. 2. Family recreation—Ohio—Cleveland Guidebooks.
II. Stoffel, Jennifer Cleveland discovery guide. III. Title.
F499.C63 S77 1999
917.71'3204'43—dc21 99-6351 CIP

ISBN 1-886228-28-0

This guide was prepared on the basis of the author's best knowledge at the time of publication. However, because of constantly changing conditions beyond the author's control, the author disclaims any responsibility for the accuracy and completeness of the information in this guide. Users of this guide are cautioned not to place undue reliance upon the validity of the information contained herein and to use this guide at their own risk.

Printed in the United States of America

10 9 8 7 6 5 4 3 2 1

Contents

Acknowledgments

This book wouldn't have seen the light of day without help. Particular thanks to Adam Robinson, Helga Wowries, and Claudia Marchewka for their dogged research help and again to our son Alex, now age 9, for his enthusiastic assistance with reviewing.

Photo Credits

p.12 *clockwise from top left:* Casey Batule/Cleveland Metroparks; Western Reserve Historical Society; Hale Farm and Village; Casey Batule/Cleveland Metroparks; Stark County Historical Society; Casey Batule/Cleveland Metroparks
p.32 Geauga Lake
p.35 Cedar Point
p.38 Geauga Lake
p.40 I-X Center
p.44 SeaWorld Cleveland
p.47 Great Lakes Science Center
p.49 Century Village
p.50 Jonathan Wayne
p.51 Matthew Kocsis/Western Reserve Historical Society
p.55 Great Lakes Science Center
p.56 Western Reserve Historical Society
p.60 Bruce Ford/City of Akron
p.62 Jonathan Wayne
p.65 *left:* Stark County Historical Society; *right:* Merry-Go-Round Museum
p.69 Rainbow Children's Museum
p.76 Jonathan Wayne
p.77 Western Reserve Historical Society
p.78 Roger Mastroiani
p.79 Akron Zoo
p.81 Geauga Park District
p.84 Burnette's
p.85 Cuyahoga Valley National Recreation Area
p.89 Cleveland Botanical Garden
p.90 Cleveland Convention & Visitors Bureau
p.93 Cuyahoga Valley Scenic Railroad
p.97 Lake Metroparks
p.104 Lake Metroparks
p.105 Lake Metroparks
p.106 Casey Batule/Cleveland Metroparks
p.107 Carol Morrison/Holden Arboretum
p.108 Casey Batule/Cleveland Metroparks
p.111 Lake Farmpark
p.112 Lake Metroparks
p.116 Casey Batule/Cleveland Metroparks
p.118 Robert Bailie/Shaker Heights Regional Nature Center
p.119 Casey Batule/Cleveland Metroparks
p.120 Casey Batule/Cleveland Metroparks
p.123 Sandy Luther/Lake Metroparks
p.126 Cleveland Metroparks
p.127 Casey Batule/Cleveland Metroparks
p.132 Geauga Park District
p.136 Cleveland San Jose Ballet
p.137 Jane Turzillo/Akron Art Museum
p.142 Doug Cox/Cleveland Center for Contemporary Art
p.144 Cleveland Museum of Art
p.146 Cleveland Orchestra
p.147 Cleveland Play House
p.148 Cleveland San Jose Ballet
p.152 Fine Arts Association
p.163 Boston Mills/Brandywine
p.164 Boston Mills/Brandywine
p.174 Lakeland Community College
p.176 Mentor Recreation Department
p.178 Greater Cleveland Growth Association
p.179 Cleveland Metroparks
p.191 Cleveland Indians
p.193 Jonathan Wayne
p.194 Gregory Drezdzon/Cleveland Indians
p.195 Cleveland Rockers
p.198 Malley's Chocolates
p.202 Cleveland Convention & Visitors Bureau
p.206 *top:* Malley's Chocolates; *bottom:* Wetzler Photography
p.210 Jonathan Wayne
p.211 Trolley Tours of Cleveland
p.212 Roger Mastroiani
p.222 Cleveland Museum of Natural History
p.240 *clockwise from top left:* Cedar Point; Geauga Park District; Cleveland Convention & Visitors Bureau; Cleveland Indians; Cleveland Metroparks; Cleveland Orchestra

Introduction

Family Time, Cleveland-Style

Nothing is more fun than a successful family outing—one that parents and children alike can truly enjoy; one you all will remember fondly, talk about, and want to do over again.

Sound impossible?

It's not, really—especially here in Greater Cleveland. Because we're fortunate: this is a wonderful place for families.

Our community is paying more attention to the educational and recreational needs of children than ever before. A whole generation of interactive museums is dramatically changing the profile of our local institutions. "Please touch" hands-on exhibits are fast replacing the roped-off, glassed-in displays. And this trend isn't just limited to museums. Now, children's activities are being planned nearly everywhere, libraries are setting aside areas for noisy youngsters, and theaters are offering special children's series.

Cleveland boasts a history of well-established family favorites, too. Just five miles east of downtown, University Circle, the city's cultural heart, has been home to world-class museums, renowned performing arts groups, and eclectic galleries for decades. An "Emerald Necklace" of Metroparks and state parks surrounds the city with a wealth of green open spaces and plenty of opportunity for nature education and outdoor recreation. Many amusement parks—some big, some little, and all within easy reach—offer lively fun for a full range of ages. Historical sites and small museums scattered throughout the area provide quieter, more educational recreation. Sporting opportunities range from major league baseball, basketball, and soccer to instructional programs at civic recreation centers. A far-reaching system of libraries brings a convenient range of thoughtful family entertainment to every community.

In fact, Greater Cleveland offers so much for families that a lot of exploring is required to really know the area well. This is true even for natives—especially so when we become parents (we're suddenly challenged to discover the city all over again!). For newcomers and visitors to Cleveland, there's so much to discover that it can be hard even to decide where to start.

That is why this book exists. I've done the work of researching, collecting, and compiling information about all the best family recreation opportunities in Greater Cleveland—so you can concentrate on the most important part: having fun together.

Planning for Quality Time

Fun and learning can sometimes happen spontaneously. But you can't count on them being a part of your next outing unless you do a little planning ahead of time.

Find out about the place you will be visiting before you go. For example, does it mix hands-on and hands-off activities? What age children is it most appropriate for? Match its features with the needs and interests of your family members.

Discuss expectations with your children. Find out what subject they want to focus on. Will it be dinosaurs or Gothic armor? You may want to select one or two specific areas or exhibits for a visit—especially at larger attractions. (Even adults get overstimulated!)

Choose the right time, and the right amount of time. Avoid scheduling visits for the end of a hectic day of errands or sightseeing, or during naptimes or mealtimes. If you will be taking a long car ride, plan to let the kids blow off some steam after they arrive and before asking them to sit quietly at a performance or walk obediently through an exhibit.

Perhaps most importantly, plan activities appropriate to your kids. As experts and parents alike will attest, all kids—go younger ones most of all—do not like just to watch and sit. They like to move and do. This is not something you should fight. Experts point to hands-on activities as the best use of our children's time; that is how kids really learn.

One of the nicest things about exploring together as a family is that if the outing is set up right, your kids can make their own discoveries. It can be a relief to find that as a parent you don't have to be constantly involved. Where does this leave you? Your biggest role is setting up those opportunities for discovery. There are plenty of things that parents and children can do together—a bookful in fact!

How to Use this Book

When you need a good idea fast:
Section 1: Instant Adventures

Stir crazy? Stuck in a rut? When you and the kids need something to do and you need it *right now*, start here.

These sixteen pre-planned outings are full of easy adventure your family can find just about anytime. Treat them like recipes for fun. You can follow them exactly, doing each activity in order; or mix and match, doing one activity at a time and combining adventures from different recipes to make up your own brand of family fun.

How you use them is up to you. But rest assured that they have been parent-tested and kid-proven to take the worry and fuss out of your plans for the day.

When you want details, and lots of 'em
Section 2: The Directory

Here are the details you need to make good, *informed* decisions about where to spend your valuable family time together.

Each of the hundreds of family attractions in this book was very carefully researched. As a parent, I know that you can't get a lot of really important information about a place from the phone book, or from an advertisement or a newspaper listing.

How do you find out if they allow strollers? Or what time they open on Sunday mornings in summer. Or if they ever offer discounted admission. Or exactly how to get there. Or—most important—if your eight-year-old is likely to enjoy it.

These are the kinds of things *parents* want to know. So that's what I researched and what I have included in each listing in the Directory section.

When you're looking for something specific:
Section 3: Indexes
Indexes are arranged alphabetically, by geographic location, by specific activities offered, and by recommended age range.

Please remember: *Always call ahead!*

This book was current and accurate at the time it went to press. But information like this—especially prices, dates, and times—is always subject to change. Call before you go to double-check the information that is most important to you.

You might also call for special events, classes, and other programs offered on an irregular basis. (I've found that some programs are so popular, you need to call on the first day of registration just to get in.)

Phone numbers are provided for each entry. Most are general information numbers and some will connect you with recordings. If you get a recording, relax and take a deep breath—you'll usually be able to speak with a real live person if you need one.

Areas Covered in This Book:

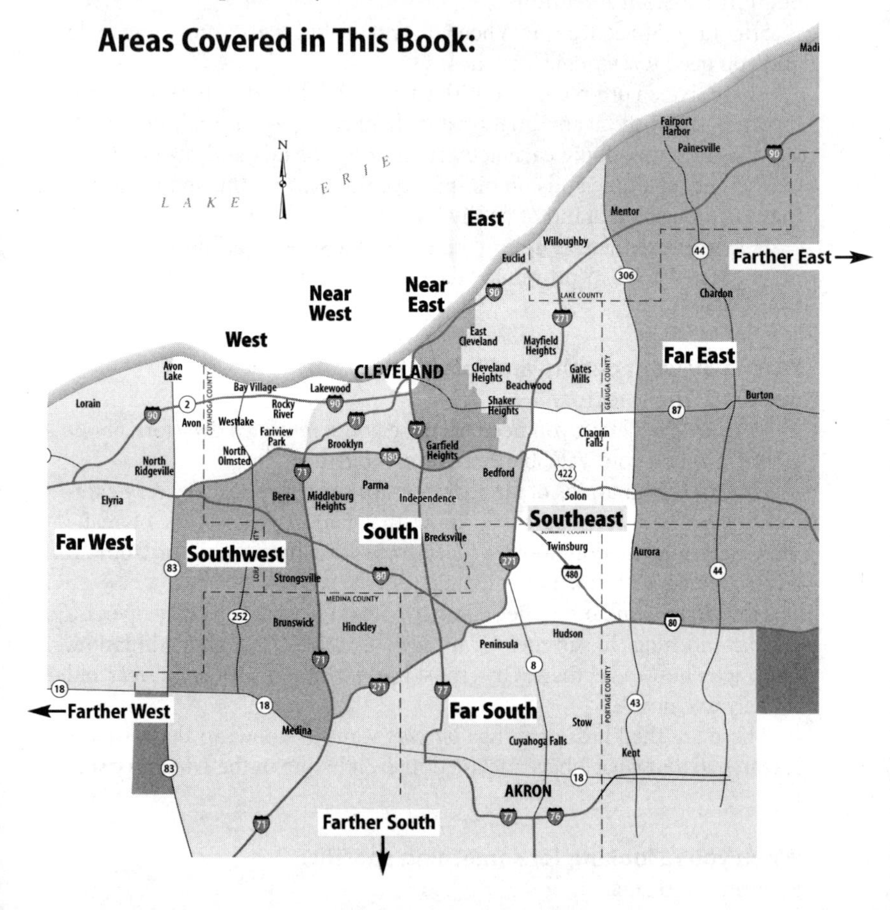

Cleveland
Family
FUN

Section 1

Instant Adventures: Just Add Kids!

Here are 16 pre-planned outings full of easy adventure your family can find just about anytime. Treat them like recipes for fun. You can follow them exactly, doing each activity in order; or mix and match, doing one activity at a time and combining adventures from different recipes to make up your own brand of family fun. How you use them is up to you. But rest assured that they have been parent-tested and kid-proven to take the worry and fuss out of your plans for the day.

The Adventures:

OUTING 1 Barnyard, Beach, and Beady Little Eyes

AREA: East • **AGES:** 1½–8 • **SETTING:** Outdoors • **SEASON:** Any
COST: Low–moderate • **TIME:** 2–7 hrs
DON'T FORGET: Camera, picnic, towels, beach gear, hiking shoes

LAKE FARMPARK (2–3 hours): What do your kids know about life on a farm? Here is your chance to introduce them to the chores and activities of rural life. There are baby chicks to hold, cows to milk (you'll probably have to do it, too), and a horse-drawn wagon ride that serves as a shuttle of sorts. Kirtland, (440) 256-2122. **SEE PAGE: 111**

While the restaurant at Lake Farmpark is great for snacks, it is a bit pricey and uninspired for lunch. A better plan would be to pack or pick up a lunch and head north to the beach.

HEADLANDS BEACH STATE PARK (2–3 hrs): Aside from being a perfect place for a picnic, this windswept, sandy beach (Ohio's largest) is popular for all of the water and nature-related activities on hand—naturalist programs are held all summer long, there are well-marked hiking trails, and chairs and umbrellas can be rented from the concessionaire (perfect for a mid-afternoon naptime). Mentor, (440) 352-8082. **SEE PAGE: 104**

Before you head home, if your troop has some energy left, stop by one more place.

CHILDREN'S SCHOOLHOUSE NATURE PARK (1–2 hrs): With snakes, lizards, and turtles, a Discovery Room filled with hands-on exhibits, and short, well-marked hiking trails outside, this is a perfect mini-zoo for young kids. Be sure to check out their special programming schedule; it is filled with nature activities for preschoolers and their families. Kirtland Hills, (440) 256-3800. **SEE PAGE: 88**

OUTING 2 Critters and Coasters

AREA: West • **AGES:** 1½–8 • **SETTING:** Mostly outdoors
SEASON: Any • **COST:** Low–moderate • **TIME:** 1–7 hrs
DON'T FORGET: Camera, picnic, towels, beach gear, hiking shoes

LAKE ERIE NATURE AND SCIENCE CENTER (1–2 hrs): Thanks to a dramatic renovation, all of the critters here have posh digs. There are deer, rabbits, and birds outside; turtles, snakes, and lizards inside. Most days young volunteers are walking around with a snake or turtle in their arms. (Be forewarned, the gift shop is really wonderful and hard to miss; luckily, there are small, inexpensive items.) Bay Village, (440) 871-2900. **SEE PAGE: 110**

While there are no food provisions at the LENSC, you need not go far for a picnic on the beach. Stop by a grocery store or restaurant for takeout and head to **HUNTINGTON RESERVATION** (2–3 hrs). There are tables and grills in the park above the beach (there's even a small snack bar, for drinks and such), but the attraction here is the expansive, natural sand beach. Bay Village, (216) 351-6300.
SEE PAGE: 108

To finish off the day, if your kids are on the younger side of this age range, there is the **MEMPHIS KIDDIE PARK** (1–2 hrs). I challenge you to find a better place to introduce the thrill ride to your toddler. Sure, it's a little hokey, and your older kids won't be caught dead on the rides here, but there is that perfect age when this place is magic. Brooklyn, (216) 941-5995. **SEE PAGE: 41**

If your kids are a bit older, add instead the **CLEVELAND METROPARKS ZOO AND RAINFOREST** (2–3 hrs). One of the best attractions here is the RainForest. It's complete with roaring waterfall, roaming animals, and free-flying birds—visitors are immersed in the habitat. Don't overlook the rest of the zoo—there is a lot to see and do. However, there is also a lot of ground to cover, and you will want to rent a stroller or wagon. Cleveland, (216) 661-7511. **SEE PAGE: 90**

OUTING 3 Play All Day

AREA: Far west • **AGES:** 1½–8 • **SETTING:** Indoors & out
SEASON: Any • **COST:** Low • **TIME:** 1–6 hrs
DON'T FORGET: Camera, picnic, towels, beach gear, hiking shoes

AVON LAKE PUBLIC LIBRARY (1–2 hrs): One of the nicest libraries around, this is a true community center, complete with live performances, lectures, and regularly scheduled programs for families. Drop in to play at Discovery Works, with its floor-to-ceiling bubble maker, small appliance take-apart area, and well-stocked dress-up clothes closet. Avon Lake, (440) 933-8128. **SEE PAGE: 213**

Never overlook an opportunity for an outdoor picnic and nap on the beach. There's a playground right on the sand at **LORAIN LAKEVIEW PARK** (1–2 hrs), as well as picnic tables and restrooms, but there's no concessionaire, so you need to stop for takeout or pack your own. Lorain, (440) 244-9000. **SEE PAGE: 113**

To complete your West Side day, stop by the **FRENCH CREEK NATURE CENTER** (1–2 hrs). Hands-on natural history displays, animals in their habitats, and short hikes combine to make this a regular stop for area families. Family programming and special exhibits are scheduled throughout the year; most require a small fee. Sheffield Village, (440) 949-5200. **SEE PAGE: 98**

OUTING 4 Blocks, Bones, and Botany

AREA: University Circle • **AGES:** 1½–8 • **SETTING:** Mostly indoors
SEASON: Any • **COST:** Moderate • **TIME:** 1–7 hrs
DON'T FORGET: Camera

RAINBOW CHILDREN'S MUSEUM AND TRW LEARNING CENTER (2-3 hrs): There is an age when this place is a parent's dream—you know what I mean. Everything is designed to be taken apart, rebuilt, and crawled over, under, and on. Warning: This is the same age that cannot walk by a gift shop, so come prepared either to buy something (and there is a lot to pick from) or practice your effective parenting skills. As this might very well end up being your whole outing, be sure to bring a book or a friend. Cleveland, (216) 791-KIDS. **SEE PAGE: 68**

If you can drag your kids away (or they're a bit on the older side), check out the **CLEVELAND MUSEUM OF NATURAL HISTORY** (2–3 hrs). With an impressive collection of dinosaur skeletons, elaborate dioramas, and planetarium shows and a super new interactive geology and astronomy display, this is clearly one of the city's finest spots for the young inquisitive mind. The Discovery Room downstairs is especially designed for the littlest visitors. Cleveland, (216) 231-4600. **SEE PAGE: 49**

Be sure to take a lunch break before adding the next two spots. There are a handful of places to eat right in the neighborhood, but there are many more just to the east in Little Italy.

When the weather is right, save some energy for the **CLEVELAND BOTANICAL GARDEN** (½–2 hrs). A very nice place for a stroll, this one-half acre children's garden may encourage your kids to develop a green thumb. Cleveland, (216) 721-1600. **SEE PAGE: 88**

Nearby and often overlooked is the **ROCKEFELLER PARK GREENHOUSE** (1–2 hrs). Completed in 1905 with funds from John D. Rockefeller, it includes a peace garden, Japanese Gardens, and indoor flower displays. Just a bit removed from the city, peaceful and serene, walks here are pleasant indeed. Cleveland, (216) 664-3103. **SEE PAGE: 125**

OUTING 5 History, Invention, and Exploration

AREA: South • **AGES:** 1½–8 yrs • **SETTING:** Indoors and out
SEASON: Any • **COST:** Moderate • **TIME:** 2–8 hrs
DON'T FORGET: Camera, picnic, hiking shoes

HALE FARM AND VILLAGE (2–3 hrs): This is a living history museum surrounded by the Cuyahoga Valley National Recreation Area. The setting, the live demonstrations, and the painstaking restorations make it a super family spot. The best times to visit—during special-event weekends—are also the busiest. (Of course, you can always find an open field for an impromptu naptime.) Bath, (330) 666-3711.
SEE PAGE: 55

If you'd rather be indoors, check out **INVENTURE PLACE** (2–3 hrs). There are so many hands-on exploration possibilities here that your kids could spend the day—science truly becomes fun—with magnets, lasers, and an inventor's workshop. (Bring a book for yourself and let them go for it.) Akron, (330) 762-4463. **SEE PAGE: 60**

Then, pack a picnic or grab some takeout and head to the **CUYAHOGA VALLEY NATIONAL RECREATION AREA** (2–3 hrs). As there are 52 square miles (that's 33,000 acres) of parkland to investigate, the Happy Days Visitor Center is a good place to start. With rangers on hand, as well as park publications, maps, and several trailheads and picnic shelters, the Center provides a great introduction to the CVNRA. Brecksville, Peninsula, Valley View, (800) 433-1986. **SEE PAGE: 92**

OUTING 6 Dinosaurs, Snakes, and a Ferris Wheel

AREA: Far south • **AGES:** 1½–8 • **SETTING:** Indoors and out
SEASON: Adaptable for any • **COST:** Moderate • **TIME:** 1–7 hrs
DON'T FORGET: Camera, picnic, hiking shoes

MCKINLEY MUSEUM (1–2 hrs): To get the car-ride kinks out, head up the towering National Memorial first; then make a beeline inside the museum to the basement for the hands-on Discovery Room with its pond life, earth station, and requisite dinosaurs. This hands-on science spot was the first to raise the level of interactivity in the area; it still ranks high for creativity. Canton, (330) 455-7043. **SEE PAGE: 64**

After dragging your kids away from the McKinley, consider stopping for some takeout and picnicking at **SIPPO LAKE PARK** (2–3 hrs). The small lake is surrounded by 278 acres with trails, a nature center, several picnic areas, a playground, and a marina. Check out the Sanders Center of Outdoor Education nature center, home to nature exhibits, including a reptarium. Massillon, (330) 477-0448.
SEE PAGE: 130

If you're napped up and still have some energy, there's a small kiddie park that'll make you feel more than a little bit nostalgic. At **TUSCORA PARK** (1-2 hrs), there is a train ride, small roller coaster, and Ferris wheel tucked in a park in the center of town. Open until 9:30 p.m. in the summer only, it's a pleasant way to end a day. New Philadelphia, (330) 343-4644. **SEE PAGE: 45**

OUTING 7 Big Lawn, Big Hill, Big Lake

AREA: East • **AGES:** 5–12 • **SETTING:** Mostly outdoors
SEASON: Adaptable for any • **COST:** Moderate to high • **TIME:** 1–8 hrs
DON'T FORGET: Snow gear or beach gear, depending on the season

LAWNFIELD, JAMES A. GARFIELD NATIONAL HISTORIC SITE (1–2 hrs) After a top-to-bottom restoration, this period home of the former president provides a great lesson in early American history. Considered the Republicans' best orator, Garfield conducted his (pre-TV) campaign for the presidency from this very front porch. Mentor, (440) 255-8722. **SEE PAGE: 62**

After the history lesson, how about blowing off some steam? Head south to **ALPINE VALLEY** (3–4 hrs) where beginners can try out their ski or snowboard legs on the small and easily accessible slopes. Group or private lessons (with equipment rental) are scheduled throughout the day; its location in prime snowbelt country guarantees at minimum several weeks of wintry days. Chesterland, (440) 285-2211.
SEE PAGE: 163

You can easily end up skiing into the evening hours or, if there's no snow, check out instead the nearby **FAIRPORT MARINE MUSEUM** (1 hour). Head here for a great view of Lake Erie and the harbor area and enough nautical equipment to launch a successful (if pretend) sea voyage. Fairport Harbor, (440) 354-4825. **SEE PAGE: 53**

A good way to end the day is a sunset beach picnic, and you don't have to venture far. The **FAIRPORT HARBOR LAKEFRONT PARK** (2–3 hrs) is spread over 20 acres with grills and sheltered picnic areas and a large playground. All sorts of game equipment (Frisbees, balls, horseshoes) is available for rental from the concessionaire. Fairport Harbor, (440) 639-9972. **SEE PAGE: 97**

OUTING 8 Skyscraper, Science, and Submarine

AREA: Downtown • **AGES:** 5–12 • **SETTING:** Mostly indoors
SEASON: Any • **COST:** Low to moderate • **TIME:** 1–7 hrs
DON'T FORGET: Camera

INSTANT ADVENTURES

TERMINAL TOWER (½ hr.): For a super, 360-degree view of the city's downtown and surrounding area, check out the observation deck on the 42nd floor. (NOTE: HOURS CHANGE SEASONALLY.) Cleveland, (216) 621-7981. **SEE PAGE: 209**

GREAT LAKES SCIENCE CENTER (2–3 hrs): With over 300 interactive exhibits, this place was designed to give families a place to safely explore how things work, and it succeeds—to a point. Kids have fun playing around with the gadgets, but it's hard to figure what they're actually learning. The OMNIMAX theater presentations are very cool. Cleveland, (216) 694-2000. **SEE PAGE: 54**

For lunch, head just across the Cuyahoga River to the **WEST SIDE MARKET** (1–2 hrs). Packed with vendors, this marketplace, a designated National Historic Landmark, provides a great introduction to the foods of the world. Inside, there is a delicious and exotic assortment of baked goods, cheeses, and meats; outside, fresh vegetables and fruits reign. (NOTE: It is only open Mon, Wed, Fri, and Sat.) Cleveland, (216) 664-3386. **SEE PAGE: 211**

Still have some energy? Then visit the **USS COD SUBMARINE** (1–2 hrs): The only surviving sub in original World War II condition, this landmark allows the nimble to climb ladders and squeeze through the hatches just as a crew of seamen had to over 50 years ago. Closed in the winter. Cleveland, (216) 566-8770. **SEE PAGE: 75**

OUTING 9 Ohio Heritage on Water and on Foot

AREA: Far south • **AGES:** 5–12 • **SETTING:** Mostly outdoors
SEASON: Spring to Fall • **COST:** Moderate • **TIME:** 4–7 hrs
DON'T FORGET: Camera, beach gear, hiking shoes

CANAL FULTON (2 hrs): This lazy, horse-drawn ride up one of the few remaining sections of the Ohio and Erie Canal provides a great look into our area's history. It's not just in the telling; the pace and setting bring an era back to life. Closed in winter. Canal Fulton, (330) 854-3808.
SEE PAGE: 71

SCHOENBRUNN VILLAGE (1 hr): This reconstructed village is run by the Ohio Historical Society. The walking tour here includes 17 log buildings, gardens, a cemetery, and a museum and visitors' center. The best time to visit is during a special-event weekend, especially the annual children's day in June. Closed in winter. New Philadelphia, (330) 339-3636.
SEE PAGE: 72

For a little more action, check out **ATWOOD LAKE PARK** (1–3 hrs). With a swimming beach, boat rentals, and hiking trails as well as a golf course, tennis courts, and playground, your family could easily spend an entire day here. Mineral City, (330) 343-6780. **SEE PAGE: 80**

OUTING 10 A Walk In the Woods, a Ride down the River

AREA: East • **AGES:** 8–15 • **SETTING:** Outdoors
SEASON: Adaptable to any • **COST:** Low to moderate • **TIME:** 2–8 hrs
DON'T FORGET: Camera, Hiking Shoes, Picnic

It's easy at this age to let everybody go in different directions. Still, a family ritual of adventuring can be a great way to keep the lines of communication open. Sometimes it's just a matter of time and opportunity.

HOLDEN ARBORETUM (2–3 hrs): Spread over 3,100 acres, Holden is the largest private arboretum in the country. This place, although large, is very accessible: Well-marked trails, activity kits, and super programs make it so. Head first to the Visitor's Center for maps, trail guides, and a rest stop. Kirtland, (440) 256-1110. **SEE PAGE: 107**

If a bit of adventure and solitude is more your speed, check out the **CAMP HI CANOE LIVERY** (3–4 hrs) and spend a day on the upper reaches of the Cuyahoga River. Be sure to bring your food, there's not much around. Hiram, (330) 569-7621. **SEE PAGE: 166**

Or, if you're looking for something more extreme, check out the trails at the **NORTH CHAGRIN RESERVATION** (2–3 hrs). Bring your own in-line skates, or rent some and take on the smooth, all-purpose trails that wind their way through the park. While you're here, check out the Nature Center and Squire's Castle. Mayfield Village, (440) 473-3370. **SEE PAGE: 119**

OUTING 11 Culture and Caverns

AREA: West • **AGES:** 8–15 • **SETTING:** Indoors and out
SEASON: Adaptable to any • **COST:** Low to moderate • **TIME:** 1–7 hrs
DON'T FORGET: Camera, Picnic, Hiking Shoes, Jacket, Beach Gear

ALLEN MEMORIAL ART MUSEUM (1–2 hrs): Containing one of the finest campus art collections in the country, this institution also maintains a high community profile with family days and community days scheduled throughout the year. Oberlin, (440) 775-8665. **SEE PAGE: 138**

If the day is right, head outside to **FINDLEY STATE PARK** (2–3 hrs). A popular spot for fishing and boating, there are boats to rent and bait to buy (bring your own tackle equipment, however) and, supposedly, fish to catch. Originally a state forest, the 10 miles of trails here are heavily wooded. Wellington, (440) 647-4490. **SEE PAGE: 97**

Or head underground. A tour of **SENECA CAVERNS** (1–2 hrs) will take you below ground to see the crystal-clear underground river at this registered state natural landmark. The hike through the cave lasts about an hour. (Even in summer, the temperature is typically in the mid–50s—bring a jacket.) Bellevue, (419) 483-6711. **SEE PAGE: 129**

OUTING 12 Around the Circle

AREA: University Circle • **AGES:** 9–15 • **SETTING:** Mostly indoors
SEASON: Any • **COST:** Moderate to high • **TIME:** 1–6 hrs
DON'T FORGET: Camera

INSTANT ADVENTURES

One of the great things about living in or near Cleveland is the wealth of cultural offerings. Try a day of art and see how your family differs in their taste and ideas.

Start at the **CLEVELAND MUSEUM OF ART** (2–3 hrs). Filled with treasures, the galleries here house one of the finest collections of art in the country. To make it more accessible for families, a wide variety of special programs are offered—most of them free. Be sure to drop in at the cafeteria for a snack and some people-watching. Cleveland, (216) 421-7340. **SEE PAGE: 144**

Several blocks west, the **CLEVELAND CENTER FOR CONTEMPORARY ART** (1–2 hrs) offers Clevelanders a chance to see some of the most modern and often controversial artists. With their schedule of changing exhibits, each trip is a chance to see something different. Guaranteed to start a conversation. Cleveland, (216) 421-8671. **SEE PAGE: 142**

For some outdoor art, head up Murray Hill to the **LAKE VIEW CEMETERY** (1–2 hrs). The highlight: the towering Garfield Monument with one of the area's best views—Lake Erie and the downtown skyline. As a 285-acre arboretum, the grounds are very pleasant indeed, and the statues and monuments to Cleveland's famous can prompt a good deal of discussion. Cleveland, (216) 421-2665. **SEE PAGE: 61**

For lunch or dinner, try one of the many restaurants in nearby Little Italy or on Coventry Rd.

OUTING 13 Downtown's Big Draws

AREA: Downtown • **AGES:** 9–15 • **SETTING:** Indoors
SEASON: Any • **COST:** Moderate to high • **TIME:** 1–6 hrs
DON'T FORGET: Camera

INSTANT ADVENTURES

FEDERAL RESERVE BANK OF CLEVELAND (½ hr) After several years and millions spent, everyone should at least step inside this National Historic Building and take a look at the marble lobby and gilded decorations. Cleveland, (216) 579-2125. **SEE PAGE: 201**

Even non–history buffs should also step inside the **OLD STONE CHURCH** (½ hr) for its stunning stained-glass windows, vaulted ceiling, and frescoed walls. Cleveland, (216) 241-6145. **SEE PAGE: 206**

Then, before heading to the next attraction, stop for lunch—there are plenty of choices in Tower City and the Galleria or, for more local history, check out the Old Arcade on Superior.

You'll either love or hate the **ROCK AND ROLL HALL OF FAME AND MUSEUM** (1–3 hrs). But there is no question that for many, the near-constant barrage of video-screen images and high-decibel music is mesmerizing; some folks don't think a whole day is long enough to see everything in this homage to rock and its roots. (For us, an hour or two at a time is plenty.) The videos are well made, if dizzying; the cafe a great spot to people-watch. A good way to go through: Your group can split up and plan to meet back here for a snack before taking on the domed Hall of Fame video exhibit together. Cleveland, (216) 781-7625. **SEE PAGE: 69**

OUTING 14 Art and Action

AREA: South • **AGES:** 9–15 • **SETTING:** Mostly outdoors
SEASON: Adaptable for any • **COST:** Low to moderate • **TIME:** 1–6 hrs
DON'T FORGET: Camera, snow gear or beach gear (seasonal), hiking shoes

AKRON ART MUSEUM (1–2 hrs): Although small, this museum consistently lines up first-class exhibits, and their hands-on arts-with-the-artists programming for kids on the weekends is super. Akron, (330) 376-9185. **SEE PAGE: 137**

There needn't be snow on the ground, but if the temperature is cold enough, take on the challenge of the **CLEVELAND METROPARKS TOBAGGAN RUN** at Mill Stream Run Reservation (2–3 hrs). The 1,000-foot, refrigerated ice chutes offer a high-speed, physically jarring and thrilling ride (you must be 42 inches tall); the hike up the stairs can be very chilling indeed. Strongsville, (440) 572-9990.
SEE PAGE: 115

In warmer weather, check out **CLEVELAND METROPARKS HINCKLEY RESERVATION** (2–4 hrs). Pack a picnic, bring along your in-line skates (or rent them), and plan to spend the rest of the day here—the all-purpose trails are perfect for skating. Not to worry, though, if you're not a skater, there's swimming in Hinckley Lake and boats are available for rental. Hinckley, (216) 351-6300. **SEE PAGE: 106**

OUTING 15 Rubber, Pigskin, and Fiberglass

AREA: Far south • **AGES:** 8–15 • **SETTING:** Indoors and out
SEASON: Adaptable to any • **COST:** Moderate • **TIME:** 1–7 hrs
DON'T FORGET: Camera, winter gear (in season), hiking shoes

Here's an opportunity to begin a day with odd trivia at the **GOODYEAR WORLD OF RUBBER** (1–2 hrs). Where else but in Akron would there be a museum dedicated to the discovery and development of rubber manufacturing? This is one place where you can be sure to learn something—however, we can't guarantee that you'll be able apply it to anything. Akron, (330) 796-7117. **SEE PAGE: 203**

PROFESSIONAL FOOTBALL HALL OF FAME (1–2 hrs): Lay to rest any doubt that our area has deep ties to and sentiment for football. Stocked with plenty of fan-rousing videos, this place succeeds in honoring the greatest players of the gridiron. (It is also one of the state's busiest attractions, so be prepared for a crowd.) Canton, (330) 456-8207. **SEE PAGE: 68**

BOSTON MILLS/BRANDYWINE (3–4 hrs): With plenty of wintry weather and snowmaking machines to help out, the slopes here could turn into your family's seasonal hangout. Sign up for a group snowboarding lesson and be prepared to spend a lot of time face down! Peninsula, (330) 467-2242. **SEE PAGE: 164**

If snow is not in the forecast, check out the **WILDERNESS CENTER** (2-3 hrs). Start at the headquarters building for trail maps and then set out on one of the six trails. There are small lakes, marshland, and forests to tromp through as well as a nature center and small planetarium (call ahead for a schedule of shows). Wilmot, (330) 359-5235. **SEE PAGE: 135**

OUTING 16 A Great Lake and a Famous Inventor

AREA: Far west • **AGES:** All • **SETTING:** Mostly outdoors
SEASON: Any • **COST:** Moderate to high • **TIME:** 1–8 hrs
DON'T FORGET: Camera, beach gear, comfortable shoes

INLAND SEAS MARITIME MUSEUM (1 hour): Models of Great Lakes vessels, a scale model of the ill-fated *Edmund Fitzgerald*, and a fully equipped freighter pilothouse overlooking the lake make this a great place for Great Lakes history. Vermilion, (440) 967-3467. **SEE PAGE: 59**

EDISON'S BIRTHPLACE (1–2 hrs): Depending on your level of interest in inventors and inventions, this short tour and small homestead may provide that needed spark. This small town has made quite a name for itself as the birthplace of Thomas Edison. (Did you know he held more than 1,000 patents?) Milan, (419) 499-2135. **SEE PAGE: 52**

MARBLEHEAD LIGHTHOUSE STATE PARK (1–2 hrs): Ohio's newest (and 73rd) state park honors the role of this historic lighthouse as protector of early Lake Erie boaters. This is your chance to see in person the lighthouse that has been commemorated on postage stamps and license plates. Marblehead, (419) 798-9777. **SEE PAGE: 64**

Head out on the lake via ferry to **PERRY'S MONUMENT** (1 hr, plus boat travel time). In a town put on the map for boaters and party-goers, this towering memorial offers visitors of all ages a superb view (as much as 10 miles) across Lake Erie, as well as the history of the War of 1812. Be forewarned, younger kids will have trouble with the climb. Put-in-Bay, (419) 285-2184. **SEE PAGE: 67**

There are plenty of places to choose from if you want to stay on the island for dinner—just keep your ferry schedule handy.

Key to Directory Listings

Age Rating is an estimate based on four things: age-appropriate activities, crowds, environment, and price.

★★★ = ideal for that age range
★★ = good for that age range
★ = okay for that age range
NR = not recommended for that age range

Cost is rated on a per-person basis:
$ = under $6
$$ = under $12
$$$ = over $12
FREE Some attractions are free only at certain times or for certain ages; If it does read "free" in the Cost section, the whole family can visit for free at one time or another.

Discovery Zone

AGES:	1½–3	3–5	5–8	8–12	12–15
RATING:	★	★★	★★	★	NR

COST: **$–$$** PREP.: **None–Some**
AREA: **South** CITY: **Akron**

ADDRESS: 1952 Bucholzer Blvd.

PHONE: (330) 630-0133

SEASON: Year round

HOURS: Mon–Thu 11 a.m.–8 p.m., Fri–Sat 10 a.m.–9 p.m., Sun 11 a.m.–7 p.m.

PRICES: 3–12 years old: $4.99; 1–2 $3.99; under 1 year old free w/ paying child

DIRECT.: SR 8 to Howe Ave.; east on Howe; right on Bucholzer Blvd.

✓ Strollers ✓ Groups ✓ Food Nearby
✓ Diap Chg Picnic ✓ Pub. Trans.
✓ Parking ✓ Food Serv. ✓ Handicapped

Discovery Zone has figured out how to bring the popular "Chutes and Ladders" game to life: kids playing pirate scale hanging nets; cylindrical slides hasten transport from high vantage points back to earth. Expect some chaos—the shrieks never stop in the main play area.

Preparation. Can we just pick up and go, or do we need reservations?

None = Just check the season and hours of operation and you're on your way!

Some = Could mean ordering tickets a day in advance or planning to arrive at a specific time to see a particular attraction.

Much = You'll need to make arrangements well in advance, like registering for a class, or getting tickets to a popular show.

Area and City. I divided Greater Cleveland into sections to make it easier to describe what part of town an attraction is located in. (See the map on page 10.)

Checklist. Dark text with a check mark means, Yes, they have it. Gray text means, No, they don't.

Directions start from the nearest major highway and use main roads to make getting there easier. They're based on the most current maps, but you should still call ahead to confirm, especially for those long drives and trips to unfamiliar places. Travel conditions, road closings, construction detours, and even street names are always subject to change. If you're not absolutely sure where you're going, call ahead!

Section 2

The Directory

Want details? Here they are. The listing tracks 25 separate bits of useful information for each attraction and describes the most important family-friendly features you'll find when you go.

The Directory is organized by type of activity. Like to romp around out in the fresh air? Flip through the Nature and Outdoors section. Enjoy introducing your kids to the fine arts? Sample the Art, Music, Theater, and Dance section. Into thrills? Look at Fun and Games. Like learning about gadgets or re-living the past? Try History, Science, and Technology.

You'll also be directed to specific pages in this section by the Instant Adventures and the indexes.

Fun & Games

Theme parks recognize that parents with younger children are important customers. In recent years, offerings for kids have been expanded and improved to include easier access, better prices and, simply, more to do. Bear Country at Cedar Point is delightful. The sand, sun, and swimming at Turtle Beach in Geauga Lake are just the right combination for youngsters. And the slides and rope climbing at Sea World's Happy Harbor can easily occupy a whole day's visit. Discovery Zone adds a convenient indoor option.

These are not places you want to visit without some preparation, though. Crowds can be daunting, and the day can become quite expensive. But take heart, use the following lists, and access information to help plan, and enjoy.

To give you the widest choice of amusements, these listings include both the large, well-recognized theme parks and the smaller, neighborhood family fun centers.

American Funland

AGES:	1½–3	3–5	5–8	8–12	12–15
RATING:	NR	★	★★	★★	★★

COST: **$$** PREP.: **None**
AREA: **Near West** CITY: **Lakewood**

ADDRESS: 12201 Berea Rd.

PHONE: (216) 476-8300

SEASON: Seasonal (Mar–Oct depending on weather, please call ahead.)

HOURS: Vary by season, please call ahead

PRICES: Vary

DIRECT.: I-90 to Exit 166 for W. 117 St.; north on W. 117; left (west) on Berea Rd.; on left.

Strollers | ✓ Groups | ✓ Food Nearby
Diap Chg | ✓ Picnic | ✓ Pub. Trans.
✓ Parking | ✓ Food Serv. | Handicapped

Primarily an outdoor spot popular for its batting cages and minigolf, this neighborhood funland also boasts a pretty extensive indoor arcade. With ice cream and hot dogs and a shaded picnic area, it is also a good place for an active birthday party.

Brookpark Fun and Games Emporium

AGES:	1½–3	3–5	5–8	8–12	12–15
RATING:	★★	★★	★★	★★	★

COST: **$–$$$** PREP.: **None**
AREA: **West** CITY: **Cleveland**

ADDRESS: 6770 Brookpark Rd.

PHONE: (216) 351-1910

SEASON: Seasonal (Spring–Fall)

HOURS: Mon–Thu 11 a.m.–10 p.m., Fri–Sat 11 a.m.–11 p.m., Sun noon–10 p.m.

PRICES: Group rates available; go-carts: $4 for 5 min.; batting cages: $5 for 7 tokens

DIRECT.: I-480 to Exit 15 for Ridge Rd.; south on Ridge; left (east) on Brookpark Rd.; on left.

✓ Strollers | ✓ Groups | ✓ Food Nearby
✓ Diap Chg | ✓ Picnic | ✓ Pub. Trans.
✓ Parking | ✓ Food Serv. | ✓ Handicapped

Two 18-hole miniature golf courses, go-carts, and batting cages are the draw at this area fun center. Several different birthday-party group-event packages are available.

Buzzard Cove

AGES:	1½–3	3–5	5–8	8–12	12–15
RATING:	NR	★	★★	★★	★★

COST: **$–$$$** PREP.: **None**
AREA: **South** CITY: **Hinckley**

ADDRESS: 1053 Bellus Rd.

PHONE: (330) 278-2384

SEASON: Seasonal (Apr–Oct; advance notice for group picnics required)

HOURS: Daily 7 a.m.–11 p.m.

PRICES: Vary; after 5 p.m. adults $4.95, teens $3.95

DIRECT.: I-71 to Exit 226 for SR 303 (Center Rd.); east on Center; right (south) on SR 606 (Hinckley Hills Rd.); left (east) on Bellus Rd.; on right.

Strollers	✓ Groups	✓ Food Nearby
Diap Chg	✓ Picnic	✓ Pub. Trans.
✓ Parking	✓ Food Serv.	✓ Handicapped

This family funland is equipped with miniature golf and a video-game arcade. In addition to the two 18-hole miniature golf courses, there is a lighted driving range with covered tees. Golf instruction is available. Adjacent is Hinckley Lake, with picnic pavilions, boating, swimming, and fishing. The *Hinckley Queen* lake boat is available for rides.

During the month of October, Buzzard Cove features a 100-year-old Haunted Barn (a covered waiting area is provided for any not-so-nice fall weather).

TIPS FOR TRIPS

SOUVENIRS

Most places these days have a well-stocked gift shop. Decide in advance how you're going to deal with your kids' impulse to buy and let them know the policy before you even go in.

Cedar Point

AGES:	1½–3	3–5	5–8	8–12	12–15
RATING:	NR	★	★★	★★★	★★★

COST: **$$$** PREP.: **None–Some**
AREA: **Farther West** CITY: **Sandusky**

ADDRESS: SR 2 (One Causeway Dr.)

PHONE: (419) 627-2350; (419) 626-0830

SEASON: Seasonal (May–Oct)

HOURS: Vary throughout season, open generally 9 a.m.–10 p.m.; gates open one hour before rides begin

PRICES: Varied prices for different ages and dates, multi-day passes, and combination packages. Separate admission for Soak City and Challenge Park (Cedar Point admission not required). Fee for parking.

DIRECT.: I-80 to Exit 118; north on US 250; right (east) on Perkins Ave,; left (north) on Remington Ave.; left (west) on US 6 (Cleveland Rd.); right (north) on Cedar Point Causeway
Or, SR 2 to Rye Beach Rd.; north on Rye Beach; left (west) on US 6 (Cleveland Rd.); right (north) on Cedar Point Causeway.

WEB: www.cedarpoint.com

✓ Strollers	✓ Groups	✓ Food Nearby
✓ Diap Chg	✓ Picnic	✓ Pub. Trans.
✓ Parking	✓ Food Serv.	✓ Handicapped

You name it, Cedar Point has it: water rides, live shows, merry-go-rounds. A new multimillion-dollar ride seems to be added each season to the more than 60 other rides, which make up the largest collection of roller coasters in the country. One of the state's most popular tourist attractions, this place can be a madhouse during July and August. If you don't like crowds, go early or late in the season.

To ride the real thrillers you must be at least 48 inches tall, but there is an area with rides for younger visitors located off the main drag. For the youngest riders (toddlers and preschoolers) there is Bear Country. Based on the Berenstain Bears stories, it is a first-rate playground complete with shady trees, piped-in music by

Fun & Games DIRECTORY

Raffi, and child-scale buildings in which to run and hide. There are also plenty of benches for parents. Kiddie Kingdom is another popular destination for the youngest children. Camp Snoopy, aimed at youngsters with their parents, will open in May of 1999 with a new coaster and seven other new rides.

Given the size of Cedar Point (it covers 364 acres) and the large crowds, you will have a better trip if on entering the park you take the time to plan what you most want to do and see. Better yet, call ahead for a map and visitor's information packet. A drawback that cannot be avoided at peak season is the lines—the most popular roller coasters can require more than an hour's wait!

There is more to Cedar Point than rides (a sandy Lake Erie beach, for example), and if you want to stay more than a day there are hotels and a campground on the premises. Next door to Cedar Point is the separate (costs extra) Challenge Park, home to Soak City water park, miniature golf, and a raceway.

Cedar Point

Conneaut Lake Park

AGES:	1½–3	3–5	5–8	8–12	12–15
RATING:	★	★★	★★★	★★	★★

COST: **$$–$$$** PREP.: **None**
AREA: **Farther East** CITY: **Conneaut Lake, PA**

ADDRESS: 12382 Center St. (SR 618)

PHONE: Hotel Conneaut: (814) 382-5115

SEASON: Seasonal (Memorial Day–Labor Day)

HOURS: Mon–Fri noon–9 p.m., Sat–Sun noon–10 p.m.; water park: noon–7 p.m.

PRICES: $14.95

DIRECT.: I-90 to Exit 235 for SR 193; south on SR 193; left (east) on SR 167; right (south) on SR 7; left (east) on US 6; left (north) on SR 618; on right.

✓ Strollers	✓ Groups	✓ Food Nearby
✓ Diap Chg	✓ Picnic	Pub. Trans.
✓ Parking	✓ Food Serv.	✓ Handicapped

It looks like an old-time park because it is one—with all the typical rides: merry-go-round, dodgems, inner-tube ride, Tilt-a-Whirl. The Blue Streak, a small wooden roller coaster, is meaner than it looks. There is also a water slide.

On the waterfront (this small amusement park is just one of several attractions surrounding Conneaut Lake, Pennsylvania's largest natural lake) there are motorboat and pontoon boat rentals, and there is a playground area on the beach. Other activities available nearby include swimming, boating, golf, and sternwheeler sightseeing cruises on the lake. (Conneaut Lake is also one of the only lakes in the area with no limit on horsepower, making it very popular with speedboaters and water-skiers.)

Annual events draw crowds. The biggest are fishing tournaments, music festivals, a frog-jumping contest, and, for winter visitors, a snowball festival.

Discovery Zone, Akron

AGES:	1½–3	3–5	5–8	8–12	12–15
RATING:	★	★★	★★	★	NR

COST: **$–$$** PREP.: **None–Some**
AREA: **Far South** CITY: **Akron**

ADDRESS: 1952 Bucholzer Blvd.

PHONE: (330) 630-0133

SEASON: Year round

HOURS: Mon–Thu 11 a.m.–8 p.m., Fri–Sat 10 a.m.–9 p.m., Sun 11 a.m.–7 p.m.

PRICES: 3–12 years old: $4.99; 1–2 $3.99; under 1 year old free w/ paying child

DIRECT.: SR 8 to Howe Ave.; east on Howe; right on Bucholzer Blvd.

✓ Strollers ✓ Groups ✓ Food Nearby
✓ Diap Chg Picnic ✓ Pub. Trans.
✓ Parking ✓ Food Serv. ✓ Handicapped

Discovery Zone has figured out how to bring the popular "Chutes and Ladders" game to life: kids playing pirate scale hanging nets; cylindrical slides hasten transport from high vantage points back to earth. Expect some chaos—the shrieks never stop in the main play area.

With 30 separate areas, each offering several activities, there is plenty to do here.

Each location has a Micro Zone, geared to toddlers, with mini-slides and crawl-in coves. A quiet area is set aside upstairs for parents who need to feed babies or just catch their breath. (There is no way, however, to escape the smell of dirty socks.)

Several Kid Coaches patrol all areas to make sure the playing is safe. The "adults play free" policy also helps ensure safety—a parent's presence seems to prevent total anarchy.

Discovery Zone occasionally schedules arts-and-crafts classes and scavenger hunts; they also do birthday parties by special arrangement.

Discovery Zone, Mayfield Hts.

AGES:	1½–3	3–5	5–8	8–12	12–15
RATING:	★	★★	★★	★	NR

COST: **$–$$** PREP.: **None–Some**
AREA: **East** CITY: **Mayfield Hts.**

ADDRESS: 6420 Mayfield Rd.

PHONE: (440) 461-8887

SEASON: Year round

HOURS: Mon–Thu 11 a.m.–8 p.m.; Fri, Sat 10 a.m.–9 p.m.; Sun 11 a.m.–7 p.m.

PRICES: Under 38 in.: $3.99; over 38 in.: $4.99; under 1 year old free

DIRECT.: I-271 to Exit 34 for US 322 (Mayfield Rd.); west on Mayfield; on left in Golden Gate Shopping Center.

✓ Strollers ✓ Groups ✓ Food Nearby
✓ Diap Chg Picnic ✓ Pub. Trans.
✓ Parking ✓ Food Serv. ✓ Handicapped

(See listing for Discovery Zone, Akron.)

Discovery Zone, Parma

AGES:	1½–3	3–5	5–8	8–12	12–15
RATING:	★	★★	★★	★	NR

COST: **$–$$** PREP.: **None**
AREA: **South** CITY: **Parma**

ADDRESS: 7601 West Ridgewood Dr.

PHONE: (440) 842-3866

SEASON: Year round

HOURS: Mon–Thu 11 a.m.–8 p.m., Fri & Sat 10 a.m.–9 p.m., Sun 11 a.m.–7 p.m.

PRICES: Under 38 inches: $3.99; over 38 inches: $4.99; under 1 year old & adults free

DIRECT.: I-480 to Exit 15 for SR 3 (Ridge Rd.); south on Ridge; right (west) on W. Ridgewood Dr.; on left.

✓ Strollers ✓ Groups ✓ Food Nearby
✓ Diap Chg Picnic ✓ Pub. Trans.
✓ Parking ✓ Food Serv. ✓ Handicapped

(See listing for Discovery Zone, Akron.)

Dover Lake Water Park

AGES:	1½–3	3–5	5–8	8–12	12–15
RATING:	★	★★	★★★	★★★	★★★

COST: **$$** PREP.: **None**
AREA: **South** CITY: **Sagamore Hills**

ADDRESS: 1150 West Highland Rd.

PHONE: 330-467-SWIM, 1-800-372-SWIM

SEASON: Seasonal (June 11–Labor Day)

HOURS: 10 a.m.–8 p.m.

PRICES: $11.95/person weekends, $8.95/person weekdays, free for children 40 in. & under, group rates available

DIRECT.: West: I-77 to Exit 149 for SR 82 (Royalton Rd.); east on Royalton; right (south) on Riverview Rd.; left (east) on Vaughn Rd.; Vaughn becomes W. Highland Rd.; on right.

East: I-271 to Exit 19 for SR 82 (Aurora Rd.); west on Aurora; left (south) on Boyden Rd.; right (west) on W. Highland Rd.; on left.

WEB: www.doverlake.com

Strollers	✓ Groups	Food Nearby
Diap Chg	✓ Picnic	Pub. Trans.
✓ Parking	✓ Food Serv.	Handicapped

If you like to party in water, here's the place for you! With seven mountain slides (not for the faint of heart), three tubing rides, and a wave pool with four-foot crests, this giant water park has plenty of opportunities to get wet. Two new speed slides drop gliders over the sidewalk and send them shooting out onto the beach.

A kiddie area features a train ride, playground, and petting zoo; a picnic grove is shady and pleasant and the concessions offer typical park food—hot dogs, ice cream, and the like.

A large manmade lake is bordered by a sandy beach—adults can sun and keep an eye on their paddle-boating kids.

It's a good idea to come early, especially on summer weekends and holidays, to grab a picnic spot and set up for the day, as the place is popular for group outings.

Erieview Park

AGES:	1½–3	3–5	5–8	8–12	12–15
RATING:	NR	★★	★★★	★★★	★

COST: **$–$$** PREP.: **None** AREA: **Farther East**
CITY: **Geneva-on-the-Lake**

ADDRESS: 5483 Lake Rd.

PHONE: (440) 466-8650

SEASON: Seasonal (Memorial Day–Labor Day)

HOURS: Daily to 10 p.m.; water slides noon–9 p.m.; other rides: 2 p.m.–10 p.m.

PRICES: $1.20 per ride, $11.75 day-long ride & slide pass, group rates available

DIRECT.: I-90 to Exit 218 for SR 534/Geneva; north on SR 534; SR 534 ends at SR 531; east on SR 531; on left.

✓ Strollers	✓ Groups	✓ Food Nearby
✓ Diap Chg	✓ Picnic	✓ Pub. Trans.
✓ Parking	✓ Food Serv.	✓ Handicapped

Located on the "strip" in Geneva-on-the-Lake, this small park hugs the Lake Erie shoreline only a short walk from the video arcades, doughnut shops, tee-shirt boutiques, and other diversions that have made this mile-long stretch of Lake Road so popular for decades. Not much has changed here over the past 35 years.

All the typical rides are here: Tilt-a-Whirl, Ferris wheel, fun house, bumper cars, and carousel. There are several kiddie rides suitable for preschoolers. The bumper cars are popular with older kids, as is the water slide (for which riders must be 42 inches tall).

TIPS FOR TRIPS

CROWDS

For those times when you can't avoid a crowd, wear matching, brightly colored hats or T-shirts. Also, always set a meeting place in case someone gets lost.

Fun N Stuff

AGES:	1½–3	3–5	5–8	8–12	12–15
RATING:	NR	★	★★	★★	★★

COST: **$$** PREP.: **None**
AREA: **South** CITY: **Macedonia**

ADDRESS: 661 E. Highland Rd.

PHONE: (330) 467-0820

SEASON: Year round

HOURS: Open daily, but hours vary by day and season. Please call ahead.

PRICES: Each attraction is priced separately. Special rates for groups and birthdays

DIRECT.: I-271 to Exit 18 for SR 8 (Boston Hts.); south on SR 8; left (east) on E. Highland Rd.; on left.

✓ Strollers	✓ Groups	✓ Food Nearby
Diap Chg	✓ Picnic	✓ Pub. Trans.
✓ Parking	✓ Food Serv.	✓ Handicapped

If you're hankering for a go-cart race or some putt-putt golf and it's February, this place brings summer indoors (there is even an on-site tanning center). Covered batting cages, bumper boats, and laser tag translate indoor fun into outdoor play with the seasons.

Geauga Lake

AGES:	1½–3	3–5	5–8	8–12	12–15
RATING:	★	★★	★★	★★	★★

COST: **$$$** PREP.: **None**
AREA: **Southeast** CITY: **Aurora**

ADDRESS: 1060 N. Aurora Rd.

PHONE: (330) 562-7131

SEASON: Seasonal (May–Oct)

HOURS: 10 a.m.–10 p.m.; hours vary early & late in season

PRICES: $25.99, $12.99 under 48 in., $14.99 seniors, free for kids under 2, no added charge for water park; stroller rental $5; wagon rental $7

DIRECT.: US 422 to SR 306 (Chillicothe Rd.); south on SR 306; left (west) on Pettibone Rd.; left (south) on Geauga Lake Rd.; left (south) on SR 43.; on left.

Turtle Beach at Geauga Lake

Or, I-271 to Exit 21 for Broadway Ave.; south on Broadway; left (east) on Pettibone Rd.; right (south) on SR 43 (Aurora Rd.); on left.

WEB: www.geaugalake.com

✓ Strollers	✓ Groups	✓ Food Nearby
✓ Diap Chg	✓ Picnic	✓ Pub. Trans.
✓ Parking	✓ Food Serv.	✓ Handicapped

Roller coasters, live entertainment, and extensive water play areas make Geauga Lake a popular summertime destination for families.

There are plenty of water-based activities. The Wave, a two-million-gallon, two-and-a-half-acre pool boasts surfs cresting up to six feet. There are five water chutes and wet slides.

As at many large amusement parks, the real thrill rides (the Big Dipper, Corkscrew, and Neptune's Falls) require that riders be at least a certain height—42, 48, or 54 inches tall. Other rides merely require that smaller children be accompanied by an adult. On busy summer weekends and holidays, don't be surprised if there are waits of an hour or so for the most popular rides, such as Raging Wolf Bob's roller coaster.

For littler folks, Turtle Beach and Rainbow Island create an aquatic playground equipped with waterfalls and water slides. (You'll want to head directly here if you have preschoolers.)

In recent years, the management has been working hard to make your stay more pleasant by adding numerous conveniences. There are lockers, life jackets, towels for rent, fitting rooms, and even swimwear for sale in the shops in case you forgot yours. (Proper swimming attire is required; tee-shirts and cut-offs are not permitted.) Near Turtle Beach there is a diaper-changing facility complete with a microwave, bassinets, high chairs, and ready-to-feed juice and milk bottles.

The food here is basic park fare—burgers, hot dogs, ice cream, pizza. It is also pricey. You'll do much better to bring your own meal in a cooler and park it in one of the nicely shaded picnic areas.

Goodtimes

AGES:	1½–3	3–5	5–8	8–12	12–15
RATING:	★	★★	★★	★★	★★

COST: **$–$$$** PREP.: **None**
AREA: **Far West** CITY: **Avon**

ADDRESS: 33777 Chester Rd.

PHONE: (440) 937-6210; (440) 937-6200

SEASON: Year round

HOURS: Vary throughout season, call for times

PRICES: Free entry admission. $6-$20 for ticket packs (rides and games require 2–4 tickets), play-all-day wristbands available; video tokens $.25; Batting Cage tokens $1; Laser Xtreme $7

DIRECT.: I-90 to Exit 153 for SR 83; north on SR 83; right (east) on Chester Rd.; on right

✓ Strollers ✓ Groups ✓ Food Nearby
✓ Diap Chg ✓ Picnic Pub. Trans.
✓ Parking ✓ Food Serv. ✓ Handicapped

This family fun center combines seasonal outdoor attractions with indoor activities to assure year-round fun. There are activities for all ages. Outside, there are bumper boats, bumper cars, and race cars (some designed for parent and tot). Preschoolers can play along on two 18-hole miniature golf courses with special clubs for pint-sized players. Inside, younger kids will head for the two-story climbing gym and go-carts. Older kids migrate to the indoor video arcade and outdoor batting cages.

I-X Center Indoor Amusement Park

AGES:	1½–3	3–5	5–8	8–12	12–15
RATING:	★	★	★	★★	★★

COST: **$$–$$$** PREP.: **None**
AREA: **West** CITY: **Brook Park**

ADDRESS: 6200 Riverside Dr.

PHONE: (800) 897-3942

SEASON: Seasonal (Late Mar–early May)

HOURS: Vary

PRICES: $15; $10 seniors; free 2 and under

DIRECT.: I-71 to Exit 239 for SR 237/Airport; south on SR 237 past airport; west on I-X Center Dr.; right (north) on Riverside Dr.

Or, I-480 to Exit 9 for Grayton Rd.; south on Grayton; left (east) on Brookpark Rd.; right (south) on SR 237 past airport; west on I-X Center Dr.; right (north) on Riverside Dr.

✓ Strollers ✓ Groups ✓ Food Nearby
✓ Diap Chg ✓ Picnic ✓ Pub. Trans.
✓ Parking ✓ Food Serv. ✓ Handicapped

This indoor amusement park has become a rite of spring with more than 150 rides, games, and live entertainment shows, and special events scheduled each weekend. A roller

I-X Center Indoor Amusement Park

coaster, video arcade, and miniature golf course are among the 20-acre indoor park's popular attractions.

For younger kids, there is a kiddie area with motorcycles, fire engines, and trains to ride, as well as a petting zoo. There are also plenty of rides for parents to enjoy with their kids.

The setting is rather like a big garage. The cavernous exhibit floor and metal siding create weird acoustics and lighting. In other words, it is dark and loud. Still, with Cleveland's spring weather, it's no surprise that the indoor park has become a popular destination—particularly on weekend evenings for teenagers and young adults.

The food is what you might expect: hot dogs, popcorn, pizza. An expanded food pavilion can accommodate lunch or dinner.

One of the biggest hits is the world's tallest indoor Ferris wheel. At 10 stories high, it literally pops out of the roof (the top's enclosed in a glass atrium). From the top of the wheel you get a good view of nearby Hopkins airport and the downtown skyline. (There is often a 20- to 30-minute wait to board the wheel.)

Jeepers

AGES:	1½–3	3–5	5–8	8–12	12–15
RATING:	★★	★★	★★	★	NR

COST: **FREE–$$** PREP.: **None**
AREA: **East** CITY: **Cleveland**

ADDRESS: Randall Park Mall, 20801 Miles Rd.

PHONE: (216) 662-9999

SEASON: Year round

HOURS: Mon–Thurs 10 a.m.–9 p.m., Fri 10 a.m.–10 p.m., Sat 10 a.m.–10 p.m., Sun 11 a.m.–8 p.m.

PRICES: $4 per child (does not include rides); all day admission plus rides: $9 ocer 36 in., $6 under 36 in.; adults free with child admission

DIRECT.: West: I-480 to Exit 25B for Northfield Rd.(north); right (east) to Miles Rd.; on right.

East: I-271 to I-480 East; I-480 to Exit 27 for Miles Rd.; on left.

East2: I-480 to Exit 25 for Aurora Rd.; right (north) on Northfield Rd.; left (west) on Miles Rd.; on left.

WEB: www.jeepers.com

Strollers	✓ Groups	✓ Food Nearby
Diap Chg	Picnic	✓ Pub. Trans.
✓ Parking	✓ Food Serv.	Handicapped

This rapidly expanding national chain is a welcome challenge to other indoor amusement parks. With more than 20,000 square feet well partitioned into a ride area, a chute, slide, and bounce playground, and a diner (featuring Pizza Hut service), the noise, distraction, and stress level here is kept to a minimum. Particularly impressive is the ImaginArea, an interactive, creative play area that is free for preschoolers. Here, the youngest visitors can play dress-up and pretend.

Aimed at kids aged 2 to 12, this is a great place to work off some of that winter steam.

Lazer Xtreme

AGES:	1½–3	3–5	5–8	8–12	12–15
RATING:	NR	NR	NR	★★	★★★

COST: **$$$** PREP.: **None–Some**
AREA: **South** CITY: **Middleburg Hts.**

ADDRESS: 13409 Smith Rd.

PHONE: (440) 842-6044

SEASON: Year round

HOURS: Mon–Thu 4:30 p.m.–10 p.m.; Fri 4:30 p.m.–midnight; Sat noon–midnight; Sun noon–8 p.m.

PRICES: $7 per mission (20 minutes)

DIRECT.: I-71 to Exit 235 for Bagley Rd.; east on Bagley; right (north) on SR 42 (Pearl Rd.); right (east) on Smith Rd.; Southland Shopping Center on left.

Strollers	✓ Groups	✓ Food Nearby
Diap Chg	✓ Picnic	✓ Pub. Trans.
✓ Parking	Food Serv.	Handicapped

While this indoor play arena is not for everyone (and definitely not for anyone under eight), it does the laser tag experience very well. Fog machines, theater lights, 20 speakers pumping out 4,000 watts of sound, and a multilevel play area make for a pretty wild experience. Be forewarned: if you play by the game, it's not inexpensive, and the game is over pretty quickly, especially once you get the hang of it. The all-day pass is a good deal.

It's a popular place for birthday parties, but kids need to be coordinated and not easily rattled—the vest and gun add up to 8 ½ pounds. After-hours rental is also offered.

Memphis Kiddie Park

AGES:	1½–3	3–5	5–8	8–12	12–15
RATING:	★	★★★	★	NR	NR

COST: **$$** PREP.: **None**
AREA: **South** CITY: **Brooklyn**

ADDRESS: 10340 Memphis Ave.

PHONE: (216) 941-5995

SEASON: Seasonal (Apr–Sep)

HOURS: Daily 10 a.m.–9 p.m. (June–Aug); Apr & Sep hours vary

PRICES: $7.50 for 10 tickets, $14 for 25 tickets (1 ticket per ride); group rates available

DIRECT.: I-480 to Exit 13 for Tiedeman Rd.; north on Tiedeman; left (west) on Memphis Rd.; on right.

OR I-71 to Exit 242 for Bellaire Rd.; northeast on Bellaire; right (southeast) on Memphis Rd.; on left before Tiedeman Rd.

Strollers	✓ Groups	✓ Food Nearby
✓ Diap Chg	✓ Picnic	✓ Pub. Trans.
✓ Parking	✓ Food Serv.	✓ Handicapped

Memphis Kiddie Park has been a Cleveland institution since its opening in 1952. In fact, many local youngsters have met their first roller coaster here. (With seats just big enough to accommodate an adult companion, the ride is certainly tame enough for a first-timer.) All the typical rides are here—in miniature versions. There's a Ferris wheel, a pony cart, rocket rides, and a merry-go-round. A mini-train circles the park with a short detour through some trees. For older kids, there is an 18-hole miniature golf course.

Mr. Divot's Sports Park

AGES:	1½–3	3–5	5–8	8–12	12–15
RATING:	NR	★	★★	★★	★★

COST: **$–$$** PREP.: **None**
AREA: **Southwest** CITY: **North Royalton**

ADDRESS: 13393 York Rd.

PHONE: (440) 237-2226

SEASON: Seasonal (Mid-Mar–Oct, weather permitting)

HOURS: Daily 10 a.m.–11 p.m.

PRICES: Vary; group rates available

DIRECT.: I-71 to Exit 231 for SR 82 (Royalton Rd.); east on Royalton Rd; left (north) on York Rd.; on right.

✓ Strollers ✓ Groups ✓ Food Nearby
Diap Chg ✓ Picnic Pub. Trans.
✓ Parking ✓ Food Serv. ✓ Handicapped

This family fun center is equipped with an 18-hole miniature golf course, a driving range, batting cage, and a tennis-ball target shoot.

Pioneer Waterland and Dry Fun Park

AGES:	1½–3	3–5	5–8	8–12	12–15
RATING:	NR	★	★★	★★★	★★★

COST: **FREE–$$$** PREP.: **None**
AREA: **Far East** CITY: **Chardon**

ADDRESS: 10661 Kile Rd.

PHONE: (440) 951-7507

SEASON: Seasonal (early June–Labor Day)

HOURS: Daily 10 a.m.–8 p.m.; water attractions 11 a.m.–8 p.m. (7 p.m. weekdays); GoKarts & other "Pay As You Play" 11 a.m.–9 p.m.

PRICES: Activity admission $11.95; GoKart & Sportsland Admission $9.95; children under 40 in. free; free parking

DIRECT.: I-271 to Exit 34 for US 322 (Mayfield Rd.); east on US 322; left (north) on SR 608; right (east) on Chardon-Windsor Rd.; left (north) on Kile Rd.; on right.

Or, I-90 to Exit 200 for SR 44; south on SR 44; left (east) on US 6; right (south) on Kile Rd.; on left.

WEB: www.pioneerwaterland.com

✓ Strollers ✓ Groups ✓ Food Nearby
✓ Diap Chg ✓ Picnic Pub. Trans.
✓ Parking ✓ Food Serv. ✓ Handicapped

Four killer water slides—the twin Banzai Speed Slides and two giant Spiraling Waterslides—share one six-story tower and act like a magnet for preteens and other daredevils. But smaller kids fare well too, especially on the Elephant Slide in the Kiddie Waterpark. There is also a kiddie train and a mini–go cart track—mighty popular with the age 3–8 grand prix set.

This water park has a large natural lake for paddleboats, a three-acre cement activity pool with water volleyball and basketball, and a lazy inner-tube ride for all ages that gently flows through the middle of the park around Adventure Island.

Elsewhere on the grounds are a Grand Prix Supertrack (go carts), batting cages, an 18-hole miniature golf course, golf cages, and an indoor game arcade.

Companies often reserve pavilions in the Group Picnic Grove for corporate picnics on weekends. Expect larger crowds on these days. There are also other activities exclusively for groups, including the Fort Pioneer Play Area, horseshoes, sand volleyball, bocce, shuffleboard, and more.

Tee-shirts and shorts are permitted in all water attractions. Pioneer Waterland has a raincheck policy, so don't worry if your trip is cut short by a summer rainstorm.

There are ample shaded and grassy picnic areas.

Putt-Putt Golf & Games

AGES:	1½–3	3–5	5–8	8–12	12–15
RATING:	NR	★	★★	★★	★

COST: **$–$$** PREP.: **None**
AREA: **Far East** CITY: **Willoughby**

ADDRESS: 38886 Mentor Ave.

PHONE: (440) 951-7888

SEASON: Seasonal (Year-round video arcade; outdoor season Apr 15–Oct 15)

HOURS: Summer: Daily 10 a.m.–midnight; off-season hours vary, please call ahead.

PRICES: Prepaid packages ($7) include arcade, putt-putt, and lunch; batting cage: 6 tokens for $5

DIRECT.: I-90 to Exit 190 for SR 306 (Reynolds Rd.); north on SR 306; north on Broadmoor Rd.; left (west) on Mentor Ave.; on left.

WEB: www.bittnerco.com/puttputt

Strollers	✓ Groups	✓ Food Nearby
Diap Chg	Picnic	Pub. Trans.
✓ Parking	✓ Food Serv.	Handicapped

Known primarily for its outdoor batting cages and minigolf, this facility also offers a video arcade, pinball, and skeeball area indoors.

Q-Zar

AGES:	1½–3	3–5	5–8	8–12	12–15
RATING:	NR	NR	NR	★	★★

COST: **$$** PREP.: **Some**
AREA: **East** CITY: **Mayfield Hts.**

ADDRESS: 1615 Golden Gate Plaza

PHONE: (440) 473-9955

SEASON: Year round

HOURS: Mon–Thu 3 p.m.–11 p.m.; Fri 3 p.m.–midnight; Sat 10 a.m.–midnight; Sun noon–11 p.m.

PRICES: 1 game: $6; 3 games: $15

DIRECT.: I-271 to Exit 34 for Mayfield Rd.; west on Mayfield; on left.

Strollers	✓ Groups	✓ Food Nearby
Diap Chg	Picnic	✓ Pub. Trans.
✓ Parking	✓ Food Serv.	Handicapped

Not for the fainthearted, this laser-tag parlor offers tag in the midst of piped-in smoke, pumped-in music, and flashing lights. This may be the perfect birthday party spot for a spirited group—you know who you are.

SeaWorld Cleveland

AGES:	1½–3	3–5	5–8	8–12	12–15
RATING:	★	★★	★★	★★	★★

COST: **$$$** PREP.: **None–Some**
AREA: **Southeast** CITY: **Aurora**

ADDRESS: 1100 SeaWorld Drive

PHONE: (800) 63-SHAMU

SEASON: Seasonal (May–Sep, weekends only in Sep)

HOURS: Vary: daily 10 a.m.–7 p.m. (closes at 11 p.m. early Jun–late Aug)

PRICES: $30.95, $22.95 ages 3–11 (+2.5% tax), no charge under age 3; parking: $5 per vehicle; strollers and wagons available for rental. Discounts for seniors.

DIRECT.: US 422 to SR 306 (Chillicothe Rd.); south on SR 306; left (west) on Pettibone Rd.; left (south) on Brewster Rd.; right (north) on SR 43.; on right.

Or, I-271 to Exit 21 for Broadway Ave.; south on Broadway; left (east) on Pettibone Rd.; right (south) on SR 43 (Aurora Rd.); on left.

WEB: www.SeaWorld.org

✓ Strollers	✓ Groups	✓ Food Nearby
✓ Diap Chg	✓ Picnic	✓ Pub. Trans.
✓ Parking	✓ Food Serv.	✓ Handicapped

Each summer, this 90-acre marine life theme park fills with families in search of Shamu the "Killer Whale" and his aquatic pals. SeaWorld, brought to you by the same folks who run Busch Gardens in Tampa, Florida, and Colonial Williamsburg, Virginia, is a slick and impressive operation—from its water shows to its playground area.

An athletic dolphin act showcases the grace and power of these mammals. Another show, featuring sea lions, penguins, otters, and walruses, plays it strictly for laughs. Other shows, featuring water-skiers, are scheduled throughout the day. To catch the most popular attractions (Shamu the killer whale, and the dolphin shows), line up early. (Oh, and if you don't want to get wet, don't sit in the front rows.) The downside of this strategy is that kids get fidgety listening to the shameless promotions that run before performances.

Shark Encounter, a recent addition, features an impressive tank that bends overhead, making it look like sharks are surrounding you. Interactive exhibits teach about sharks, including how they swim.

A big hit with children is Shamu's Happy Harbor, a three-acre nautical playground. It is complete with boat deck (with water cannons), a huge net to climb on, clear plastic tubes to crawl through (with water cascading over them), and air mattresses to fall on. Even toddlers will find some entertainment here. Parents can and often do squeeze through the tubes and clamber up the rope ladders themselves.

SeaWorld Cleveland

Also a hit with the kids is the new *Pirates* movie, starring Leslie Neilsen and filled with off-color slapstick. Some adults will like it—you know who you are.

Don't miss the World of Sea Aquarium. Though small, it is Northeast Ohio's best aquarium, complete with a touch pool filled with starfish, jellyfish, anemones, crabs, and coral reef fish. Another popular exhibit, Dolphin Cove, allows kids to get personal with dolphins (fish food is sold at posted intervals).

As at other theme parks, food and drink, while plentiful, are not cheap; if you are willing to carry them, bring your own.

School groups looking for an animal program should consider either a field trip or a visit from the educational outreach program—both options are offered, and both are very popular.

Swings-N-Things Family Fun Park

AGES:	1½–3	3–5	5–8	8–12	12–15
RATING:	★	★★	★★	★	★

COST: **$$–$$$** PREP.: **None**
AREA: **Southwest** CITY: **Olmsted Twp.**

ADDRESS: 8501 Stearns Rd.

PHONE: (440) 235-4420; (440) 235-4469

SEASON: Year round (Summer season Memorial Day to Labor Day)

HOURS: In season: Sun–Thu 11 a.m.–11 p.m., Fri–Sat 11 a.m.–midnight; off season: hours vary greatly, please call ahead (usually open daily).

PRICES: Vary; packages available starting at $5

DIRECT.: I-480 to Exit 3 for Stearns Rd.; south on Stearns; on left.

WEB: www.swings-n-things.com

✓ Strollers	✓ Groups	✓ Food Nearby
✓ Diap Chg	✓ Picnic	Pub.Trans.
✓ Parking	✓ Food Serv.	✓ Handicapped

Outside, there are two miniature golf courses, complete with short clubs for short kids and a cordoned-off area, Fun Junction Kiddie Park, for small children, where they can ride in electric-powered cars and bumper boats and take a short train ride. If smaller kids stick with a parent, they can also get wet in gasoline-powered

Fun & Games DIRECTORY

bumper boats and yell at their parents to outmaneuver wily teens in two-person go-carts that never go quite as fast as the single-person versions.

Indoors there is a video arcade, an ice-cream parlor, and a new laser-tag arena, popular for birthday parties.

Tuscora Park

AGES:	1½–3	3–5	5–8	8–12	12–15
RATING:	★★	★★★	★★★	★★	★

COST: **$–$$** PREP.: **None**
AREA: **Farther South** CITY: **New Philadelphia**

ADDRESS: 161 Tuscora Ave., NW

PHONE: (330) 343-4644

SEASON: Seasonal (Memorial Day–mid-Sep)

HOURS: Weekdays: 5 p.m.–9:30 p.m.; weekends: noon–9:30 p.m.

PRICES: 25¢ tickets or package rates

DIRECT.: I-77 to Exit 81 for SR 39; east on SR 39; left (north) on SR 416; left (west) on Tuscora Ave.; on right.

✓ Strollers ✓ Groups ✓ Food Nearby
Diap Chg ✓ Picnic Pub. Trans.
✓ Parking ✓ Food Serv. Handicapped

Packed with small-town flavor, this local park is a gem. It has a train ride, a small roller coaster, a Ferris wheel, miniature golf, and an outdoor swimming pool. Its permanence and its park setting make this much nicer than the typical carnival. Tucked in the center of town, it's easy to miss. Don't.

Wildwood Water Park

AGES:	1½–3	3–5	5–8	8–12	12–15
RATING:	NR	★	★	★★★	★★★

COST: **$$** PREP.: **None**
AREA: **Southwest** CITY: **Columbia Station**

ADDRESS: 11200 E. River Rd.

PHONE: (440) 236-3944

SEASON: Seasonal (Mid-Jun–Labor Day)

HOURS: Daily 10:30 a.m.–8 p.m.

PRICES: Mon–Fri $8, Sat–Sun $10, no charge age 4 & under

DIRECT.: I-480 to Exit 6 for SR 252 (Great Northern Blvd.); south on Great Northern; on right after Sprague Rd.

WEB: www.wildwoodwaterpark.com

✓ Strollers ✓ Groups ✓ Food Nearby
✓ Diap Chg ✓ Picnic ✓ Pub. Trans.
✓ Parking ✓ Food Serv. ✓ Handicapped

This shady and noncommercial water park is a neighborhood favorite, especially for older school-age kids. There's plenty to do: six big slides, five kiddie slides, a playground, miniature golf, five new volleyball courts, and other "on-the-lake" rides. A mini-arcade, sunny beach, horseshoe pit, and ample grassy area surrounded by 12 scenic lakeside picnic pavilions with grills provide leisure (and easy car access) for those who wish to stay dry. On the green lake, nearly as deep as Lake Erie, the park rents paddleboats and canoes for a dollar. If you decide not to picnic, cheap, full-service catering can be arranged at the park's year-round banquet hall. Music and special events are scheduled for summer weekends.

We were glad to see that there are many more lifeguards watching the rides than in years past. Expect crowds. On a hot day at noontime, you'll likely dry off waiting in line. You can easily spend the entire day here, but you will need a shower when returning home. (The slide pumps water from the lake.)

History, Science, & Technology

You might think of museums as difficult to visit with young children. Think again. True, some youngsters wouldn't pick a museum exhibit over their favorite video. But if they've been to a museum before and had a good time, they will probably want to go back. It's up to parents, though, to ensure a successful visit by planning ahead.

Be aware when visiting large institutions with children that weekends can be quite crowded. If weekends are your only opportunity, try to go first thing in the morning and quit by lunchtime. You may not see the entire collection in one visit, but that's okay; you can come back.

If you find yourself returning again and again to a particular museum, look into becoming members. Memberships often include free or reduced admission prices, preferred enrollment in classes (a chance to sign up before the general public), and savings in gift shops (often stocked with unusual toys and games).

African American Museum

AGES:	1½–3	3–5	5–8	8–12	12–15
RATING:	NR	NR	★★	★★	★★

COST: **$** PREP.: **None–Some**
AREA: **Near East** CITY: **Cleveland**

ADDRESS: 1765 Crawford Rd.

PHONE: (216) 791-1700

SEASON: Year round

HOURS: Tue–Fri 10 a.m.–3 p.m., Sat 11 a.m.–3 p.m.; closed Sun–Mon

PRICES: $4 adults; $3 students 17 & under, $3.50 seniors; Group rates available (group tours should be scheduled approximately 2 weeks in advance)

DIRECT.: I-90 to Exit 173B for Chester Ave.; east on Chester; left on Crawford at E. 92 St.; on right.

WEB: www.ben.net/aamuseum

✓ Strollers ✓ Groups ✓ Food Nearby
Diap Chg Picnic ✓ Pub. Trans.
✓ Parking Food Serv. Handicapped

Founded in 1953, the African American Museum was one of the first museums of its kind to open in the U.S. Its special offerings for school-age children include a Saturday "Shule" (school) during the school year that focuses on African history and heritage, and activities in the arts, history, and dance. Annual celebrations of particular interest to families include Black History Month (February) and the Carter G. Woodson celebration in December.

Ashtabula, Carson & Jefferson Scenic Line

AGES:	1½–3	3–5	5–8	8–12	12–15
RATING:	NR	NR	★	★★	★★

COST: **$$** PREP.: **Some**
AREA: **Farther East** CITY: **Jefferson**

ADDRESS: E. Jefferson St.

PHONE: (440) 576-6346

SEASON: Seasonal (Jun–Oct)

HOURS: Sat, Sun 12:30 p.m., 2 p.m., 3:30 p.m.

PRICES: $7 adults, $6 seniors, $5 ages 3–12, under 3 free when held

DIRECT.: I-90 to Exit 229 for SR 11; south on SR 11; south on SR 46; left (east) on E. Jefferson St.

✓ Strollers ✓ Groups ✓ Food Nearby
Diap Chg Picnic Pub. Trans.
✓ Parking ✓ Food Serv. Handicapped

On summer and fall weekends, this fully operating freight line becomes a six-mile-long scenic rail ride. Engineer Bob Callahan and his daughter, Heather, operate three partially restored passenger cars dating from the 1920s. The train rolls mostly through old country farms, fields, and woods, but also crosses a couple of streams and passes the loading docks in Ashtabula Harbor.

Special events include Family Halloween Theme Trains in October and murder mysteries several times a year. Fall rides when the leaves change are especially beautiful.

Butterfly Box

AGES:	1½–3	3–5	5–8	8–12	12–15
RATING:	★	★	★	★	NR

COST: **$** PREP.: **None**
AREA: **Farther West** CITY: **Kelleys Island**

ADDRESS: 604 Division St.

PHONE: (419) 746-2454

SEASON: Seasonal (Memorial Day–Labor Day)

HOURS: Open seven days a week, 10 a.m.–6:30 p.m.

PRICES: Adults $2.50, kids $1.50, seniors $1.50; group rates: adults $1.50, kids/seniors $1

DIRECT.: SR 2 to SR 269; north on SR 269 to SR 163; east on SR 163 to Marblehead; Neuman Boat Line/Kelleys Island Ferry on left.

Strollers ✓ Groups ✓ Food Nearby
Diap Chg Picnic Pub. Trans.
✓ Parking ✓ Food Serv. Handicapped

The gardens are pleasant and the butterflies peaceful at this small tourist trap, a nice, not-too-expensive diversion on the island.

Century Village

Geauga County Historical Society

AGES:	1½–3	3–5	5–8	8–12	12–15
RATING:	NR	★	★★	★★	★★

COST: **$** PREP.: **None–Much**
AREA: **Far East** CITY: **Burton**

ADDRESS: 14653 E. Park St.

PHONE: (440) 834-4012

SEASON: Seasonal (Mar 1–Oct 31)

HOURS: Tue–Fri: 9:30 a.m.–4 p.m., tours at 10:30 a.m., 1 p.m., and 3:30 p.m.; Sat, Sun: 9:30 a.m.–4 p.m., tours at 1 p.m. and 3 p.m.

PRICES: $5, $3 ages 6–12, free for ages 5 & under

DIRECT.: I-271 to Exit 29 for Chagrin Blvd.; east on Chagrin; east on SR 87.

Or, US 422 to SR 700; north on SR 700; left (northeast) on SR 168 (Tavern Rd.).

✓ Strollers ✓ Groups ✓ Food Nearby
Diap Chg ✓ Picnic Pub. Trans.
✓ Parking ✓ Food Serv. Handicapped

This is the place for an afternoon of playing pioneer. Created by the Geauga Historical Society, it includes 21 reassembled buildings from the Western Reserve era (1798–1900), complete with antiques, and a working farm with barn, orchards, fields, and animals.

Any one of the society's annual festivals will whisk you back to *Little House on the Prairie* days as people dressed in period costume go about their business.

In the center of the town square, a log cabin offers craft boutiques, maple-sugar samples, or hot apple butter—depending on the season. Food always seems to motivate our family, so, not surprisingly, our favorite event here is the Apple Butter Festival. Held at the peak of apple-picking season, usually in late September, it coats the village with the scent of cinnamon-spiced apples. You can watch volunteers stir the tangy brown concoction in huge wooden barrels over open-flame pits.

But the best part is not visual: slices of warm, freshly baked bread are for sale, topped with ladles full of hot apple butter.

If your children are interested in getting more than just a taste of this village, Pioneer School Camp is held each summer in July for ages 9–11. Workshops include whitewashing, ink making, gingerbread baking, jam making, and square dancing.

Other events of special interest include a Civil War show. Tours through the schoolhouse, stores, and other buildings are usually available during the events, but don't expect to climb cannons or practice sharp-shooting; most of the exhibits are set up for looking, listening, and, well, eating.

Century Village

Cleveland Museum of Natural History

AGES:	1½–3	3–5	5–8	8–12	12–15
RATING:	★	★★	★★★	★★★	★★★

COST: **FREE–$$** PREP.: **None–Some**
AREA: **Near East** CITY: **Cleveland**

ADDRESS: 1 Wade Oval Dr.

PHONE: (800) 317-9155

SEASON: Year round

HOURS: Mon–Sat 10 a.m.–5 p.m.; Sun noon–5 p.m.; Wed (Sept–May) 10 a.m.–10 p.m.; closed holidays. Discovery Center Mon–Fri 2 p.m.–5 p.m.; Sat 10 a.m.–4 p.m.; Sun 1 p.m.–4 p.m.

PRICES: $6.50, $4.50 for ages 5–17, seniors, & students with ID; free under age 5; prices subject to change

DIRECT.: West: I-90 to Exit 173B for Chester Ave.; east on Chester; left on Euclid Ave; left on East Blvd; left on Wade Oval; on left.

East: I-90 to Exit 177 for Martin Luther King Blvd.; south on MLK; left (northeast) on Euclid Ave; left (north) on East Blvd; left on Wade Oval; on left.

South: I-271 to Exit 32 for Cedar Rd.; west on Cedar to University Circle; right (northeast) on Euclid Ave; left (north) on East Blvd.; left on Wade Oval; on left.

WEB: www.cmnh.org

✓ Strollers	✓ Groups	✓ Food Nearby
✓ Diap Chg	✓ Picnic	✓ Pub. Trans.
✓ Parking	✓ Food Serv.	✓ Handicapped

Into dinosaurs? No problem. Head to Kirtland Hall, which has complete skeletons of a mastodon, an allosaurus, and a nanotyrannus, among others. Astronomy? For an additional $1.50, 30-minute-long planetarium shows are well worth the money. Archaeology? The cavernous Sears Hall houses multilevel exhibits about indigenous peoples from all over the world in historical surroundings. Mounted wolves and mountain lions lurk above glass-enclosed cases of masks, amulets, figurines, and pottery. At toddler level, dioramas depict hunts, different styles of shelter, and fire building. While some exhibits may seem a bit static, "Planet e," a multisensory exhibit, has transformed Reinberger Hall into a state-of-the-art interactive display featuring geology and astronomy. Don't miss the Wade Gallery's display of precious gems.

Be prepared to spend some time here, because there is a lot to see for youngsters and parents alike. Especially popular with families are the regularly scheduled live animal programs. Also very popular are year-round classes for ages 4–18 covering everything from astronomy to rain-forest ecosystems.

The museum can easily handle

Cleveland Museum of Natural History

weekend crowds, but the same cannot be said for its modest parking lot; expect a hike if you come after 11:30 a.m. Don't forget to browse the museum store—it's a good one.

Cleveland Police Historical Society, Inc. & Museum

AGES:	1½–3	3–5	5–8	8–12	12–15
RATING:	NR	NR	★	★★	★★

COST: **FREE** PREP.: **None–Some**
AREA: **Downtown** CITY: **Cleveland**

ADDRESS: Clevleand Police Headquarters 1300 Ontario St.

PHONE: (216) 623-5055

SEASON: Year round

HOURS: Mon–Fri 10 a.m.–4 p.m.; guided tours by reservation only

PRICES: Free, donations accepted

DIRECT.: East/West: SR 2 to E. 9 St.; south on E. 9; right (west) on St. Clair Ave.; right (north) on Ontario St.; on left.

West: I-90 to Exit 171B for Ontario St.; on left.

Strollers	✓ Groups	✓ Food Nearby
Diap Chg	Picnic	✓ Pub. Trans.
✓ Parking	Food Serv.	✓ Handicapped

This museum houses a growing collection of historical items pertaining to Cleveland's public safety history, specifically the role of the Cleveland Police Department. Collection items include a revolver signed out to Eliot Ness, a 1920s jail cell, lots of confiscated weapons, uniform displays, and two vintage Harley Davidson motorcycles.

As there are no real kids' programs or hands-on activities here, this museum is better suited for elementary-school children or school groups especially interested in the subject matter.

Crawford Auto-Aviation Museum

Western Reserve Historical Society

AGES:	1½–3	3–5	5–8	8–12	12–15
RATING:	NR	NR	★	★★	★★

COST: **$–$$** PREP.: **None**
AREA: **Near East** CITY: **Cleveland**

ADDRESS: 10825 East Blvd.

PHONE: (216) 721-5722

SEASON: Year round

HOURS: Mon–Sat 10 a.m.–5 p.m.; Sun noon–5 p.m.

PRICES: $6.50, $5.50 for seniors, $4.50 students and children ages 6–12 (free age 5 and under); members admitted free

DIRECT.: East: I-90 to Exit 177 for Martin Luther King Blvd.; south on MLK; east on East Blvd.; on left

West: I-90 to Exit 173B for Chester Ave.; east on Chester; left (east) on Euclid Ave.; left (north) on East Blvd.; on right after Hazel Dr.

WEB: www.wrhs.org

✓ Strollers	✓ Groups	✓ Food Nearby
Diap Chg	✓ Picnic	✓ Pub. Trans.
✓ Parking	✓ Food Serv.	✓ Handicapped

Industrialist Frederick Crawford collected early automobiles because they, unlike today's models, always looked distinctive. No two models were exactly alike. Therein lies the strength of this museum: each of the dozens of cars on display represents a distinct form of early automotive excellence.

The museum's collection features hundreds of automobiles, aircraft, bicycles, and other vehicles. Split between two levels, this eclectic collection boasts leaders in a variety of categories, including the oldest known car in North America, the Parisian-made 1895 Panhard et Levassor. On the top floor, special emphasis is given to the automobiles produced in Northeast Ohio in the late 1800s and early 1900s, when Cleveland was a leading national automotive center. A 1932 Peerless (the last passenger car made in Cleveland) is the centerpiece. A prototype, it is the only one of its kind and has an estimated value of $2.5 million. Two exhibits featuring White Motors and the National Air Races also occupy the upper floor. They are interactive (with computer monitors and recorded interviews) as well as memorabilia-filled, with authentic trucks and airplanes on display. "Working at White" also features interactive art for children.

Downstairs you will find most of the older cars (up to 1930), along with a full-size replica of a late 1800s Main Street. Rotating exhibits of motorcycles, roadsters, race cars, concept cars, model trains, and other transportation-related items also appear on the lower level.

While many of the exhibits here are static and a few displays could use a face-lift, the museum will appeal to the budding car buff. To appeal to younger visitors, special demonstrations and make-and-take workshops are periodically scheduled as part of the Crawford Kids Club. Plans for major changes are in the works—including a move to E. 9th Street in the coming years.

Crawford Auto-Aviation Museum

Dittrick Museum of Medical History

AGES:	1½–3	3–5	5–8	8–12	12–15
RATING:	NR	NR	NR	★★	★★

COST: **FREE** PREP.: **None**
AREA: **Near East** CITY: **Cleveland**

ADDRESS: Allen Medical Library building, CWRU campus, 11000 Euclid Ave.

PHONE: (216) 368-3648

SEASON: Year round

HOURS: Mon–Fri 10 a.m.–5 p.m.; closed Saturday, Sunday, and most holidays

PRICES: Free

DIRECT.: East: I-90 to Exit 177 for Martin Luther King Blvd.; south on MLK; left (east) on Euclid Ave.; right (south) on Adelbert Rd.; on left.

West: I-90 to Exit 173B for Chester Ave.; east on Chester; left (east) on Euclid Ave.; right (south) on Adelbert Rd.; on left.

Strollers	✓ Groups	✓ Food Nearby
Diap Chg	Picnic	✓ Pub. Trans.
Parking	Food Serv.	✓ Handicapped

Small but informative, the Dittrick is stocked with items and exhibits pertaining to the early practice of medicine, both locally and nationally.

As there are no real kids' programs or hands-on activities here, this museum is better suited for elementary-school children, school groups, or teens especially interested in science and medicine.

Dunham Tavern Museum

AGES:	1½–3	3–5	5–8	8–12	12–15
RATING:	NR	NR	★★	★★	★

COST: **$** PREP.: **None–Some**
AREA: **Near East** CITY: **Cleveland**

ADDRESS: 6709 Euclid Ave.

PHONE: (216) 431-1060

SEASON: Year round

HOURS: Wed & Sun 1–4 p.m., groups by arrangement

PRICES: $2, $1 ages 6–16, no charge under age 6

DIRECT.: I-90 to Exit 173B for Chester Ave.; east on Chester; right (south) on E. 55 St.; left (east) on Euclid Ave.; on left.

WEB: www.multiverse.com:80/tavern/

Strollers	✓ Groups	✓ Food Nearby
Diap Chg	✓ Picnic	✓ Pub. Trans.
✓ Parking	Food Serv.	Handicapped

The Dunham Tavern is the oldest building in Cuyahoga County still standing in its original location. The main clapboard structure, completed in 1824, survived Euclid Avenue's many changes—first from rough path to Cleveland's most glamorous residential street, later into a bustling commercial thoroughfare. The Tavern operated originally as a stagecoach stop on the Buffalo-Cleveland-Detroit Road and was quite a busy place. Converted to a museum in 1938, it still preserves the atmosphere of an early meeting place. With heavy timbers held in place by wooden pins and spikes, it is one of the few remaining pre–Civil War structures in Cleveland. The Dunham staff customizes activities for the age range and size of visiting groups.

Edison's Birthplace

AGES:	1½–3	3–5	5–8	8–12	12–15
RATING:	NR	★	★★★	★★★	★★★

COST: **$** PREP.: **None–Some**
AREA: **Far West** CITY: **Milan**

ADDRESS: 9 Edison Dr.

PHONE: (419) 499-2135

SEASON: Year round

HOURS: April, May, Sept, Oct: Tues–Sun, 1 p.m.–5 p.m.; June, July, Aug: Tues–Sat, 10 a.m.–5 p.m.; Sunday 1 p.m.–5 p.m.; Feb, March, Nov, Dec: by appointment only; Closed Jan, Mondays & Easter

PRICES: $5 adults, $4 seniors, $2 children 6–12

DIRECT.: I-90 to SR 2; west on SR 2 to SR 13; south on SR 13 to US 250; south on US 250 to SR 113; east on SR 113; left (north) on Edison Dr.; on right.

WEB: www.tomedison.org

Strollers	✓ Groups	✓ Food Nearby
Diap Chg	Picnic	Pub. Trans.
✓ Parking	Food Serv.	Handicapped

For anyone interested in inventors and inventions, this is a great place. The small town of Milan has made quite a name for itself as the birthplace of Thomas Edison.

The rather unassuming homestead, a National Historic Landmark, is a small brick colonial on a tree-lined street overlooking a grassy ravine—a perfect place to sit and dream up inventions. The museum features a small collection of Edison's early inventions and family mementos.

A short walk away, the Milan Historical Museum is a seven-building complex including exhibits on Milan Canal history, glass-blowing, and blacksmithing, all within a one-acre garden.

Fairport Marine Museum

Fairport Harbor Historical Society

AGES:	1½–3	3–5	5–8	8–12	12–15
RATING:	NR	★★	★★	★★	★

COST: **$** PREP.: **None**
AREA: **Far East** CITY: **Fairport Harbor**

ADDRESS: 129 Second St.

PHONE: (440) 354-4825

SEASON: Seasonal (Memorial Day to Labor Day)

HOURS: Wed, Sat, Sun, holidays 1–6 p.m.

PRICES: $2, $1 students & seniors, free under age 6

DIRECT.: SR 2 to Richmond Rd. (Fairport Harbor); north on Richmond; Richmond becomes High St.; north on High; left (west) on Second St.; on right.

✓ Strollers	✓ Groups	✓ Food Nearby
Diap Chg	Picnic	Pub. Trans.
✓ Parking	Food Serv.	Handicapped

A ship's wheel in a re-created pilothouse is the best attraction here for kids. The entire exhibit is equipped with nautical instruments from the early 1900s, more than enough for a successful pretend sea voyage.

With a 60-foot spiral staircase of 69 steps, the route up to the top of the lighthouse can be challenging. There is a reward: the observation platform offers a splendid view of Lake Erie and the harbor.

Navigation instruments, marine charts, paintings of ships, tools, models, and half-hulls of lake freighters are just a few of the items in the museum's collection.

Fort Laurens State Memorial

Ohio Historical Society

AGES:	1½–3	3–5	5–8	8–12	12–15
RATING:	NR	★	★	★	★

COST: **FREE–$** PREP.: **None–Some**
AREA: **Far South** CITY: **Bolivar**

ADDRESS: 11067 Fort Laurens Blvd., NW

PHONE: (800) 283-8914

SEASON: Seasonal (April–Oct)

HOURS: Park: April–Oct: daily 9:30 a.m. –dusk. Museum: Memorial Day–Labor Day, Wed–Sat, 9:30 a.m.–5 p.m., Sun & holidays, noon–5 p.m.; After Labor Day–Oct, Sat 9:30 a.m.–5 p.m., Sun. noon–5 p.m.

PRICES: Park free except for special events: $3 adults, $2.70 seniors, $1.25 children 6-12

DIRECT.: I-77 to Exit 93 for SR 212; east on SR 212; left (south) on Fort Laurens Rd.; on left.

✓ Strollers	✓ Groups	✓ Food Nearby
Diap Chg	✓ Picnic	Pub. Trans.
✓ Parking	Food Serv.	✓ Handicapped

While there is no remaining fort here, there are artifacts remaining from archaeological digs and a shallow trench that traces the dimensions of the original fort. A small museum, sitting near what once was the fort's west side, includes weapons from the Revolutionary War period and uniforms of the soldiers who built the fort. A short video describes the history of the war and the role of the Fort Laurens campaign. The entire place really comes to life during one of the regularly scheduled reenactments.

Frostville Museum

Olmsted Historical Society

AGES:	1½–3	3–5	5–8	8–12	12–15
RATING:	NR	★★	★★	★★	★★

COST: **FREE** PREP.: **None**
AREA: **West** CITY: **North Olmsted**

ADDRESS: 24101 Cedar Point Rd.

PHONE: (440) 777-0059

SEASON: Seasonal (Memorial Day–Oct; special events during week)

HOURS: Sun 2–5 p.m. & by special appointment; group tours available

PRICES: Free

DIRECT.: I-480 to Exit 6 for SR 252 (Great Northern Blvd.); south on Great Northern; left (east) on Butternut Ridge Rd.; left (north) on Columbia Rd.; right (east) on Cedar Point Rd.; on right.

✓ Strollers ✓ Groups Food Nearby
Diap Chg ✓ Picnic Pub. Trans.
✓ Parking Food Serv. ✓ Handicapped

This collection of early-19th-century buildings depicts early life in the Western Reserve. It includes a one-room cabin with a center-cooking fireplace, a furnished Victorian farmhouse display, and a general store. This is mostly a look-not-touch group of exhibits, so families might choose to visit during one of the various annual celebrations. Summer brings Friday-night square dances; Christmas is celebrated with hot cider, cookies, and decorations. (Although there are gravel walkways, be sure to wear boots in the winter months.) A general store offers period items for sale.

The museum is named for Elias Carrington Frost, who settled in Olmsted in 1819. It is located in the Rocky River Reservation of the Cleveland Metroparks (see separate listing), and run by the dedicated volunteers of the Olmsted Historical Society.

Great Lakes Science Center

AGES:	1½–3	3–5	5–8	8–12	12–15
RATING:	★	★★★	★★★	★★	★★

COST: **$$** PREP.: **None–Some**
AREA: **Downtown** CITY: **Cleveland**

ADDRESS: 601 Erieside Ave.

PHONE: (216) 694-2000

SEASON: Year round

HOURS: Daily 9:30 a.m.–5:30 p.m.; OMNIMAX shows vary. Closed Thanksgiving and Christmas.

PRICES: Adults $7.75 for exhibits or OMNIMAX, $10.95 for both; Children (ages 3-17) $5.25 for exhibits or OMNIMAX, $7.75 for both

DIRECT.: East/West: SR 2 to E. 9th St.; north on E. 9th; left (west) on Erieside Ave.; on right.

WEB: www.greatscience.com

✓ Strollers ✓ Groups ✓ Food Nearby
✓ Diap Chg ✓ Picnic ✓ Pub. Trans.
✓ Parking ✓ Food Serv. ✓ Handicapped

Encompassing 165,000 square feet with 300 interactive exhibits, the Great Lakes Science Center is this region's big daddy of interactive museums. Everything from the museum's ample windows overlooking Lake Erie to the exhibits themselves is designed to give families a better understanding of how things work in and around the Great Lakes.

By early afternoon, it can get crowded with school groups, so the early hours are best for visits with small children and preschoolers.

The Science Center's environmental exhibits, located in the lower level, take up one-third of the museum's space. There, families can pilot an ore boat up a scaled-down replica of the

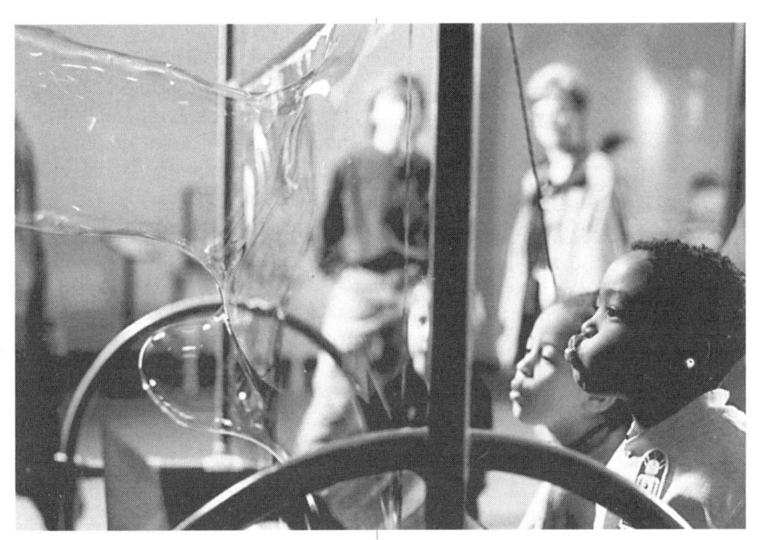

Great Lakes Science Center

Cuyahoga River or play a 20-foot-long sculpture that uses vertical pipes to demonstrate aurally the size of the Great Lakes. Next door is the auditorium-like Situation Room, where 25 computer terminals are linked to each other and to a 25-foot video grid at the front of the room, on which families can play Great Lakes Jeopardy or Environmental Bingo.

Upstairs, at ground level, are the Biomedical and Infotech areas, where a computer-aided batting cage can assess your swing and where, thanks to digital technology, you can move your eyes and ears and other facial features around on a computer screen. On the top level, step inside a cauldron and watch how steel is made, or lift a 2,000-pound crushed car by a single strand of kevlar. In cooperation with other science museums, special exhibits are scheduled throughout the year.

The six-story-tall OMNIMAX Theater, which can be visited separately without having to enter the museum, shows science, natural history, and technology films, all manipulating OMNIMAX's own multisensation technology. A lower-level restaurant area, with ample outdoor lakeside seating and walkways, is a popular gathering place. The gift shop is a good one. Unfortunately, the food both upstairs and down is not.

Birthday parties here are a virtual science bash. Party-goers have the run of the place, with a staff guide, and conduct age-appropriate experiments in a private party room.

Hale Farm and Village

Western Reserve Historical Society

AGES:	1½–3	3–5	5–8	8–12	12–15
RATING:	NR	★	★★	★★★	★★

COST: **FREE–$** PREP.: **None–Some**
AREA: **Far South** CITY: **Bath**

ADDRESS: 2686 Oak Hill Rd., P.O. Box 296

PHONE: (800) 589-9703

SEASON: Seasonal (May–Oct, plus special events)

HOURS: Tue–Sat 10 a.m.–5 p.m.; Sun noon–5 p.m.

PRICES: $9, $7.50 seniors, $5.50 ages 6–12, free 5 and under

DIRECT.: I-77 to Exit 143 for Richfield; west on Wheatley Rd.; left (south) on Brecksville Rd.(becomes Cleveland-Massillon Rd.); left (east) on Ira Rd.; left (north) on Oak Hill Rd.; on left.

✓ Strollers	✓ Groups	Food Nearby
✓ Diap Chg	✓ Picnic	Pub. Trans.
✓ Parking	✓ Food Serv.	Handicapped

This replicated village, dubbed a living history museum, allows you to imagine the everyday lives of Ohio's settlers in the mid-1800s. The buildings were moved from all over Northeast Ohio to re-create a working village. Painstaking restoration of homes, gardens, barns, and even a little one-room log schoolhouse makes it work.

Scattered throughout the village are live demonstrations by blacksmiths, glassblowers, cheesemakers, and other period craftspeople. Guides are stationed in the homes and gardens to answer questions. The setting in Cuyahoga Valley is wooded, hilly, and serene, and although the houses and demonstrations are not set up for the youngest visitors, running and touching are encouraged outside.

Hale Farm and Village

On one visit, we came prepared with a picnic lunch and settled on a hill overlooking the woods. Later we stopped for a treat at the small store and snack bar. We extended our stay to listen to an impromptu concert of folk music.

Hale Farm's special events are very popular. An annual Children's Day in midsummer features 19th-century games and activities; a folk festival brings musicians to the site.

Hayes Presidential Center

Ohio Historical Society

AGES:	1½–3	3–5	5–8	8–12	12–15
RATING:	NR	★	★★	★★	★★

COST: **$–$$** PREP.: **None–Some**
AREA: **Far West** CITY: **Fremont**

ADDRESS: Spiegel Grove (at Hayes and Buckland)

PHONE: (800) 998-PRES

SEASON: Year round

HOURS: Mon–Sat, 9 a.m.–5 p.m.; Sundays and holidays, noon–5 p.m.; closed Thanksgiving, Christmas & New Year's Day

PRICES: Home or Museum $5 adults, $1.25 children 6–12; combination ticket to both sites $8.50 adults, $2.50 children 6–12; children under 6 are free; Senior, Foodtown & AAA discounts; free to OHS members; group rates available upon request.

DIRECT.: I-80/I-90 to Exit 6/91 for SR 53 (Rawson Ave.); south on Rawson; right (west) on Napolean St.; left (south) on Washington St.; left (east) on Hayes Ave.; right (south) on Buckland Ave.; on right.

WEB: www.rbhayes.org

✓ Strollers	✓ Groups	Food Nearby
✓ Diap Chg	Picnic	Pub. Trans.
✓ Parking	Food Serv.	✓ Handicapped

The shady park grounds of Spiegel Grove, once owned by the 19th president of the U.S., features a multilevel Library/Museum with self-guided or arranged tours of past and present presidential belongings. The museum

History, Science & Technology DIRECTORY

has hand-crafted furniture and doll houses, U.S. memorabilia including cannons, artillery, a hand-pump fire engine, and a presidential coach, and interactive displays of the Civil War.

Visitors opt for separate or combination tours which also include the Victorian home and gardens where Hayes and his large family lived. His tomb is also on site.

Picnicking is not allowed on the grounds, but another park has benches close by. Joggers and strollers frequent the grounds to take advantage of a 3/4-mile trail.

History buffs and those looking for an informative afternoon can spend several hours here. Displays are well kept and innovative. The annual Civil War Encampment is well known and well attended.

Health Museum of Cleveland

AGES:	1½–3	3–5	5–8	8–12	12–15
RATING:	NR	★	★	★	★

COST: **$** PREP.: **None–Much**
AREA: **Near East** CITY: **Cleveland**

ADDRESS: 8911 Euclid Ave.

PHONE: (216) 231-5010

SEASON: Year round

HOURS: Mon–Fri 9 a.m.–5 p.m.; Sat 10 a.m.–5 p.m.; Sun noon–5 p.m.

PRICES: $4.50 adults, $3 ages 5–17, college students w/ ID, and seniors; free age 3 & under with adult family member

DIRECT.: West: I-90 to Exit 173B for Chester Ave.; east on Chester; right (south) on E. 55 St.; left (east) on Euclid Ave.; on left.

East: I-90 to Exit 177 for Martin Luther King Blvd.; south on MLK; left on Euclid Ave.; on right.

WEB: www.healthmuseum.org

✓ Strollers ✓ Groups ✓ Food Nearby
✓ Diap Chg Picnic ✓ Pub. Trans.
✓ Parking Food Serv. ✓ Handicapped

If your child has been barraging you with questions about how babies are born, how the human ear hears, or how the heart works, this is the place to go. The Health Museum of Cleveland's exhibits are matter-of-fact and loaded with detail.

Several exhibits, such as Touch Island and the Children's Health Fair, will interest 3- or 4-year-olds, but this museum is best suited for children age 6 and up. And though the layout is logical and there are things to do and learn about, most of the exhibits are in need of modernization: the audio cones that explain how things work are at least a decade old, descriptions of how to use exhibits are cumbersome, and the computers and videotapes need several minutes to reboot or rewind. Much better are the frequently featured traveling exhibits and programs that supplement the 150 permanent exhibits. (The Health Museum—as of this writing—plans to close down and rebuild. The last major renovation was in 1972.)

Special programs for families are scheduled throughout the year and are worth investigating, as is a summer program for preschoolers and up. Year round, the museum staff conducts classes exploring such subjects as sight, hearing, and smell. Classes for school groups are numerous and range from heredity to fitness to substance abuse. Also available are day camps, birthday parties, and several family and older children/teen programs designed to promote fitness and health education.

Historic Sauder Village

AGES:	1½–3	3–5	5–8	8–12	12–15
RATING:	NR	★	★★	★★	★

COST: **$–$$** PREP.: **None–Some**
AREA: **Farther West** CITY: **Archbold**

ADDRESS: SR 2/P.O. Box 235

PHONE: (800) 590-9755

SEASON: Seasonal (Mid-Apr–Nov.1)

HOURS: Mon–Sat 10 a.m.–5 p.m.; Sun 1– 5 p.m.

PRICES: $9.50 adults, $9 seniors, $4.75 students 6–16, no charge under age 5

DIRECT.: I-80/I-90 to Exit 25 for SR 66; south on SR 66; left (east) on SR 2.

WEB: www.saudervillage.com

✓ Strollers ✓ Groups ✓ Food Nearby
✓ Diap Chg ✓ Picnic Pub. Trans.
✓ Parking ✓ Food Serv. ✓ Handicapped

Erie Sauder, who still lives in the area, founded this living history village. It is hands-on history at its best. Special seasonal programs highlight life in the 1860s and allow visitors to take part in typical chores, such as hand-washing clothes on a scrubboard and spinning wool. Other activities include stilt walking and candle making (these seem like more fun). There are many animals, ranging from horses and cows to peacocks and oxen, in the homestead area.

Check out their schedule in advance; many special celebrations take place throughout the year, including the Quilt Show in April, Butchering Day, a Woodcarving Fair, Summer on the Farm, and the Children's Fall Festival (a family favorite). You can spend three hours or more touring the village and watching craft demonstrations. No reservations are required.

Hower House Victorian Mansion

AGES:	1½–3	3–5	5–8	8–12	12–15
RATING:	NR	NR	★	★★	★★

COST: **$** PREP.: **None–Some**
AREA: **Far South** CITY: **Akron**

ADDRESS: 60 Fir Hill (University of Akron)

PHONE: (330) 972-6909

SEASON: Year-round (closed Jan)

HOURS: Tours: Wed–Sat noon–3:30 p.m., Sun 1 p.m.–4 p.m.

PRICES: $5 adults, $4 seniors, $2 students, children 6 & under free; closed in January

DIRECT.: SR 8 to E. Butchel Ave.; west on E. Butchel; right (north) on Fir Hill; on left.

Strollers ✓ Groups ✓ Food Nearby
Diap Chg Picnic ✓ Pub. Trans.
✓ Parking Food Serv. Handicapped

Wealthy and well traveled, the Howers fitted out their home lavishly. A cupboard is inlaid with mother-of-pearl. Chandeliers hang from the ceiling in every room. The sloping mansard roof covers a wraparound porch and is capped by a soaring tower. Inside and out, the home gleams and shines just as it did when industrialist John Henry Hower lived there in the 1870s.

That this historic home remains preserved is an accomplishment in itself. Instead of letting the 28-room mansion become a fraternity house, Grace Hower Crawford deeded it to the University of Akron. After her death in the 1980s, the school restored the house using donated funds and volunteer labor.

For families with younger kids less keen on hands-off history, there are special events (such as storytimes) throughout the year, and a Christmas display and celebration with cookies and wassail for everyone. Call for the most current schedule information.

Indian Museum of Lake County

AGES:	1½–3	3–5	5–8	8–12	12–15
RATING:	NR	★	★★	★★	★★

COST: **$** PREP.: **None–Some**
AREA: **Far East** CITY: **Painesville**

ADDRESS: 391 W. Washington St.

PHONE: (440) 352-1911

SEASON: Year round

HOURS: Sept–Apr Mon–Fri 9 a.m.–4 p.m., Sat–Sun 1 p.m.–4 p.m.; May–Aug Mon–Fri 10 a.m.–4 p.m., Sat–Sun 1 p.m.–4 p.m.; closed major holiday weekends and Lake Erie College's Winter Break (mid-Dec–mid-Jan) and Spring Break (last week in March)

PRICES: $2 adults, $1 students, $1.50 seniors, preschool ages free. Call for group rate and reservation.

DIRECT.: SR 2 to Richmond St; south on Richmond; right (west) on US 20 (Mentor Ave.); on left (west end of Lake Erie College campus).

✓ Strollers ✓ Groups ✓ Food Nearby
Diap Chg Picnic ✓ Pub. Trans.
✓ Parking Food Serv. ✓ Handicapped

This museum traces the development of Indian tribal groups who lived nearby between 22,000 B.C. and 1600 A.D.; it also covers the history of today's Native Americans from 1800 to the present. Several hands-on activities are excellent for parents and children to work on together. Our favorite was a large wooden learning board filled with colorful pictures of Indian dwellings. The goal: match tribes with their homes.

School-age children (grades 4 and up) are invited to participate in a mini-archaeological dig. Several sandboxes—each containing bones, teeth, or arrowheads—come equipped with brushes so that children can gently brush off the sand to reveal what lies beneath. For preschoolers, there are grinding bins equipped with stones and dried corn to grind into corn flour.

Although the museum is housed in just one room, its exhibits are well laid out and extensive. Displays cover an array of artifacts from North American indigenous cultures, including ceremonial masks, baskets, beadwork, and other crafts. A reproduction of a Hopewell Shaman (a highly decorated medicine man) and colorful totem pole are striking—toddlers will be either fascinated or terrified. Some displays are changed annually to feature unique Native American cultures.

Tour programs can be arranged for adults and children ages 4 and up by reservation only.

Inland Seas Maritime Museum

Great Lakes Historical Society

AGES:	1½–3	3–5	5–8	8–12	12–15
RATING:	★	★	★★	★★	★★

COST: **$** PREP.: **None–Much**
AREA: **Far West** CITY: **Vermilion**

ADDRESS: 480 Main St.

PHONE: (800) 893-1485

SEASON: Year round

HOURS: Daily 10 a.m.–5 p.m.

PRICES: $5 adults, $4 seniors, $3 ages 6–16, free ages 5 & under

DIRECT.: SR 2 to SR 60 (Savannah Vermilion Rd.); north on SR 60; SR 60 becomes Main St.; on left at end of Main St.

✓ Strollers ✓ Groups ✓ Food Nearby
Diap Chg ✓ Picnic Pub. Trans.
✓ Parking Food Serv. ✓ Handicapped

If you're interested in Great Lakes history, this is your place. There are paintings, artifacts (such as marine engines and tools), and detailed models of Great Lakes vessels. Vermilion, possessing one of the best natural harbors on Lake Erie, once competed with Cleveland for maritime traffic. Now, visitors can watch that traffic pass by from the museum's fully equipped freighter pilothouse overlooking the lakefront.

The Inland Seas Maritime Museum was created in 1953 and housed in the converted Commodore Wakefield Mansion. Acquisitions increased and, in 1968, a modern two-story section was added. The museum now boasts one of the largest collections of marine engines in the United States, including a 14-foot-high harbor-tug steam engine built in 1913. Other good stuff: the lighthouse exhibit and a scale model of the 729-foot *Edmund Fitzgerald*, the ill-fated freighter that went down in Lake Superior in 1975. An adult-child boat-building program results in a seaworthy boat built from scratch over a weekend.

Inventure Place & The National Inventors Hall of Fame

AGES:	1½–3	3–5	5–8	8–12	12–15
RATING:	★	★★	★★★	★★★	★★

COST: **FREE–$$** PREP.: **None**
AREA: **Far South** CITY: **Akron**

ADDRESS: 221 S. Broadway

PHONE: (800) 968-IDEA

SEASON: Year round

HOURS: Mon–Sat 9 a.m.–5 p.m.; Sun noon–5 p.m.

PRICES: $7.50 adults, $6 seniors and ages 3-17, under 3 free; group rate $5.50; family rate (2 adults & unlimited children of same household) $25

DIRECT.: I-76/I-77 to Exit 22 for Main St./Broadway Ave.; north on Broadway; on right.

WEB: www.invent.org/

✓ Strollers	✓ Groups	✓ Food Nearby
✓ Diap Chg	Picnic	✓ Pub. Trans.
✓ Parking	✓ Food Serv.	✓ Handicapped

The mission of this $38-million museum is to get children to play science the way they would play games or sports. It has succeeded. Inventure Place is one of Ohio's premier hands-on institutions. Everything from its slick exhibits to its first-rate architecture has raised the level of family museum experience in this state to new heights.

Inventure Place and National Inventors Hall of Fame

The museum layout funnels traffic in two directions: up to the National Inventors Hall of Fame, and down to the main exhibit area located beneath street level. Once below, kids will immediately be drawn to a frame holding a series of simple plumbing tubes and stainless steel detours that, if connected properly, will allow gravity to keep a golf ball in motion, or to a K'nex Table for free-form building. (Off to the right is a rest area for adults, furnished with comfortable chairs and an eclectic collection of coffee-table books.) Next is a series of exhibits devoted to fiber optics, magnetics, and lasers.

The genius of the place is that it truly makes science fun. Our son, then six years old, spent 20 minutes alone repositioning little mirrors refracting beams of red light through a steamy mist. This of course prompted a series of questions about lasers, lights, and beams that unfortunately could not be answered. If there is a weakness here, it is the lack of explanation (an element designed "to spur creativity"). If you were clueless on the way in as to how things such as a magnetic resonance scanner work, you may exit in almost as much ignorance—there is not a lot of explanatory material. (A couple of freestanding personal computers do offer some help.)

Other exhibit highlights include a workshop area where kids can dissect old electronic castaways such as typewriters and computers or assemble new creations using any one of dozens of parts from the material-rich bins.

The National Inventors Hall of Fame occupies several levels that overlook the main exhibit space. Compared to all the action in the exhibition area, the Hall is rather sleepy and low tech, with pictures of inductees hanging on the walls. There are several interesting video displays, including one on how a market was created for the Polaroid camera and another on how a pair of scissors is not just a pair of scissors, but these are too sparse.

While there is no parking that doesn't require a walk, the neighboring lots are free with a stamped entry—be sure to call ahead for directions to the lots.

Lake County Historical Society & History Center

AGES:	1½–3	3–5	5–8	8–12	12–15
RATING:	NR	★	★★	★★	★★

COST: **FREE–$** PREP.: **None–Some**
AREA: **Far East** CITY: **Kirtland Hills**

ADDRESS: 8610 King Memorial Rd.

PHONE: (440) 255-8979

SEASON: Year round

HOURS: Tue–Fri 9 a.m.–5 p.m.; Sat, Sun 1 p.m.–5 p.m. (closed weekends Jan–Mar)

PRICES: Donation requested for museum tour; nominal fee for youth, preschool programs

DIRECT.: I-90 to Exit 190 for SR 306; north on SR 306; right (east) on SR 84; right (south) on Little Mountain Rd.; right (south) on Mentor Rd.

✓ Strollers ✓ Groups ✓ Food Nearby
✓ Diap Chg ✓ Picnic Pub. Trans.
✓ Parking Food Serv. ✓ Handicapped

From September to November and again from April to June, children can be transported back in time with the "Pioneer School" program, where staff members decked out in pioneer garb let kids experience everything from candle making to colonial-style lunch preparation. No microwaves here; kids must make, then bake, their own johnnycakes, starting with hand-grinding the corn. This program offers maximum "hands-on."

Non-school groups and visitors of all ages get some of the same experiences by visiting the main museum and its galleries, two Indian cabins, log cabins, and a one-room schoolhouse in the 15-acre, nine-building living history compound. Antique music boxes and toys are also part of the museum's collection.

Christmas on the Western Reserve, with the staff aided by high-school volunteers, offers a day of crafts and cookies for ages 5–12. During the summer (late July), look for the Little Mountain Folk Festival, which features craft demonstrations, music, and living history exhibits and performances. All summer long, 1860s-style Base Ball is played, and in September hundreds of Civil War reenactors gather for the largest Civil War encampment and battle reenactment in Northeast Ohio.

Lake View Cemetery

AGES:	1½–3	3–5	5–8	8–12	12–15
RATING:	★	★	★★	★★	★★

COST: **FREE–$** PREP.: **None**
AREA: **East** CITY: **Cleveland**

ADDRESS: 12316 Euclid Ave.

PHONE: (216) 421-2665

SEASON: Year round

HOURS: Daily 7:30 a.m.–5:30 p.m.

PRICES: Donation requested

DIRECT.: I-90 to Exit 173B for Chester Ave. (eastbound: left (south) on E. 24 St.; left (east) on Chester; left (northeast) on Euclid Ave.; right (east) on US 322 (Mayfield Rd.); on left.

✓ Strollers	✓ Groups	✓ Food Nearby
Diap Chg	Picnic	✓ Pub. Trans.
✓ Parking	Food Serv.	✓ Handicapped

History and nature are combined at Lake View. Many famous people are buried in this historic cemetery, from President James Garfield to sports figures to Cleveland mayors and business tycoons (including John D. Rockefeller). Many native plants, trees, and shrubs are also collected here—it is a 285-acre arboretum. While you can see much on your own, a guided tour here runs from 45 minutes to an hour and typically includes a walk through the landscape, the Gothic and Romanesque-style Garfield Monument, and Wade Chapel, which features exceptional glass tilework by Louis Tiffany.

Garfield Monument, Lake View Cemetery

Children may be interested in the very old trees (most marked by botanical tags), statues and monuments, and a quarry located on the grounds. There is also a good view of Lake Erie and the downtown skyline—especially after a climb up the towering Garfield Monument (open April–mid-November).

Rubbings of gravestones are allowed with adult supervision; the cemetery provides the supplies. Reservations are advised for everyone and are necessary for groups, which can include 10 to 30 people. Annual celebrations and holiday programs are well worth a visit.

Lawnfield, James A. Garfield National Historic Site and Visitor Center

Western Reserve Historical Society

AGES:	1½–3	3–5	5–8	8–12	12–15
RATING:	NR	★★	★★	★★★	★★★

COST: **$** PREP.: **None**
AREA: **Far East** CITY: **Mentor**

ADDRESS: 8095 Mentor Ave.

PHONE: (440) 255-8722

SEASON: Year round

HOURS: Mon–Sat 10 a.m.–5 p.m.; Sun noon–5 p.m.

PRICES: $6 adults, $5 seniors, $4 ages 6–12, no charge under age 6

DIRECT.: SR 2 to SR 306; south on SR 306; left (east) on Mentor Ave.; on left.

Or, SR 2 to SR 615; south on SR 615; right (west) on Mentor Ave.; on right.

Or, I-90 to Exit 190 for SR 306; north on SR 306; right (east) on Mentor Ave.; on left.

WEB: www.wrhs.org

✓ Strollers	✓ Groups	✓ Food Nearby
✓ Diap Chg	✓ Picnic	✓ Pub. Trans.
✓ Parking	Food Serv.	✓ Handicapped

The spirit of James A. Garfield, the nation's 20th president, lives on in Lawnfield, home of the former president. The entire mansion reopened after an eight-year-long intensive restoration.

This one-story farmhouse was built in 1832 and expanded in the 1870s and 1880s. It was bought by the future 20th president of the United States in 1876; while campaigning in 1880, he used the front porch for speech making. Each of 12 rooms is dressed in late-19th-century style, and many of the furnishings belonged to the Garfield family. The library is a favorite spot, with walls of books from Garfield's own collection; it was the first presidential memorial library ever built. The carriage house is complete with five period carriages. (Children often ask whether the house has secret passages; the answer is no.) The museum/visitor center, built inside the 1893 carriage house on the property, features historic exhibits and other audio/visual information about President Garfield and the period. Audio components allow visitors to listen to Garfield's speech to the 1880 Republican convention or hear Garfield's thoughts on slavery.

Mad River & NKP Railroad Society Museum

AGES:	1½–3	3–5	5–8	8–12	12–15
RATING:	NR	NR	★★	★★	★

COST: **$** PREP.: **None**
AREA: **Farther West** CITY: **Bellevue**

ADDRESS: 233 York St.

PHONE: (419) 483-2222

SEASON: Seasonal (Memorial Day–Labor Day)

HOURS: Daily 1 p.m.–5 p.m.; weekends only May, Sep–Oct

PRICES: Admission charged

DIRECT.: I-80/I-90 to Exit 6A for SR 4 (Columbus Sandusky Rd.); south on SR 4; right (west) on SR 113 (Edison Highway); left (south) on Southwest St.; on left.

✓ Strollers ✓ Groups ✓ Food Nearby
✓ Diap Chg ✓ Picnic Pub. Trans.
✓ Parking Food Serv. ✓ Handicapped

This restored 19th-century depot has become the last stop for many of the railroad cars that once passed through in active service. Diesel engines, refrigerated produce cars, freight cars, dining cars, mail cars—there are 35 vintage rail cars and engines in all. Among the highlights are a caboose (in which conductors lived), a troop transport filled with wartime memorabilia, and the nation's first domed observation car. The museum's collection also includes a watchman's tower, uniforms, timetables, lanterns, china, locks, and, of course, a gift shop.

Malabar Farm State Park

AGES:	1½–3	3–5	5–8	8–12	12–15
RATING:	★	★★	★★	★★	★★

COST: **$** PREP.: **None**
AREA: **Farther West** CITY: **Lucas**

ADDRESS: 4050 Bromfield Rd.

PHONE: (800) 642-8282

SEASON: Year round

HOURS: Vary

PRICES: Vary. Admission: Big House Tour: $3 adults, $1 children 6-18; Wagon Tours: $1 over age 6

DIRECT.: I-71 to Exit 169 for SR 13; south on SR 13; left (east) on Hanley Rd.; right (south) on Little Washington Rd.; left (east) on Pleasant Valley Rd.; right on Bromfield Rd.

Strollers ✓ Groups ✓ Food Nearby
Diap Chg ✓ Picnic Pub. Trans.
✓ Parking ✓ Food Serv. ✓ Handicapped

The dream of author Louis Bromfield, Malabar Farm is a beautiful and stately 32-room country home standing amidst 900 acres with several farm ponds and 12 miles of hiking trails. The house, with furniture and paintings, remains much as it was at the time of Bromfield's death in 1956. Narrated tractor-drawn wagon rides provide history of Ohio's agriculture as well as information about the celebrated author.

Not to be overlooked are the many

outbuildings that also remain: a sugar camp, petting farm, sawmill, and dairy barn. The park is also popular for its annual celebrations including Maple Sugar time and pumpkin harvest, and its naturalist-led hikes. Over ten miles of cross-county ski trails are groomed in the winter; equipment rental is also available.

Marblehead Lighthouse State Park

AGES:	1½–3	3–5	5–8	8–12	12–15
RATING:	NR	NR	★	★	★

COST: **FREE** PREP.: **None**
AREA: **Farther West** CITY: **Marblehead**

ADDRESS: Lighthouse Dr. (off SR 163)

PHONE: (419) 797-4530

SEASON: Seasonal (Memorial Day–Labor Day)

HOURS: Mon–Fri 1 p.m.–5 p.m.; also open 10 a.m.–3 p.m. on the second Saturdays of June–Sept

PRICES: Free

DIRECT.: SR 2 to SR 269; east on SR 269; right (east) on SR 163; on left.

WEB: www.marbleheadpenninsula.com

Strollers | Groups | ✓ Food Nearby
Diap Chg | ✓ Picnic | Pub. Trans.
✓ Parking | Food Serv. | Handicapped

To honor the role of this historic lighthouse as protector of Lake Erie boaters for 176 years, the simple tower, framed by trees and perched on the rocky coast, was declared surplus in 1996 by the U.S. Coast Guard. And while the USCG continues to operate the tower, the Ohio Department of Natural Resources has taken ownership with plans to improve visitors' facilities. For its opening in the 1999 season, tours up the 87 winding steps allow a magnificent lake view.

McKinley Museum of History, Science, and Industry

AGES:	1½–3	3–5	5–8	8–12	12–15
RATING:	★★	★★★	★★★	★★	★

COST: **FREE–$$** PREP.: **None–Some**
AREA: **Farther South** CITY: **Canton**

ADDRESS: 800 McKinley Monument Dr. NW

PHONE: (330) 455-7043

SEASON: Year round

HOURS: Mon–Sat 9 a.m.–5 p.m., Sun noon–5 p.m.; Summer hours (mid-Jun–Labor Day): Mon–Sat 9 a.m.–6 p.m, Sun noon–6 p.m.

PRICES: Museum: $6, $5 seniors, $4 ages 3–18, no charge under age 3; National Memorial: free

DIRECT.: I-77 to Exit 106 for 13 St./12 St.; east on 12 St.; right (south) on Stadium Park Dr.; right (north) on McKinley Monument Dr.

WEB: www.mckinleymuseum.org

✓ Strollers | ✓ Groups | ✓ Food Nearby
✓ Diap Chg | ✓ Picnic | Pub. Trans.
✓ Parking | ✓ Food Serv. | ✓ Handicapped

With the addition of the hands-on science Discover World, this small museum has become a winner for families and well worth a special trip. The original part of the museum is devoted to re-creating the late-Victorian era of President William McKinley. Upstairs, the Museum of History includes several replicated early-American rooms along with a Street of Shops lined with life-size stores.

Your kids, however, will want to head straight to the basement. (You should, too, if your time is limited to an hour or so.) First stop: Natural History Island, a land of fossils and skeletons guarded by a roaring, life-size allosaurus named Alice. (Alice is programmed to stop every three minutes, to allow younger kids to pass.) A cave-like burrow allows you to climb up and try on the skeleton head of a tyrannosaurus rex. At Ecology Island, a massive oak tree, trickling water, and bird sounds set the mood. A series of ponds equipped with inverted periscopes allow even the smallest of visitors to glimpse the underwater life. We spent the most time at Spacestation Earth, tinkering with the various lasers, magnets, and pumps.

Before you visit, call to check on special activities. There are regularly scheduled sound shows, electric shows, and sessions with live animals, as well as a make-and-take project series for ages five and up.

In the adjacent Hoover-Prive Planetarium, sky productions change regularly. (Children under five are not permitted in the planetarium.) The towering McKinley National Memorial provides a good climb for all ages—a great way to work out the kinks from a car ride.

McKinley Museum and Memorial

Merry-Go-Round Museum

AGES:	1½–3	3–5	5–8	8–12	12–15
RATING:	NR	★	★	★	★

COST: **$** PREP.: **None**
AREA: **Farther West** CITY: **Sandusky**

ADDRESS: W. Washington & Jackson Sts.

PHONE: (419) 626-6111

SEASON: Year round

HOURS: Mon–Sat 11 a.m.–5 p.m., Sun noon–5 p.m.; open weekends only Jan & Feb, daily Memorial Day–Labor Day, Wed–Sun other times of the year.

PRICES: $4 adults, $3 seniors, $2 ages 4–14, no charge under age 3

DIRECT.: I-90 to SR 2; west on SR 2 to Rye Beach Rd.; north on Rye Beach; left (west) on US 6 (becomes Washington in Sandusky); on left at Jackson St.

WEB: www.carousel.net/org/sandusky/index.htm

✓ Strollers ✓ Groups ✓ Food Nearby
Diap Chg Picnic Pub. Trans.
✓ Parking Food Serv. ✓ Handicapped

Merry-Go-Round Museum

Carved carousel animals are now an endangered species; of the more than 7,000 merry-go-rounds built, only 200 are still in existence. Sandusky's Merry-Go-Round Museum, located in a former post office, is home to the collection of carved animals, tools, and workbenches of the Gustav Dentzel Caroussell Builder shop, re-created here from the 1800s Philadelphia original. Visitors will also find traveling exhibits on display from other museums around the world, such as a recent exhibit from the National Folk Art Museum in Paris.

While the carvings themselves may not entice all youngsters, a tour includes a look at a carousel carver at work and a ride on a fully restored Allen Herschell carousel.

Reservations are not required. Tour groups qualify for special rates if prior arrangements are made.

NASA Glenn Research Center

AGES:	1½–3	3–5	5–8	8–12	12–15
RATING:	NR	★	★★	★★★	★★

COST: **FREE** PREP.: **Some**
AREA: **Near West** CITY: **Cleveland**

ADDRESS: 21000 Brookpark Rd.

PHONE: (216) 433-2001; (216) 433-2000

SEASON: Year round

HOURS: Mon–Fri 9 a.m.–5 p.m.; Sat 10 a.m.–3 p.m.; Sun 1 p.m.–5 p.m.

PRICES: Free

DIRECT.: I-480 to Exit 9 for Grayton Rd.; south on Grayton; right (west) on Brookpark; on left.

WEB: www.grc.nasa.gov

Strollers	✓ Groups	✓ Food Nearby
Diap Chg	Picnic	Pub.Trans.
✓ Parking	Food Serv.	✓ Handicapped

A nifty collection of space stuff includes the Apollo Skylab 3 capsule, a moon rock, and a space station model. A comparison of John Glenn's two missions includes replicas of his two space suits. Nearly 8,000 square feet of this 350-acre NASA complex are devoted to educating the public about space exploration, jet propulsion, aeronautics, and research.

The Visitor Center is at its best when it sticks to the nuts and bolts of space technology, such as how a jet engine functions, or what the various layers of an Apollo space suit are, or how metal reacts to heat and stress in space travel. The interactive exhibits are less effective and a bit out of date.

The staff here shines: A short presentation about space travel was very worthwhile. These folks understand how things work and can convey that understanding to youngsters. The presentation is frequently followed by a video, "Astrosmiles," which consisted of 15 minutes of Space Shuttle gravity jokes and was a big hit with the kids. For older visitors (ages 13 and up), there is a guided tour of the test facilities on Wednesdays and one Saturday each month. Call ahead for exact date and time.

Also, make sure you bring your driver's license; it is asked for at the front gate as a security precaution. Be aware, you and your car may be searched.

Oldest Stone House Museum

Lakewood Historical Society

AGES:	1½–3	3–5	5–8	8–12	12–15
RATING:	★	★	★★	★★	★★

COST: **FREE** PREP.: **None–Much**
AREA: **Near West** CITY: **Lakewood**

ADDRESS: 14710 Lake Ave.

PHONE: (216) 221-7343

SEASON: Seasonal (Closed Dec & Jan)

HOURS: Wed 1 p.m.–4 p.m., Sun 2–5 p.m.; closed holidays

PRICES: Free

DIRECT.: I-90 to Exit 165 for Warren Rd.; north on Warren; right (east) on Clifton Blvd.; left (north) on Belle Ave.; left (west) on Lake Ave.; on right.

Strollers	✓ Groups	Food Nearby
Diap Chg	✓ Picnic	✓ Pub.Trans.
✓ Parking	Food Serv.	Handicapped

The Oldest Stone House, built in 1838, illustrates life in pioneer days through displays and tours. Children can experience the pioneer lifestyle directly in the Ohio Heritage classes held each June. Offered in conjunction with the Lakewood Recreation Department, this week-long course (morning or afternoon sessions) gets children involved with pioneer crafts, games, activities, and chores. Brownie Teas, for Brownie troops, encourage girls ages 7–10 to bring their favorite stuffed or plastic friend to tea parties to sip "Stone House" tea from old china teacups and learn about the history of dolls.

Perry's Cave

AGES:	1½–3	3–5	5–8	8–12	12–15
RATING:	NR	★	★★	★★	★★

COST: **$–$$** PREP.: **Some**
AREA: **Farther West** CITY: **Put-in-Bay**

ADDRESS: 979 Catawba Ave., P.O. Box 335

PHONE: (419) 285-2405

SEASON: Seasonal (May–Nov)

HOURS: Tours: daily 10:30 a.m.–6 p.m. (summer), limited off-season hours

PRICES: $4.50 adults; $2.25 children 5–11

DIRECT.: SR 2 to SR 163; west on SR 163 for Port Clinton; right (north) on N. Jefferson St.; Jet Express Boat for Put-in-Bay on right.

OR SR 2 to SR 53; north on SR 53 for Catawba Island; left (west) on Sloan St.; right (north) on Crogh St.; left (west) on Water St.; Miller Boat Line for Put-in-Bay on right.

Strollers	✓ Groups	✓ Food Nearby
Diap Chg	✓ Picnic	Pub. Trans.
✓ Parking	✓ Food Serv.	Handicapped

Watch your step in this active limestone cave 52 feet below ground. Lake Erie battle hero Commodore Oliver Hazard Perry once used its crystal-clear drinking water to heal his wounded men. The water is probably quite drinkable, but the facility no longer allows it. The slippery and sometimes low-ceilinged cavern remains at a constant 50 degrees Fahrenheit. The cold temperatures will likely make your nose run by the end of the short but informative lantern tour. The guides are cheerful islanders. Groups witness beautiful stalactites and stalagmites produced by the accumulation of 100 years of dripping water. Located outside the cave, a gem-sifting tank allows children to find "real gems" (beach-glass)—rough mix bags can be purchased in the gift shop. Visitors are not permitted to touch the crystal formations, as the oil from your fingers stops the process. The temptation to rub your hands on the ceiling is enticing. The entry portal into the cave is barely four feet high, and on an incline. Visitors with bad backs beware.

Perry's Victory & International Peace Memorial

AGES:	1½–3	3–5	5–8	8–12	12–15
RATING:	NR	★	★★	★★	★★

COST: **$** PREP.: **None**
AREA: **Farther West** CITY: **Put-in-Bay**

ADDRESS: 93 Delaware

PHONE: (419) 285-2184

SEASON: Seasonal (April–mid-Oct)

HOURS: Late April–mid-Oct 10 a.m.–5 p.m., rest of year by appointment

PRICES: Small fee: observation deck. $3 adults, free for children 16 and under accompanied by an adult.

DIRECT.: SR 2 to SR 163; west on SR 163 for Port Clinton; right (north) on N. Jefferson St.; Jet Express Boat for Put-in-Bay on right.

OR SR 2 to SR 53; north on SR 53 for Catawba Island; left (west) on Sloan St.; right (north) on Crogh St.; left (west) on Water St.; Miller Boat Line for Put-in-Bay on right.

Strollers	Groups	✓ Food Nearby
Diap Chg	Picnic	Pub. Trans.
✓ Parking	Food Serv.	Handicapped

A massive memorial that towers over Put-in-Bay, this national monument, managed by the U.S. Department of the Interior, honors Commodore Oliver Perry's naval victory over a British fleet in the War of 1812. An observation deck is perched 317 feet above Lake Erie; the monument is capped in bronze. On a clear day you can see 10 miles northwest to the battle site.

With 37 steps leading from a small elevator, the site can be slippery and hazardous; children are only allowed with an adult.

A small visitor's center at street

level explains the battle and the military strategies employed on Lake Erie. (Eating, drinking, and smoking are prohibited.)

Professional Football Hall of Fame

AGES:	1½–3	3–5	5–8	8–12	12–15
RATING:	NR	★	★★	★★	★★

COST: **$$–$$$** PREP.: **None**
AREA: **Farther South** CITY: **Canton**

ADDRESS: 2121 George Halas Dr. NW

PHONE: (330) 456-8207; (330) 456-7762

SEASON: Year round

HOURS: Memorial Day–Labor Day daily 9 a.m.–8 a.m.; remainder of the year daily 9 a.m.–5 p.m.

PRICES: $10 adults, $6.50 seniors, $5 ages 6–14, $25 families

DIRECT.: I-77 to Exit 107 for SR 687 (Fulton Dr.);

WEB: www.profootballhof.com

✓ Strollers ✓ Groups ✓ Food Nearby
✓ Diap Chg Picnic Pub. Trans.
✓ Parking ✓ Food Serv. ✓ Handicapped

The Hall is first and foremost a shrine to the greatest players of the gridiron. Indeed, there are enough bronze busts, shriveled pads, faded shoes, and dirty jerseys to numb even the heartiest fan. But after attendance tapered in the early 1990s, management huddled and emerged with a $9.1-million renovation that put motion back in the backfield and added 4,500 square feet of new exhibit space.

Most prominent in the expansion is "Game Day Stadium," a turntable theater film that puts visitors in the locker room as the Kansas City Chiefs and Pittsburgh Steelers prepare for a game at Arrowhead Stadium. As the teams leave the locker room, the theater floor turns 180 degrees to face a darkened wall and the sound of cleats clattering on the runway toward the field. Highlights of several other teams are shown, ending with clips from a recent Super Bowl. Three TV monitors play locker room celebrations as you walk out. Fans will appreciate the fact that NFL Films put together the entire sequence. (For the uninitiated, these are the guys who made football highlight films into struggles of epic proportions complete with pulse-quickening music, on-field sound effects, and slow-motion recaps of on-field brilliance.) The experience lasts 30 minutes.

The museum also added a research center, which is not open to the public for browsing. However, if you or your school-age child have a specific player or topic you want to investigate, make an appointment upon entering.

If you prefer an interactive approach, head to the lower level of the new addition. There, plays from the 24 Super Bowls are cued up on video screens. An announcer sets up each play; visitors guess, via a computer keyboard, what play, for example, then-49ers quarterback Joe Montana decided to call during the last 2 minutes of Super Bowl XXIII. Also located in the same area is a multiple-choice game of football trivia. The annual induction ceremony attracts a big crowd of fans from across the country.

Rainbow Children's Museum and TRW Learning Center

AGES:	1½–3	3–5	5–8	8–12	12–15
RATING:	★★★	★★★	★	★	NR

COST: **$** PREP.: **None–Some**
AREA: **Near East** CITY: **Cleveland**

ADDRESS: 10730 Euclid Ave.

PHONE: (216) 791-KIDS; office: (216) 791-7114

SEASON: Year round

HOURS: 10 a.m.–5 p.m.; Tot time: Mon 1 p.m.–5 p.m.; Tues 10 a.m.–4 p.m.

PRICES: $5 adults, $4.50 seniors, $4 children ages 2–15, no charge under age 2; $1 every 2nd Wed of month 5–8 p.m. only

DIRECT.: East: I-90 to Exit 177 for Martin Luther King Blvd.; south on MLK to Stearns Rd. (after Euclid Ave.); on right.

West: I-90 to Exit 173 for Chester Ave.; east on Chester; right (south) on Stearns Rd.; on right after Euclid Ave.

✓ Strollers	✓ Groups	✓ Food Nearby
✓ Diap Chg	✓ Picnic	✓ Pub. Trans.
✓ Parking	Food Serv.	✓ Handicapped

Everything here is designed to be taken apart, rebuilt, and crawled over, under, and on. At every turn kids can explore, learn, and have fun. Museum volunteers staff nearly every exhibit to offer assistance.

The long-running "Over and Under Bridges" exhibit boasts everything from small-scale bridges that kids can run across to a huge pit of blocks where they can design and build their own. A weather studio allows kids to play forecaster, and the Water-Go-Round is a big hit.

There is a separate area for toddlers for quiet play, but the museum can get crowded and rowdy on weekends and on school days when there are large groups. So for the younger ones, try Tuesday mornings or Monday afternoons, when the museum is open only to preschoolers. Weekday afternoons also tend to be more relaxed. Also, the Tot Spot is a safe, carpeted area filled with Little Tikes equipment geared to the preschool set.

The museum's special events are interactive celebrations with singing, dancing, storytelling, toy making, bead stringing . . . the list goes on. Check out the seasonal calendar for special programs.

The museum store is tough to miss. It is stocked with unusual toys, books, and games.

Rainbow Children's Museum

Rock and Roll Hall of Fame and Museum

AGES:	1½–3	3–5	5–8	8–12	12–15
RATING:	NR	NR	★	★★	★★★

COST: **$$$** PREP.: **None**
AREA: **Downtown** CITY: **Cleveland**

ADDRESS: 1 Key Plaza

PHONE: (888) 764-ROCK

SEASON: Year round

HOURS: Daily 10 a.m.–5:30 p.m., Wed 10 a.m.–9 p.m.

PRICES: $14.95 adults, $11.50 seniors (55+) and children ages 4-11

DIRECT.: SR 2 to E. 9 St.; north on E. 9; left (west) on Erieside Ave.; on right.

WEB: www.rockhall.com

✓ Strollers	✓ Groups	✓ Food Nearby
Diap Chg	Picnic	✓ Pub. Trans.
✓ Parking	✓ Food Serv.	✓ Handicapped

I. M. Pei's pyramid-shaped glass-faced Rock Hall rises up dramatically from Lake Erie at the E. 9th Street Pier. Inside, much of the action is below street level. There you are greeted by black-and-white photos of rock's early influences and, just beyond, a section called "The Beat Goes On" where you can tap computer screens and call up song snippets and film clips and follow a musical family tree to see, for example, that Fats Domino was influenced by Amos Milburn and that Muddy Waters motivated Jimi Hendrix.

There are plenty of rock artifacts to gaze at—the Temptations' blue tuxedos, Alice Cooper's boots, Madonna's bustier, and Jim Morrison's Cub Scout shirt, to mention only a few. There is no shortage of guitars and shoes.

And you are never far from the music. Another bank of interactive computer screens features performers discussing their lives and music. "What'd I Say?" dissects how several songs were made through interviews with performers, producers, and songwriters.

Woven into this mix are several movie-like exhibits, one of which explains how songs were inspired. Another room boasts two walls of TV monitors, one displaying modern American history, the other music and musicians of the times. It is simultaneously disturbing and entertaining.

While lots of families were there on our visit, we were hard-pressed to find a reason to bring our six-year-old along—there is little to touch or do. As for even littler kids, leave them at home; they just won't get it. Upstairs, the cafe serves spotty fare, but its view of Lake Erie is great, no matter what the season.

As this place is new, its rhythm isn't well established. Daily attendance varies from 1,000 to 9,000, while the average stay is about three hours. There are three nearby parking lots: one directly to the north of the museum on E. 9th St.; one south, also on E. 9th; and one at the Cleveland-Cuyahoga Port Authority (plan on spending about $5). For those really brutal days, the Port Authority has valet service.

Roscoe Village Foundation

AGES:	1½–3	3–5	5–8	8–12	12–15
RATING:	★	★	★★	★★	★★

COST: **FREE–$$** PREP.: **None–Some**
AREA: **Farther South** CITY: **Coshocton**

ADDRESS: 381 Hill St.

PHONE: (800) 877-1830

SEASON: Year round (special events Feb–Dec)

HOURS: Sun–Thu 10 a.m.–6 p.m., Fri–Sat 10 a.m.–8 p.m.; Living History Tour 10 a.m.–5 p.m.

PRICES: Village admission: free; tour: $8.95 adults, $3.95 children ages 5–12

DIRECT.: I-77 to Exit 65 for US 36; west on US 36 into Coshocton.

WEB: www.roscoevillage.com

✓ Strollers ✓ Groups ✓ Food Nearby
Diap Chg ✓ Picnic ✓ Pub. Trans.
✓ Parking ✓ Food Serv. ✓ Handicapped

Roscoe was once a thriving commercial center along the Ohio and Erie Canal (which was built to connect the Ohio River with Lake Erie). The village fell on hard times after the canal closed in 1913. Since 1968, though, a historic re-creation has allowed visitors to experience life in the early canal days, circa 1830. Living History Buildings include a printshop, a blacksmith shop, and a schoolhouse. The Living History Tour offers demonstrations of broom-, toy-, and barrel-making, and other period crafts. The tour includes hands-on activities for kids.

A visitor center includes a theater with a 15-minute slide show about canal life in the 1830s. The exhibit hall below has a room full of dioramas—miniatures depicting details of early American life.

The biggest hit for kids is the canal boat *Monticello III*, which provides rides from Memorial Day through Labor Day. This replica canal boat, drawn by horses, takes you up the canal and back on a 45-minute tour. Reservations are not required, and there is no minimum group size. Horse-drawn trolleys also operate during the summer months.

Special events typically focus on music, food, and crafts of early Americans.

Rose Hill Museum

Bay Village Historical Society

AGES:	1½–3	3–5	5–8	8–12	12–15
RATING:	NR	NR	★	★	★

COST: **FREE** PREP.: **Some**
AREA: **West** CITY: **Bay Village**

ADDRESS: 27715 Lake Rd.

PHONE: (440) 871-7338

SEASON: Seasonal (April–Dec)

HOURS: Sun 2 p.m. to 4:30 p.m. (call ahead to confirm); groups should call ahead for appointments

PRICES: Free

DIRECT.: I-90 to Exit 159 for Columbia Rd.; north on Columbia; left (west) on Lake Rd.; on left.

Strollers	✓ Groups	✓ Food Nearby
Diap Chg	✓ Picnic	✓ Pub. Trans.
✓ Parking	Food Serv.	✓ Handicapped

Near the shore of Lake Erie, Rose Hill preserves the history of the Cahoon family homestead and farm from the late 1800s. Renovation has restored the house to its original design; period Empire and Victorian furniture is featured in each room. A walk through the site evokes a sense of pioneer life.

As there are no real kids' programs or hands-on activities here, this museum is better suited for elementary-school children or school groups especially interested in the subject matter.

St. Helena III and Canal Fulton Heritage Society

AGES:	1½–3	3–5	5–8	8–12	12–15
RATING:	NR	★	★★	★★	★★

COST: **$–$$** PREP.: **None–Some**
AREA: **Farther South** CITY: **Canal Fulton**

ADDRESS: 103 Tuscarawas St. (off SR 93 in downtown Canal Fulton)

PHONE: (800) HELENA-3

SEASON: Seasonal (May–Oct)

HOURS: Jun–Aug daily 1–3 p.m., May, Sept & Oct weekends 1–3 p.m. (boat rides leave hourly); museum open 1–4 p.m.

PRICES: $6.50 adults, $5.50 seniors, $4.50 children ages 4–12

DIRECT.: I-77 to Exit 135 for SR 21; south on SR 21; north on SR 93; right (east) on Cherry St.; on right.

Strollers	✓ Groups	✓ Food Nearby
Diap Chg	✓ Picnic	Pub. Trans.
✓ Parking	Food Serv.	Handicapped

When roads were little more than paths full of muddy potholes and the nation's railroad system was still on the drawing board, canal riverboats shuttled goods and people throughout much of the eastern half of the United States. A replica riverboat offers a chance for modern passengers to sample the ride.

Representative of a typical flat-bottomed canal boat circa 1860, the *St. Helena III* takes a lazy trip up one of the few sections of the Ohio and Erie Canal that hasn't been filled in within the past 150 years.

Designed to haul barrels of corn and other goods to points east, the *St. Helena III* can easily fit a few dozen people. The boat travels the same way boats of the 1800s did—pulled by hefty Belgian horses that walk alongside the canal. The world passes lazily by at the laconic speed of two miles per hour. On one side of the canal is a wall of trees; on the other, the backs of Canal-Fultonite homes. The whole trip takes about 45 minutes. A pair of pubescent Huck Finn clones man the boat and recite the rise and fall of Ohio's canal industry. While it is safe to walk or run around, parents of crawlers should remember that this is a boat and make sure their progeny don't fall overboard.

Schoenbrunn Village

Ohio Historical Society

AGES:	1½–3	3–5	5–8	8–12	12–15
RATING:	NR	★	★	★	★

COST: **$–$$** PREP.: **None**
AREA: **Farther East** CITY: **New Philadelphia**

ADDRESS: East High Ave., P.O. Box 129

PHONE: (800) 752-2711

SEASON: Seasonal (Memorial Day–Oct)

HOURS: Memorial Day Weekend–Labor Day: Mon–Sat 9:30 a.m.–5 p.m., Sun noon–5 p.m.; after Labor Day–Oct: Sat 9:30 a.m.–5 p.m., Sun noon–5 p.m.

PRICES: $5 adults, $1.25 children ages 6-12, senior & AAA discounts available. Ticket sales stop at 4 p.m.

DIRECT.: I-77 to Exit 81 for US 250; east on US 250 to SR 259; north on SR 259; on left.

WEB: www.ohiohistory.org/places/schoenbr

✓ Strollers ✓ Groups ✓ Food Nearby
Diap Chg ✓ Picnic Pub. Trans.
✓ Parking Food Serv. ✓ Handicapped

The story here is of the rare meeting of European and Indian cultures—a meeting that was ended by the American Revolution. Founded in 1772 as a mission to the Delaware Indians, this small settlement grew to include 60 buildings. Today, the reconstructed village includes 17 log buildings, gardens, a cemetery, and a visitor center and museum.

A short video at the gift shop is informative; a tape recorder is also available to provide narration on a self-guided walk through the grounds (though the recorder is rather cumbersome).

Shaker Historical Society Museum

AGES:	1½–3	3–5	5–8	8–12	12–15
RATING:	NR	NR	★★	★★	★★

COST: **FREE–$** PREP.: **None–Some**
AREA: **East** CITY: **Shaker Hts.**

ADDRESS: 16740 S. Park Blvd.

PHONE: (216) 921-1201

SEASON: Year round

HOURS: Tue–Fri 2–5 p.m.; Sun 2–5 p.m.

PRICES: Free; charge for group tours

DIRECT.: I-271 to Exit 32 for Brainard/Cedar Rd.; left (south) on Brainard; right (west) on Cedar; left (south) on Lee Rd.; left (east) on South Park Blvd.; on right.

I-271 to Exit 29 for Chagrin Blvd.; west on Chagrin; right (north) on Lee Rd.; right (east) on South Park Blvd.; on right.

WEB: www.cwru.edu/orgs/shakhist/shaker.htm

✓ Strollers ✓ Groups ✓ Food Nearby
Diap Chg Picnic ✓ Pub. Trans.
✓ Parking Food Serv. Handicapped

Many local schools teach Shaker history in the third grade, so the Shaker Historical Society Museum will likely appeal to this age group. The museum building is a stately old house that is not of Shaker heritage (it was built as part of the original Van Sweringen brothers' "Garden Community" of Shaker Heights), but curators say its design provides a provocative contrast to the Shaker ideal of simplicity and stimulates conversation about what is "real Shaker." Nearby, between North Park and South Park boulevards, some vestiges remain of the North Union Shaker community that prospered here from

1822 to 1889. The house stands on the site of an original Shaker apple orchard, opposite Shaker Horseshoe Lake (Upper Shaker Lake).

Inside there are displays of Shaker furniture, artifacts, and memorabilia. There is not much in the way of hands-on exhibits, so children under age 4 may get a little squirmy. There *is* much in the way of Shaker inventions: the modern flat broom, tilter chairs, clothespins, and seed packets. On the landing there are dioramas of Shaker life, complete with miniature wooden people. The gift shop is stocked with stencils, herbs, candles, books, music, and miniature furniture—all of Shaker design.

Keep an eye out for the apple festival scheduled each October.

Shandy Hall

Western Reserve Historical Society

AGES:	1½–3	3–5	5–8	8–12	12–15
RATING:	NR	NR	★	★★	★

COST: **$** PREP.: **None–Some**
AREA: **Far West** CITY: **Geneva**

ADDRESS: 6333 South Ridge Rd., West

PHONE: (440) 466-3680

SEASON: Seasonal (May–October)

HOURS: Tues–Sat 10 a.m.–5 p.m.; Sunday noon–5 p.m.

PRICES: $3 adults, $2 seniors and children

DIRECT.: I-90 to Exit 212 for SR 528; north on SR 528; east on SR 84; on right

WEB: www.whrs.org

Strollers ✓ Groups ✓ Food Nearby
Diap Chg Picnic Pub. Trans.
✓ Parking Food Serv. Handicapped

Four generations of the Harper family made this 17-room house their home; now, its original furnishings, tools, and records are preserved and on display. Group tours include a look at the circa 1815 home and its grounds, and tales of the family's history and adventures as early residents of the Western Reserve.

Spring Hill Historic Home

AGES:	1½–3	3–5	5–8	8–12	12–15
RATING:	NR	★	★	★	★

COST: **$** PREP.: **None–Some**
AREA: **Farther South** CITY: **Massillon**

ADDRESS: 1401 Spring Hill Lane NE

PHONE: (330) 833-6749

SEASON: Seasonal (Jun–Aug)

HOURS: Jun–Aug: Wed, Thurs & Sun 1–4 p.m.; Group tours for 10 or more available by appointment year round

PRICES: $3 Adults, $1 ages 6–17, under 6 free

DIRECT.: I-77 to Exit 105 for SR 172 (Lincoln St.); west on SR 172; right (north) on SR 241 (Wales Ave.); right (east) on Spring Hill Lane to Lake Ave.

Strollers ✓ Groups ✓ Food Nearby
Diap Chg ✓ Picnic Pub. Trans.
✓ Parking Food Serv. Handicapped

This historic home, built in the 1820s (and once a station on the Underground Railroad), is filled with interesting items like a bee room, a secret stairway, wig and false teeth drawers, a playroom, and a basement kitchen with a cooking fireplace, one of the oldest in Ohio. A tour of the grounds includes the springhouse, smokehouse, woolhouse, and milkhouse. Trails wind through gardens and woods.

Annual special events include an Easter-egg hunt, children's fun and games day, Fall Fest, and a Christmas party.

Stan Hywet Hall and Gardens

AGES:	1½–3	3–5	5–8	8–12	12–15
RATING:	NR	NR	★	★★	★★

COST: **$$** PREP.: **None–Some**
AREA: **Far South** CITY: **Akron**

ADDRESS: 714 N. Portage Path

PHONE: (330) 836-5533

SEASON: Year round (NOTE: Closed January)

HOURS: Jan–Mar 31: Tue–Sat 10 a.m.–4 p.m., Sun 1–4 p.m.; open seven days a week after Apr 1

PRICES: $8 adults, $7 seniors, $4 children 6–12, under 6 free (gardens & grounds can be toured separately at a reduced charge)

DIRECT.: I-77 to Exit 138 for Ghent Rd.; south on Ghent; left (east) on Smith Rd.; right (east) on Riverview Rd./Merriman Rd.; right (south) on N. Portage Path; on right.

WEB: www.stanhywet.org

✓ Strollers ✓ Groups ✓ Food Nearby
✓ Diap Chg ✓ Picnic ✓ Pub. Trans.
✓ Parking ✓ Food Serv. ✓ Handicapped

There are several nifty *little* things in this 65-room Tudor mansion—the library bookcase that opens into a secret passageway and telephones tucked behind carved wood panels—but just about everything else here is big.

Built in 1915 on a 3,000-acre bluff, Stan Hywet Hall and its adjacent gardens now take up 70 acres. A mansion with formal gardens, grape arbor, greenhouse, lagoon, and a parade of white birch trees needs that much space. Everything about Frank and Gertrude Seiberling's house makes a grand statement, from the three-story-tall ceilings in the great room to the 16th-century tapestries and European antiques that Seiberling, co-founder of the Goodyear Tire and Rubber Co., imported to re-create the feel of the 1700s.

Depending on your guide, the tour can be an entertaining peep show into the lives of one of Ohio's most famous industrialists, replete with tidbits such as why the stone on the hallway floor is worn in spots (Gertrude wanted the place to look a little broken in). Guides take a dim view of younger children who want to handle the silverware and wander past the ropes.

On-site attractions also include seasonal flower displays and annual events, such as the Decorated Egg Show, Shakespeare at Stan Hywet, Arts and Crafts Fair, Miniature Faire, and Christmas Then and Now, which features a 14-foot Christmas tree in the Great Hall.

Steamship William G. Mather Museum

Harbor Heritage Society

AGES:	1½–3	3–5	5–8	8–12	12–15
RATING:	NR	NR	★★	★★	★★

COST: **$** PREP.: **None–Some**
AREA: **Downtown** CITY: **Cleveland**

ADDRESS: 1001 E. 9 St. (on the E. 9 St. Pier)

PHONE: (216) 574-6262

SEASON: Seasonal (May–Oct)

HOURS: Memorial–Labor Day: Mon–Sat 10 a.m.–5 p.m., Sun noon–5 p.m.; Fri–Sun in May, Sept, and Oct

PRICES: $5 adults, $4 seniors, $3 children ages 5–12, free children under 5

DIRECT.: I-90- to SR2; west on SR 2 to E. 9 St.; north on E. 9; left (west) on Erieside Ave.; on right.

WEB: little.nhlink.net/wgm/wgmhome.html

Strollers ✓ Groups ✓ Food Nearby
Diap Chg Picnic ✓ Pub. Trans.
✓ Parking Food Serv. Handicapped

The *Steamship William G. Mather* is the former flagship of the Cleveland Cliffs Iron Company's freighter line. When christened in 1925, this behemoth craft that combined cavernous cargo holds (capable of holding 13,300 tons of iron ore) with elegant

History, Science & Technology DIRECTORY

oak-paneled guest dining rooms and cozy staterooms.

The tour begins through a cut-away cargo hold and winds through small crew bunk rooms, across the top of the ship, into the state rooms and engine room, and back across the top to the pilothouse. The dining room has been painstakingly restored.

Staff members are second to none when it comes to knowledge of the freighter; many worked aboard this 618-foot-long ship or similar vessels that hauled loads of ore from northern Minnesota to the steel mills of Cleveland and other Great Lakes ports. A short film runs throughout the day.

The vessel tour requires climbing several sets of steep steps. Strollers and child-carrying backpacks are not allowed. Although the guardrails have been significantly reinforced and augmented, parents of toddlers and small children will want to hang on to their offspring when walking atop the ship.

Trolleyville USA

AGES:	1½–3	3–5	5–8	8–12	12–15
RATING:	★★	★★	★★	★	★

COST: **$** PREP.: **None–Some**
AREA: **Southwest** CITY: **Olmsted Township**

ADDRESS: 7100 Columbia Rd.

PHONE: (440) 235-4725

SEASON: Seasonal (May–Dec)

HOURS: Wed, Fri 10 a.m.–3 p.m., Sat–Sun and holidays noon–5 p.m.; groups by appt. only

PRICES: $5 adults, $4 seniors, $3 children, no charge under age 2

DIRECT.: I-480 to Exit 6 for SR 252 (Columbia Rd.)/Great Northern Blvd.; south on Columbia; on right.

✓ Strollers ✓ Groups ✓ Food Nearby
Diap Chg ✓ Picnic ✓ Pub. Trans.
✓ Parking Food Serv. Handicapped

Cleveland was once lined with many miles of trolley tracks, a fact you can explore thoroughly at Trolleyville USA. The museum, begun in 1954, and really named after its founder, is officially titled the Gerald E. Brookins Museum of Electric Railways, Inc.—but everyone calls it Trolleyville. The collection displays more than 34 pieces of historic electric railway equipment, such as interurbans and streetcars—many of which can be ridden—that are hooked up and hauled through a neighboring trailer park. Yes, trailer park. Midway,the convoy of trains stops at a railway depot and gift shop before venturing home.

Kids will be interested in the winter holiday celebrations here. At Christmastime, the place is filled with lights; the cars are running (most are heated), and there is free cider and goody bags. Santa is often stationed at the depot on weekends.

USS COD Submarine

AGES:	1½–3	3–5	5–8	8–12	12–15
RATING:	★	★★★	★★★	★★★	★

COST: **$** PREP.: **None**
AREA: **Downtown** CITY: **Cleveland**

ADDRESS: 1089 E. 9 St.

PHONE: (216) 566-8770

SEASON: Seasonal (May–Sep)

HOURS: Daily 10 a.m.–5 p.m.

PRICES: $4, $2 students, free under age 5

DIRECT.: SR 2 to E. 9 St.; north on E. 9; right (east) on N. Marginal; on left.

WEB: www.usscod.org

Strollers ✓ Groups ✓ Food Nearby
Diap Chg ✓ Picnic ✓ Pub. Trans.
✓ Parking Food Serv. Handicapped

This veteran of South Pacific action is the only submarine surviving in original World War II condition. This means if you want to visit this

DIRECTORY History, Science & Technology

landmark (it is listed in the National Register of Historic Ships), you had better be able to climb ladders and squeeze through the same hatches that a crew of 155 navy seamen had to negotiate over 50 years ago.

Inside, you have the run of the place, with the exception of the conning tower, the head (it took seven steps to flush the toilet), and the mess. But don't try to backtrack, because traffic flows only from the rear torpedo room to the forward torpedo room, where you climb another ladder to get out.

There are no hands-on exhibits. Atop the *COD* sits a 5-inch gun that can no longer fire but can still be turned and adjusted. Nearby on the grounds, the periscope is set up for viewing. Signs and lighting are decent but not exceptional. Still, if you want a feel for life on a sub, this is the place. If you have questions, ask one of the old salts who man the gate.

USS Cod Submarine

Western Reserve Historical Society

AGES:	1½–3	3–5	5–8	8–12	12–15
RATING:	NR	★	★★	★★★	★★

COST: **$$** PREP.: **None–Some**
AREA: **Near East** CITY: **Cleveland**

ADDRESS: 10825 East Blvd.

PHONE: (216) 721-5722

SEASON: Year round

HOURS: Mon-Sat 10 a.m.–5 p.m., Sun noon–5 p.m.; tours of the mansion are offered daily noon–5 p.m.

PRICES: $6.50 adults, $5.50 seniors, $4.50 students; free under 6; free admission Tue 3-5 p.m.

DIRECT.: East: I-90 to Exit 177 for Martin Luther King Blvd.; south on MLK; right (east) on East Blvd.; on left.

West: I-90 to Exit 173B for Chester Ave.; east on Chester; left (east) on Euclid Ave.; left (north) on East Blvd.; on right after Hazel Dr.

WEB: www.wrhs.org

✓ Strollers	✓ Groups	✓ Food Nearby
Diap Chg	✓ Picnic	✓ Pub. Trans.
✓ Parking	✓ Food Serv.	✓ Handicapped

While adults may easily get caught up in the elegant interiors of the restored Hay-McKinney and Bingham-Hanna mansions (which make up the history portion of the Western Reserve Historical Society), to make the most of a family visit here make sure you ask a staff member for a tour. The staff's wealth of knowledge goes well beyond the posted information plaques. And get a map at the admissions desk.

The museum has made attempts to be child-friendly: exhibits contain interactive components from puzzles to computers. Children's programming is scheduled monthly, and there is a new Education Center at the bottom of the Hay Mansion that is open to school tours and visitors (check in advance with the Education Department). Special children's tours on Saturday include hands-on tours and activities for ages 6-12.

An annual Family Day celebration (the weekend after Thanksgiving) includes craft demonstrations, entertainment, and special events designed around a different theme each year.

Every year the Hay-McKinney mansion is trimmed for the holidays with decorations appropriate for the period, chronicling the traditions brought to Cleveland by its many diverse immigrants.

The Bingham-Hanna Mansion has been converted into gallery space, and while visitors can still enjoy the beauty of the structure and its ornate ceilings, only the dining room and breakfast nook remain in their original condition. This part of the museum contains rotating history exhibits on an array of diverse Northeast Ohio topics, which have in recent years featured baseball history, African-American churches, Cleveland music history, and leisure-time history, to name a few. The History Museum also houses the Chisholm-Halle Costume Wing. Its rotating exhibitions feature historic design styles and illustrate how one's choice of clothing can be as telling as a personal diary.

Also part of the Historical Society at University Circle are the Frederick C. Crawford Auto-Aviation Collection (see separate listing) and the Library of the Western Reserve Historical Society, which specializes in history and genealogy—just the place to chart your family tree (ask for a starter kit).

Western Reserve Historical Society

Zoar Village

Ohio Historical Society

AGES:	1½–3	3–5	5–8	8–12	12–15
RATING:	NR	NR	★	★	★

COST: **$** PREP.: **None–Some**
AREA: **Farther South** CITY: **Zoar**

ADDRESS: P.O. Box 404/SR 212

PHONE: (800) 262-6195

SEASON: Seasonal (Apr–Oct)

HOURS: Apr 3–May 28: Sat 9:30 a.m.–5 p.m., Sun noon–5 p.m.; May 29–Sep 6: Wed–Sat 9:30 a.m.–5 p.m., Sun & holidays noon–5 p.m.; Sept 7–Oct 31 Sat 9:30 a.m.–5 p.m., Sun noon–5 p.m.; Groups by appointment on weekdays

PRICES: $5 adults, $1.25 children 6–12, free children 5 and under, $4.50 seniors

DIRECT.: I-77 to Exit 93 for SR 212; south on SR 212; on left.

Strollers	✓ Groups	✓ Food Nearby
Diap Chg	Picnic	Pub. Trans.
✓ Parking	Food Serv.	Handicapped

You can walk through many of the ten buildings in this restored village on your own, but the guides here offer a wealth of information about this settlement, which was home to German Separatists in the early days of our country. Better yet, try to visit during one of the annual weekend festivals for more craft demonstrations and family activities.

TIPS FOR TRIPS

EPIPHANIES

Special places often inspire special activities. Try to leave a little flexible time in case your child falls in love with something.

DIRECTORY
History, Science & Technology

Nature and outdoors

Kids learn best from hands-on experiences, and nature makes a great teacher. That's why a trip to a nearby park for a hike or swim or nature class can be so satisfying. Other activities are almost unlimited, including kiting, birding, biking, cross-country skiing, sledding, tubing, environmental programs, volunteer conservation work, and more.

We're surrounded by parklands. The Cleveland Metroparks alone cover 19,000 acres around the city; the Cuyahoga Valley National Recreation Area covers another 33,000 acres. There are also several state parks, including nearby Lakefront State Parks, and the county park systems of Geauga, Lake, and Lorain counties.

As with other activities, keep in mind your children's ages and abilities when choosing a park to visit. It's also a good idea to leave home well stocked with supplies; some parks are relatively remote and have limited facilities. And, remember to bring and wear appropriate clothes—children need protection from the elements.

If you're looking for some ground to explore, what follows is a list of parks, nature centers, and nature-oriented programs for children, most of which offer guided walks, group outings, and demonstrations, in addition to plenty of opportunities for outdoor discovery.

Petting zoo, Akron Zoological Park

Akron Zoological Park

AGES:	1½–3	3–5	5–8	8–12	12–15
RATING:	★★	★★★	★★	★★	★

COST: **$** PREP.: **None**
AREA: **Far South** CITY: **Akron**

ADDRESS: 500 Edgewood Ave.

PHONE: (330) 375-2525; (330) 375-2550

SEASON: Seasonal (Apr–Oct)

HOURS: Mon–Sat 10 a.m.–5 p.m., Sun & holidays 10 a.m.–6 p.m.

PRICES: $7.50 adults, $6 seniors, $5 ages 2–14, under 2 Free; $1.50 parking fee

DIRECT.: I-77 to Exit 131 for Copley Rd.; east on Copley; right (south) on Edgewood; on right.

WEB: www.neo.lrun.com/akzoo

✓ Strollers	✓ Groups	✓ Food Nearby
✓ Diap Chg	✓ Picnic	✓ Pub. Trans.
✓ Parking	✓ Food Serv.	✓ Handicapped

This zoo has the feel of many smaller, older urban zoos. Even though it is five minutes away from downtown, it has lots of tall trees to filter sunlight, adding to the feeling that you are taking a pleasant walk in the park. One-dollar pony rides, strollers at every turn, and plenty of park benches (made from recycled plastic refuse) help to reinforce the feeling.

The selection of animals here is not huge, but few other zoos allow visitors to get as close to animals as this. When the eight macaws start squawking, the entire zoo reverberates.

Annual special events include Boo at the Zoo trick-or-treating in October and a Holiday Lights Celebration in December.

Atwood Lake Park

Muskingum Watershed Conservancy District

AGES:	1½–3	3–5	5–8	8–12	12–15
RATING:	★	★★	★★	★★	★★

COST: **FREE–$$** PREP.: **None**
AREA: **Far South** CITY: **Mineral City**

ADDRESS: 4956 Shop Rd. NE

PHONE: (330) 343-6780

SEASON: Year round

HOURS: Vary

PRICES: Vary

DIRECT.: I-77 to to Exit 93 for SR 212; south on SR 212; on left after SR 800.

WEB: www.mwcdlakes.com

✓ Strollers ✓ Groups ✓ Food Nearby
Diap Chg ✓ Picnic Pub. Trans.
✓ Parking ✓ Food Serv. Handicapped

This lake resort area is popular, especially on summer weekends. With a swimming beach, boat rentals, and hiking trails, along with a golf course, tennis courts, and concessions, there is plenty to do. The horsepower limit on the lake makes it a pleasant place indeed, even for non-boaters.

Bedford Reservation

Cleveland Metroparks

AGES:	1½–3	3–5	5–8	8–12	12–15
RATING:	★★	★★	★★	★★	★★

COST: **FREE** PREP.: **None**
AREA: **Southeast** CITY: **Bedford**

ADDRESS: Gorge Pkwy.

PHONE: (216) 351-6300; Shawnee Hills Golf Course (440) 232-7184

SEASON: Year round

HOURS: Daily 6 a.m.–11 p.m.

PRICES: Free

DIRECT.: I-77 to Exit 155 for Rockside Rd.; east on Rockside; right (south) on Dunham Rd.; left (east) on Gorge Pkwy.

Or, I-480/I-271 to Exit 23 for SR 14 (Broadway Ave.); west on Broadway; left (west) on Union St.; left (west); on Egbert Rd.; right (north) on Gorge Pkwy.

✓ Strollers ✓ Groups ✓ Food Nearby
Diap Chg ✓ Picnic ✓ Pub. Trans.
Parking Food Serv. ✓ Handicapped

This 2,109-acre reservation has several all-purpose trails (including Tinker's Creek Gorge Scenic Overlook, a national Natural Landmark, and Bridal Veil Falls), cross-country ski trails, Shawnee Hills Golf Course, ball fields, designated sledding hills, and six picnic areas.

Bessie Benner Metzenbaum Park

Geauga Park District

AGES:	1½–3	3–5	5–8	8–12	12–15
RATING:	★★	★★	★★	★★	★★

COST: **FREE–$** PREP.: **None**
AREA: **Far East** CITY: **Chester Twp.**

ADDRESS: 7940 Cedar Rd.

PHONE: (440) 285-2222

SEASON: Year round

HOURS: Daily, 6 a.m.–11 p.m.

PRICES: Free

DIRECT.: I-271 to Exit 34 for US 322 (Mayfield Rd.);

east on Mayfield; right (south) on County Line Rd.; left (east) on Cedar Rd.; on left.

✓ Strollers ✓ Groups Food Nearby
✓ Diap Chg ✓ Picnic Pub. Trans.
Parking Food Serv. ✓ Handicapped

This 65-acre park has picnicking and hiking, with one mile of paved trails.

Big Creek Park and Donald W. Meyer Center

Geauga Park District

AGES:	1½–3	3–5	5–8	8–12	12–15
RATING:	★★	★★	★★	★★	★★

COST: **FREE–$$$** PREP.: **None–Some**
AREA: **Far East** CITY: **Chardon**

ADDRESS: 9160 Robinson Rd.

PHONE: (440) 285-2222

SEASON: Year round

HOURS: Park: 6 a.m.–11 p.m.; Meyer Center: Mon–Fri 8 a.m.–4:30 p.m.; Sat–Sun 10 a.m.–6 p.m.

PRICES: Free, fee for some classes

DIRECT.: I-90 to Exit 200 for SR 44; south on SR 44; left (east) on Clark Rd.; right (southeast) on Robinson Rd.; on right.

Or, US 422 to SR 44; north on SR 44 through Chardon; north on North St./Ravenna Rd.; right (east) on Woodin Rd.; left (north) on Robinson Rd.; on left.

✓ Strollers Groups Food Nearby
✓ Diap Chg ✓ Picnic Pub. Trans.
✓ Parking Food Serv. ✓ Handicapped

The Donald W. Meyer Center, headquarters for the Geauga Park District, is the only nature center in Geauga County. It offers nature-oriented exhibits and classes, and wildlife programs such as Timbertots, which introduces children ages 3–5 and parents to birdwatching, animals, and hiking. This is the place to pick up trail maps for the entire Geauga Park District.

The 642-acre wooded reservation includes 6½ miles of well-marked trails, fishing in ponds, cross-country ski trails, and a playground.

Big Creek Park and Donald W. Meyer Center

Big Creek Reservation

Cleveland Metroparks

AGES:	1½–3	3–5	5–8	8–12	12–15
RATING:	★★	★★	★★	★★	★★

COST: **FREE** PREP.: **None** AREA: **South**
CITY: **Parma Hts., Middleburg Hts.**

ADDRESS: Big Creek Pkwy.

PHONE: (216) 351-6300

SEASON: Year round

HOURS: Daily 6 a.m.–11 p.m.

PRICES: Free

DIRECT.: I-480 to Exit 13 for Tiedeman Rd.; south on Tiedeman; left (east) on Brookpark Rd.; right (south) on Big Creek Pkwy.

Or, I-71 to Exit 235 for Bagley Rd.; east on Bagley to Big Creek Pkwy.

✓ Strollers ✓ Groups ✓ Food Nearby
Diap Chg ✓ Picnic ✓ Pub. Trans.
Parking Food Serv. ✓ Handicapped

All-purpose trails (including cross-country ski trails) on 566 acres, three picnic areas with grills and shelters, ball fields, sledding at Memphis Picnic Area (lighted at night) and Snow Road Picnic Area. The Lake Isaac Waterfowl Sanctuary is bordered by a hiking trail that offers great looks at migratory birds—a great family hike.

Black River Reservation

Lorain County Metro Parks

AGES:	1½–3	3–5	5–8	8–12	12–15
RATING:	★★	★★★	★★★	★★★	★★★

COST: **FREE–$** PREP.: **None–Some**
AREA: **Far West** CITY: **Elyria**

ADDRESS: Ford Rd.

PHONE: (800) LCM-PARK

SEASON: Year round

HOURS: Daily 8 a.m.–9:30 p.m.

PRICES: Free

DIRECT.: Norfolk: I-90 to Exit 145 for SR 87 (Lorain Rd.); north on Lorain; right on E. 31 St. to Norfolk Ave.

Ford: I-90 to Exit 148 for SR 254 (North Ridge Rd.); west on North Ridge; left (south) on Gulf Rd.; right (west) on Ford Rd.

✓ Strollers ✓ Groups ✓ Food Nearby
✓ Diap Chg ✓ Picnic Pub. Trans.
✓ Parking Food Serv. ✓ Handicapped

Hiking trails, three picnic areas with shelters, and a playground are located on 900 acres along the Black River. A 3.5-mile asphalt hike/bike trail winds through open fields and wooded areas; guided hikes are offered by Metroparks staff. An electric tram takes visitors into the valley.

Boston Store

CVNRA

AGES:	1½–3	3–5	5–8	8–12	12–15
RATING:	NR	★	★★	★★	★★

COST: **FREE** PREP.: **None**
AREA: **Far South** CITY: **Boston Twp.**

ADDRESS: 1548 Boston Mills Rd.

PHONE: (800) 433-1986

SEASON: Year round

HOURS: Summer Mon–Fri 8 a.m.–5 p.m.; Fall Mon–Fri 10 a.m.–5 p.m.; Winter Sat–Sun 10 a.m.–5 p.m.; Spring Wed–Sun 10 a.m.–5 p.m.

PRICES: Free

DIRECT.: I-271 to Exit 12 for SR 303 (Streetsboro Rd.); east on Streetsboro; left (north) on Riverview Rd.; right (east) on Boston Mills Rd.; on left.

WEB: www.nps.gov/cuva

✓ Strollers ✓ Groups Food Nearby
Diap Chg ✓ Picnic Pub. Trans.
✓ Parking Food Serv. ✓ Handicapped

Exhibits in this small information center, originally built in 1836 and now restored, focus on canal history and boats with a number of hands-on exhibits. It is also a perfect meeting place—its porch is well known to hikers and bikers along the Towpath Trail.

Bradley Woods Reservation

Cleveland Metroparks

AGES:	1½–3	3–5	5–8	8–12	12–15
RATING:	★★	★★	★★	★★	★★

COST: **FREE** PREP.: **None**
AREA: **West** CITY: **Westlake**

ADDRESS: Bradley Rd.

PHONE: (216) 351-6300

SEASON: Year round

HOURS: Daily 6 a.m.–11 p.m.

PRICES: Free

DIRECT.: I-90 to Exit 156 for Crocker Rd./Bassett Rd.; south on Crocker; right (west) on Detroit Rd.; left (south) on Bradley Rd.; on left.

Nature & Outdoors DIRECTORY

Or, I-480 to Exit 1 for SR 10 (Lorain Rd.); east on Lorain; left (west) on Barton Rd.; right (north) on Bradley Rd.; on right.

✓ Strollers	✓ Groups	✓ Food Nearby
Diap Chg	✓ Picnic	✓ Pub. Trans.
✓ Parking	Food Serv.	✓ Handicapped

Hiking trails, cross-country ski trails, waterfowl and wildlife areas with fishing and ice fishing (Bunns Lake), picnic area, small playground with swings and a sandbox.

Brecksville Nature Center

Cleveland Metroparks

AGES:	1½–3	3–5	5–8	8–12	12–15
RATING:	★★★	★★★	★★★	★★★	★★★

COST: **FREE–$** PREP.: **None–Much**
AREA: **South** CITY: **Brecksville**

ADDRESS: Chippewa Creek Dr.

PHONE: (440) 526-1012

SEASON: Year round

HOURS: Daily 9:30 a.m.–5 p.m. except Thanksgiving, Christmas, New Year's Day

PRICES: Free; fees for some special programs

DIRECT.: I-77 to Exit 149 for SR 82 (Royalton Rd.); east on Royalton; right (south) on Chippewa Creek Dr.; on right.

✓ Strollers	✓ Groups	✓ Food Nearby
✓ Diap Chg	Picnic	✓ Pub. Trans.
✓ Parking	Food Serv.	✓ Handicapped

Inside the Brecksville Nature Center is a Children's Corner featuring hands-on activities with shells, fossils, hives, and nests. While there are no live animals here, a stuffed red fox and quail exhibit allows kids to "search" for other animals hiding in the area.

Animal Crackers, a monthly program for ages 3–5, involves a nature hike and craft activity. During the summer months, other naturalist programs involve hikes and crafts for school-age children. Preregistration required; check the *Emerald Necklace* monthly newsletter for details.

The Brecksville Nature Center was opened in 1939 as part of a Works Progress Administration project and is now a part of the Cleveland Metroparks Brecksville Reservation (see separate listing).

Brecksville Reservation

Cleveland Metroparks

AGES:	1½–3	3–5	5–8	8–12	12–15
RATING:	★★	★★	★★	★★	★★

COST: **FREE** PREP.: **None**
AREA: **South** CITY: **Brecksville**

ADDRESS: Chippewa Creek Dr. & Valley Pkwy.

PHONE: (216) 351-6300; nature center (440) 526-1012; Historical Society (440) 526-7165; stables (440) 526-6767 (no trail rides)

SEASON: Year round

HOURS: Daily 6 a.m.–11 p.m.

PRICES: Free

DIRECT.: I-77 to Exit 149 for SR 82 (Royalton Rd.); east on Royalton Rd.; right (south) on Chippewa Creek Dr.

Or, I-77 to Exit 149 for SR 82 (Royalton Rd.); east on Royalton; right (south) on SR 21 (Brecksville Rd.); left (east) on Valley Pkwy.

✓ Strollers	✓ Groups	✓ Food Nearby
✓ Diap Chg	✓ Picnic	Pub. Trans.
✓ Parking	Food Serv.	✓ Handicapped

This is a great place for younger hikers. Trails (which include the Chippewa Creek Gorge Scenic Overlook) are well marked, and with map in hand it is easy to create your own short loop because the paths intersect often.

Breckville Reservation also has ball fields, sledding, eight picnic areas, Sleepy Hollow Public Golf Course, Brecksville Stables, and the Brecksville Nature Center (see separate listing) on 3,392 acres.

Brookside Reservation

Cleveland Metroparks

AGES:	1½–3	3–5	5–8	8–12	12–15
RATING:	★★	★★	★★	★★	★★

COST: **FREE** PREP.: **None**
AREA: **Near West** CITY: **Cleveland**

ADDRESS: Ridge Rd.

PHONE: (216) 351-6300

SEASON: Year round

HOURS: 6 a.m.–11 p.m.

PRICES: Free

DIRECT.: I-71 to Exit 245 for Fulton Rd.; south on Fulton; right on John Nagy Blvd. at Denison Ave.

Or, I-71 to 242 for Bellaire Rd.; north on Bellaire; right (south) on Memphis Rd.; left (north) on Ridge Rd.; right on John Nagy Blvd.

Strollers	✓ Groups	✓ Food Nearby
Diap Chg	✓ Picnic	✓ Pub. Trans.
✓ Parking	✓ Food Serv.	✓ Handicapped

Brookside Reservation was one of the city of Cleveland's oldest parks before it was acquired by Cleveland Metroparks in 1993. Within its 143 acres are football, baseball, and soccer fields; the Meadow Ridge picnic area; and an all-purpose trail that connects Brookside Reservation to the Cleveland Metroparks Zoo. Cross-country skiing is permitted when conditions are favorable.

Burnette's Pet Farm and Educational Center

AGES:	1½–3	3–5	5–8	8–12	12–15
RATING:	★★	★★	★	★	NR

COST: **$–$$** PREP.: **Some**
AREA: **Southwest** CITY: **Olmsted Twp**

ADDRESS: 6940 Columbia Rd.

PHONE: (440) 235-4050

SEASON: Seasonal (mid-May–Oct)

HOURS: Tours Tues–Sat 10 a.m. & 2 p.m., Sun 2 p.m.; please call ahead

Burnette's Pet Farm and Educational Center

PRICES: $5 adults, $4 students, no charge for infants; group discounts for 30 or more

DIRECT.: I-480 to Exit 6A for Great Northern Blvd./Columbia Rd; south on Great Northern/Columbia; on right.

Or, I-71 to Exit 235 for Bagley Rd.; west on Bagley; left (north) on Columbia Rd.; on left.

✓ Strollers	✓ Groups	✓ Food Nearby
✓ Diap Chg	✓ Picnic	✓ Pub. Trans.
✓ Parking	Food Serv.	✓ Handicapped

With petable bunnies, chicks, and ducks, owner Dr. Jim Burnett, a former teacher, designed this farm as a hands-on place to learn about animals. The tour includes a look at life on a working farm with traditional farm animals (goats, sheep, and horses); it also offers a look at emus, bearcats, prairie dogs, South American opossum, monkeys, and other exotic species. The pet farm includes a small vineyard and herb and flower gardens—with a gazebo, pond, and bridge—that children can wander through. For an additional charge, there are pony rides. Bring your own bread or fruit to feed the animals. Reservations are preferred.

Caley National Wildlife Woods

Lorain County Metro Parks

AGES:	1½–3	3–5	5–8	8–12	12–15
RATING:	NR	NR	★★	★★	★★

COST: **FREE** PREP.: **None**
AREA: **Far West** CITY: **Pittsfield Township**

ADDRESS: West Rd. (southeast of Oberlin)

PHONE: (800) LCM-PARK

SEASON: Year round

HOURS: Daily 8 a.m.–dusk

PRICES: Free

DIRECT.: I-480 to Exit 1 for SR 20; west on SR 20; left (south) on SR 58; right (east) on Whitney Rd.; right (south) on West Rd.; on left.

Strollers ✓ Groups Food Nearby
Diap Chg ✓ Picnic Pub. Trans.
✓ Parking Food Serv. Handicapped

This mostly undeveloped reservation features hiking trails and fishing on an eight-acre lake. For those seeking an opportunity to view migrating waterfowl, guided hikes are offered here, as they are throughout the Lorain County Metroparks.

Canal Visitor Center

Cuyahoga Valley National Recreation Area

AGES:	1½–3	3–5	5–8	8–12	12–15
RATING:	★	★★	★★★	★★★	★★★

COST: **FREE–$$$** PREP.: **None–Some**
AREA: **South** CITY: **Valley View**

ADDRESS: 7104 Canal Rd. (at Hillside Rd.)

PHONE: (800) 445-9667

SEASON: Year round

HOURS: Daily 8 a.m.–5 p.m.; closed Thanksgiving, Christmas, New Year's Day

PRICES: Free; fee for special events

DIRECT.: I-77 to Exit 155 for Rockside Rd.; east on Rockside; right (south) on Canal Rd.; on left

WEB: www.nps.gov/cuva

✓ Strollers ✓ Groups ✓ Food Nearby
Diap Chg ✓ Picnic Pub. Trans.
✓ Parking Food Serv. ✓ Handicapped

The Canal Visitor Center building was at various times a private home, a general store, a tavern, a hotel, and a dance hall. It prospered from its location when the canal was open and passengers waited to pass through the nearby lock. These days, it is home to the National Park Service's ranger office and exhibits on canal history and the settlement of the Cuyahoga

The Canal Visitor Center, Cuyahoga Valley National Recreation Area

DIRECTORY
Nature & Outdoors

Valley. It is also a great place to find out about the features of the Cuyahoga Valley National Recreational Area. Canal lock demonstrations are scheduled on summer weekends with volunteers dressed in period clothing.

Year round, there are special programs here for children ages 4 and up. Preschoolers in the Park, for ages 4–6 (with a parent), includes a short hike, talk, and an activity with a nature theme.

Carlisle Reservation and Visitors Center

Lorain County Metro Parks

AGES:	1½–3	3–5	5–8	8–12	12–15
RATING:	★★	★★	★★	★★	★★

COST: **FREE–$** PREP.: **None–Some**
AREA: **Far West** CITY: **Lagrange**

ADDRESS: 12882 Diagonal Rd.

PHONE: (800) LCM-PARK

SEASON: Year round

HOURS: Daily 8 a.m.–4:30 p.m.; Thu 8 a.m.–9 p.m.

PRICES: Free; fees for some classes & special events

DIRECT.: I-480 to Exit 1 for SR 10; south on SR 10 to SR 301 (Lagrange Rd.); south on Lagrange; right (west) on Nickelplate Diagonal Rd.; on right.

✓ Strollers ✓ Groups ✓ Food Nearby
✓ Diap Chg ✓ Picnic Pub. Trans.
✓ Parking Food Serv. ✓ Handicapped

Hikes, special events, and family programs for all ages are hosted throughout the year at the Carlisle Visitors Center, which houses the administrative offices of the park district. Programs for preschoolers and parents are offered monthly and include a short hike, crafts, and a discussion. Other attractions include the Wildlife Observation Area and Children's Nature Space. Also on the grounds are all-purpose trails (including horse trails), picnic areas with shelters, fishing ponds, baseball fields, the 18-hole Forest Hills Golf Center, and a show ring at the Equestrian Center.

Cascade Valley Metro Park

Metro Parks Serving Summit County

AGES:	1½–3	3–5	5–8	8–12	12–15
RATING:	★	★	★	★★	★★

COST: **FREE** PREP.: **None**
AREA: **Far South** CITY: **Akron**

ADDRESS: 837 and 1061 Cuyahoga St. (Chuckery Area and Oxbow Area)

PHONE: (330) 867-5511

SEASON: Year round

HOURS: Dawn–dusk

PRICES: Free

DIRECT.: SR 8 to SR 261 (Tallmadge Rd.); west on Tallmadge; right (north) on Cuyahoga St.; on left.

Or, I-77 to Exit 132 for White Pond Dr.; northeast on White Pond; right (east) on Mull Ave.; right (southeast) on SR 18 (E. Market St.); left (north) on Portage Path; right (east) on Memorial Pkwy; left (north) on Cuyahoga St.; on left.

Strollers Groups ✓ Food Nearby
Diap Chg ✓ Picnic Pub. Trans.
✓ Parking Food Serv. Handicapped

This reservation's Chuckery Trail is 3.6 miles of steep hiking and skiing terrain. The 1.2-mile Oxbow Trail and 3.2-mile Highbridge Trail connect to Gorge Metro Park (see separate listing).

Chagrin River Park

Lake Metroparks

AGES:	1½–3	3–5	5–8	8–12	12–15
RATING:	★	★★	★★	★★	★★

COST: **FREE–$$** PREP.: **None**
AREA: **East** CITY: **Willoughby/Eastlake**

ADDRESS: 3100 Reeves Rd.

PHONE: (440) 639-7275

SEASON: Year round

HOURS: Daily, 8 a.m.–sunset

PRICES: Free; some programs have fees

DIRECT.: SR 2 to Lost Nation Rd.; north on Lost Nation; left (west) on Reeves Rd.; on left.

WEB: www.lakemetroparks.com

Strollers	✓ Groups	✓ Food Nearby
Diap Chg	✓ Picnic	Pub. Trans.
✓ Parking	Food Serv.	✓ Handicapped

This 101-acre park has an all-purpose trail, ball fields, and a picnic area with shelters and grills, sledding hills, playground, and fishing.

Chapin Forest Reservation and Pine Lodge Ski Center

Lake Metroparks

AGES:	1½–3	3–5	5–8	8–12	12–15
RATING:	★	★★	★★	★★	★★

COST: **FREE–$$** PREP.: **None–Some**
AREA: **Far East** CITY: **Kirtland**

ADDRESS: 10373 Hobart Rd.

PHONE: (440) 639-7275; ski center: (440) 256-3810; hotline: (440) 256-2255

SEASON: Year round

HOURS: Daily, daylight–dusk. Pine Lodge: Mon–Thu 11 a.m.–6 p.m., Fri 11 a.m.–8 p.m., Sat–Sun 9 a.m.–6 p.m.

PRICES: Free, fee for classes & equipment rentals

DIRECT.: I-90 to Exit 190 for SR 306; south on SR 306; right (west) on US 6 (Chardon Rd.); right (north) on Hobart Rd.; on right

WEB: www.lakemetroparks.com

✓ Strollers	✓ Groups	Food Nearby
✓ Diap Chg	✓ Picnic	Pub. Trans.
✓ Parking	✓ Food Serv.	✓ Handicapped

A former state forest, this 390-acre reservation includes well-marked hiking trails, ball and game fields, a playground, a designated sledding area, and picnic areas with shelters and fire pits. Panoramic vistas are abundant atop bluffs and ledges—many are slippery when muddy, making some trails a bit dangerous for younger hikers. Guided tours are offered periodically.

At Pine Lodge, classes are scheduled year round for ages 3–adult. These typically include a story, craft, and hike. In winter, cross-country ski and snowshoe rentals are available, and the well-groomed trails are perfect for families and beginners. The Lodge is perfect for warming up—with a fire always lit and hot chocolate brewing.

Charlemont Reservation

Lorain County Metro Parks

AGES:	1½–3	3–5	5–8	8–12	12–15
RATING:	NR	NR	NR	★★	★★

COST: **FREE** PREP.: **None**
AREA: **Far West** CITY: **Wellington**

ADDRESS: New London-Eastern Rd. (S. of Wellington)

PHONE: (800) LCM-PARK

SEASON: Year round

HOURS: Daily 8 a.m.–dusk

PRICES: Free

DIRECT.: I-71 to Exit 209 for US 224; east on US 224; right (north) on SR 301; left (west) on New London-Eastern Rd.; on right.

Strollers	✓ Groups	Food Nearby
Diap Chg	Picnic	Pub. Trans.
✓ Parking	Food Serv.	Handicapped

This reservation provides 540 acres of undeveloped natural wildlife habitat. For rugged hikes only—it has no trails. It is open for hunting during rabbit and pheasant seasons.

Children's Schoolhouse Nature Park

Lake Metroparks

AGES:	1½–3	3–5	5–8	8–12	12–15
RATING:	★★★	★★★	★★	★	★

COST: **FREE–$$** PREP.: **None–Some**
AREA: **Far East** CITY: **Kirtland Hills**

ADDRESS: 9045 Baldwin Rd.

PHONE: (440) 256-3808

SEASON: Year round

HOURS: Scheduled classes or by appt.

PRICES: Fee for classes

DIRECT.: I-90 to Exit 190 for SR 306; south on SR 306; left (east) on Kirtland-Chardon Rd.; left (north) on Chillicothe Rd.; right (east) on Baldwin Rd.; on left.

Or, I-90 Exit 190 for SR 306; north on SR 306; right (east) on SR 84; right (south) Little Mountain Rd.; right (south) on Hart Rd.; left on Baldwin Rd; on left.

WEB: www.harborcom.net/parks/parkinfo.html

✓ Strollers ✓ Groups Food Nearby
Diap Chg Picnic Pub. Trans.
✓ Parking Food Serv. ✓ Handicapped

With short, well-marked hiking trails, hands-on exhibits, and small classrooms housed in a 100-year-old school, this nature center is ideal for young naturalists. The Discovery Room is full of "please touch" activities, including a Microscope Zoo (with more than 20 easy-to-use power scopes showing slides of pond water, fur, and more) and 14 Discovery Boxes from which kids can remove and examine different materials (furs, skulls, feathers). A wildlife observation room, equipped with glass walls and microphones, lets kids listen to and see birds up close. Live snakes, salamanders, and box turtles live in a 52-gallon stream aquarium.

The Look and See program, for 2- and 3-year-olds with adult, includes a short hike, craft, and snack. Magic Moments, for ages 4–5 with adult, includes a short hike, crafts, discussion, and snack. Trailside Tales, for ages 3–5 with adult, includes a story, craft, and snack with an optional hike or outdoor activity. Natural Wonders, for ages 6–7, features a craft, story or puppets, song, game or other activity, and a hike. Discovery Walks, for ages 6–10, and special programs for older school-age children combine outdoor scavenging with hiking and nature lessons. Short-term summer camps for school-agers focus on nature activities.

Cleveland Botanical Garden

AGES:	1½–3	3–5	5–8	8–12	12–15
RATING:	★★	★★	★★	★★	★★

COST: **FREE–$$** PREP.: **None–Much**
AREA: **Near East** CITY: **Cleveland**

ADDRESS: 11030 East Blvd.

PHONE: (216) 721-1600

SEASON: Year round

HOURS: Building: Mon–Fri 9 a.m.–5 p.m., Sat 9 a.m.–5 p.m., Sun noon–5 p.m.; grounds: daily dawn–dusk

PRICES: Free; fees for special events

DIRECT.: West: I-90 to Exit 173B for Chester Ave.; east on Chester; left on Euclid Ave; left on East Blvd; on left.

East: I-90 to Exit 177 for Martin Luther King Blvd.; south on MLK; left (northeast) on Euclid Ave; left (north) on East Blvd; on left.

South: I-271 to Exit 32 for Cedar Rd.; west on Cedar to University Circle; right (northeast) on Euclid Ave; left (north) on East Blvd.; on left.

✓ Strollers ✓ Groups ✓ Food Nearby
Diap Chg ✓ Picnic ✓ Pub. Trans.
✓ Parking Food Serv. ✓ Handicapped

Founded in 1930, this is the oldest civic garden in the United States. Wildflower, herb, rose, perennial, and Japanese gardens are included among the 3,000 meticulously maintained plants and shrubs on the Cleveland Botanical Garden's 7.5 acres. Inside is one of the country's largest garden libraries—including a special children's section.

The Cleveland Botanical Garden

Throughout the year, special classes for ages 3 and up are offered with either a garden theme or make-and-take project. Library story sessions for preschoolers usually have a nature theme. A gardening program for school-age children is offered each spring. Scheduled to open in Spring 1999 is the Hershey Children's Garden, designed to be an interactive outdoor area with a treehouse, cave, bog, and pond.

Annual events at Valentine's Day, Easter, and Christmas are especially popular and fill up fast, so register early. The annual winter holiday show here is especially nice and typically includes special children's activities as well as entertainment.

Cleveland Metroparks

AGES: 1½–3 3–5 5–8 8–12 12–15
RATING: (see individual parks for age ratings)

COST: **FREE–$** PREP.: **None–Some**
AREA: **Various** CITY: **Cleveland**

ADDRESS: 4101 Fulton Pkwy. (Admin. offices)
PHONE: (216) 351-6300
SEASON: Year round
HOURS: Vary throughout Park District
PRICES: Free admission to reservation & nature centers; fees for some special programs & classes
WEB: www.clemetparks.com

Strollers	✓ Groups	Food Nearby
Diap Chg	✓ Picnic	Pub. Trans.
✓ Parking	Food Serv.	Handicapped

The Cleveland Metroparks system was established in 1917 to ensure public access to open spaces and conserve the many natural valleys of this area. Dubbed the "Emerald Necklace" because its 14 reservations of green space encircle the city, it presently includes more than 19,000 acres.

A map of the Cleveland Metroparks is available at any nature center or at the administrative offices, or by mail. For updated lists of Metroparks events and activities, ask to be added to the mailing list for the monthly *Emerald Necklace* newsletter.

Other general phone numbers:

Ranger Headquarters:
9301 Pearl Rd., Strongsville, (440) 243-7860
Swimming: (216) 351-6300
Winter Recreation Info Line: (216) 351-6300
Cross-Country Ski Ctr. (440) 946-7669 (Sat, Sun)
Permits, picnic area reservations: (216) 351-6300

The following Cleveland Metroparks facilities are described separately in this book:

RESERVATIONS:
Rocky River Reservation
Bradley Woods Reservation
Bedford Reservation
Big Creek Reservation
Brecksville Reservation
Cleveland Metroparks Zoo
Euclid Creek Reservation
Garfield Park Reservation
Huntington Reservation
Mill Stream Run Reservation
North Chagrin Reservation
Ohio & Erie Canal Reservation
South Chagrin Reservation

NATURE CENTERS:
Brecksville Nature Center
Garfield Park Nature Center
Lake Erie Nature and Science Center
Rocky River Nature Center
North Chagrin Nature Center

Cleveland Metroparks Zoo and RainForest

AGES:	1½–3	3–5	5–8	8–12	12–15
RATING:	★★	★★★	★★★	★★★	★★

COST: **$–$$** PREP.: **None–Some**
AREA: **South** CITY: **Cleveland**

ADDRESS: 3900 Wildlife Way

PHONE: (216) 661-7511; office: 661-6500

SEASON: Year round

HOURS: Zoo: daily 9 a.m.–5 p.m.; RainForest: daily 10 a.m.–5 p.m., Wed 10 a.m.–9 p.m.; both closed Christmas and New Year's Day

PRICES: Zoo & RainForest: $7 adults, $4 ages 2–11, no charge under age 2; free Mon 9 a.m.–noon for Cuyahoga County & Hinckley Township. residents (not holidays); RainForest: $5 adults, $3 ages 2–11, free under age 2

DIRECT.: I-71 to Exit 245 for Fulton Rd.; south on Fulton; right (east) on Brookside Park Dr.; on left.

Or, I-480 to Exit 16 for SR 94 (State Rd.); north on State; right (north) on Pearl Rd.; left (west) on Brookside Park Dr.; on right.

WEB: www.clemetzoo.com

✓ Strollers	✓ Groups	✓ Food Nearby
✓ Diap Chg	✓ Picnic	✓ Pub. Trans.
✓ Parking	✓ Food Serv.	✓ Handicapped

The RainForest, one of the Zoo's splashiest attractions, ranks as one of the city's most advanced interactive educational institutions. It's also a lot of fun.

Upon entering, visitors are directed past a roaring waterfall and up a winding staircase to enter an elaborately staged jungle laboratory, complete with microscopes and a computer. Outside the lab, the action really begins: anteaters roam behind glass fences; birds are free to fly above or walk across the floor. Good news for families with small children: there are places to climb up for good views and low-level portholes to see inside caves.

On the lower level, after meeting a colony of bats, you come upon a rain forest "island" that literally explodes into a rainstorm every few minutes. (Our then-toddler cowered. As with many children his age, thunderclaps are not his favorite noise.) The exhibit downstairs tends to be more serious. Interspersed throughout the animal habitats are exhibits explaining the importance of the rain forest in the ecosystem and how the forest is endangered.

Don't overlook the rest of the Zoo. Its lower level is accessible via the main gate, on the same level as the RainForest. From there you can easily

Entrance to the RainForest exhibit at the Cleveland Metroparks Zoo

get to the waterfowl lake. Also accessible from the main gate are the lions, elephants, bird house, and the Zoo train ride. A log cabin sets the stage for the Wolf Wilderness exhibit, designed to look like a trapper's home. From the back porch visitors try to pick out the wolves—sometimes hard to do as they have the run of this two-acre wooded area.

The Zoo Adventure Series, for children ages 3–12, introduces animals and their habits. The most popular of the series is Breakfast with Animals. Families also get either a full breakfast or a snack, depending on the size of the featured animal. This series is a lot of fun, very popular, and often fills quickly, because Zoo members are offered advanced registration.

Concord Woods Nature Park

Lake Metroparks

AGES:	1½–3	3–5	5–8	8–12	12–15
RATING:	★	★	★	★	★

COST: **FREE** PREP.: **None**
AREA: **Far East** CITY: **Concord Township**

ADDRESS: 11211 Spear Rd.

PHONE: (440) 639-PARK

SEASON: Year round

HOURS: Daily dawn–dusk; office: Mon–Fri 8 a.m.–4:30 p.m.

PRICES: Free

DIRECT.: I-90 to Exit 200 for SR 44; south on SR 44; left (north) on Auburn Rd.; right (east) on Spear Rd.; on left.

WEB: www.lakemetroparks.com

✓ Strollers ✓ Groups ✓ Food Nearby
Diap Chg ✓ Picnic Pub. Trans.
✓ Parking Food Serv. ✓ Handicapped

The administrative offices of Lake Metroparks are located here on a 20-acre park with hiking trails, a playground, and picnic areas with grills, fireplaces, and shelters.

Crane Creek State Park

AGES:	1½–3	3–5	5–8	8–12	12–15
RATING:	★	★	★★	★★	★★

COST: **FREE** PREP.: **None**
AREA: **Farther West** CITY: **Oak Harbor**

ADDRESS: 13229 West State Rt. 2

PHONE: (419) 898-2495

SEASON: Seasonal (Summer)

HOURS: Park: Daily 6 a.m.–dusk; Wildlife Center Mon.–Sat. 8 a.m.–5 p.m., Sunday noon–6 p.m.

PRICES: Free

DIRECT.: SR 2 through Port Clinton; on right.

✓ Strollers Groups Food Nearby
Diap Chg ✓ Picnic Pub. Trans.
✓ Parking Food Serv. ✓ Handicapped

The 3,500-foot sandy beach on the shores of Lake Erie is a popular spot for area families in the summer. A half-mile boardwalk trail winds its way through the park, skirting ponds, woodland, and marsh and giving bird-watchers a good view of migratory birds. Picnic tables with grills are scattered on the shoreline and tucked under trees; there is one shelter. At the main entrance road is the Sportsmen's Migratory Bird Center with wildlife displays and an observation platform; next door is the Magee Marsh Wildlife Area and the Ottawa National Wildlife Refuge (the largest federal refuge in the state).

TIPS FOR TRIPS

ATTENTION SPAN

Recommended age ranges are tied to attention spans and hands-on potential; they're not meant to be rigid – you know your family best.

DIRECTORY

Nature & Outdoors

Crown Point Ecology Center

AGES:	1½–3	3–5	5–8	8–12	12–15
RATING:	NR	★	★★	★★	★★

COST: **FREE–$$** PREP.: **Some–Much**
AREA: **Far South** CITY: **Bath**

ADDRESS: 3220 Ira Rd./P.O. Box 484

PHONE: (330) 666-9200

SEASON: Year round

HOURS: Program hours vary, office hours 9 a.m. to 5 p.m.

PRICES: Vary

DIRECT.: I-77 to Exit 143 for Wheatley Rd.; west on Wheatley; left (south) on SR 21 (Brecksville Rd.); left (east) on Ira Rd.; on right.

Strollers ✓ Groups ✓ Food Nearby
Diap Chg Picnic Pub. Trans.
✓ Parking Food Serv. Handicapped

Certified organic farmers staff this 130-acre farm, a nonprofit activity of the Sisters of Saint Dominic. The farm includes a barn (where summertime activities are held) and the Orchard House (winterized for colder months). A variety of children's programming is offered year round; an Earth Camp is run every summer. Past events have ranged from flower printing and art projects to canning and herb growing.

Cuyahoga Valley National Recreation Area

CVNRA

AGES:	1½–3	3–5	5–8	8–12	12–15
RATING:	★★★	★★★	★★★	★★★	★★★

COST: **FREE–$$$** PREP.: **None–Much**
AREA: **South** CITY: **Brecksville**

ADDRESS: 15610 Vaughn Rd. (park headquarters)

PHONE: (800) 445-9667

SEASON: Year round

HOURS: Vary; see individual listings

PRICES: Free; fee for train, picnic shelters, special events, & some programs

DIRECT.: I-77 to Exit 149 for SR 82 (Royalton Rd.); east on Royalton; right (south) on Riverview Rd.; left (east) on Vaughn Rd.; on right.

WEB: www.nps.gov/cuva

Strollers ✓ Groups Food Nearby
Diap Chg ✓ Picnic Pub. Trans.
✓ Parking Food Serv. Handicapped

Covering 33,000 acres along 22 miles of the Cuyahoga River between Cleveland and Akron, this great nearby natural resource offers woods, prairies, freshwater ponds . . . and plenty of opportunities for outdoor recreation.

The Ohio and Erie Canal Towpath Trail, completed in 1993, is a 20-mile multi-use trail stretching from Rockside Rd. in Independence to Bath Rd. north of Akron. It runs the length of the park and follows the remnants of the old canal.

A park-maintained special events site is home to a variety of folk, blues, and jazz performances in the summer months.

The Environmental Education Center (3675 Oak Hill Rd., Peninsula)—open only to school groups and private parties—has introduced "A River Runs Through It," a full-fledged environmental curriculum equipped with laboratories and computers. For information, call (800) 642-3297. A young archeologist/naturalist program for ages 7–12 introduces the disciplines through guided hikes during the summer months.

Visitors to the Cuyahoga Valley National Recreation Area may want to begin at one of the park's visitor centers to pick up trail maps.

Cuyahoga Valley Scenic Railroad

AGES:	1½–3	3–5	5–8	8–12	12–15
RATING:	NR	★	★★★	★★★	★

COST: **$$–$$$** PREP.: **Much**
AREA: **South** CITY: **Independence**

ADDRESS: Rockside Rd. at Canal Rd.

PHONE: (800) 468-4070

SEASON: Seasonal (Mid-Feb–Dec)

HOURS: Vary

PRICES: Prices vary according to destination: $11–20 adults, $10–18 seniors, $7–12 ages 3–12. Group discounts available; special prices for Polar Express & special events

DIRECT.: Main station: I-77 to Exit 155 for Rockside Rd.; east on Rockside; north on Canal Rd.; left (west) on Old Rockside Rd.; on left.

WEB: www.cvsr.com

✓ Strollers ✓ Groups Food Nearby
Diap Chg Picnic Pub. Trans.
✓ Parking ✓ Food Serv. ✓ Handicapped

The Cuyahoga Valley Scenic Railroad offers scenic rides on restored, climate-controlled railway coaches (from the 1930s and 1940s) through the Cuyahoga Valley National Recreation Area (CVNRA). Rides vary in length from 16 to 52 miles. Stops include Hale Farm and Village, the Canal Visitor Center in the CVNRA, downtown Akron, and Stan Hywet Hall and Gardens (see separate listings).

There are several routes. The main ones are: Independence to Hale Farm and Village (departing from Old Rockside Rd., west of Canal Rd.); and Independence (departing from the station at Ira and Riverview roads) to Akron (Howard and Ridge streets). The Scenic Ltd. travels between Independence and Peninsula.

Special rides include the Valley Explorer, a naturalist-led, 41-mile, 5-hour round-trip tour departing at Independence and stopping for lunch in Akron before returning. This trip promises a close-up look at wildlife, including beaver, deer, and waterfowl; there are impromptu, unscheduled stops. The most popular ride for youngsters, the Polar Express, boasts Santa Claus aboard. Running in late November through December, the trip is 24 miles long and lasts a more child-friendly 90–120 minutes. It also includes hot chocolate, Christmas carols, and stories.

Other seasonal and family-oriented train runs include special fall foliage trips, a Christmas Tree Adventure, and a warm-weather Bike and Hike.

Cuyahoga Valley Scenic Railroad

Deep Lock Quarry Metro Park

Metro Parks Serving Summit County

AGES:	1½–3	3–5	5–8	8–12	12–15
RATING:	★	★	★	★★	★★

COST: **FREE** PREP.: **None**
AREA: **Far South** CITY: **Peninsula**

ADDRESS: Riverview Rd.

PHONE: (330) 867-5511

SEASON: Year round

HOURS: Dawn–dusk

PRICES: Free

DIRECT.: I-271 to Exit 12 for SR 303 (Streetsboro Rd.); right (south) on Riverview Rd.; on left.

Strollers	Groups	✓ Food Nearby
Diap Chg	✓ Picnic	Pub. Trans.
✓ Parking	Food Serv.	Handicapped

Fishing is permitted on this reservation encircled by more than 15 miles of gentle loop trails. It is the site of the deepest lock on the Ohio & Erie Canal.

East Harbor State Park

AGES:	1½–3	3–5	5–8	8–12	12–15
RATING:	★★	★★	★★	★★	★★

COST: **FREE–$$** PREP.: **None–Much**
AREA: **Farther West**
CITY: **Lakeside-Marblehead**

ADDRESS: 1169 N. Buck Rd.

PHONE: (419) 734-4424

SEASON: Year round (fully operational Apr–Oct)

HOURS: Daily 7 a.m.–10 p.m.(7 a.m.–11 p.m., weekends); lifeguard daily Memorial Day–Labor Day 10 a.m.–6 p.m.

PRICES: Park admission free; fee for campsite: $12–$17

DIRECT.: SR 2 to SR 269; east on SR 269; on right, after SR 163

✓ Strollers	✓ Groups	✓ Food Nearby
Diap Chg	✓ Picnic	Pub. Trans.
✓ Parking	✓ Food Serv.	✓ Handicapped

The nearly mile-long sandy beach at East Harbor State Park offers swimming with a lifeguard on duty, boating, and fishing. For children, there is also a playground and seven miles of clearly marked hiking trails through marsh and wooded areas. Nature programs are taught by specialists, hired by the Ohio Department of Natural Resources, for families and children ages 10 and up during mornings from Memorial Day to Labor Day. Programs range from Swamp Stomps to observing birds and bugs. (Participate in three and earn a badge.) No preregistration is necessary. An indoor recreation room with video games is open from 8 a.m. to 10 p.m.

Winter activities include three trails for a total of 3½ miles of cross-country skiing with a good view of the harbor. Access to Blackberry Trail (½ mile) is at the campground office; Middle Harbor Trail (2 miles) starts at Exit Rd.; Red Bird Trail (1 mile) starts at the campground boat ramp. Snowmobile access to frozen Lake Erie is possible from the beach, the campground boat ramp, and the water plant.

The 1,831-acre park is set up with 570 sites for tents and recreational vehicles, the largest campground in the state park system. Facilities include bathhouses with flush toilets and showers, laundry, telephone, a small grocery store, ice, food service, and fire rings. A "Rent-A-Camp" program is also offered. Be forewarned: even as large as it is, the park fills up on summer weekends.

Edgewater Park

Cleveland Lakefront State Park

AGES:	1½–3	3–5	5–8	8–12	12–15
RATING:	★★	★★	★★	★★	★★

COST: **FREE** PREP.: **None**
AREA: **West** CITY: **Cleveland**

ADDRESS: 8107 Lakeshore Blvd. (office)

PHONE: (216) 881-8141

SEASON: Year round

HOURS: Lifeguard noon–dusk daily Memorial Day–Labor Day

PRICES: Free

DIRECT.: SR 2 to West Blvd.; north on West Blvd.; right (east) on Edgewater Dr.

Strollers	✓ Groups	✓ Food Nearby
Diap Chg	✓ Picnic	✓ Pub. Trans.
✓ Parking	✓ Food Serv.	✓ Handicapped

This 131-acre park offers swimming at a 900-foot-long sandy Lake Erie beach, as well as a fishing pier, boating, a fitness trail, and plenty of space for general recreation (such as kite-flying). A boat ramp is located just east of Edgewater marina. Two side-by-side pavilions are reservable for large family or group outings. Call park offices for information. The view of the city's skyline from the Upper Park's bluff is arguably the best in Cleveland.

There is a playground with slides and jungle gyms. During the summer months, a naturalist program involves children in conservation projects and other nature activities. Edgewater is also the site for the annual July Fourth Festival of Freedom fireworks extravaganza and the annual Kite Festival.

Eldon Russell Park

Geauga Park District

AGES:	1½–3	3–5	5–8	8–12	12–15
RATING:	★★	★★	★★	★★	★★

COST: **FREE–$** PREP.: **None**
AREA: **Far East** CITY: **Troy Township**

ADDRESS: 16315 Rapids Rd.

PHONE: (440) 285-2222, (440) 564-7131, (440) 834-1856

SEASON: Year round

HOURS: Daily 6 a.m.–11 p.m.

PRICES: Free

DIRECT.: US 422 to Rapids Rd.; north on Rapids; on right.

Or, I-90 to Exit 200 for SR 44; south on SR 44; right (east) on SR 87 (Kinsman Rd.); right (south) on Rapids Rd.; on left.

✓ Strollers	✓ Groups	Food Nearby
Diap Chg	✓ Picnic	Pub. Trans.
✓ Parking	Food Serv.	Handicapped

Bring your own canoe here, and paddle on the Cuyahoga River, which runs through this 132-acre park. There are hiking trails (cross-country skiing in the winter), fishing areas, and picnic facilities.

Euclid Beach

Cleveland Lakefront State Park

AGES:	1½–3	3–5	5–8	8–12	12–15
RATING:	★★	★★	★★	★★	★★

COST: **FREE** PREP.: **None**
AREA: **East** CITY: **Cleveland**

ADDRESS: 16300 Lakeshore Blvd.

PHONE: (216) 881-8141

SEASON: Year round

HOURS: Daily 6 a.m.–11 p.m.; lifeguard noon–dusk daily Memorial Day–Labor Day

PRICES: Free

DIRECT.: I-90 to Exit 182A for E. 185 St. / Nottingham Rd.; north on Nottingham; left (west) on Lakeshore Blvd.; right (north) on E. 169 St.; on left.

Strollers	Groups	✓ Food Nearby
Diap Chg	✓ Picnic	✓ Pub. Trans.
✓ Parking	✓ Food Serv.	✓ Handicapped

The 650-foot-long sandy beach at Euclid Beach Park is popular for swimming. It is mainly a day-use picnic area. Facilities include bathhouses equipped with showers, restrooms, and changing areas. There is a playground and a scenic pier, as well as lampposts, benches, and a grand entrance gate that are vestiges of the old amusement park from a century ago.

Euclid Creek Reservation

Cleveland Metroparks

AGES:	1½–3	3–5	5–8	8–12	12–15
RATING:	★★	★★	★★	★★	★★

COST: **FREE** PREP.: **None**
AREA: **East** CITY: **Euclid**

ADDRESS: Euclid Creek Pkwy.

PHONE: (216) 351-6300

SEASON: Year round

HOURS: Daily 6 a.m.–11 p.m.

PRICES: Free

DIRECT.: I-90 to Exit 182A for E. 185 St./ Nottingham Rd.; south on Nottingham; Nottingham becomes Dille Rd.; Dille becomes Highland Rd.; left (south) on Euclid Creek Pkwy.

✓ Strollers	✓ Groups	✓ Food Nearby
Diap Chg	✓ Picnic	✓ Pub. Trans.
✓ Parking	Food Serv.	✓ Handicapped

Euclid Creek Reservation is home to a quarry featuring the only remaining exposure of bluestone in the area. It also offers all-purpose trails (including cross-country ski trails), five picnic areas, ball fields, and designated sledding (at Kelly Picnic Area).

F. A. Seiberling Naturealm

Metro Parks Serving Summit County

AGES:	1½–3	3–5	5–8	8–12	12–15
RATING:	★★	★★★	★★	★★	★

COST: **FREE** PREP.: **None**
AREA: **Far South** CITY: **Akron**

ADDRESS: 1828 Smith Rd.

PHONE: (330) 865-8065

SEASON: Year round

HOURS: Mon–Sat 10 a.m.–5 p.m., Sun noon–5 p.m.; grounds open from 8 a.m. to sunset

PRICES: Free

DIRECT.: I-77 to Exit 136 for SR 18 (Medina Rd.); east on Medina; left (north) on Smith Rd.; on right.

✓ Strollers	✓ Groups	✓ Food Nearby
✓ Diap Chg	✓ Picnic	Pub. Trans.
✓ Parking	Food Serv.	✓ Handicapped

This place has some of the best nature exhibits in northern Ohio. Stuffed owls and prairie dogs stare down at toddlers, and no, the rope in front of them does not stop kids from petting these inanimate animals. "Please-touch" exhibits range from turtles to leaf bark. Among our favorites are an interactive computer game in which users are asked to match footprints to their owners, and leaves to their trees. The best display, however, was a bug's-eye view of a typical pond from under the water. This room boasts crayfish models blown up from their regular size to the size of a five-year-old.

Bird-watchers can sit in front of a huge picture window overlooking a series of bird feeders, trees, and a manmade babbling brook. Like most kids, ours cared less about the birds than about the huge black binoculars on the window sill.

The naturealm also has paths, including a rock-and-herb garden and a tree walk. Both are less than half a mile long and are handicap- as well as family-friendly.

Fairport Harbor Lakefront Park

Lake Metroparks

AGES:	1½–3	3–5	5–8	8–12	12–15
RATING:	★★	★★	★★	★★	★★

COST: **FREE–$$** PREP.: **None–Some**
AREA: **Far East** CITY: **Fairport Harbor**

ADDRESS: 301 Huntington Beach Dr.

PHONE: (440) 639-7275; hotline: (440) 639-9972

SEASON: Year round (fully operational Memorial Day–Labor Day)

HOURS: Daily dawn–dusk; lifeguards 11 a.m.–7 p.m. daily (in season)

PRICES: Free admission; $2 parking; fees for some classes

DIRECT.: SR 2 to Richmond Rd. (Fairport Harbor); north on Richmond; Richmond becomes High St.; north on High; on right.

WEB: www.lakemetroparks.com

✓ Strollers ✓ Groups Food Nearby
✓ Diap Chg ✓ Picnic Pub. Trans.
✓ Parking ✓ Food Serv. ✓ Handicapped

Attractions at the 20-acre Fairport Harbor Lakefront Park include fishing, picnic areas with grills and shelters, a large playground, and volleyball courts.

Of note for families is the Sunday in the Park summer concert series. For kids, there are organized programs for infants to high-school age, such as Beach Babies playtime, sand crafts, obstacle courses, Hobie Cat lessons, and sailing.

Fairport Harbor Lakefront Park

At the beach, rental equipment is available for volleyball, badminton, softball, soccer, horseshoes, frisbee, and bocce. Facilities also include restrooms, changing rooms, and showers.

Findley State Park

AGES:	1½–3	3–5	5–8	8–12	12–15
RATING:	★★	★★	★★	★★	★★

COST: **FREE–$$** PREP.: **None–Much**
AREA: **Far West** CITY: **Wellington**

ADDRESS: 25381 SR 58

PHONE: (440) 647-4490

SEASON: Year round (fully operational Apr–Oct)

HOURS: Daily 6 a.m.–11 p.m.; 24 hrs. on request

PRICES: Free park admission; fee for campsites: $12

DIRECT.: I-480 to Exit 1 for SR 10; southwest on SR 10; SR 10 becomes SR 20; SR 20 to SR 58; south on SR 58 through Wellington; on left.

✓ Strollers ✓ Groups Food Nearby
Diap Chg ✓ Picnic Pub. Trans.
✓ Parking ✓ Food Serv. ✓ Handicapped

The big attraction here is Findley Lake. At 93 acres and with a relatively shallow depth (up to 25 feet), it offers a grassy beach, swimming with a lifeguard on duty, and boating—with boat rentals. Fishing, mainly for bass, bluegill, catfish, and northern pike, is also available. Bait is sold at the concession stand, but bring your own rod and reel. Because this state park was originally a state forest, the 10 miles of well-marked hiking trails are heavily wooded, and stunning in the fall. A nature trail of 1.2 miles is perfect for families.

In the winter months, six miles of ski trails run through rolling wooded terrain suitable for both beginning and advanced cross-country skiers. Approximately half the trail is groomed. Access points are provided at the park office and the camp check-in station (no ski rental is available). There is also ice-skating on the lake.

For children there is a playground, and nature programs are offered from Memorial Day to Labor Day. There are no age restrictions for most of the programs, and older children can earn Junior Naturalist badges by attending three courses at any state park or combination of parks. There is no need to register.

The park has 275 tent and recreational vehicle sites. Park facilities include fire rings, flush and pit toilets, showers, laundry, phone, and a small grocery store. The "Rent-A-Camp" program is also offered.

Firestone Metro Park

Metro Parks Serving Summit County

AGES:	1½–3	3–5	5–8	8–12	12–15
RATING:	★★	★★	★★	★★	★★

COST: **FREE** PREP.: **None**
AREA: **Far South** CITY: **Akron**

ADDRESS: Harrington and Warner Rds.

PHONE: (330) 867-5511

SEASON: Year round

HOURS: Dawn–dusk

PRICES: Free

DIRECT.: I-77 to I-277; west on I-277 to Exit 3 for S. Main St.; south on S. Main; left (east) on Swartz Rd.; right (south) on Harrington Rd.; on left.

Strollers | Groups | ✓ Food Nearby
✓ Diap Chg | ✓ Picnic | Pub. Trans.
✓ Parking | Food Serv. | Handicapped

In addition to several hiking and fitness trails, this park has the Coventry Oaks Pavilion (off South Main St.) available for rental. There's also play equipment, a sledding hill, and cross-country skiing (when conditions permit). Little Turtle Pond is reserved for fishing for ages 15 and under. The park contains a river, two ponds, and a marsh in its 255 acres.

French Creek Nature Center

Lorain County Metro Parks

AGES:	1½–3	3–5	5–8	8–12	12–15
RATING:	★★	★★★	★★★	★★	★★

COST: **FREE–$** PREP.: **None–Some**
AREA: **Far West** CITY: **Sheffield Village**

ADDRESS: 4530 Colorado Ave. (SR 611)

PHONE: (800) LCM-PARK

SEASON: Year round

HOURS: Daily 8 a.m.–4:30 p.m.

PRICES: Free; fees for some classes & special events

DIRECT.: I-90 to Exit 151 for SR 611 (Colorado Ave.); west on SR 611; on left.

✓ Strollers | ✓ Groups | ✓ Food Nearby
✓ Diap Chg | ✓ Picnic | Pub. Trans.
✓ Parking | Food Serv. | ✓ Handicapped

The French Creek Nature Center has two rooms of natural history displays with several interactive exhibits (a hollowed-out tree to climb into, cards to flip, buttons to push) and a few live animals (a rather big snake, turtles, and frogs).

For ages 4–5 with parents, the Park Pals program includes a short hike, simple crafts, and a discussion with a nature focus. Other workshops are designed for school-age kids and can include tree identification, making milk-carton bird feeders, and nature art. Organized hikes are offered year round for all age levels. Registration is required for most activities, and these programs are popular.

The Nature Center is located in the French Creek Reservation (listed separately).

French Creek Reservation

Lorain County Metro Parks

AGES:	1½–3	3–5	5–8	8–12	12–15
RATING:	★★	★★	★★	★★	★★

COST: **FREE** PREP.: **None**
AREA: **Far West** CITY: **Sheffield Village**

ADDRESS: French Creek Rd.

PHONE: (800) LCM-PARK

SEASON: Year round

HOURS: Daily 8 a.m.–dusk

PRICES: Free

DIRECT.: I-90 to Exit 151 for SR 611 (Colorado Ave.); west on SR 611; left (south) on Abbe Rd.; right (west) on French Creek Rd.; on right.

✓ Strollers ✓ Groups ✓ Food Nearby
Diap Chg ✓ Picnic Pub. Trans.
✓ Parking Food Serv. ✓ Handicapped

Four and a half miles of hiking trails, picnic areas with shelters, large playground, French Creek Nature Center (listed separately).

The trails here are ideal for younger hikers because they are well marked and include some very short loops over the creek, through the woods, and back to the Nature Center.

Furnace Run Metro Park

Metro Parks Serving Summit County

AGES:	1½–3	3–5	5–8	8–12	12–15
RATING:	★	★	★	★★	★★

COST: **FREE** PREP.: **None–Some**
AREA: **South** CITY: **Richfield**

ADDRESS: 4955 Townsend Rd.

PHONE: (330) 867-5511

SEASON: Year round

HOURS: Dawn–dusk

PRICES: Free

DIRECT.: Daffodil: I-77 to Exit 145 for SR 21 (Brecksville Rd.); south on Brecksville; left (east) on Brush Rd.; on right.

Other Trails: I-77 to Exit 145 for SR 21 (Brecksville Rd.); south on Brecksville; right (north) on Townsend Rd.; on right.

Strollers ✓ Groups ✓ Food Nearby
✓ Diap Chg ✓ Picnic Pub. Trans.
✓ Parking ✓ Food Serv. Handicapped

There are 3.2 miles of easy-to-follow trails within the 890 acres of this park. (Though two-thirds of the park is off limits, an annual Stream Stomp allows a glimpse into the restricted area.) During the winter months there is ice-skating on Brushwood Lake and cross-country skiing. The Stream Stomp is a guided hike through portions of the park that are off limits to the public.

Gardenview Horticultural Park

AGES:	1½–3	3–5	5–8	8–12	12–15
RATING:	NR	★	★★	★★	★★

COST: **$–$$** PREP.: **None**
AREA: **Southwest** CITY: **Strongsville**

ADDRESS: 16711 Pearl Rd.

PHONE: (440) 238-6653

SEASON: Seasonal (Apr 1–mid-Oct)

HOURS: Sat–Sun noon–6 p.m. (non-members); members admitted any time 7 days a week; groups by appointment

PRICES: Adults $5, children $3; $25 membership

DIRECT.: I-71 to Exit 231 for SR 82 (Royalton Rd.); west on Royalton; right (south) on US 42 (Pearl Rd.); on left

WEB: www.geocities.com/heartland/cottage/9303/index.htm

✓ Strollers ✓ Groups ✓ Food Nearby
✓ Diap Chg Picnic ✓ Pub. Trans.
✓ Parking Food Serv. Handicapped

Tucked in the midst of a fast-growing suburb, this not-for-profit horticultural park makes for a peaceful break from the outside world. Ten acres of crabapple trees and six acres of gardens are ribboned with winding paths; it's a great place to take a walk.

Garfield Park Nature Center

Cleveland Metroparks

AGES:	1½–3	3–5	5–8	8–12	12–15
RATING:	★★	★★	★★	★★	★★

COST: **FREE–$$** PREP.: **None–Much**
AREA: **South** CITY: **Garfield Hts.**

ADDRESS: 11350 Broadway Ave.

PHONE: (216) 341-3152

SEASON: Year round

HOURS: Daily 9:30 a.m.–5 p.m. except Thanksgiving, Christmas, New Year's Day

PRICES: Free; fees for special programs

DIRECT.: I-480 to Exit 23 for Broadway Ave.; north on Broadway; on left.

✓ Strollers ✓ Groups ✓ Food Nearby
✓ Diap Chg ✓ Picnic Pub. Trans.
✓ Parking Food Serv. ✓ Handicapped

Kids particularly enjoy the collection of live animals—turtles, fish, frogs, toads, snakes, beehive—at this nature center. Programs designed for young children include Forest Adventures and Night Crawlers (ages 3–5); Junior Naturalists (ages 6–7); and Explorers (ages 8–10). All are led by naturalists and include stories, short hikes, and crafts. Registration is required for all programs. Check the *Emerald Necklace* monthly newsletter for details.

Garfield Park Reservation

Cleveland Metroparks

AGES:	1½–3	3–5	5–8	8–12	12–15
RATING:	★★★	★★★	★★★	★★★	★★★

COST: **FREE** PREP.: **None**
AREA: **South** CITY: **Garfield Hts.**

ADDRESS: Garfield Park Dr.

PHONE: (216) 351-6300; nature center: (216) 341-3152

SEASON: Year round

HOURS: Daily 6 a.m.–11 p.m.

PRICES: Free

DIRECT.: I-480 to Exit 23 for Broadway Ave.; north on Broadway; left on Garfield Park Dr.

✓ Strollers ✓ Groups ✓ Food Nearby
✓ Diap Chg ✓ Picnic Pub. Trans.
✓ Parking Food Serv. ✓ Handicapped

The nature trails here are especially good for youngsters, because Garfield Park is one of the smaller reservations in the Emerald Necklace. The Ridgetop trail and the North Ravine trail cover only about ½ mile each. There is also a small public garden, a loop all-purpose trail, ball fields, four picnic areas, Iron Spring Wildlife Preserve, and the Garfield Park Nature Center (see separate listing).

Geauga Park District

AGES: 1½–3 3–5 5–8 8–12 12–15
RATING: (see individual park listings for age ratings)

COST: **FREE–$** PREP.: **None**
AREA: **Far East** CITY: **Chardon**

ADDRESS: 9160 Robinson Rd.

PHONE: (440) 285-2222

SEASON: Year round

HOURS: 6 a.m.–11 p.m.

PRICES: Free, fees for special programs

DIRECT.: I-90 to Exit 200 for SR 44; south on SR 44; left (east) on Clark Rd.; right (southeast) on Robinson Rd.; on right.

Or, US 422 to SR 44; north on SR 44 through Chardon; north on North St./Ravenna Rd.; right (east) on Woodin Rd.; left (north) on Robinson Rd.; on left.

Strollers ✓ Groups Food Nearby
Diap Chg ✓ Picnic Pub. Trans.
✓ Parking Food Serv. Handicapped

More than 4,600 acres of forests, wetlands, lakes, rivers, and streams make up this excellent park system, complete with fishing, hiking, and picnic areas throughout. Expansion provided a 926-acre Headwaters Park and the 792-acre West Woods track. Also part of the park is Auburn's Beartown Lakes Reservation and 410 acres of the White Pine Bog Forest in the Burton Wetlands, a combined effort with the Nature Conservancy (public access to the Wetlands, however, is restricted).

Maps and directions to the park area are available from the park office. For updated lists of special events, ask to be added to the mailing list for the bimonthly newsletter.

The following Geauga Park District facilities are described separately in this book:

Bessie Benner Metzenbaum Park
Big Creek Park and Donald W. Meyer Nature Center
Eldon Russell Park
Swine Creek Reservation
Walker C. Best Preserve
WhitlamWoods

Geneva State Park

AGES:	1½–3	3–5	5–8	8–12	12–15
RATING:	★★	★★	★★	★★	★★

COST: **FREE–$$$** PREP.: **None**
AREA: **Farther East** CITY: **Geneva**

ADDRESS: 6412 Lake Rd. West (camp office)

PHONE: (440) 466-8400

SEASON: Year round (fully operational Apr–Oct)

HOURS: Rangers: 24 hours Sat, Sun; lifeguard: Mon–Fri noon–6 p.m.; Sat, Sun 1 p.m.–7 p.m. Memorial Day–Labor Day

PRICES: Free park admission; fee for campsites: $18

DIRECT.: I-90 to Exit 218 for SR 534; north on SR 534; on left.

Strollers	✓ Groups	✓ Food Nearby
Diap. Chg	✓ Picnic	Pub. Trans.
✓ Parking	✓ Food Serv.	✓ Handicapped

The beachfront at Geneva State Park is a 1,500-foot-long mix of sand and rock. The park offers swimming with lifeguards on duty, boating, and fishing. There is also a marina with a bait shop, boat-trailer parking, and six launching ramps. The park is set up with 91 tent and RV sites. Facilities include flush toilets, showers, laundry, telephone, and fire rings. The Ohio Department of Natural Resources also offers "Rent-A-Camp" and "Rent-A-RV" programs. Seasonal cabins are open May through September. Call for reservations. Typically, the park fills in the summer on weekends.

There is a playground for children and seven miles of hiking trails (but the trails are not well marked). Rangers also caution that the wooded trails go through areas in which hunting is permitted.

Winter recreation includes five miles of cross-country skiing trails that are mainly flat and excellent for beginners. Access to the trail is at the park office. The staging area for the 3½-mile trail is located on Lake Rd. across from Deer Lake Golf Course on the north end of the park. (Park at the old park office lot.) No equipment rental is available, so bring your own skis. Snowmobiling is also available.

Girdled Road Reservation, South

Lake Metroparks

AGES:	1½–3	3–5	5–8	8–12	12–15
RATING:	★★	★★	★★	★★	★★

COST: **FREE** PREP.: **None**
AREA: **Far East** CITY: **Concord**

ADDRESS: Radcliffe Rd. at SR 608

PHONE: (440) 639-7275

SEASON: Year round

HOURS: Daily dawn–dusk

PRICES: Free

DIRECT.: I-90 to Exit 200 for SR 44; south on SR 44; left (east) on Girdled Rd.; right (south) on SR 608; left (east) on Radcliffe Rd.; on left.

WEB: www.lakemetroparks.com

✓ Strollers ✓ Groups ✓ Food Nearby
Diap Chg ✓ Picnic Pub. Trans.
✓ Parking Food Serv. Handicapped

This 643-acre reservation has all-purpose trails (including hiking, horseback riding, cross-country skiing), fishing, ball and game fields, picnic areas with grills and shelters, and a playground. Bounded by the Big Creek, the park is popular with birds and birders—over 70 species have been identified here.

Goodyear Heights Metro Park

Metro Parks Serving Summit County

AGES:	1½–3	3–5	5–8	8–12	12–15
RATING:	★★	★★	★★	★★	★★

COST: **FREE** PREP.: **None**
AREA: **Far South** CITY: **Akron**

ADDRESS: 2077 Newton St.

PHONE: (330) 867-5511

SEASON: Year round

HOURS: Dawn–dusk

PRICES: Free

DIRECT.: I-77 to I-76 east; I-76 to Exit 27 for Gilchrist Rd.; northwest on Gilchrist; right (north) on Darrow Rd.; left (west) on Newton St.; (Goodyear Memorial Pavilion on right); right (north) on Frazier Ave.

Strollers Groups ✓ Food Nearby
✓ Diap Chg ✓ Picnic ✓ Pub. Trans.
✓ Parking Food Serv. Handicapped

Goodyear Heights is a 410-acre playground for children and adults. The park has a ball field, fishing, hiking and fitness trails, play equipment, open and closed shelters, sledding, ice-skating, restrooms, and cross-country skiing. Pavilion and shelter rental is also an option.

Gorge Metro Park

Metro Parks Serving Summit County

AGES:	1½–3	3–5	5–8	8–12	12–15
RATING:	★★	★★	★★	★★	★★

COST: **FREE** PREP.: **None**
AREA: **Far South** CITY: **Cuyahoga Falls**

ADDRESS: 1160 Front St.

PHONE: (330) 867-5511

SEASON: Year round

HOURS: Dawn–dusk

PRICES: Free

DIRECT.: I-271 to Exit 18 for SR 8; south on SR 8 to Cuyahoga Falls Ave./Howe Ave.; west on Cuyahoga Falls; right; north on Front St.; on right.

Strollers Groups ✓ Food Nearby
Diap Chg ✓ Picnic ✓ Pub. Trans.
✓ Parking Food Serv. Handicapped

This 205-acre park contains several gentle hiking trails, play equipment, an open shelter, and restrooms. The 3.2-mile Highbridge Trail connects with Cascade Valley Metro Park.

Hach-Otis State Nature Preserve

AGES:	1½–3	3–5	5–8	8–12	12–15
RATING:	NR	NR	★★	★★	★★

COST: **FREE** PREP.: **None–Some**
AREA: **East** CITY: **Willoughby Twp.**

ADDRESS: SR 174 & Skyline Dr.

PHONE: (440) 563-9344; (614) 265-6453 (Ohio Dept. of Natural Resources)

SEASON: Year round

HOURS: Dawn–dusk

PRICES: Free

DIRECT.: I-90 to Exit 189 for SR 91 (SOM Center Rd.); south on SR 91; left (east) on US 6; left (north) on SR 174 (Chagrin River Rd.); right (east) on Skyline Dr.

Strollers Groups ✓ Food Nearby
Diap Chg Picnic Pub. Trans.
✓ Parking Food Serv. Handicapped

Two loop trails provide dramatic overlooks on the Chagrin and Grand rivers. (The 150-foot South Trail bluff rim can be unstable, so it's not good for youngsters.) Nature programs, such as the popular full-moon night hikes, are scheduled year round by Audubon Society members. Open to the public since 1944, this 82.4-acre sanctuary and interpretive nature preserve is owned by the Cleveland Audubon Society and managed by the Ohio Department of Natural Resources.

Hampton Hills Metro Park

Metro Parks Serving Summit County

AGES:	1½–3	3–5	5–8	8–12	12–15
RATING:	★★	★★	★★	★★	★★

COST: **FREE** PREP.: **None**
AREA: **Far South** CITY: **Akron**

ADDRESS: Akron-Peninsula Rd. at Steels Corners Rd.

PHONE: (330) 867-5511

SEASON: Year round

HOURS: Dawn–dusk

PRICES: Free

DIRECT.: I-77 to Exit 138 for Ghent Rd.; north on Ghent; right (east) on Yellow Creek Rd.; right (west) on W. Bath Rd.; left on Akron Peninsula Rd.

Or, SR 8 to Steels Corners Rd.; west on Steels Corners; left (south) on Akron Peninsula Rd.

Strollers | Groups | ✓ Food Nearby
Diap Chg | ✓ Picnic | Pub. Trans.
✓ Parking | Food Serv. | Handicapped

Hampton Hills offers a ball field and soccer field, hiking trails (which are rather steep), and restrooms.

Happy Days Visitor Center

CVNRA

AGES:	1½–3	3–5	5–8	8–12	12–15
RATING:	★	★★	★★★	★★★	★★★

COST: **FREE–$$$** PREP.: **None–Much**
AREA: **South** CITY: **Peninsula**

ADDRESS: SR 303

PHONE: (800) 257-9477

SEASON: Year round

HOURS: Daily 8 a.m.–5 p.m.; closed Mon–Tue Nov through Mar

PRICES: Free; fee for special events

DIRECT.: I-90 to Exit 189 for SR 91 (SOM Center Rd.); south on SR 91; left (east) on US 6 (Chardon Rd.); left (north) on SR 174 (Chagrin River Rd.); right (east) on Skyline Dr.

WEB: www.hps.gov/cuva

✓ Strollers | ✓ Groups | ✓ Food Nearby
Diap Chg | ✓ Picnic | Pub. Trans.
✓ Parking | Food Serv. | ✓ Handicapped

The Happy Days Visitor Center of the Cuyahoga Valley National Recreation Area offers a slide show about the park's history. Park publications are available here, and rangers are always on hand. Three other Civilian Conservation Corps structures are nearby: Ledges Shelter, with open playing fields and trails leading to rock ledges; the Octagon Shelter, with playing fields and picnic areas; and Kendall Lake Shelter, a winter sports shelter and picnic area (see separate listing). In all, there are 52 square miles of parkland to explore. The center was built in the 1930s by the Civilian Conservation Corps as a day camp.

Special programs are offered year round for children ages 3–6 and for older school-age children. They typically include short hikes, talks, and an activity. The Young Naturalist Series, for example, is a year-round program that offers both indoor instruction and field experience to children ages

7–12. There are workshops on family camping, hiking, biking, and canoeing. Special Olympics–related events are held here annually. A schedule of events is published quarterly; call for details.

Headlands Beach State Park

AGES: 1½–3 3–5 5–8 8–12 12–15
RATING: ★★ ★★ ★★ ★★ ★★

COST: **FREE** PREP.: **None**
AREA: **Far East** CITY: **Mentor**

ADDRESS: 9601 Headlands Rd.

PHONE: (440) 352-8082, (216) 881-8141

SEASON: Year round

HOURS: Mon–Sat 8 a.m.–sunset; lifeguard on duty Mon–Fri 11 a.m.–7 p.m.; Sat–Sun noon–8 p.m. Memorial Day–Labor Day

PRICES: Free

DIRECT.: SR 2 to SR 44 (Headlands Beach State Park); north on SR 44.

✓ Strollers ✓ Groups ✓ Food Nearby
Diap Chg ✓ Picnic Pub. Trans.
✓ Parking ✓ Food Serv. ✓ Handicapped

Looking for a large expanse of soft sand and shallow water? You'll find it here. Headlands, Ohio's largest natural sandy beach, stretches for a mile and is bounded by the last remaining natural sand dunes along the shores of Lake Erie.

Summer weekends are popular for swimming, fishing, wind surfing (lessons and rentals available), and sand volleyball (equipment rental available). Lawn chairs and umbrellas can also be rented. There is a first-aid station. Prepare to spend the day.

There are also three miles of well-marked hiking trails, including the northern terminus of the Buckeye Trail and several trails through the Headlands Dunes State Nature Preserve, where there is also a Coast Guard lighthouse. (Be careful: the rocks are uneven.) Naturalist programs are held here in the summer.

During winter months, there are designated areas for sledding, ice-skating, and cross-country skiing.

Helen Hazen Wyman Park

Lake Metroparks

AGES: 1½–3 3–5 5–8 8–12 12–15
RATING: ★★ ★★ ★★ ★★ ★★

COST: **FREE** PREP.: **None**
AREA: **Far East** CITY: **Painesville**

ADDRESS: SR 86

PHONE: (440) 639-7275

SEASON: Year round

HOURS: Daily dawn–dusk

PRICES: Free

DIRECT.: I-90 to Exit 205 for Vrooman Rd.; south on Vrooman; right (west) on Carter Rd.; right (north) on SR 86 (Painesville Warren Rd.) on right.

Or, I-90 to Exit 200 for SR 44; north on SR 44; right (east) on SR 84 (Johnnycake Ridge Rd.); right (south) on SR 86 (Painesville Warren Rd.); on left.

Or, SR 2 to SR 44; south on SR 44; left (east) on SR 84 (Johnnycake Ridge Rd.); right (south) on SR 86 (Painesville Warren Rd.); on left.

WEB: www.lakemetroparks.com

Helen Hazen Wyman Park

✓ Strollers ✓ Groups ✓ Food Nearby
Diap Chg ✓ Picnic Pub. Trans.
✓ Parking Food Serv. Handicapped

Fishing, ball fields, playground, picnic areas with fire pits, grills, and shelters on 60 acres.

Hell Hollow Wilderness Area

Lake Metroparks

AGES:	1½–3	3–5	5–8	8–12	12–15
RATING:	★★	★★	★★	★★	★★

COST: **FREE** PREP.: **None**
AREA: **Far East** CITY: **Leroy**

ADDRESS: Leroy Center Rd.

PHONE: (440) 639-7275

SEASON: Year round

HOURS: Daily dawn–dusk

PRICES: Free

DIRECT.: I-90 to Exit 205 for Vrooman Rd.; south on Vrooman; left (east) on Leroy Center Rd.; on left.

WEB: www.lakemetroparks.com

✓ Strollers ✓ Groups ✓ Food Nearby
Diap Chg ✓ Picnic Pub. Trans.
✓ Parking Food Serv. Handicapped

Hiking trails, game fields, picnic areas with playgrounds, grills, shelters, and fire pits on 643 acres.

TIPS FOR TRIPS

FOOD

It can't be stressed enough: your energy level is directly determined by your fuel level. Don't forget the emergency snack supply.

Hidden Valley Park

Lake Metroparks

AGES:	1½–3	3–5	5–8	8–12	12–15
RATING:	★★	★★	★★	★★	★★

COST: **FREE** PREP.: **None**
AREA: **Far East** CITY: **Madison**

ADDRESS: 4880 Klasen Rd.

PHONE: (440) 639-7275

SEASON: Year round

HOURS: Daily 9 a.m.–dusk

PRICES: Free

DIRECT.: I-90 to Exit 212 for SR 528; south on SR 528; right (west) on Klasen Rd.; on left.

WEB: www.lakemetroparks.com

✓ Strollers ✓ Groups ✓ Food Nearby
Diap Chg ✓ Picnic Pub. Trans.
✓ Parking Food Serv. ✓ Handicapped

All-purpose trails (hiking, cross-country skiing), fishing, designated sledding area, canoe access, picnic areas with grills, shelters, fire pits, and playground on 147 acres. Hugging the Grand River, a state-designated scenic river, this park is a hideout for some of the state's rarest plants and animals. More easily spotted are the salamanders and newts that hug the river.

Hidden Valley Park

DIRECTORY Nature & Outdoors

Hinckley Reservation

Cleveland Metroparks

AGES:	1½–3	3–5	5–8	8–12	12–15
RATING:	★★★	★★★	★★★	★★★	★★★

COST: **FREE–$$** PREP.: **None**
AREA: **South** CITY: **Hinckley**

ADDRESS: Off Bellus and State Rds.

PHONE: (216) 351-6300; boathouse: (330) 278-2122; Historical Society (330) 278-2154; Ledge Pool and Recreation Area: (216) 351-6300

SEASON: Year round (lifeguard on duty Jun–Labor Day)

HOURS: Reservation: 6 a.m.–11 p.m. daily; lifeguard 9 a.m.–9 p.m. daily (seasonal)

PRICES: Free; some rental fees; admission fee at Ledge Pool

DIRECT.: I-71 to Exit 145 for Brecksville Rd.; south on Brecksville; right (west) on SR 303 (Streetsboro Rd.); left (south) on SR 94 (State Rd.); after Bellus Rd.

✓ Strollers	✓ Groups	✓ Food Nearby
Diap Chg	✓ Picnic	Pub.Trans.
✓ Parking	✓ Food Serv.	✓ Handicapped

Best known as the place where the buzzards summer (there is even a mid-March celebration of their return), Hinckley Reservation offers swimming (with lifeguards on duty) at Hinckley Lake and Ledge Lake, changing rooms, restrooms, and concessions.

Hinckley Lake Boathouse on West Drive has a boat launch and offers rentals (canoes, electric motorboats, kayaks, in-line skates) available April 1st to November 1st.

There are also all-purpose trails, cross-country ski trails, sledding (off State Rd.; lit at night), skating on Hinckley Lake, fishing and ice fishing on Hinckley, Judge's, and Ledge lakes, and eight picnic areas. Whipp's Ledges rock formation overlooks Hinckley Lake from a height of 350 feet.

Hogback Ridge

Lake Metroparks

AGES:	1½–3	3–5	5–8	8–12	12–15
RATING:	★	★	★	★	★

COST: **FREE** PREP.: **None**
AREA: **Far East** CITY: **Madison**

ADDRESS: Emerson Rd.

PHONE: (440) 639-7275

SEASON: Year round

HOURS: Daily dawn–dusk

PRICES: Free

DIRECT.: I-90 to Exit 212 for SR 528; south on SR 528; left (east) on Griswold Rd.; left (north) on Emerson Rd.

WEB: www.lakemetroparks.com

Hinckley Reservation

Nature & Outdoors DIRECTORY

✓ Strollers ✓ Groups ✓ Food Nearby
Diap Chg ✓ Picnic Pub. Trans.
✓ Parking Food Serv. ✓ Handicapped

Hiking trails (including the All People's Trail), fishing, picnic areas with grills and shelters on 418 acres.

Holden Arboretum

AGES:	1½–3	3–5	5–8	8–12	12–15
RATING:	★★	★★	★★★	★★★	★★★

COST: **$** PREP.: **None–Some**
AREA: **Far East** CITY: **Kirtland**

ADDRESS: 9500 Sperry Rd.

PHONE: ~~(440) 256-1110;~~ (440) 946-4400

SEASON: Year round

HOURS: Tue–Sun 10 a.m.–5 p.m.

PRICES: $4 adults, $2 ages 6–15, $3 seniors w/ Buckeye Card, free under age 6

DIRECT.: I-90 to Exit 190 for SR 306; south on SR 306; right (southeast) on Kirtland-Chardon Rd.; right (northeast) on Sperry Rd.; on right.

WEB: www.holdenarb.org

✓ Strollers ✓ Groups ✓ Food Nearby
✓ Diap Chg ✓ Picnic Pub. Trans.
✓ Parking Food Serv. ✓ Handicapped

Encompassing over 3,100 acres, Holden is the largest private arboretum in the United States. Its wide, well-marked trail system helps make it a family-friendly place. There are signs posted on each trail explaining the ecosystems as well as naming wildflowers and native birds—making it easier to answer children's questions. Even better, youngsters can receive a loaner backpack with an audiotape and an activity kit for the hike. (A parent must leave behind a driver's license as collateral.) Start any visit at the visitor's center for maps, trail guides, and a rest stop.

Holden also boasts fine parent-and-child programs. During the fall, for example, one program invites youngsters to collect leaves, berries, and bark and use them to prepare dye baths to color tee-shirts. Campfire story and song programs are a big hit with all ages. Advance registration is required for all classes, and be forewarned that classes are popular and class sizes are limited. Most have a seasonal theme; look for bird feeding, snowshoeing, tracking, and gardening. The class schedule is available quarterly.

During weekday visits, you will likely encounter a school group. More than 9,000 children visit Holden Arboretum annually on field trips.

Holden Arboretum

Hunt Farm Visitor Information Center

CVNRA

AGES:	1½–3	3–5	5–8	8–12	12–15
RATING:	NR	★	★★	★★	★★

COST: **FREE** PREP.: **None**
AREA: **Far South** CITY: **Peninsula**

ADDRESS: Bolanz Rd.

PHONE: (800) 433-1986

SEASON: Seasonal (Summer)

HOURS: Vary

PRICES: Free

DIRECT.: I-271 to Exit 12 for SR 303 (Streetsboro Rd.); east on SR 303; right (south) on Riverview Rd.; left (east) on Bolanz Rd.; on left.

WEB: www.nps.gov/cuva

Strollers	Groups	Food Nearby
Diap Chg	✓ Picnic	Pub. Trans.
✓ Parking	Food Serv.	Handicapped

The life of a farming community is depicted in a small exhibit at this restored late-19th-century farm complex, open during the summer months. It is typical of many of the small family farms that populated the valley at the turn of the century. The information center is a great place to pick up a map or refill your water bottle.

Huntington Reservation

Cleveland Metroparks

AGES:	1½–3	3–5	5–8	8–12	12–15
RATING:	★★★	★★★	★★★	★★★	★★★

COST: **FREE** PREP.: **None**
AREA: **West** CITY: **Bay Village**

ADDRESS: Porter Creek Dr.

PHONE: (216) 351-6300; Lake Erie Nature and Science Center: (440) 871-2900; Baycrafters: (440) 871-6543; Huntington Playhouse: (440) 871-8333

SEASON: Year round (lifeguard on duty June–Labor Day)

HOURS: Daily 6 a.m.–11 p.m.; lifeguard 9 a.m.–9 p.m. daily (seasonal)

PRICES: Free

DIRECT.: I-90 to Exit 159 for SR 252 (Columbia Rd); north on Columbia; left (west) on Lake Rd.

Or, I-90 to Exit 156 for Crocker/Bassett Rd.; north on Crocker; Crocker becomes Bassett; north on Bassett; right (east) on Lake Rd.

✓ Strollers	Groups	✓ Food Nearby
✓ Diap Chg	✓ Picnic	✓ Pub. Trans.
✓ Parking	✓ Food Serv.	✓ Handicapped

This popular and sandy Lake Erie beach has a shallow walk-in and sandbars—helpful for new swimmers. There are picnic tables and grills, a small playground, bathhouse, and restrooms. On a clear day the downtown skyline is easily visible to the east.

Huntington Reservation also has hiking trails, ball fields, sledding (east of Porter Creek Drive), the Lake Erie Nature and Science Center (off Porter Creek Drive—see separate listing), and Baycrafters (see separate listing).

Huntington Reservation

Indian Hollow Reservation

Lorain County Metro Parks

AGES:	1½–3	3–5	5–8	8–12	12–15
RATING:	★★	★★	★★	★★	★★

COST: **FREE** PREP.: **None**
AREA: **Far West** CITY: **Grafton**

ADDRESS: at Parsons Rd. and Indian Hollow Rd.

PHONE: (800) LCM-PARK

SEASON: Year round

HOURS: Daily 8 a.m.–dusk

PRICES: Free

DIRECT.: I-480 to Exit 1 for SR 10; south on SR 10; south on SR 57; right (west) on Parsons Rd.; on right.

✓ Strollers	✓ Groups	✓ Food Nearby
Diap Chg	✓ Picnic	Pub. Trans.
✓ Parking	Food Serv.	Handicapped

Hiking trails, horseshoe courts, picnic areas with shelters, playground.

Indian Point Park

Lake Metroparks

AGES: 1½–3 | 3–5 | 5–8 | 8–12 | 12–15
RATING: ★ | ★ | ★ | ★ | ★

COST: **FREE** PREP.: **None**
AREA: **Far East** CITY: **Leroy**

ADDRESS: Seeley Rd.

PHONE: (440) 639-7275

SEASON: Year round

HOURS: Daily dawn–dusk

PRICES: Free

DIRECT.: I-90 to Exit 205 for Vrooman Rd.; north on Vrooman; right (east) on Seeley Rd.; on left.

WEB: www.lakemetroparks.com

✓ Strollers · Groups · ✓ Food Nearby · Diap Chg · ✓ Picnic · Pub. Trans. · ✓ Parking · Food Serv. · Handicapped

Hiking trails, fishing, picnic areas with grills on 261 acres.

Kelleys Island State Park

AGES: 1½–3 | 3–5 | 5–8 | 8–12 | 12–15
RATING: ★★ | ★★ | ★★ | ★★ | ★★

COST: **FREE–$$** PREP.: **None–Much**
AREA: **Farther West** CITY: **Kelleys Island**

ADDRESS: Division St.

PHONE: (419) 746-2546; off-season (419) 797-4530

SEASON: Seasonal (fully operational Apr–Oct)

HOURS: First aid & rangers: Daily, 24 hrs.

PRICES: Free park admission; fee for campsites

DIRECT.: SR 2 to SR 269; north on SR 269 to SR 163; east on SR 163 to Marblehead; Neuman Boat Line/Kelleys Island Ferry on left.

WEB: winslo.ohio.gov/ohswww/places/grooves.html

✓ Strollers · Groups · ✓ Food Nearby · Diap Chg · ✓ Picnic · Pub. Trans. · ✓ Parking · Food Serv. · ✓ Handicapped

The 1½-mile sandy beach at Kelleys Island State Park offers swimming (no lifeguards), boating (with boat launch), and fishing (mainly for small-mouthed bass and walleye). Amazing glacial grooves and Inspiration Rock are among the must-see sites on the island. There is also a playground for children and five or six miles of well-marked wooded hiking trails. Also of interest is an abandoned quarry that can be explored for fossils. Swimming in the quarry is prohibited, except during special group arrangements. The 4-H club, for example, learns to scuba dive here. A naturalist program includes hikes and nature talks for children. During summer months there are also Saturday-night movies, geared toward the family, that focus on nature.

The park is set up for 129 tent and recreational vehicle sites. Facilities include bathhouse with flush toilets, showers and changing rooms, telephone, and fire ring. The "Rent-A-Camp" program is offered May 15 through September 15. Call ahead for availability information.

Kendall Lake Area and Winter Sports Center

Cuyahoga Valley National Recreation Area

AGES: 1½–3 | 3–5 | 5–8 | 8–12 | 12–15
RATING: ★ | ★★ | ★★★ | ★★★ | ★★★

COST: **FREE** PREP.: **None**
AREA: **South** CITY: **Peninsula**

ADDRESS: Truxell Rd.

PHONE: (800) 257-9477

SEASON: Year round

HOURS: Shelter: Sat, Sun 10 a.m.–5 p.m. (some holidays) in Jan & Feb

PRICES: Free

DIRECT.: I-271 to Exit 18 for SR 8; SR 8 to SR 303/Akron Cleveland Rd.; south on Akron Cleveland; right (west) on Truxell Rd.; on left.

WEB: www.nps.gov/cuva

Strollers	✓ Groups	Food Nearby
✓ Diap Chg	✓ Picnic	Pub. Trans.
✓ Parking	Food Serv.	✓ Handicapped

The Kendall Area is one of the oldest parts of the Cuyahoga Valley National Recreation Area; the center was built by the Civilian Conservation Corps in the late 1930s. It's particularly popular in winter, as it is a hub for sledding and tubing. Snowshoes are available for a fee. (You must leave your driver's license behind for collateral.) The park has rolling hills, the lake, and spectacular ledges. There are well-marked all-purpose trails, and snowshoeing and cross-country ski trails that go through woods, meadows, and several caves, and near sandstone rock ledges.

In the summer, there is fishing in the lake; there are also ball playing fields and picnic areas. The center is used for special workshops, such as boomerang construction and bird-watching (snowshoe instruction in winter). Nearby are open recreation areas for kite flying and frisbee throwing.

Lake Erie Nature and Science Center

AGES:	1½–3	3–5	5–8	8–12	12–15
RATING:	★★★	★★★	★★★	★★★	★★★

COST: **FREE–$** PREP.: **None–Some**
AREA: **West** CITY: **Bay Village**

ADDRESS: 28728 Wolf Rd.

PHONE: (440) 871-2900

SEASON: Year round

HOURS: Mon–Sat 10 a.m.–5 p.m.; Sun 1–5 p.m.; planetarium: 1st & 3rd Saturdays of each month.

PRICES: Free admission; planetarium: $3, $1 under age 10 & seniors, free to members

DIRECT.: I-90 to Exit 159 for SR 252 (Columbia Rd); north on Columbia; left (west) on Wolf Rd., on right. Or, I-90 to Exit 156 for Crocker/Bassett Rd.; north on Crocker; Crocker becomes Bassett; north on Bassett; right (east) on Wolf Rd.; on left.

WEB: bbs2.rmrc.net/~lensc

✓ Strollers	✓ Groups	✓ Food Nearby
Diap Chg	✓ Picnic	✓ Pub. Trans.
✓ Parking	Food Serv.	✓ Handicapped

The Lake Erie Nature and Science Center is just as a nature center should be: cozy, with lots of little critters sliding, sniffing, and scurrying about. It is also a beautiful, modern facility, thanks to a recently completed renovation. It is well stocked with deer, rabbits, ducks, and chickens outside; turtles, iguanas, snakes, and fish inside. Many animals in the center's collection have been brought in wounded or sick by area residents and nursed back to health. This is a wonderful place for smaller children. It is popular, but never really crowded.

Year-round special nature programs for children begin with ages 3–4, and typically include crafts, songs, stories, and exploring the adjacent trails.

The Schuele Planetarium offers programs geared for a family audience or smaller children. Annual family events range from seminars on wildlife to hands-on crafts and storytelling around a seasonal theme.

The Nature Center is located on the Metroparks' Huntington Reservation (see separate listing), so there are also trails here that lead through the woods and along the creek. Ask for directions if you want to make the longer hike that ends up on Lake Erie at Huntington Beach.

Lake Farmpark

Lake Metroparks

AGES: 1½–3 3–5 5–8 8–12 12–15
RATING: ★★★ ★★★ ★★ ★ ★

COST: **$–$$$** PREP.: **None–Some**
AREA: **Far East** CITY: **Kirtland**

ADDRESS: 8800 Chardon Rd. (US 6)

PHONE: (800) 366-3276

SEASON: Year round

HOURS: Daily 9 a.m.–5 p.m.; closed Christmas & New Year's Day, Mondays in January and February

PRICES: $6 adults, $5 seniors, $4 ages 2–11, free under age 2

DIRECT.: I-90 to Exit 190 for SR 306; south on SR 306; left (east) on US 6 (Chardon Rd.); on right.

WEB: www.lakemetroparks.com

✓ Strollers ✓ Groups Food Nearby
✓ Diap Chg Picnic Pub. Trans.
✓ Parking ✓ Food Serv. ✓ Handicapped

Lake Farmpark offers the best way to see, chase, and pet farm animals short of buying your own farmstead. In addition to the main building, which features a daily milking demo (a hands-on original) and changing exhibits about life on the farm, there is a huge barn and open barnyard a short hike down the road. The easiest way to get to the barn—and an event in itself—is to ride the farm's horse-drawn covered wagon, which leaves every 15 minutes from the back of the main building.

The barn is home to baby farm animals (chickens, pigs, goats, lambs) and is where you'll spend most of your time—especially when there are newborns. The amiable staff makes a point of ensuring that each child has seen and touched enough. (Our son talked for months about the baby chick that hopped and peeped in his hands.) The barn also houses quarter horses and a large show ring that is used for special exhibits and farm machinery demonstrations.

This is one of the few family attractions that opens at 9:00 a.m. on Sundays.

Each month brings a new activity or special event, such as bluegrass concerts, tractor displays, a fall harvest festival, and country lights and decorations during the winter holidays. For younger visitors, special programs include Chores at the Crack of Dawn for ages 8–12 with an adult, a farm life series for preschoolers, and a variety of short-term summer camps.

Remember: This is a farm, so shoes will get dusty or muddy.

Lake Farmpark

Lake Metroparks

AGES: 1½–3 3–5 5–8 8–12 12–15
RATING: (see individual park listings for age ratings)

COST: **FREE–$$$** PREP.: **None–Much**
AREA: **Far East** CITY: **Kirtland**

ADDRESS: 8800 Chardon Rd. (US 6)

PHONE: (440) 639-7275; class registration: (440) 358-7275; cross-country ski hotline: (440) 256-2255

SEASON: Year round

HOURS: Daily 9 a.m.–5 p.m.

PRICES: Fees for classes & special events

WEB: www.lakemetroparks.com

Strollers ✓ Groups Food Nearby
Diap Chg ✓ Picnic Pub. Trans.
✓ Parking Food Serv. Handicapped

Lake Metroparks offers a wide array of first-class recreational opportunities, nature programs, and many other family-oriented activities year round at their various scenic park facilities. The headquarters for Lake Metroparks is located adjacent to Concord Woods Nature Park in Concord Township (see separate listing). Registration for activities is held at Lake Farmpark (see separate listing).

Lake Metroparks

The following Lake Metroparks locations are featured separately in this book:

Chagrin River Park
Chapin Forest Reservation and Pine Lodge
Children's Schoolhouse and Nature Center
Concord Woods Nature Park
Fairport Harbor Lakefront Park
Girdled Road Reservation, South
Helen Hazen Wyman Park
Hell Hollow Wilderness Area
Hidden Valley Park
Hogback Ridge
Indian Point Park
Lake Farmpark
Lakeshore Reservation
Mason's Landing Park
Paine Falls Park
Painesville Township Park
Parson's Gardens
Penitentiary Glen Reservation and Nature Center
Riverview Park
Veterans Park

Lakeshore Reservation

Lake Metroparks

AGES: 1½–3 3–5 5–8 8–12 12–15
RATING: ★★ ★★ ★★ ★★ ★★

COST: **FREE** PREP.: **None**
AREA: **Far East** CITY: **Perry**

ADDRESS: 4799 Lockwood Rd.

PHONE: (440) 639-7275

SEASON: Year round

HOURS: Daily dawn–dusk

PRICES: Free

DIRECT.: SR 2 to US 20 (North Ridge Rd.); left (north) on Antioch Rd.; right (east) on Lockwood Rd.; on left.

WEB: www.lakemetroparks.com

✓ Strollers ✓ Groups ✓ Food Nearby
Diap Chg ✓ Picnic Pub. Trans.
✓ Parking Food Serv. ✓ Handicapped

Hiking trails (including an All People's Trail), fishing, sculpture garden, picnic areas with grills on 86 acres.

Lorain County Metropolitan Park District

AGES: 1½–3 | 3–5 | 5–8 | 8–12 | 12–15
RATING: ★★ | ★★★ | ★★★ | ★★★ | ★★

COST: **FREE–$** PREP.: **None**
AREA: **West** CITY: **Lagrange**

ADDRESS: 12882 Diagonal Rd.

PHONE: (800) LCM-PARK

SEASON: Year round

HOURS: Vary.

PRICES: Free; fees for classes and events

DIRECT.: I-480 to Exit 1 for Sr 10; west on SR 10 to Lagrange Rd.; south on Lagrange; right (west) on Nickelplate Diagonal Rd.; 2nd entrance on right.

✓ Strollers ✓ Groups ✓ Food Nearby
✓ Diap Chg ✓ Picnic Pub. Trans.
✓ Parking Food Serv. ✓ Handicapped

Uncrowded and accessible, the Lorain County Metroparks include eight varied facilities that offer families a glimpse of native wildlife, Ohio history, and outdoor experiences. Maps of parks and various trails are available at any of the parks. For updated lists of special events and programs, ask to be added to the mailing list of the bimonthly newsletter, *The Arrowhead.*

The following Lorain County Metroparks are featured in this book:

Black River Reservation
Caley National Wildlife Woods
Carlisle Reservation and Visitors Center
Charlemont Reservation
French Creek Nature Center
French Creek Reservation
Indian Hollow Reservation
Mill Hollow-Bacon Woods Memorial Park
Schoepfle Arboretum

Lorain Lakeview Park

AGES: 1½–3 | 3–5 | 5–8 | 8–12 | 12–15
RATING: ★★★ | ★★★ | ★★ | ★★ | ★

COST: **FREE** PREP.: **None–Some**
AREA: **Far West** CITY: **Lorain**

ADDRESS: W. Erie Ave. at Lakeview Dr. & Parkview Ave. (just east of SR 58)

PHONE: (440) 244-9000

SEASON: Year round

HOURS: Daily sunrise–11 p.m.; lifeguard on duty Memorial Day–Labor Day 11 a.m.–7 p.m.

PRICES: Free

DIRECT.: I-90 to SR 2; west on SR 2 to SR 58 (Leavitt Rd.); north on Leavitt; right (east) on W. Erie Ave.; on left.

Strollers ✓ Groups ✓ Food Nearby
✓ Diap Chg ✓ Picnic ✓ Pub. Trans.
✓ Parking ✓ Food Serv. ✓ Handicapped

There is an elegance to the setting here: a boardwalk overlooking the lakefront stretches 1,200 feet; rose gardens, a fountain, and a latticed gazebo provide the setting for outdoor concerts on Sundays in the summer.

There is swimming in Lake Erie off a sandy beach and fishing off nearby Municipal Pier. The 42-acre park is set up for lawn bowling, softball, baseball, beach volleyball, and tennis. Bring your own equipment, and call in advance to reserve a court. (The tennis courts are lit for night use.)

There is a playground right on the beach. In summertime, craft programs run daily for school-age children.

Ice-skating, depending on weather conditions, is offered during the winter on a small pond.

Magee Marsh Wildlife Area

AGES:	1½–3	3–5	5–8	8–12	12–15
RATING:	NR	★	★★	★★	★★

COST: **FREE** PREP.: **None**
AREA: **Farther West** CITY: **Oak Harbor**

ADDRESS: 13229 West State Rt. 2

PHONE: (419) 898-0960

SEASON: Year round

HOURS: Mon–Fri 8 a.m.–5 p.m.; Sat–Sun in spring and summer noon–6 p.m.

PRICES: Free

DIRECT.: SR 2 through Port Clinton; on right.

✓ Strollers Groups Food Nearby
Diap Chg Picnic Pub. Trans.
✓ Parking Food Serv. ✓ Handicapped

Start a visit here at the Sportsmen's Center for maps, wildlife exhibits, and trail heads that lead to the marsh and lakefront. This is a favorite spot for migratory birds and birders—more than 300 kinds of birds have been spotted here. Also on hand are marsh residents such as rabbits, deer, raccoons, snakes, frogs, and turtles. Views of the marsh are dramatic—the swamp is literally teaming with wildlife. The accessible boardwalk bird trail is a nice walk for everyone.

Mason's Landing Park

Lake Metroparks

AGES:	1½–3	3–5	5–8	8–12	12–15
RATING:	NR	★★	★★	★★	★★

COST: **FREE** PREP.: **None**
AREA: **Far East** CITY: **Perry**

ADDRESS: Vrooman Rd.

PHONE: (440) 639-7275

SEASON: Year round

HOURS: Daily dawn–dusk

PRICES: Free

DIRECT.: I-90 to Exit 205 for Vrooman Rd.; north on Vrooman; on left.

WEB: www.lakemetroparks.com

✓ Strollers ✓ Groups ✓ Food Nearby
Diap Chg ✓ Picnic Pub. Trans.
✓ Parking Food Serv. Handicapped

Fishing, canoe access, picnic areas with grills on 133 acres.

Mentor Marsh State Nature Preserve

AGES:	1½–3	3–5	5–8	8–12	12–15
RATING:	NR	★	★	★	★

COST: **FREE** PREP.: **None**
AREA: **Far East** CITY: **Mentor**

ADDRESS: 5185 Corduroy Ave.

PHONE: (440) 257-0777

SEASON: Seasonal (Apr–Oct, Nature Center; trails open year round)

HOURS: Sat–Sun noon–5 p.m., trails dawn–dusk

PRICES: Free; programs for groups available for a fee

DIRECT.: SR 2 to SR 44 (Heisley Rd.); north on Heisley; west on SR 283 (Lake Shore Blvd.); right (north) on Corduroy Rd.

Strollers ✓ Groups ✓ Food Nearby
Diap Chg ✓ Picnic Pub. Trans.
✓ Parking Food Serv. ✓ Handicapped

Although it is just 30 miles northeast of downtown Cleveland, Mentor Marsh is really a world away. This state nature preserve is co-owned by the Cleveland Museum of Natural History and the Ohio Department of Natural Resources; it is a National Natural Landmark. Its 644 acres are home to beaver, mink, deer, fox, and 125 species of birds. Of course, spotting them behind the eight-foot-tall reeds, and among hidden ponds and feeder streams, requires some patience, timing, and luck.

Unfortunately, with the growth of the suburban neighborhood bordering the Marsh, some portions of the trails feel as though you're in someone's backyard. More disappointing, the neighbors also seem to be using portions of the Marsh as a dump.

Five self-guided tours range from the blacktopped Newhouse Overlook Trail—just one-tenth of a mile—to the more robust Zimmerman Trail, which crosses streams, shallow ravines, and swamp forests. At two miles in length through an especially soggy part of the preserve, the Zimmerman Trail might not be well suited to families with small children. Also, as this is a marsh, mosquitoes thrive here. (The handy "Mentor Marsh State Nature Preserve" brochure and map available at Mentor Marsh House does a good job of sizing up the trails.)

The area is rich with history as well as wildlife. The marsh began under a glacier before becoming a small lake and later evolving into a meandering branch of the Grand River. The area was once home to Native American tribes and also to surveyor crews occupying the area at the same time Moses Cleaveland settled Cleveland.

Metro Parks Serving Summit County

AGES: 1½–3 3–5 5–8 8–12 12–15
RATING: (see individual park listings for age ratings)

COST: **FREE–$** PREP.: **None–Some**
AREA: **Far South** CITY: **Akron**

ADDRESS: 975 Treaty Line Rd.

PHONE: (330) 867-5511

SEASON: Year round

HOURS: 8 a.m.–4:30 p.m. (office); dawn–dusk (trails)

PRICES: Free

DIRECT.: I-77 to Exit 132 for White Pond Dr.; north on White Pond; right (east) on Mull Ave.; right (southeast) on E. Market St.; left (north) on N. Portage Path; right (east) on Treaty Line Rd. on left.

Strollers	✓ Groups	Food Nearby
Diap Chg	✓ Picnic	Pub. Trans.
✓ Parking	Food Serv.	Handicapped

This 6,700-acre park system has 12 developed parks, more than 86 miles of trails (some stroller and wheelchair accessible), and nature programs for all ages. The Bike & Hike Trail, which also allows skiing, is an easy, traffic-free trail that follows old railroad right-of-ways. Participants in the annual Fall Hiking Spree hike 8 of 12 designated trails to earn a walking staff or a metal shield for their staff. A seasonal information line gives details about Metroparks conditions (330-865-8060). A program information line lists upcoming programs and special events (330-865-8064).

The following Metro Park locations are described separately in this book:

Cascade Valley Metro Park
Deep Lock Metro Park
Firestone Metro Park
Furnace Run Metro Park
Goodyear Heights Metro Park
Gorge Metro Park
Hampton Hills Metro Park
Munroe Falls Metro Park
F. A. Seiberling Metro Park
O'Neil Woods Metro Park
Sand Run Metro Park
Silver Creek Metro Park

Mill Stream Run Reservation

Cleveland Metroparks

AGES: 1½–3 3–5 5–8 8–12 12–15
RATING: ★★★ ★★★ ★★★ ★★★ ★★★

COST: **FREE–$$** PREP.: **None**
AREA: **West** CITY: **Strongsville**

ADDRESS: Valley Pkwy. (S. of Bagley Rd., N. of Drake Rd.)

PHONE: (216) 351-6300; Chalet: (440) 572-9990; Wallace Lake: (440) 826-1682

SEASON: Year round (tobogganing Nov–Feb; hayrides Sept & Oct; swimming June–Labor Day; lifeguards on duty when posted)

HOURS: Reservation: daily 6 a.m.–11 p.m.; Chalet: Thu 6–10 p.m., Fri 6–10:30 p.m., Sat 10 a.m.–10:30 p.m.; Sun noon–10 p.m. (holiday hours are longer; Chalet is sometimes closed during private rental)

PRICES: Free; fee for tobogganing & hayrides

DIRECT.: I-71 to Exit 231 for SR 82 (Royalton Rd.); east on Royalton; right (south) on Valley Pkwy.; on right.

✓ Strollers	✓ Groups	Food Nearby
Diap Chg	✓ Picnic	✓ Pub. Trans.
✓ Parking	✓ Food Serv.	✓ Handicapped

Trails in the Mill Stream Run Reservation are well marked and cover a variety of terrain to accommodate hikers and cross-country skiers. Hayrides through the reservation and square dancing are offered at the Chalet in October on Sundays 1–4 p.m. and during Haywagon Hoedown celebrations (which also include square dancing) on Saturdays 6–10 p.m. Hayrides are available year round to groups and for parties.

From November through February (no snow necessary), a pair of 1,000-foot toboggan chutes open for a thrilling ride. This is not for the faint of heart—or for children under 42 inches tall. Inside the Chalet, two large stone fireplaces (and a large-screen TV) serve as popular winter warm-up spots. Year round, the Chalet can be reserved for large picnics. There are grills, a playground, and a sand volleyball court.

Toboggan chute, Mill Stream Run Reservation

Baldwin and Wallace lakes, formed from former quarries, offer boating (nonmotorized), fishing, and swimming. Paddleboats can be rented at Wallace Lake Concessions, off Valley Pkwy. south of Bagley Rd. (216-826-1682), from Memorial Day to Labor Day. In winter, there is skating on both lakes (Wallace Lake is lit at night).

There are also ball fields, the Strongsville Wildlife Area, nine picnic areas, and sledding at Pawpaw Picnic Area (lit at night).

Mohican State Park

AGES:	1½–3	3–5	5–8	8–12	12–15
RATING:	★	★★	★★★	★★★	★★★

COST: **FREE–$$** PREP.: **None–Some**
AREA: **Farther South** CITY: **Loudonville**

ADDRESS: 914

PHONE: (800) ATA-PARK

SEASON: Year round

HOURS: Vary

PRICES: Vary

DIRECT.: I-71 to Exit 169 for SR 13; south on SR 13; east on SR 97; on left after Butler.

✓ Strollers	✓ Groups	Food Nearby
✓ Diap Chg	✓ Picnic	Pub. Trans.
✓ Parking	✓ Food Serv.	✓ Handicapped

With an abundance of rivers and streams, the town of Loudonville has earned its name as Ohio's Canoe Capital. While it's pretty sleepy during the off-season, the population booms during canoe season. Trips on the Mohican River, with its 1,000-foot-wide gorge (formed by glacial carving 12,000 years ago), are aimed at pleasure cruises—there is no white water here. As it is highly popular with college students and young adults, if you're seeking peace and quite, go midweek, or better yet, just before closing time.

Park trails are well maintained and

marked, and the landscape is hilly and wooded. Scavenger hunts, water games, hikes, and movies are scheduled during the summer through the park naturalist. A lazy inner-tube trip down a sunny and shady part of the river is especially fun for kids old enough to swim.

The resort lodge is among Ohio's nicest with two swimming pools, a sauna, tennis courts, and a basketball court. Be forewarned, it fills up quickly and early in the season. There are campgrounds here, too, which fill daily from Memorial Day to Labor Day.

Mosquito Lake State Park

AGES:	1½–3	3–5	5–8	8–12	12–15
RATING:	★	★★	★★	★★	★★

COST: **FREE–$$** PREP.: **None–Some**
AREA: **Farther East** CITY: **Cortland**

ADDRESS: 1439 SR 305

PHONE: (330) 637-2856

SEASON: Year round (fully operational Apr–Oct)

HOURS: First aid & rangers: 24 hrs.; lifeguard on duty daily 11 a.m.–7 p.m. Memorial Day–Labor Day; Park office Mon.–Fri., 8 a.m.–noon & 1 p.m.–5 p.m.

PRICES: Free park admission; fee for campsites

DIRECT.: US 422 to SR 305; east on SR 305; on left.

WEB: www.dnr.state.oh.us/odnr/parks

Strollers	Groups	Food Nearby
Diap Chg	✓ Picnic	Pub. Trans.
✓ Parking	Food Serv.	✓ Handicapped

Mosquito Lake, the second-largest artificial lake in Ohio (it covers 7,800 acres with an average depth of 10 feet), offers swimming with lifeguards on duty, a 600-foot sandy beach, boating, fishing (14-foot aluminum fishing boats are available for rental), a playground, and hiking trails. (There are also horse trails, but no horses available for the public.)

Kids can enjoy nature classes taught by a naturalist, and there is an amphitheater where wildlife programs are held Saturday nights during the summer.

During winter, cross-country ski trails (3–4 miles) range from open meadow to mature woodland starting at the main park entrance and traveling through the campground area. Fourteen miles of frozen lake surface are available for snowmobiling. No rentals are available.

The park is a popular place for summer overnights and is set up with 234 tent and recreational vehicle sites. Facilities include bathhouses with flush toilets and showers, a telephone, and fire rings.

Munroe Falls Metro Park

Metro Parks Serving Summit County

AGES:	1½–3	3–5	5–8	8–12	12–15
RATING:	★★	★★	★★	★★	★★

COST: **$** PREP.: **None**
AREA: **Far South** CITY: **Munroe Falls**

ADDRESS: 521-605 S. River Rd.

PHONE: (330) 867-5511

SEASON: Seasonal (Memorial Day–Labor Day swimming available; rest of park open year round)

HOURS: Daily 10 a.m.–9 p.m. swimming area (Aug & Sep close at 8 p.m.)

PRICES: $3 adults, $2 for children 2–12, under 2 free

DIRECT.: I-271 to Exit 18 for SR 8; south on SR 8 to Graham Rd.; east on Graham; right (south) on SR 91 (Darrow Rd.); left (east) on S. River Rd.; on right.

✓ Strollers	✓ Groups	✓ Food Nearby
✓ Diap Chg	✓ Picnic	Pub. Trans.
✓ Parking	✓ Food Serv.	✓ Handicapped

Munroe Falls offers a ball field, hiking trail, fishing, play equipment, three open shelters, sledding hill, soccer field, swimming lake, tennis court, volleyball court, cross-country skiing, and restrooms.

Nature Center at Shaker Lakes

AGES:	1½–3	3–5	5–8	8–12	12–15
RATING:	★	★★	★★	★★	★★

COST: **FREE–$** PREP.: **None–Much**
AREA: **East** CITY: **Cleveland**

ADDRESS: 2600 S. Park Blvd.

PHONE: (216) 321-5935

SEASON: Year round

HOURS: Nature center: Mon–Fri 9 a.m.–5 p.m., Sat 10 a.m.–5 p.m., Sun 1–5 p.m.; Trails: daily 6 a.m.–9 p.m

PRICES: Free; fee for special programs

DIRECT.: I-271 to Exit 29 for Chagrin Blvd.; west on Chagrin; right (north) on Warrensville Center Rd.; left (west) on S. Park Blvd.; on left.

✓ Strollers ✓ Groups ✓ Food Nearby
Diap Chg ✓ Picnic ✓ Pub. Trans.
✓ Parking ✓ Food Serv. ✓ Handicapped

The Shaker Lakes Nature Center is ideal for young hikers. It is surrounded by well-marked trails through wooded hillside, marshland, and gardens along the Doan Brook and Shaker Lakes. (The 1/3-mile-long All People's Trail is also wheelchair and stroller accessible.)

Programs for children ages 2–11 specialize in early childhood education and explore the natural world through hikes, talks, and projects. Saturday parent-and-child classes are particularly popular, as are the summer programs. Watch for special annual events, including family holiday celebrations and a bird-seed sale.

Be sure to pick up a trail map before you set out.

Nature Center at Shaker Lakes

Nickel Plate Beach

AGES:	1½–3	3–5	5–8	8–12	12–15
RATING:	★★	★★	★★	★★	★★

COST: **$** PREP.: **None**
AREA: **Farther West** CITY: **Huron**

ADDRESS: 417 Main St.

PHONE: (419) 433-8487

SEASON: Seasonal (Memorial Day through Labor Day)

HOURS: Dawn–dusk

PRICES: Parking: $1 motorcycles, $3 cars, $3 campers; Season passes: $15 resident, $25 non-resident

DIRECT.: SR 2 to Berlin Rd.; north on Berlin; right (north) on Tiffin Ave.; left (west) on Nickel Plate Dr.; on right.

Strollers ✓ Groups ✓ Food Nearby
Diap Chg ✓ Picnic Pub. Trans.
✓ Parking ✓ Food Serv. Handicapped

Nickel Plate is a popular summer picnic spot because of its mile-long natural sand beach. Swimmers can enjoy the waters of Lake Erie, but there are no lifeguards, only buoys designating the swimming area. Volleyball nets are set up around the area; balls can be rented from the concession stand. There is also a small playground.

North Chagrin Nature Center

Cleveland Metroparks

AGES:	1½–3	3–5	5–8	8–12	12–15
RATING:	★★★	★★★	★★★	★★★	★★★

COST: **FREE–$** PREP.: **None**
AREA: **East** CITY: **Mayfield Village**

ADDRESS: 3037 SOM Center Rd. (North Chagrin Reservation)

PHONE: (440) 473-3370

SEASON: Year round

HOURS: 9:30 a.m.–5 p.m. daily except Thanksgiving, Christmas, New Year's Day

PRICES: Free; fees for some special programs

North Chagrin Nature Center

DIRECT.: I-271 to Exit 36 for Wilson Mills Rd.; east on Wilson Mills; left (north) on SR 91 (SOM Center Rd.); right (east) on Sunset Ln.

Or, I-90 to Exit 189 for SR 91 (SOM Center Rd.); south on SR 91; left (east) on Sunset Ln.

✓ Strollers ✓ Groups ✓ Food Nearby
✓ Diap Chg ✓ Picnic Pub. Trans.
✓ Parking Food Serv. ✓ Handicapped

North Chagrin Nature Center, located in the North Chagrin Reservation (see separate listing), houses an indoor play area that offers environment-oriented games and puzzles. The live snake and turtle exhibits are a child-pleaser. Adults as well as children are likely to learn something from the displays of bird photographs, antlers, and wetlands wildlife; they are targeted to all ages and teach about the ecosystem of the surrounding area.

We visited on a wintry day and so spent most of our time playing indoors with the big wooden Concentration game. Its removable wooden blocks cover pairs of outdoor scenes that children have to remember and match.

EarthWords (440-449-0511), the nature center's bookstore, is well stocked with nature picture books and stories about the environment and animals. A storytime is offered twice a month featuring environmental themes.

Outside the nature center, friendly ducks waddle nearby. Accustomed to curious children, they are not shy about asking for handouts. However, no feeding allowed!

For older children (and parents), in-line skates are available here for rental in the summer. Smooth trails offer an easy hike as well.

North Chagrin Reservation

Cleveland Metroparks

AGES:	1½–3	3–5	5–8	8–12	12–15
RATING:	★★	★★	★★	★★	★★

COST: **FREE–$$** PREP.: **None**
AREA: **East** CITY: **Mayfield Village**

ADDRESS: Buttermilk Falls Pkwy.

PHONE: (216) 351-6300; nature center: (440) 473-3370; Manakiki Golf Course (440) 942-2500

SEASON: Year round

HOURS: Daily 6 a.m.–11 p.m.

PRICES: Free

DIRECT.: Willoughby Entrance: I-90 to Exit 189 for SR 91 (SOM Center Rd.); south on SR 91; left (east) on Chardon Rd.; right (south) on Buttermilk Falls Pkwy.

Mayfield Hts. Entrance: I-271 to Exit 36 for Wilson Mills Rd.; east on Wilson Mills; left (north) on Buttermilk Falls Pkwy.

✓ Strollers	✓ Groups	✓ Food Nearby
✓ Diap Chg	✓ Picnic	Pub. Trans.
✓ Parking	✓ Food Serv.	✓ Handicapped

All-purpose trails (including Buttermilk Falls), fishing and ice fishing (Oxbow Lagoon), ball fields, basketball court, ice-skating (at Strawberry Pond and Oxbow Lagoon—both lit at night), sledding hills (at the River Grove Winter Recreation Area and Old River Farm Picnic Area—both lit at night), five picnic areas, and Manakiki Public Golf Course. A Junior Naturalist program includes a hike and instruction around a theme for grade schoolers. Check the *Emerald Necklace* newsletter for registration information.

Squire's Castle is fun to investigate before or after a picnic. It is also the site of an annual Halloween celebration with songs and stories.

The North Chagrin Nature Center is located here (see separate listing).

Squire's Castle, North Chagrin Reservation

O'Neil Woods Metro Park

Metro Parks Serving Summit County

AGES:	1½–3	3–5	5–8	8–12	12–15
RATING:	NR	★	★★	★★	★★

COST: **FREE** PREP.: **None**
AREA: **Far South** CITY: **Bath Twp.**

ADDRESS: Martin Rd.

PHONE: (330) 867-5511

SEASON: Year round

HOURS: Dawn–dusk

PRICES: Free

DIRECT.: I-271 to Exit 12 for SR 303; east on SR 303; right (south) on Riverview Rd.; right (west) on Ira Rd.; left (southwest) on Martin Rd.; on left.

Or, I-77 to Exit 138 for Ghent Rd.; northeast on Ghent; right (east) on Shade Rd.; left (east) on Martin Rd.; on right.

Or, SR 8 to Steels Corners Rd.; west on Steels Corners; right (north) on Akron Peninsula Rd.; left (west) on Ira Rd.; right (south) on Martin Rd.; on left.

Strollers	Groups	✓ Food Nearby
Diap Chg	✓ Picnic	Pub. Trans.
✓ Parking	Food Serv.	Handicapped

O'Neil Woods is a hilly 274 acres, known for deer and birds. A 1.8-mile loop hike follows the Yellow Creek.

Ohio & Erie Canal Reservation

Cleveland Metroparks

AGES:	1½–3	3–5	5–8	8–12	12–15
RATING:	★★	★★	★★	★★	★★

COST: **FREE** PREP.: **None–Some**
AREA: **South** CITY: **Cuyahoga Hts.**

ADDRESS: E. 49 St. (south of Harvard Ave., north of Rockside Rd.)

PHONE: (216) 351-6300

SEASON: Year round (Opening fall of 1999)

HOURS: Vary

PRICES: Free

DIRECT.: I-77 to Exit 159 for Harvard Rd.; west on Harvard Rd.; left (south) on E. 49 St.

Or, I-77 to Exit 155 for Rockside Rd.; east on Rockside Rd.; left (north) on Canal Rd. (becomes E. 49 St.).

✓ Strollers ✓ Groups ✓ Food Nearby
✓ Diap Chg ✓ Picnic ✓ Pub. Trans.
✓ Parking Food Serv. ✓ Handicapped

A slice of nature in the midst of the city's industrial Flats, featuring a 4.5-mile stretch of the 166-year-old Ohio & Erie Canal, this reservation promises to be of great interest. Stop first at the visitor center (due to open in mid-1999) where exhibits will focus on the history of Cleveland, another branch of EarthWords bookshop will be open, and classrooms will accommodate school groups for an extensive schedule of educational programs.

The all-purpose trail here will connect to the existing 20-mile Towpath Trail of the Cuyahoga Valley National Recreation Area. There are also picnic areas, fishing spots, and playing fields.

Old Woman Creek State Nature Preserve

AGES:	1½–3	3–5	5–8	8–12	12–15
RATING:	NR	★	★★	★★	★★

COST: **FREE** PREP.: **None**
AREA: **Farther West** CITY: **Huron**

ADDRESS: 2514 Cleveland Rd. East (SR 6)

PHONE: (419) 433-4601

SEASON: Year round

HOURS: Visitor center: Wed–Sun 1 p.m.–5 p.m.

PRICES: Free

DIRECT.: SR 2 to SR 61 (Ceylon Rd.); north on SR 61; left (west) on US 6 (Cleveland-Sandusky Rd.); on left.

Strollers Groups Food Nearby
Diap Chg Picnic Pub. Trans.
✓ Parking Food Serv. ✓ Handicapped

Bordering Lake Erie with 1.5 miles of trails through forest, swamp, and marsh and over sand dunes, this state preserve is a favorite with bird-watchers. A 2,000-foot boardwalk makes the walk perfect for families.

Paine Falls Park

Lake Metroparks

AGES:	1½–3	3–5	5–8	8–12	12–15
RATING:	NR	★	★	★	★

COST: **FREE** PREP.: **None**
AREA: **Far East** CITY: **Leroy**

ADDRESS: Paine Rd.

PHONE: (440) 639-7275

SEASON: Year round

HOURS: Daily dawn–dusk

PRICES: Free

DIRECT.: I-90 to Exit 205 for Vrooman Rd.; south on Vrooman; left (east) on Carter Rd.; left (north) on Paine Rd. on left.

WEB: www.lakemetroparks.com

✓ Strollers ✓ Groups ✓ Food Nearby
Diap Chg ✓ Picnic Pub. Trans.
✓ Parking Food Serv. Handicapped

Hiking trails and picnic areas with grills on 56 acres, near a scenic waterfall.

Painesville Township Park

Lake Metroparks

AGES:	1½–3	3–5	5–8	8–12	12–15
RATING:	★★	★★	★★	★★	★★

COST: **FREE–$$** PREP.: **None–Much**
AREA: **Far East** CITY: **Painesville Township**

ADDRESS: 1025 Hardy Rd.

PHONE: (440) 639-7275; community center info: (440) 354-3885; softball info: (440) 639-9930

SEASON: Year round

HOURS: Daily dawn–dusk

PRICES: Vary

DIRECT.: SR 2 to SR 535 (Fairport Nursery Rd.); right (north) on Hardy Rd.; on left.

WEB: www.lakemetroparks.com

✓ Strollers ✓ Groups ✓ Food Nearby
Diap Chg ✓ Picnic ✓ Pub. Trans.
✓ Parking ✓ Food Serv. ✓ Handicapped

Family events at the 37-acre Painesville Township Park include ballroom and country dances and picnics held in the community center. Programs for kids include a Jazzer Kamp for ages 4–11 and sessions in arts and crafts, fitness, and food preparation centered around holidays. Nearby are softball fields, playgrounds, and picnic areas.

Parsons Gardens

Lake Metroparks

AGES:	1½–3	3–5	5–8	8–12	12–15
RATING:	NR	★	★	★	★

COST: **FREE** PREP.: **None–Some**
AREA: **East** CITY: **Willoughby**

ADDRESS: Erie Rd.

PHONE: (440) 639-7275

SEASON: Year round

HOURS: Daily dawn–dusk

PRICES: Free

DIRECT.: SR 2 to Lost Nation Rd.; south on Lost Nation; right (west) on St. Clair St.; on left.

WEB: www.lakemetroparks.com

✓ Strollers ✓ Groups ✓ Food Nearby
Diap Chg ✓ Picnic Pub. Trans.
✓ Parking Food Serv. Handicapped

Picnic areas and rental garden plots on seven acres.

TIPS FOR TRIPS

SEASONS

one of the best reasons to live in northeast ohio is the dramatic season changes. It's also a perfect reason to set up an annual celebration.

Penitentiary Glen Reservation and Nature Center

Lake Metroparks

AGES:	1½–3	3–5	5–8	8–12	12–15
RATING:	★★★	★★★	★★★	★★	★★

COST: **FREE–$$** PREP.: **None–Much**
AREA: **Far East** CITY: **Kirtland**

ADDRESS: 8668 Kirtland-Chardon Rd.

PHONE: Nature Center: (440) 256-1404; Wildlife Helpline: (440) 256-2131

SEASON: Year round

HOURS: Nature Center: daily 9 a.m.–5 p.m.; Wildlife Center: daily 9 a.m.–5 p.m.; gift shop: Tue–Sun noon–5 p.m.; closed Mon

PRICES: Free; fees for some classes & special programs

DIRECT.: I-90 to Exit 190 for SR 306; south on SR 306; left (east) on Kirtland-Chardon Rd.; on left.

WEB: www.lakemetroparks.com

✓ Strollers Groups Food Nearby
✓ Diap Chg ✓ Picnic Pub. Trans.
✓ Parking Food Serv. ✓ Handicapped

The 385-acre Penitentiary Glen has all-purpose trails (including hiking, horse, and cross-country ski trails, and an All People's Trail) and picnic areas with grills. Its wildlife center and amphitheater, in what was once the summer estate of Halle Bros. co-owner Samuel Halle, make it an especially popular family park.

Family programs such as star searches (the astronomical kind), family hikes, slide shows, and lectures in the auditorium are scheduled throughout the year. Programs for children include orienteering for school-age children, fishing workshops for ages 10 and up, and hikes for preschoolers and up.

The annual Bug Day is a popular, all-ages, family event with a bug show, exhibits, bug bingo, and other buggy games.

Lake Shore Live Steamers offers free 10-minute, volunteer-operated public train rides on miniature-scale trains that run on a half-mile tract through a wooded section of the Glen on selected weekends throughout the summer.

Inside the separate wildlife center is a quiet area off limits to the public, where injured animals can recover. Outside, when weather permits, a red-tailed hawk, other birds, and squirrels can be observed in the animal yard.

Penitentiary Glen Reservation and Nature Center

Portage Lakes State Park

AGES:	1½–3	3–5	5–8	8–12	12–15
RATING:	★	★★	★★	★★	★★

COST: **FREE–$$** PREP.: **None–Much**
AREA: **Far South** CITY: **Akron**

ADDRESS: 5031 Manchester Rd.

PHONE: (330) 644-2220

SEASON: Year round

HOURS: First aid: 24 hrs.; office: Mon–Fri 8 a.m.–noon, 1–5 p.m.

PRICES: Free park admission; fee for campsites

DIRECT.: I-277 to Exit 2 for Waterloo Rd.; east on Waterloo; right (south) on Manchester Rd.; on left after Vanderhoof Rd.

WEB: www.dnr.state.oh.us/odnr/parks

✓ Strollers ✓ Groups ✓ Food Nearby
✓ Diap Chg ✓ Picnic Pub. Trans.
✓ Parking Food Serv. ✓ Handicapped

A string of 13 lakes—all slightly different but averaging about 20 feet in depth—offers swimming with a lifeguard on duty, boating, and fishing. There is an area designated for boat launching on each lake. Turkey Foot Lake has a sandy beach ideal for swimmers and sun worshippers, as well as several picnic areas. There are five miles of marked hiking trails that pass mainly through wooded areas, and 104 tent and trailer sites. Facilities include pit toilets, telephone, and fire rings.

Classes are taught in the offices, on the beach, or at the campgrounds by a naturalist during the summer. Programming and schedules change, so call ahead. Also, the Astronomy Club of Akron offers monthly evening programs at the observatory.

In winter, cross-country skiing is available if you bring your own equipment. Snowmobiles can use lake surfaces throughout the lake chain. Access is from designated boat launch areas, but exercise caution and consult with a park employee about ice thickness.

Punderson State Park

AGES:	1½–3	3–5	5–8	8–12	12–15
RATING:	★	★★	★★	★★	★★

COST: **FREE–$$$** PREP.: **None–Some**
AREA: **Far East** CITY: **Newbury**

ADDRESS: 11755 Kinsman Rd./P.O. Box 338

PHONE: chalet: (440) 564-5246;
lodge front desk: (440) 564-9144;
lodge & cabin rental: (800) 282-7275

SEASON: Year round

HOURS: First aid & rangers: 24 hrs.; Park office: Mon.–Fri., 8 a.m.–noon & 1 p.m.–5 p.m.

PRICES: Free park admission; fee for campsites, cabins and lodge accommodations

DIRECT.: US 422 to SR 44 (Ravenna Rd.); north on SR 44; left (east) on SR 87 (Kinsman Rd.); on left.

Or, I-271 to Exit 29 for Chagrin Blvd.; east on Chagrin; at Lander Circle, east on SR 87 (Pinetree Rd.); Pinetree becomes S. Woodland Rd., then Kinsman Rd.; on right.

WEB: www.dnr.state.oh.us/odnr/parks

✓ Strollers	✓ Groups	✓ Food Nearby
✓ Diap Chg	✓ Picnic	Pub. Trans.
✓ Parking	✓ Food Serv.	✓ Handicapped

Punderson, almost a thousand acres, is a park for all seasons. In summer, it is set up for 201 tent and recreational vehicle sites (all with electrical hookups). (Twenty-six cabins are also available for rental, usually by the week in the summer.) The 90-acre lake is the largest natural lake in Ohio; it has a sandy-bottomed swimming beach with lifeguards on duty. Rowboats, paddleboats, canoes, and electric motors can be rented. (Bring your own equipment and license if you want to fish.) There are also several playgrounds, tennis courts, an 18-hole golf course, a shuffleboard area, and 14 miles of well-marked hiking trails. The "Rent-A-Camp" and "Rent-A-RV" programs are also available.

In the winter months, there is cross-country skiing (rentals available) on two designated trails stretching eight kilometers through thick woods and around the perimeter of the golf course. Equipment can be rented at the chalet; call ahead for details. Winter sports also include ice-skating on the lake and tobogganing on a sledding hill (bring your own equipment). Several roads and trails are open to snowmobilers.

The naturalist program here is the same as at other state parks, including Saturday movies and campfires, with a naturalist on-site various days from Memorial Day through Labor Day.

Park facilities include flush toilets, showers, laundry, telephone, and fire rings. The Manor House, once a private residence, is a resort lodge with 31 rooms, an outdoor pool, and a restaurant and lounge that are open to the public.

Pymatuning State Park

AGES:	1½–3	3–5	5–8	8–12	12–15
RATING:	★	★★	★★	★★	★★

COST: **FREE–$$$** PREP.: **None**
AREA: **Farther East** CITY: **Andover Township**

ADDRESS: Pymatuning Lake Rd./Route 1

PHONE: cabin rental: (800) 282-7275

SEASON: Year round

HOURS: Daily 8 a.m.–11 p.m.; lifeguard on duty Sat, Sun 11 a.m.–7 p.m. Memorial Day–Labor Day

PRICES: Free; fees for campsite & cabin rental

DIRECT.: I-90 to Exit 200 for SR 44; south on SR 44 to Chardon; east on US 6 to Andover; east on SR 85; left (north) on Pymatuning Lake Rd.

WEB: www.dnr.state.oh.us/odnr/parks

Strollers	✓ Groups	Food Nearby
Diap Chg	✓ Picnic	Pub. Trans.
✓ Parking	✓ Food Serv.	✓ Handicapped

In summer, the big attraction at Pymatuning is the 14,650-acre reservoir with three swimming beaches (Main Beach, near the offices; Cabin Beach, near the cabins; and Campground Beach, reserved for campers). Kids will especially like the fish hatchery tour, with its spillway and "duck walk"—so named because the ducks walk the spillway in search of fish. There is also a small waterfowl museum and a nature program that includes hikes, workshops, wildlife clinics, and fishing derbies. An amphitheater features movies and slide shows for overnighters.

Three miles of hiking trails are well marked, but be sure to pick up an interpretive brochure at the main office before you set out. The Beaver Dam trail loops for just under a mile and leads past a stream where, appropriately enough, beavers are busy building dams.

In winter months, there are cross-country ski trails and snowmobiling; bring your own equipment.

The park is set up with 373 campsites, most with electrical hookups, and 60 cabins. There is some playground equipment near the campgrounds. Pontoons and motorized boats can be rented.

Quail Hollow State Park

AGES:	1½–3	3–5	5–8	8–12	12–15
RATING:	★	★★	★★	★★	★★

COST: **FREE** PREP.: **None**
AREA: **Farther South** CITY: **Hartville**

ADDRESS: 13340 Congress Lake Ave.

PHONE: (330) 877-6652

SEASON: Year round

HOURS: Daily 6 a.m.–11 p.m.; Park office Mon.–Fri. 8 a.m.–noon & 1 p.m.–5 p.m.

PRICES: Free

DIRECT.: I-77 to Exit 119 for SR 241; north on SR 241; east on SR 619; north on SR 43; right (east) on Pontius Rd.; right (south) on Congress Lake Ave.; on left.

WEB: www.dnr.state.oh.us/odnr/parks

✓ Strollers ✓ Groups ✓ Food Nearby
Diap Chg ✓ Picnic Pub. Trans.
✓ Parking ✓ Food Serv. ✓ Handicapped

The main attraction at Quail Hollow is the 10-mile system of hiking trails. The trails are well marked and travel through forest and field, meadow and swamp. There is a small wildlife pond here with fishing (no swimming is allowed). The former Stewart Family Manor, now named the Natural History Study Center, traces the lives of two early Ohio families. The small cemetery's headstones date to the 1890s. A naturalist is on duty year round, but programs for kids (ages 9–14) are offered only during summer. Although 4 miles of bridle trails are available, horses are not. Bring your own mount.

During winter months, you can cross-country ski on several miles of interpretive, hiking, and bridle trails with gently rolling terrain. Ski rental is available through the park office, and there is a winter warm-up center at the manor house.

Campsites are available for organized groups only.

Riverview Park

Lake Metroparks

AGES:	1½–3	3–5	5–8	8–12	12–15
RATING:	NR	★	★★	★★	★★

COST: **FREE** PREP.: **None**
AREA: **Far East** CITY: **Madison**

ADDRESS: Bailey Rd.

PHONE: (440) 639-7275

SEASON: Year round

HOURS: Daily dawn–dusk

PRICES: Free

DIRECT.: I-90 to Exit 212 for SR 528; south on SR 528; left (east) on River Rd.; right (south) on Bailey Rd.

WEB: www.lakemetroparks.com

✓ Strollers ✓ Groups ✓ Food Nearby
Diap Chg ✓ Picnic Pub. Trans.
✓ Parking Food Serv. Handicapped

This 45-acre park includes hiking trails, fishing, sledding areas, picnic areas with fire pits and grills, and overnight camping.

Rockefeller Park Greenhouse

City of Cleveland

AGES:	1½–3	3–5	5–8	8–12	12–15
RATING:	★★	★★	★★	★★	★★

COST: **FREE** PREP.: **None**
AREA: **Near East** CITY: **Cleveland**

ADDRESS: 750 E. 88 St.

PHONE: (216) 664-3103

SEASON: Year round

HOURS: Daily 10 a.m.–4 p.m.

PRICES: Free

DIRECT.: I-90 to Exit 177 for Martin Luther King Blvd.; south on MLK to E. 88 St.; left (north) on E. 88; on left.

Strollers	✓ Groups	✓ Food Nearby
✓ Diap Chg	✓ Picnic	✓ Pub. Trans.
✓ Parking	Food Serv.	✓ Handicapped

Extensive indoor and outdoor collections of flowers and plants are well maintained and attractively displayed in this City of Cleveland greenhouse. Detailed fountains and sculptures lend a sense of history.

Four acres of outdoor grounds provide ample running room, plus a path through a Japanese garden that includes a small bridge—always a hit with the toddler and preschool set. (There are also several wishing ponds—bring pennies.) In addition to the seasonal plantings, there is the Betty Ott Talking Garden for the Blind, which offers walk-by-activated audio explanations of the visual displays in the garden.

Inside, the greenhouse displays ferns, cacti, orchids, and tropical plants, as well as changing exhibits. All are easy to see—some are also easy to touch, though not by design. These hothouses are a great place to escape a raw winter day for an hour or so.

Each year, the Friends of the Greenhouse schedule a variety of special events, including an annual June Garden Party and plant sale and a Christmas-preview poinsettia party.

The greenhouses were completed in 1905 on land donated by John D. Rockefeller.

Rocky River Nature Center

Cleveland Metroparks

AGES:	1½–3	3–5	5–8	8–12	12–15
RATING:	★★★	★★★	★★★	★★★	★★★

COST: **FREE–$** PREP.: **None–Much**
AREA: **West** CITY: **North Olmsted**

ADDRESS: 24000 Valley Pkwy.

PHONE: (440) 734-6660

SEASON: Year round

HOURS: Daily 9:30 a.m.–5 p.m. except Thanksgiving, Christmas, New Year's Day

PRICES: Free; fees for some special programs

DIRECT.: I-480 to Exit 6 for Great Northern Blvd.; south on Great Northern; left (east) on Butternut Ridge Rd.; left (north) on Columbia Rd.; right (east) on Cedar Point Rd.; left on Valley Pkwy.; on left.

✓ Strollers	✓ Groups	✓ Food Nearby
Diap Chg	Picnic	Pub. Trans.
✓ Parking	Food Serv.	✓ Handicapped

Inside the nature center are a few small animal displays (turtles, frogs, and fish) and a topographical map of the area. A huge stone fireplace is the site for special storytimes. Each month there are programs for children. The Fun to Be Three program and Fundays (for 4–5-year-olds) are great ways to introduce younger kids

Rocky River Nature Center

to nature. They typically include a short hike, a nature talk, and a make-and-take craft, all centered around a specific topic. Junior and Senior Leafkickers (ages 6–8 and 9–12 respectively) are topic-related hikes guided by naturalists. All of these programs are very popular and reservations are required. Check the *Emerald Necklace* newsletter for details.

The Rocky River Nature Center is located in the Cleveland Metroparks Rocky River Reservation (listed separately).

Rocky River Reservation

Cleveland Metroparks

AGES:	1½–3	3–5	5–8	8–12	12–15
RATING:	★★	★★	★★	★★	★★

COST: **FREE** PREP.: **None–Some**
AREA: **West** CITY: **Rocky River**

ADDRESS: 24000 Valley Pkwy.

PHONE: (216) 351-6300; Nature Center: (440) 734-6660; Stables: (216) 267-2525; Marina: (216) 226-2233; Big Met Golf Course (440) 331-1070; Little Met Golf Course (216) 941-9672; Mastick Woods Golf Course (216) 267-5626

SEASON: Year round

HOURS: Daily 6 a.m.–11 p.m.

PRICES: Free; fee for golf courses, stables, marina

DIRECT.: I-480 to Exit 6 for Great Northern Blvd.; south on Great Northern; left (east) on Butternut Ridge Rd.; left (north) on Columbia Rd.; right (east) on Cedar Point Rd.; left on Valley Pkwy.; on left.

✓ Strollers ✓ Groups ✓ Food Nearby
Diap Chg ✓ Picnic Pub. Trans.
✓ Parking ✓ Food Serv. ✓ Handicapped

Rocky River Reservation has an all-purpose trail, ball fields, fishing (several locations), ice fishing and ice-skating (Rocky River Lagoon), sledding hills, Little Met, Big Met, and Mastick Woods golf courses, Rocky River Stables (listed separately), nine picnic areas, Rocky River Nature Center (listed separately), and the Frostville Museum (listed separately) within its 2,540 acres.

The Emerald Necklace Marina at the northern end of the reservation near Detroit Rd. (1500 Scenic Park Dr., 216-226-3030) supplies a boat launch and trailer parking, and sells bait, tackle, and supplies. Recently rebuilt, the marina store also includes a snack-bar restaurant with a very pleasant outdoor patio. It is a great place to aim for after a family hike or bike ride.

The well-marked trails of the Rocky River Reservation are perfect for younger hikers. One short (but strenuous) walk leads up a grand staircase for a great view of the Rocky River; another winds alongside the river—a good place for waterfowl sightings. The three-quarter-mile Solar System Walk (with informational signs that describe the planets) traverses a scaled-down model of the universe. (One foot is equal to one million miles, so you can really do a lot of walking!)

Rocky River Reservation

Rookery

Geauga Park District

AGES:	1½–3	3–5	5–8	8–12	12–15
RATING:	★★	★★	★★	★★	★★

COST: **FREE–$** PREP.: **None**
AREA: **Far East** CITY: **Munson Twp.**

ADDRESS: 10110 Cedar Rd.

PHONE: (440) 285-2222

SEASON: Year round

HOURS: Daily 6 a.m.–11 p.m.

PRICES: Free

DIRECT.: I-90 to Exit 190 for SR 306; south on SR 306; left (east) on US 322 (Mayfield Rd.); right (south) on Rockhaven Rd.; right (west) on Cedar Rd.

Or, I-271 to Exit 34 for US 322 (Mayfield Rd.); east on US 322; right (south) on Rockhaven Rd.; right (west) on Cedar Rd.

Or, US 422 to SR 44 (Ravenna Rd.); north on SR 44; left (west) on Butternut Rd.; left (south) on Auburn Rd.; right (west) on Cedar Rd.

Strollers	✓ Groups	Food Nearby
Diap Chg	Picnic	Pub. Trans.
✓ Parking	Food Serv.	Handicapped

One of the largest great blue heron nesting colonies in Northeast Ohio can be found at this 446-acre nature preserve. The Chagrin River runs through a 200-acre wetlands habitat, and there are beaver ponds, fields, forests, and an abundance of wildlife including deer, waterfowl, mink, and turtles.

Sand Run Metro Park

Metro Parks Serving Summit County

AGES:	1½–3	3–5	5–8	8–12	12–15
RATING:	★★	★★	★★	★★	★★

COST: **FREE** PREP.: **None**
AREA: **Far South** CITY: **Akron**

ADDRESS: 1475 Sand Run Pkwy.

PHONE: (330) 867-5511

SEASON: Year round

HOURS: Dawn–dusk

PRICES: Free

DIRECT.: I-77 to Exit 138 for Ghent Rd.; south on Ghent; left (east) on Sand Run Pkwy.

✓ Strollers	✓ Groups	✓ Food Nearby
✓ Diap Chg	✓ Picnic	✓ Pub. Trans.
✓ Parking	Food Serv.	Handicapped

Sand Run offers a fitness and hiking trail, ice-skating, play equipment, open shelters and closed pavilions, a sledding hill, a soccer field, and restrooms for guests. Pavilion rental is available.

Schoepfle Garden

Lorain County Metroparks

AGES:	1½–3	3–5	5–8	8–12	12–15
RATING:	★	★★	★★★	★★★	★

COST: **FREE** PREP.: **None**
AREA: **Far West** CITY: **Birmingham**

ADDRESS: 1106 Market St.

PHONE: (440) 965-7237

SEASON: Year round

HOURS: Daily 8 a.m.–dusk

PRICES: Free

DIRECT.: SR 2 to Baumhart Rd.; south on Baumhart; right (west) on SR 113; left (south) on Market St.; on left.

✓ Strollers	✓ Groups	✓ Food Nearby
✓ Diap Chg	Picnic	Pub. Trans.
✓ Parking	Food Serv.	✓ Handicapped

More than 70 acres of shrubs and trees, rhododendrons, roses, hostas, and topiaries grace this garden fronting three-quarters of a mile on the Vermilion River. A winding river walk is a nice one for families—it is easy on smaller hikers. The garden was created by Otto B. Schoepfle in 1936.

Secrest Arboretum

Ohio Agricultural Research and Development Center

AGES:	1½–3	3–5	5–8	8–12	12–15
RATING:	★	★	★★★	★★★	★★★

COST: **FREE** PREP.: **None–Some**
AREA: **Farther South** CITY: **Wooster**

ADDRESS: 1680 Madison Ave.

PHONE: (330) 263-3700

SEASON: Year round

HOURS: Year round dawn–dusk; guided tours by appointment

PRICES: Free

DIRECT.: I-71 to Exit 204 for SR 83; south on SR 83; east on US 30; south on Madison Ave.; on left.

WEB: www.oardc.ohio-state.edu/biohio

✓ Strollers ✓ Groups ✓ Food Nearby
Diap Chg Picnic Pub. Trans.
✓ Parking Food Serv. Handicapped

A research arboretum affiliated with Ohio State University, the Secrest gardens' 85 acres are filled with more than 2,000 different trees, shrubs, and plants. Plantings here, continuous since 1909, are used to evaluate plants from Ohio, the country, and around the world. An annual calendar allows visitors to plan for a tour during some of the most spectacular displays—the rose gardens, azaleas, and rhododendrons.

Guided tours offered throughout the year by arrangement with the Ohio Agricultural Research and Development Center cover plants as well as dairy farming and lambing. A self-guided driving tour through the gardens and research facilities is also open to the public.

Seneca Caverns

AGES:	1½–3	3–5	5–8	8–12	12–15
RATING:	NR	NR	★	★★★	★★★

COST: **$$** PREP.: **None–Some**
AREA: **Farther West** CITY: **Bellevue**

ADDRESS: 15248 E. Township Rd. #178

PHONE: (419) 483-6711

SEASON: Seasonal (May–mid-Oct: weekends only in May before Memorial Day, Sep–mid-Oct; daily Memorial Day–Labor Day)

HOURS: Summer hours 9 a.m.–7 p.m.; May, Sep–mid-Oct 10 a.m.–5 p.m.

PRICES: Adults $8.50, children $4.50

DIRECT.: I-80/I-90 to Exit 6A for SR 4 (Columbus Sandusky Rd.); south on SR 4; right (west) on Seel Rd. (becomes Lee Rd.); on the left after Frank Rd.

Strollers ✓ Groups Food Nearby
Diap Chg ✓ Picnic Pub. Trans.
✓ Parking ✓ Food Serv. Handicapped

Here is an easy way to visit the world below without becoming a mole.

The tour of Seneca Caverns, which lasts about one hour, covers about one-half mile, consisting of seven rooms, or levels—the biggest about 250 feet in length; the deepest about 110 feet under the ground.

While Seneca Caverns does not boast colorful formations, it does have a crystal-clear underground river. The cave is unusual in that it was created when the limestone bedrock below it collapsed, resulting in its formation along a fracture plane—otherwise known as a crack in the earth. The separated limestone is expected to come together again—but don't worry about it for the next million years or so. In October 1996, Seneca Caverns was declared a registered State of Ohio Natural Landmark.

The average temperature inside the cave is 54 degrees Fahrenheit. Wear a light jacket and decent walking shoes.

Sheldon Marsh State Nature Preserve

AGES:	1½–3	3–5	5–8	8–12	12–15
RATING:	NR	NR	★	★★	★★

COST: **FREE** PREP.: **None**
AREA: **Farther West** CITY: **Huron**

ADDRESS: 2715 Cleveland Rd. West
PHONE: (419) 433-4919
SEASON: Year round
HOURS: Daily, dawn–dusk
PRICES: Free
DIRECT.: SR 2 to Rye Beach Rd.; north on Rye Beach; left (west) on US 6; on right.
WEB: www.dnr.state.oh.us/odnr/dnap/dnap.html

✓ Strollers ✓ Groups ✓ Food Nearby
Diap Chg Picnic Pub. Trans.
✓ Parking Food Serv. ✓ Handicapped

Since 1970, the Natural Areas Preservation Act has been ensuring the protection of Ohio's natural heritage with a system of nature preserves. The Sheldon Marsh includes some of the last remaining undeveloped stretch of Lake Erie shore in the region—once an expansive wetland. The elaborate gates at the preserve entrance are what remain of the original auto entrance to Cedar Point Amusement Park; remnants of the road are now a hiking trail through the preserve. More than 300 bird species visit the marsh in the spring.

Silver Creek Metro Park

Metro Parks Serving Summit County

AGES:	1½–3	3–5	5–8	8–12	12–15
RATING:	★★	★★	★★	★★	★★

COST: **$** PREP.: **None**
AREA: **Far South** CITY: **Norton**

ADDRESS: Medina Line Rd.
PHONE: (330) 867-5511
SEASON: Year round (swimming Memorial Day to Labor Day)
HOURS: 10 a.m.–9 p.m. (in season)
PRICES: $3 adults, $2 children 2–12, under 2 free (for swimming); other areas of the park are free
DIRECT.: I-77 to Exit 135 for SR 21; south on SR 21; east on SR 585; north on Hametown Rd.; on left.

✓ Strollers Groups ✓ Food Nearby
✓ Diap Chg ✓ Picnic Pub. Trans.
✓ Parking ✓ Food Serv. ✓ Handicapped

This park has a bridle trail, fishing, two hiking trails, play equipment, swimming lake, cross-country skiing, restrooms, and an open shelter.

Sippo Lake Park

Stark County Parks

AGES:	1½–3	3–5	5–8	8–12	12–15
RATING:	★	★★★	★★★	★★★	★★★

COST: **FREE** PREP.: **None**
AREA: **Farther South** CITY: **Massillon**

ADDRESS: 800 Genoa Rd., NW
PHONE: (330) 477-3552; Sanders Nature Center: (330) 477-0448
SEASON: Year round
HOURS: Daily 10 a.m.–6 p.m.; Sat, Sun & holidays noon–5 p.m.
PRICES: Free
DIRECT.: I-77 to Exit 105 for Tuscarawas St.; west on Tuscarawas (becomes Lincoln St. at Whipple Ave.); north on Genoa St.; on right.

✓ Strollers ✓ Groups ✓ Food Nearby
Diap Chg ✓ Picnic Pub. Trans.
✓ Parking ✓ Food Serv. ✓ Handicapped

Sippo Lake Park is a 278-acre park with four hiking trails. The Sanders Center of Outdoor Education, like other nature centers in the area, is designed to better inform visitors about endangered species, the food chain, animal classification, ecosystems, environmental pollution, and other aspects of nature study.

The center also provides medical attention to injured animals and supplies live traps for nuisance animals. (The staff suggests calling ahead before bringing in animals or borrowing its traps.) During spring and summer, the center opens an outdoor area for reptiles known as the reptarium.

Outside are a wide variety of activities: a marina with boat rental and a tackle and bait shop; stocked lakes; a playground; perception park designed for handicapped access; hiking trails; volleyball courts; and an observation tower. Future plans call for the extension of the Towpath Trail through all of Stark County.

South Bass Island State Park

AGES:	1½–3	3–5	5–8	8–12	12–15
RATING:	★	★★	★★	★★	★★

COST: **FREE–$$** PREP.: **None**
AREA: **Farther West** CITY: **Put-in-Bay**

ADDRESS: Catawba Ave.

PHONE: (800) BUCKEYE;
Miller Boat Line: (419) 285-2421;
Put-in-Bay Jet Express Boat Line: (800) 245-1538

SEASON: Year round

HOURS: Park: daily, sunrise–sunset; office: 8 a.m.–5 p.m.

PRICES: Free; campsite fee $16

DIRECT.: SR 2 to SR 163; west on SR 163 for Port Clinton; right (north) on N. Jefferson St.; Jet Express Boat for Put-in-Bay on right.

OR SR 2 to SR 53; north on SR 53 for Catawba Island; left (west) on Sloan St.; right (north) on Crogh St.; left (west) on Water St.; Miller Boat Line for Put-in-Bay on right.

WEB: www.dnr.state.oh.us/odnr/parks

Strollers	Groups	✓ Food Nearby
Diap Chg	✓ Picnic	Pub Trans
✓ Parking	Food Serv.	✓ Handicapped

Located on the largest of the Lake Erie islands, this small park includes a half-mile-long stone beach with public swimming (no lifeguard on duty). The campground is popular because it is just west of the village of Put-in-Bay, which has many playgrounds, restaurants, and shops.

Of the 135 campsites located on a bluff overlooking Lake Erie, 32 are considered cliffside sites and are limited to tent campers (with no more than one vehicle per site). There are also four small efficiency cabins. Cabin rental is very popular and is available only by the week from Memorial Day to the last weekend in September. Cabins are rented on a lottery basis; contact the Catawba Island State Park. Facilities include showers and toilets.

There is fishing for perch, crappies, walleye, and small-mouthed bass at various times from April to June in the shallow waters surrounding the park. Ice-fishing guides are available in winter.

If you decided to leave your car on the mainland, bikes and golf carts are available for rental, allowing you to cruise the 17 miles of road on the island.

South Chagrin Reservation

Cleveland Metroparks

AGES:	1½–3	3–5	5–8	8–12	12–15
RATING:	★★	★★	★★	★★	★★

COST: **FREE–$$** PREP.: **None–Much**
AREA: **Far East** CITY: **Solon**

ADDRESS: Sulphur Springs Dr. & Hawthorn Pkwy.

PHONE: (216) 351-6300; Look About Lodge (440) 247-7075

SEASON: Year round

HOURS: Daily 6 a.m.–11 p.m.

PRICES: Free; fee for special programs

DIRECT.: US 422 to SR 91 (SOM Center Rd.); north on SR 91; right (east) on Hawthorne Pkwy.

✓ Strollers	✓ Groups	✓ Food Nearby
Diap Chg	✓ Picnic	✓ Pub. Trans.
✓ Parking	Food Serv.	✓ Handicapped

This reservation consists of all-purpose trails (including cross-country ski trails), ball fields, and fishing and ice-skating at Shadow Lake. Designated sledding hills are located off Hawthorn Pkwy., south of Solon Rd., and at the corner of Sulphur Springs Dr. and Chagrin River Rd. There are also six picnic areas.

One of the trails here leads along the Chagrin River to Squaw Rock, a large stone outcrop that bears the remains of a 19th-century carving by Henry Church.

Family programs are scheduled at the WPA-era Look About Lodge (216) 247-7075, a former private club that is now reopened to the public.

Swine Creek Reservation

Geauga Park District

AGES:	1½–3	3–5	5–8	8–12	12–15
RATING:	★★	★★	★★	★★	★★

COST: **FREE–$** PREP.: **None–Some**
AREA: **Far East** CITY: **Middlefield Twp.**

ADDRESS: 16004 Hayes Rd.

PHONE: (440) 285-2222

SEASON: Year round

HOURS: Daily, 6 a.m.–11 p.m.

PRICES: Free

DIRECT.: US 422 to SR 528 (Madison Rd.) at Parkman; north on SR 528; at SR 608, right (east) on Swine Creek Rd.; left on Hayes Rd.; on left.

✓ Strollers ✓ Groups ✓ Food Nearby
✓ Diap Chg ✓ Picnic Pub. Trans.
✓ Parking Food Serv. ✓ Handicapped

Named for the hogs that once searched its bank for hickory nuts, Swine Creek passes through this 331-acre reservation, which includes a picnic area and a catch-and-release fishing pond. The lodge, with its fireplace, videos, and warm beverages, is used as a warm-up center in the winter months after skating on the pond or enjoying a sleigh ride. During March there are maple sugaring demonstrations. Ten trails covering six miles loop through the woods and run alongside the creek.

Collecting maple sap, Swine Creek Reservation

Tinker's Creek State Park

AGES:	1½–3	3–5	5–8	8–12	12–15
RATING:	★	★★	★★	★★	★★

COST: **FREE** PREP.: **None**
AREA: **Southeast** CITY: **Aurora, Streetsboro**

ADDRESS: Aurora-Hudson Rd.

PHONE: (800) BUCKEYE

SEASON: Year round

HOURS: Daily dawn–dusk; lifeguard on duty weekends only

PRICES: Free

DIRECT.: I-480 to Exit 41 for Aurora Hudson Rd./Frost Rd.; east on Aurora Hudson; left (north) on Aurora Hudson at Frost; right (east) on Aurora Hudson at Wellman Rd.; on left.

WEB: www.dnr.state.oh.us/odnr/parks

Strollers Groups ✓ Food Nearby
Diap Chg ✓ Picnic Pub. Trans.
✓ Parking Food Serv. Handicapped

Almost three miles of hiking trails travel through Tinker's Creek State Park, a small satellite of the West Branch State Park that includes a nature preserve. The trails are well marked, wooded, and pass by active beaver ponds. There is also a small (10-acre) lake for swimming. (A lifeguard is only on duty weekends.)

During winter months, a 1.5-mile cross-country ski trail combines woods and a field for a good beginner outing. No equipment rental is available.

Vermilion River Reservation

Lorain County Metro Parks

AGES:	1½–3	3–5	5–8	8–12	12–15
RATING:	★★	★★	★★	★★	★★

COST: **FREE** PREP.: **None**
AREA: **Far West** CITY: **Brownhelm Twp.**

ADDRESS: N. Ridge & Vermilion Rds.

PHONE: (800) LCM-PARK

SEASON: Year round

HOURS: Daily 8 a.m.–dusk; nature center, museum: Fri–Sun & holidays 1–5 p.m.

PRICES: Free

DIRECT.: I-90 to SR 2; west on SR 2 to Baumhart Rd.; south on Baumhart Rd.; right (west) on North Ridge Rd.; Reservation at Vermilion Rd.

✓ Strollers	✓ Groups	✓ Food Nearby
✓ Diap Chg	✓ Picnic	Pub. Trans.
✓ Parking	Food Serv.	✓ Handicapped

Here you will find hiking trails, picnic areas with shelters, open playing fields, a designated sledding hill, and duck ponds. Three well-marked trails ideal for young hikers provide views of the Vermilion River Valley, shale cliffs, and sandstone formations. Self-guided-tour maps are available with information about each trail; seasonally printed guides offer help with identification of a few common plants and animals.

Also on the park grounds is the Benjamin Bacon Museum (open Memorial Day through mid-October and for holiday special events). Originally a homestead built in 1845, the museum preserves furnishings and artifacts of daily life from that period.

A Carriage Barn, open year round (staffed by a park district naturalist), features educational displays and information. An amphitheater has been added for an all-ages summer concert series and educational lectures.

Veterans Park

Lake Metroparks

AGES:	1½–3	3–5	5–8	8–12	12–15
RATING:	★★	★★	★★	★★	★★

COST: **FREE** PREP.: **None**
AREA: **Far East** CITY: **Mentor**

ADDRESS: 5740 Hopkins Rd.

PHONE: (440) 639-7275

SEASON: Year round

HOURS: Daily dawn–dusk

PRICES: Free

DIRECT.: SR 2 to SR 615 (Center St.); north on Center; right (east) on Hendricks Rd.; left (north) on Hopkins Rd.; on left.

WEB: www.lakemetroparks.com

✓ Strollers	✓ Groups	✓ Food Nearby
Diap Chg	✓ Picnic	Pub. Trans.
✓ Parking	Food Serv.	✓ Handicapped

The facilities at this 93-acre park include hiking trails, fishing pier, ball fields, picnic areas, and a playground.

Villa Angela

Cleveland Lakefront State Park

AGES:	1½–3	3–5	5–8	8–12	12–15
RATING:	★★	★★	★★	★★	★★

COST: **FREE** PREP.: **None–Much**
AREA: **East** CITY: **Cleveland**

ADDRESS: Lake Shore Blvd. at E. 162 St.

PHONE: (216) 881-8141

SEASON: Year round

HOURS: 6 a.m.–11 p.m.

PRICES: Free

DIRECT.: I-90 to Exit 182 for E. 185 St.; north on E. 185.; left (west) on Marcella Rd.; left (west) on Lakeshore Blvd.; on right.

✓ Strollers	✓ Groups	✓ Food Nearby
✓ Diap Chg	✓ Picnic	✓ Pub. Trans.
✓ Parking	✓ Food Serv.	✓ Handicapped

Villa Angela is an extension of Euclid Beach State Park. It is a 1,000-foot-long sand beach with a picnic area developed on the former campus of a young women's boarding school. Lifeguards are on duty Memorial Day–Labor Day. A park naturalist schedules programming for children and families in the summer. For in-line skaters, runners, and bicyclists, a one-mile trail connects Villa Angela with Euclid Beach on the west and Wildwood on the east.

Walter C. Best Wildlife Preserve

Geauga Park District

AGES:	1½–3	3–5	5–8	8–12	12–15
RATING:	★★	★★	★★	★★	★★

COST: **FREE–$** PREP.: **None**
AREA: **Southeast** CITY: **Munson Twp.**

ADDRESS: 11620 Ravenna Rd. (SR 44)
PHONE: (440) 285-2222
SEASON: Year round
HOURS: Daily 6 a.m.–11 p.m.
PRICES: Free
DIRECT.: I-90 to Exit 200 for SR 44; south on SR 44 through Chardon; on left after Bass Lake Rd.

✓ Strollers ✓ Groups ✓ Food Nearby
Diap Chg Picnic Pub. Trans.
✓ Parking Food Serv. ✓ Handicapped

This 101-acre wildlife preserve has hiking trails and a 30-acre lake that's great for fishing and bird-watching.

West Branch State Park

AGES:	1½–3	3–5	5–8	8–12	12–15
RATING:	★★	★★	★★	★★	★★

COST: **FREE–$$** PREP.: **None**
AREA: **Far South** CITY: **Ravenna**

ADDRESS: 5708 Esworthy Rd./SR5
PHONE: (330) 296-3239
SEASON: Year round (fully operational Apr–Oct)
HOURS: Rangers: 24 hrs.
PRICES: Free park admission; fee for campsites
DIRECT.: I-77 to I-76; east on I-76 to Exit 38 for SR 44; north on SR 44; east on SR 5; right (south) on Esworthy Rd.

✓ Strollers Groups ✓ Food Nearby
Diap Chg ✓ Picnic Pub. Trans.
✓ Parking ✓ Food Serv. ✓ Handicapped

The central attraction at West Branch State Park is the 2,650-acre Kirwan Lake. Speedboaters and water-skiers often frequent the murky waters because there are no restrictions on engine horsepower. There is a small sandy swimming beach with a lifeguard on duty. Fishing is allowed.

Kids will enjoy the playground and four short one-mile hiking trails. In summer, a naturalist offers various programs for children, and there are Friday-night family movies. No need to register. For more hiking, there is an 8.5-mile stretch of the Buckeye Trail. Even though this trail is well marked, the park manager suggests picking up a trail guide at the office.

In winter, West Branch offers 20 miles of cross-country ski trails that are generally hilly and wooded, as well as 25 miles of snowmobiling trails, which are straight and fairly level. (No rental equipment is available.)

The park is set up with 103 tent and recreational vehicle sites. Park facilities include pit toilets, telephone, and fire rings. Rent-A-Camps are available.

Whitlam Woods

Geauga Park District

AGES:	1½–3	3–5	5–8	8–12	12–15
RATING:	★★	★★	★★	★★	★★

COST: **FREE–$** PREP.: **None**
AREA: **Far East** CITY: **Hambden Twp.**

ADDRESS: 12500 Pearl Rd.
PHONE: (440) 285-2222
SEASON: Year round
HOURS: Daily 6 a.m.–11 p.m.
PRICES: Free

DIRECT.: I-90 to Exit 200 for SR 44; south on SR 44; left (east) on Clark Rd.; right (south) on Robinson Rd.; left (east) on Pearl Rd.; on left.

Or, US 422 to SR 44; north on SR 44 through Chardon; north on North St./Ravenna Rd.; right (east) on Woodin Rd.; left (north) on Robinson Rd.; right (east) on Pearl Rd.; on left.

Strollers	✓ Groups	Food Nearby
Diap Chg	Picnic	Pub. Trans.
✓ Parking	Food Serv.	Handicapped

This 110-acre park includes 1.5 miles of hiking trails through scenic forests and ravines.

Wilderness Center

AGES:	1½–3	3–5	5–8	8–12	12–15
RATING:	★★	★★	★★	★★	★★

COST: **$–$$** PREP.: **None–Some**
AREA: **Far South** CITY: **Wilmot**

ADDRESS: 9877 Alabama Ave., P.O. Box 202

PHONE: (330) 359-5235

SEASON: Year round

HOURS: Building hours: Tues–Sat 9 a.m.–5 p.m., Sun 1 p.m.–5 p.m.; closed Mon; Trails open daily dawn–dusk.

PRICES: Vary. Donation to visit; registration & fee for scheduled event

DIRECT.: I-77 to Exit 87 for US 250; northwest on US 250 through Wilmot; right (east) on Alabama Ave.; on left.

WEB: www.wildernesscenter.org

Strollers	✓ Groups	✓ Food Nearby
Diap Chg	✓ Picnic	Pub. Trans.
✓ Parking	Food Serv.	✓ Handicapped

A good place to start here is at the Center's headquarters building for trail maps and information about this nonprofit nature education center. There are six trails covering seven miles, varying from an easy boardwalk trail to others that are a mile or more over seven separate paths. Connected sites here cover 883.5 acres in three counties. There are small lakes, marshlands, and forests, as well as large boulders left from the last ice age. For wildlife, head for Sigrist Woods, a designated Natural Landmark. This 30-acre woods includes 300-year-old trees: sugar maples, beeches, and hickories that close the forest canopy by late spring.

The nature center has an observation tower and viewing pier overlooking a manmade lake. A small planetarium has a regular schedule of shows. Activities here include guided hikes, holiday crafts, and story times.

TIPS FOR TRIPS

SIBLINGS

Make time for whole-family activities as well as special times for some one-on-one interaction. For reluctant participants, set up days when friends are also invited.

Art, Music, Theater, and Dance

Apart from their value in teaching us about ourselves and the world, the arts are simply a lot of fun. The benefits of exposing children to the arts, both as audience members and as participants, are sure to last them a lifetime. Taking part does not have to be expensive. There are free concerts, special performances for younger audiences, and a wide variety of classes. And, no matter what your preference may be—sculpture, puppets, the ballet—you'll find it in Greater Cleveland.

Unsure of where to get started? What follows is a comprehensive list of arts organizations with specific programming for children. As always, it's important to pick activities that are appropriate for your family. Performances intended for adults are not the best way to interest and involve children; look instead for performances aimed specifically at your children's age group. It also helps if youngsters are prepared a bit. Try talking about the program first—what is the storyline, what to expect from the experience. Many area institutions also offer programs that include both parent and child and provide a first-class way of sharing a first-time arts experience. These are especially worthwhile.

Akron Art Museum

AGES:	1½–3	3–5	5–8	8–12	12–15
RATING:	NR	★	★★★	★★★	★★★

COST: **FREE** PREP.: **None–Some**
AREA: **Far South** CITY: **Akron**

ADDRESS: 70 E. Market St.

PHONE: (330) 376-9185

SEASON: Year round

HOURS: Daily 11 a.m.–5 p.m.

PRICES: Free (donations accepted); on-site parking available

DIRECT.: I-77 to SR 59 (Martin Luther King Blvd.);north on SR 59; right (south) on SR 261 (S. Main St.); left (east) on Market St.; on right.

Or, SR 8 to Perkins St. exit.; right (west) on Perkins; left (south) on Broadway St.; right (west) on Market St.; on left.

WEB: www.akronartmuseum.org

✓ Strollers ✓ Groups ✓ Food Nearby
Diap Chg Picnic ✓ Pub. Trans.
✓ Parking Food Serv. ✓ Handicapped

This smaller museum has shown a consistent ability to line up first-class art exhibitions that other area museums overlook. Housed in an Italian Renaissance Revival structure built in 1899, the museum was extensively renovated in 1981.

Family Art Class at the Akron Art Museum

Focused on modern art and photography, its permanent collection boasts works by Frank Stella and Andy Warhol. In the courtyard there is a modern sculpture collection, which was a big hit and conversation-starter with our family. Arts festivals and a regular Saturday family workshop series blend exhibits with hands-on creative activities; Sundays at 2:30 p.m. the museum offers a special program, tour, or talk.

Akron Civic Theatre

The University of Akron/Civic Theatre

AGES:	1½–3	3–5	5–8	8–12	12–15
RATING:	NR	★	★★	★★	★★

COST: **FREE–$$** PREP.: **Some**
AREA: **Far South** CITY: **Akron**

ADDRESS: 182 S. Main St.

PHONE: (330) 253-2488

SEASON: Seasonal (Oct–May)

HOURS: Vary

PRICES: Vary

DIRECT.: SR 8 to E. Butchell Ave.; west on E. Butchell to Hill St.

✓ Strollers ✓ Groups ✓ Food Nearby
Diap Chg Picnic ✓ Pub. Trans.
✓ Parking Food Serv. ✓ Handicapped

From *Gone With the Wind* on the big screen to the free annual *TUBACHRISTMAS* featuring nearly 400 tubas playing carols at a sing-along, the Akron Civic Theatre's annual season of performances is well known and appreciated in the community. The Children's Ballet Theatre, the Cuyahoga Valley Youth Ballet, and guest performers fill out the year's schedule.

TIPS FOR TRIPS

CAR RIDES

If you're caravanning with another family, take walkie-talkies with you for communicating between cars.

Allen Memorial Art Museum

AGES:	1½–3	3–5	5–8	8–12	12–15
RATING:	★	★	★★★	★★★	★★★

COST: **FREE** PREP.: **None–Much**
AREA: **Far West** CITY: **Oberlin**

ADDRESS: 87 N. Main St.

PHONE: (440) 775-8665

SEASON: Year round

HOURS: Tue–Sat 10 a.m.–5 p.m., Sun 1–5 p.m. (closed major holidays)

PRICES: Free

DIRECT.: I-480 to Exit 1 for SR 10 ; west on SR 10 (becomes US 20) to SR 511; west on SR 511 to campus; on left.

WEB: www.oberlin.edu/~allenart

✓ Strollers ✓ Groups ✓ Food Nearby
✓ Diap Chg Picnic Pub. Trans.
✓ Parking Food Serv. ✓ Handicapped

One of the finest college or university collections in the nation is housed at Oberlin College's Allen Memorial Art Museum. Opened in 1917, it now includes some 14,000 objects, ranging from Modigliani's *Naked Woman* to Japanese woodblocks, Islamic carpets, and Old Master prints. There always seems to be an interesting temporary exhibition.

Special children's programs, including art workshops and art appreciation tours, are scheduled throughout the year, after school, and on Saturdays. Family days and community days are also scheduled and typically spill over into the small city's streets and the campus of Oberlin College.

Tours of the Frank Lloyd Wright–designed Weltzheimer/Johnson House, an example of the architect's moderately priced Usonian House, are scheduled through the museum on weekends or by special arrangement.

Ashtabula Arts Center

AGES:	1½–3	3–5	5–8	8–12	12–15
RATING:	NR	★★	★★	★★	★★

COST: **FREE–$$** PREP.: **Some**
AREA: **Farther East** CITY: **Ashtabula**

ADDRESS: 2928 W. 13 St.

PHONE: (440) 964-3396

SEASON: Year round

HOURS: Mon–Thu 9 a.m.–9 p.m., Fri 9 a.m.–7 p.m., Sat 9 a.m.–5 p.m.

PRICES: Vary

DIRECT.: I-90 to Exit 223 for SR 45; north on SR 45; right (east) on SR 521 (Lake Rd.) past KSU-Ashtabula campus; right (south) on Norwood Rd.; right (west) on W. 13 St.

✓ Strollers ✓ Groups ✓ Food Nearby
Diap Chg ✓ Picnic Pub. Trans.
✓ Parking Food Serv. ✓ Handicapped

Theater, dance, art, and music programs are offered at this community arts center. In addition to the school-year programs, there is a summer arts camp as well as the Grand Valley Theatre Company for school-age kids. Annual special events include the Free Kids Fest in summer, family matinee performances in the spring and fall, and the traveling Ashtabula Arts Center on Tour.

Baldwin-Wallace College Conservatory of Music

AGES:	1½–3	3–5	5–8	8–12	12–15
RATING:	NR	★★	★★★	★★★	★★★

COST: **FREE–$$** PREP.: **Some–Much**
AREA: **Southwest** CITY: **Berea**

ADDRESS: 96 Front St.

PHONE: (440) 826-2365, (440) 826-2330 (events line), (440) 826-2369

SEASON: Year round

HOURS: Vary

PRICES: Vary

DIRECT.: I-71 to Exit 235 for Bagley Rd.; west on Bagley; left (south) on Front St.; on left before Center St.

WEB: www.bw.edu

Strollers Groups ✓ Food Nearby
Diap Chg Picnic ✓ Pub. Trans.
✓ Parking ✓ Food Serv. ✓ Handicapped

Well known for its music program, the preparatory department of the Conservatory of Music at Baldwin-Wallace offers a varied program of music lessons for children starting at age 3. Faculty recitals and performances by the College Choir, Baldwin-Wallace Symphony, and other groups are a great introduction to music for families.

Baycrafters

AGES:	1½–3	3–5	5–8	8–12	12–15
RATING:	NR	★★	★★★	★★★	★★

COST: **FREE–$$$** PREP.: **Some–Much**
AREA: **West** CITY: **Bay Village**

ADDRESS: 28795 Lake Rd.

PHONE: (440) 871-6543

SEASON: Year round

HOURS: Gallery and station shop daily noon–5 p.m.; class times vary

PRICES: Gallery Free; fee for classes

DIRECT.: I-90 to Exit 156 for Crocker Rd./Bassett Rd.; north on Crocker (becomes Bassett); right on Lake Rd.; on right.

✓ Strollers ✓ Groups ✓ Food Nearby
Diap Chg ✓ Picnic ✓ Pub. Trans.
✓ Parking ✓ Food Serv. Handicapped

Tucked away among a collection of turn-of-the-century frame buildings on the grounds of the Cleveland Metroparks Huntington Reservation is Baycrafters, a local gem devoted to the visual arts. Painting, cartooning, clay sculpture, drama, and puppetry are among the year-long classes offered there for school-age children. A summer program includes preschoolers. Classes are kept small and are popular—so register early. Tearoom birthday parties are a treat.

Many special arts-and-crafts events are held throughout the year, including Renaissance Fayre (Labor Day weekend), a true family festival. Three days full of entertainment—jousting, theater, puppetry, music—in a lush meadow just a short hike from the lakefront offer enough activity to please an all-ages group. There are also plenty of hands-on opportunities: on one visit we tried juggling, and our three-year-old became part of a puppet show. Because this is a very popular event, be prepared for traffic congestion, especially later in the day. Call for a schedule beforehand so that you can be sure to catch the performances that look like the most fun.

Beck Center for the Arts

AGES:	1½–3	3–5	5–8	8–12	12–15
RATING:	NR	★★	★★	★★★	★★★

COST: **FREE–$$$** PREP.: **Some–Much**
AREA: **Near West** CITY: **Lakewood**

ADDRESS: 17801 Detroit Rd.

PHONE: (216) 521-2540

SEASON: Year round

HOURS: Center: Mon–Fri 9 a.m.–5 p.m.; weekends vary; Performances: Thu–Sat 8 p.m.; Sun 2 p.m.

PRICES: Gallery free; fees for classes & performances

DIRECT.: I-90 to Exit 164 for McKinley Ave.; north on McKinley; McKinley becomes Larchmont Ave.; right (east) on Detroit Ave.; on left.

WEB: www.lkwdpl.org/beck

✓ Strollers ✓ Groups ✓ Food Nearby
✓ Diap Chg ✓ Picnic ✓ Pub. Trans.
✓ Parking Food Serv. ✓ Handicapped

West Side families know this place well for the variety and quality of classes offered year round for preschoolers and up, including dance, dramatics, and a variety of fine arts. Sessions run fall, winter, spring, and summer.

Particularly popular with younger children is the Little Folks Theatre (LFT) program. LFT introduces 4- and 5-year-olds to creative dramatics and S.M.I.L.E. (Sensory Motor Integrated Learning Experience), which combines movement with positive self-image for preschoolers.

As for the regular theater season, most productions would be enjoyable for older school-age children; families with younger children should look for performances by the Beck Center Theater School for Children and Teens. The school typically presents two major stage productions a year—winter and spring—performed for children and by children.

Brecksville Center for the Arts

AGES:	1½–3	3–5	5–8	8–12	12–15
RATING:	NR	★★★	★★★	★★★	★★★

COST: **$–$$** PREP.: **Much**
AREA: **South** CITY: **Brecksville**

ADDRESS: 8997 Highland Dr. (Old Library Building)

PHONE: (440) 526-6232

SEASON: Year round

HOURS: 9:30 a.m.–3:30 p.m. Mon–Fri (office hours); class schedule varies

PRICES: Vary per activity

DIRECT.: I-77 to Exit 149 for SR 82 (Royalton Rd.); east on Royalton; right (south) on Highland Dr.; on left.

✓ Strollers ✓ Groups ✓ Food Nearby
Diap Chg Picnic ✓ Pub. Trans.
✓ Parking Food Serv. ✓ Handicapped

While specific schedules change, classes have included ceramics, dance, painting, photography, basket weaving, paper making, quilting, calligraphy, music, kids' crafts, drawing, Ukrainian egg decorating, origami, ballroom dancing, floral design, glass bead making, a variety of seminars and workshops, and more.

Cain Park

City of Cleveland Heights

AGES:	1½–3	3–5	5–8	8–12	12–15
RATING:	NR	★	★★★	★★★	★★★

COST: **FREE–$$$** PREP.: **Some–Much**
AREA: **East** CITY: **Cleveland Hts.**

ADDRESS: Superior Rd. between Lee & S. Taylor

PHONE: (216) 291-5796; summer: (216) 371-3000; winter: (216) 291-2828

SEASON: Seasonal (Jun–Aug)

HOURS: Event times vary

PRICES: Fees vary for concerts, theater, classes; some events free

DIRECT.: West: I-90 to Exit 173B for Chester Ave. (Eastbound: left (south) on E. 24 St.; left (east) on Chester); east on Chester; left northeast on Euclid Ave.; right (east) on US 322 (Mayfield Rd.); right (south) on Superior Rd., on left.

East: I-271 to Exit 32 for Cedar/Brainard Rd. (Southbound: left (south) on Brainard; right (west) on Cedar); west on Cedar; right (north) on S. Taylor; left (west) on Superior Rd.; on right.

✓ Strollers ✓ Groups ✓ Food Nearby
Diap Chg ✓ Picnic ✓ Pub. Trans.
✓ Parking ✓ Food Serv. ✓ Handicapped

An extensive summer calendar of activities has made this arts park a Heights-area favorite. Exhibits, theater, concerts, and dance—many activities designed for family audiences and some of them free—are scheduled, using the park's outdoor amphitheater and other facilities.

A series of summer classes offered through the City of Cleveland Heights (which operates the park) and specifically targeted for school-age children includes full- and half-day classes in theater, visual arts, music, writing, and movement.

The annual Cain Park Arts Festival offers a wide variety of free entertainment, typically including one matinee children's concert and a kids' area with arts and crafts activities. Of note for older school-age children and teens, the Alma Forum series, also free, highlights different alternative art forms with a combination of lectures and performances.

Be forewarned that there is no on-site parking facility, so come early for nearby street parking or call ahead for a map to take advantage of one of the city's lots and use the park's shuttle service, which runs during the festival.

In winter, the hill at Cain Park is a popular site for sledding.

Chagrin Valley Youth Theatre

AGES:	1½–3	3–5	5–8	8–12	12–15
RATING:	NR	NR	NR	★★	★★

COST: **$–$$** PREP.: **Some–Much**
AREA: **Southeast** CITY: **Chagrin Falls**

ADDRESS: 40 River St.

PHONE: (440) 247-8955

SEASON: Year round

HOURS: Shows: Fri–Sat 8 p.m.; box office: Mon–Sat 1–6 p.m.

PRICES: Vary

DIRECT.: I-271 to Exit 29 for SR 87 (Chagrin Blvd.); east on Chagrin to Chagrin Falls; right (south) on West St.; right (west) on River St.; on right.

✓ Strollers ✓ Groups ✓ Food Nearby
Diap Chg Picnic ✓ Pub. Trans.
✓ Parking Food Serv. ✓ Handicapped

This youth theater program is designed to introduce children ages 10–18 to music, drama, and performance in live theater productions. Each year's series of workshops—typically two eight-week sessions—culminates in a student performance.

Clague Playhouse

AGES:	1½–3	3–5	5–8	8–12	12–15
RATING:	NR	★	★★	★★	★★

COST: **$–$$** PREP.: **Some–Much**
AREA: **West** CITY: **Westlake**

ADDRESS: 1371 Clague Rd.

PHONE: (440) 331-0403

SEASON: Seasonal (Sept–May)

HOURS: Wed–Sat 1 p.m.–6 p.m.

PRICES: $10 adults, $9 seniors & students, $7 group discount

DIRECT.: I-480 to Exit 7 for Clague Rd.; north on Clague; on right.

Or, I-90 to Exit 160 for Clague Rd.; south on Clague; on left.

Strollers	✓ Groups	✓ Food Nearby
Diap Chg	✓ Picnic	✓ Pub. Trans.
✓ Parking	Food Serv.	✓ Handicapped

Clague Playhouse offers performances and theater classes for children and teens in basic theatrical techniques, including lighting, makeup, costuming, props, set work, acting, music, and stage direction. The auditorium seats 93.

Cleveland Center for Contemporary Art

AGES:	1½–3	3–5	5–8	8–12	12–15
RATING:	NR	★	★★	★★★	★★★

COST: **FREE–$$** PREP.: **None–Some**
AREA: **Near East** CITY: **Cleveland**

ADDRESS: 8501 Carnegie Ave.

PHONE: (216) 421-8671

SEASON: Year round

HOURS: Tues–Thur 11 a.m.–6 p.m.; Fri 11 a.m.–9 p.m.; Sat–Sun noon–5 p.m.

PRICES: Free, with prices for special events and educational programs

DIRECT.: West: I-90 to Exit 172D for Carnegie Ave.; on left.

East: I-90 to Exit 173A for Prospect Ave; east on Prospect; right (south) on E. 55 St.; left (east) on Carnegie Ave.; on left.

South: I-77 to Exit 161B for E. 55 St.; north on E. 55; right (east) on Carnegie Ave.; on left.

WEB: www.contemporaryart.org

✓ Strollers	✓ Groups	✓ Food Nearby
Diap Chg	Picnic	✓ Pub. Trans.
✓ Parking	Food Serv.	✓ Handicapped

Each trip here offers a chance to see something different. Past exhibits have ranged from life-size porcelain pigs facing a lectern to television monitors chanting "wal, wal, wal . . . nut, nut, nut . . . ." With children in tow, be prepared for plenty of questions—answering them can be an interesting lesson in art. And be forewarned that the Center's commitment to the new can also be shocking.

Exhibits here are well marked, and as a rule you are your own guide. The staff can be helpful or not so helpful. On one visit, they volunteered stories about the artists and their works while answering odd questions from our then-toddler son.

There is also a fine gift shop (with some fun children's items), an art rental program (for members), organized lectures, school programs, outdoor sculptures, and occasional special events and concerts suitable for family outings.

Workshop at Cleveland Center for Contemporary Art

Art, Music, Theater & Dance DIRECTORY

Cleveland Institute of Art

AGES:	1½–3	3–5	5–8	8–12	12–15
RATING:	NR	★	★★	★★★	★★★

COST: **FREE–$$$** PREP.: **Some–Much**
AREA: **Near East** CITY: **Cleveland**

ADDRESS: 11141 East Blvd.

PHONE: (216) 421-7000

SEASON: Year round

HOURS: Gallery: Mon 9 a.m.–4 p.m., Tues–Sat 9 a.m.–9 p.m., Sun 1–4 p.m.

PRICES: Free; fee for classes

DIRECT.: West: I-90 to Exit 173B for Chester Ave.; east on Chester; left on Euclid Ave; left on East Blvd; on right.

East: I-90 to Exit 177 for Martin Luther King Blvd.; south on MLK; left (northeast) on Euclid Ave; left (north) on East Blvd; on right.

South: I-271 to Exit 32 for Cedar Rd.; west on Cedar to University Circle; right (northeast) on Euclid Ave; left (north) on East Blvd.; on right.

WEB: www.cia.edu

✓ Strollers ✓ Groups ✓ Food Nearby
Diap Chg Picnic ✓ Pub. Trans.
✓ Parking Food Serv. ✓ Handicapped

This private professional college of fine arts, crafts, and design has offerings for the general public, including exhibits, films, lectures, and classes through the continuing education program. For school-age children (grades 3–12), the Institute also offers a year-round schedule of classes in arts basics, drawing, painting, fiber, bookmaking, photography, computer graphics, and more.

The special "Saturdays with the Children" series—offered twice a year, in fall and spring—is a wonderful introduction to the arts for younger children (ages 5–8) with their parents; newer "Sunday Afternoon Family Art Sessions" are geared to families with children ages four and above. A wide variety of arts are included, such as collage, masks, and simple sculpture. Class size is limited, so reserve a spot early.

Cleveland Institute of Music

AGES:	1½–3	3–5	5–8	8–12	12–15
RATING:	★★	★★	★★★	★★★	★★★

COST: **FREE–$$$** PREP.: **Some–Much**
AREA: **Near East** CITY: **Cleveland**

ADDRESS: 11021 East Blvd.

PHONE: (216) 791-5000

SEASON: Year round

HOURS: Vary

PRICES: Vary

DIRECT.: West: I-90 to Exit 173B for Chester Ave.; east on Chester; left on Euclid Ave; left on East Blvd; on right.

East: I-90 to Exit 177 for Martin Luther King Blvd.; south on MLK; left (northeast) on Euclid Ave; left (north) on East Blvd; on right.

South: I-271 to Exit 32 for Cedar Rd.; west on Cedar to University Circle; right (northeast) on Euclid Ave; left (north) on East Blvd.; on right.

WEB: www.cim.edu

✓ Strollers ✓ Groups ✓ Food Nearby
Diap Chg ✓ Picnic ✓ Pub. Trans.
✓ Parking ✓ Food Serv. ✓ Handicapped

Founded in 1920 to provide world-class education in music, the Cleveland Institute of Music delivers just that. For children ages 3–18, the Preparatory and Community Education divisions offer classes in instruments, voice, theory, and movement (Dalcroze Eurhythmics). For school-age students, performance experience includes two Suzuki Studies string orchestras, a percussion ensemble, and the Cleveland Youth Wind Symphony.

Many of the Institute's regular free concerts are matinees and would be interesting to older children. They are very popular, and seating is on a first-come, first-served basis. Be prompt. A special series of family concerts is designed to expose younger children to the performing arts.

Branches:
22441 Lorain Rd., Fairview Park, (440) 734-3120
32000 Chagrin Blvd., Pepper Pike, (216) 831-0697
21600 Shaker Blvd., Shaker Heights, (216) 283-2699

Cleveland Museum of Art

AGES:	1½–3	3–5	5–8	8–12	12–15
RATING:	★	★★	★★★	★★★	★★★

COST: **FREE** PREP.: **None–Some**
AREA: **Near East** CITY: **Cleveland**

ADDRESS: 11150 East Blvd.

PHONE: (216) 421-7340; 1-800-CMA-0033

SEASON: Year round

HOURS: Tues–Sun 10 a.m.–5 p.m.; Wed & Fri 10 a.m.–9 p.m.

PRICES: Free, except for special exhibits and events

DIRECT.: I-90 to Exit 177 for Martin Luther King Blvd.; south on MLK; left (east) on Jeptha Dr.; right (south) on Wade Oval Dr.; on right.

WEB: www.clemusart.com

✓ Strollers ✓ Groups ✓ Food Nearby
✓ Diap Chg ✓ Picnic ✓ Pub. Trans.
✓ Parking ✓ Food Serv. ✓ Handicapped

A visit to the Cleveland Museum of Art is like a treasure hunt. If you are good with maps, or lucky, or both, you will make some wonderful discoveries. This is, after all, one of the finest art collections in the country. But the maze of galleries that house these treasures makes it easy to get lost and a little frustrated. It's a good idea to pick up the map, "Finding Your Way," at the information desk, or you can just ask. (The guards are friendly and helpful.) Two educational workbook packets published by the museum ("Looking Together: Introducing Young Children to the Cleveland Museum of Art" and the "Museum Sleuth Workbook") are for sale.

Still, when visiting with younger children, we recommend having a plan of attack. For example, if medieval battle gear, with its sabers, daggers, and armor, is of interest to you or your child, head straight for the Armor Court. As with any museum, alarms do go off if you venture too close to exhibits or attempt to climb enticing statues—we know first hand.

The very best way we found to get to know the museum is through its Saturday program of classes designed for everyone from toddlers to teens. (Kids seem to own the place on Saturdays.) Art for Parent and Child (which we took twice) was one of the best museum experiences we have had together. For a taste of the classes, try Family Express, offered every third Sunday. It is a free program for parents and children that introduces art appreciation with a make-and-take project.

Other treasures for families are the annual offbeat Parade the Circle celebration in the summer, Chalk Festival in the fall, and candlelit Holiday CircleFest in the winter. Also, the museum cafeteria, located in the lower level, is a cut above most. The courtyard, too, is a very pleasant place indeed, especially during the evenings with scheduled entertainment.

Cleveland Museum of Art

Cleveland Music School Settlement

AGES: 1½–3 3–5 5–8 8–12 12–15
RATING: ★★★ ★★★ ★★★ ★★★ ★★★

COST: **FREE–$$$** PREP.: **Some–Much**
AREA: **Near East** CITY: **Cleveland**

ADDRESS: 11125 Magnolia Dr.

PHONE: (216) 421-5806

SEASON: Year round

HOURS: Office: 9 a.m.–7:30 p.m.

PRICES: Vary

DIRECT.: East: I-90 to Exit 177 for Martin Luther King Blvd.; south on MLK; east on Wade Park Ave.; right (south) on E. 108 St.; right (east) on Magnolia Dr.; on left.

West: I-90 to Exit 173B for Chester Ave.; east on Chester; left (east) on Euclid Ave.; left (north) on East Blvd. right (north) on Hazel Dr.; right (west) on Magnolia Dr.; on left.

✓ Strollers ✓ Groups ✓ Food Nearby
✓ Diap Chg Picnic ✓ Pub. Trans.
✓ Parking Food Serv. ✓ Handicapped

The Cleveland Music School Settlement, one of the largest community music schools in the country, is committed to providing music education to everyone—regardless of age, skill, background, or means. The performing arts department offers private lessons as well as classes in a variety of musical styles. The Early Childhood Department includes a preschool day school.

Classes in music and dance for preschoolers include Suzuki-method violin and piano for ages 3–8, Music Explorers (Orff-Schulwerk) for ages 3–6, and movement (Dalcroze Eurythmics) for ages 3–6. There is also ballet, drama, kinderdance, tap, and more. A Music Builders summer camp is especially popular.

Young musicians should look into the youth orchestra, which has two groups: one for ages 7–11, one for ages 12–18. Rehearsals are on Saturday mornings; performances are scheduled three times a year.

For families interested in attending performances, the school regularly offers free concerts that feature faculty, students, and guest artists.

Branches:

19000 Libby Rd., Maple Heights, (216) 662-6227

Cleveland Orchestra

AGES: 1½–3 3–5 5–8 8–12 12–15
RATING: NR ★★★ ★★★ ★★★ ★★★

COST: **$–$$$** PREP.: **Much**
AREA: **Near East** CITY: **Cleveland**

ADDRESS: Severance Hall, 11001 Euclid Ave.

PHONE: (800) 686-1141

SEASON: Seasonal (Sep–May, Severance; Jul–Aug, Blossom)

HOURS: Vary

PRICES: Vary, group discount

DIRECT.: West: I-90 to Exit 173B for Chester Ave.; east on Chester; left on Euclid Ave; left on East Blvd; on right.

East: I-90 to Exit 177 for Martin Luther King Blvd.; south on MLK; left (northeast) on Euclid Ave; left (north) on East Blvd; on right.

South: I-271 to Exit 32 for Cedar Rd.; west on Cedar to University Circle; right (northeast) on Euclid Ave; left (north) on East Blvd.; on right.

WEB: www.clevedorch.com

Strollers ✓ Groups ✓ Food Nearby
Diap Chg ✓ Picnic ✓ Pub. Trans.
✓ Parking ✓ Food Serv. ✓ Handicapped

Extensive (and popular) offerings for children help open this venerable Cleveland institution—a world-class musical experience—to families.

For school-age children or teenagers, performances by the Cleveland Youth Orchestra are especially suitable. They offer a traditional concert experience, but at more affordable prices than those of the regular orchestra.

Families with preschoolers flock to the Musical Rainbows series.

Designed specifically for ages 3–6, each program lasts 30 minutes and focuses on individual instruments as demonstrated by orchestra members. In addition to demonstration, explanation, and audience participation, there are also stories using the instruments.

Family Concerts, for ages 5–9, last an hour and feature the entire orchestra playing shorter pieces; preconcert activities include hands-on projects and entertainment—sometimes even a few surprise visitors.

Another good way to introduce your children to the orchestra is to attend one of the free public concerts scheduled throughout the year. These are very popular but are not recommended for young children because crowds are often very large.

The orchestra performs outdoors during the summer months at Blossom Music Center in the Cuyahoga Valley National Recreation Area. Picnics are allowed—even encouraged—for the summertime performances under the stars.

Cleveland Play House

AGES:	1½–3	3–5	5–8	8–12	12–15
RATING:	NR	NR	★★★	★★★	★★★

COST: **$$–$$$** PREP.: **Some–Much**
AREA: **Near East** CITY: **Cleveland**

ADDRESS: 8500 Euclid Ave.

PHONE: (216) 795-7000

SEASON: Seasonal (Sept–June)

HOURS: Vary

PRICES: Vary

DIRECT.: West: I-90 to Exit 172C for Carnegie Ave.; east on Carnegie; on left.

East: I-90 to Exit 175 for E. 55 St.; south on E. 55; left (east) on Euclid Ave.; on right.

South: I-77 to Exit 161 for E. 55 St.; north on E. 55; right (east) on Carnegie Ave.; on left.

WEB: www.cleveplayhouse.org

Strollers	✓ Groups	✓ Food Nearby
Diap Chg	Picnic	✓ Pub. Trans.
✓ Parking	Food Serv.	✓ Handicapped

The regular performance series at this collection of four theaters may not be suitable for younger audiences, but a separate schedule of plays has been developed for school-age children. It offers lower-priced tickets and

Cleveland Orchestra "Musical Rainbow" concert for kids

matinees in the smaller 120-seat Studio One Theatre.

For children interested in learning more about the theater, there is a schedule of classes that run in the fall, winter, and spring and cover improvisation, writing, dance, and drama. Curtain Pullers offers acting and technical theater classes for children ages 5 and up on Saturdays during the school year, with sessions running 10 weeks. Camp Cleveland Play House, a popular summer program, is organized by age: Creative Drama for ages 5–7; Creative Workshops or Performance Workshops for ages 8–12; and Performance Workshops and Writing for ages 13–17.

Cleveland Play House

Cleveland Public Theatre

AGES:	1½–3	3–5	5–8	8–12	12–15
RATING:	NR	NR	★★	★★	★★★

COST: **$–$$** PREP.: **Some–Much**
AREA: **Near West** CITY: **Cleveland**

ADDRESS: 6415 Detroit Ave.

PHONE: (216) 631-2727

SEASON: Year round

HOURS: Vary

PRICES: Vary

DIRECT.: I-90 to Exit 169 for W. 41 St.; north on W. 41; left (west) on Lorain Ave.; right (north) on W. 65 St.; right (east) on Detroit Ave; on right.

WEB: www.clevelandartists.net/cpt

Strollers	Groups	✓ Food Nearby
Diap Chg	✓ Picnic	✓ Pub. Trans.
✓ Parking	✓ Food Serv.	Handicapped

Works specifically designed for a family audience are often presented at this showcase for alternative and experimental theater. The education program involves young people age 14 to 21 in the process of creating original plays.

Cleveland San Jose Ballet

AGES:	1½–3	3–5	5–8	8–12	12–15
RATING:	NR	NR	★★	★★	★★

COST: **$–$$$** PREP.: **Some–Much**
AREA: **Downtown** CITY: **Cleveland**

ADDRESS: 3615 Euclid Ave. (offices)

PHONE: (216) 426-2500; school: (216) 426-2500, x2900

SEASON: Year round

HOURS: Box office: Mon–Fri 10 a.m.–6 p.m., Sat 10 a.m.–2 p.m.

PRICES: Vary

DIRECT.: West: I-90 to Exit 172A for E. 9 St.; north on E. 9; right (east) on Euclid Ave.; on left.

East: I-90 to Exit 173A for Prospect Ave.; west on Prospect; right (north) on E. 18 St.; left (west) on Euclid Ave.; on right.

WEB: www.csjballet.org

✓ Strollers	✓ Groups	✓ Food Nearby
Diap Chg	Picnic	✓ Pub. Trans.
✓ Parking	✓ Food Serv.	✓ Handicapped

Taking a youngster to the ballet may seem daunting, but the Cleveland San Jose Ballet has paved a more child-friendly way over the past few years. Special prices, special school matinees, a Kids Club, children's parties, and family days have been offered. Each December, many Cleveland families include in their holiday tradition the annual performance of *The Nutcracker*, a wonderful introduction to dance for school-age children.

Classes offered through the School of the Cleveland Ballet begin with ages 4–10 and are held once or twice a week as part of the Community Program. Classes become more serious and advanced, with instruction in technique and pointe, for ages 10–18, with sessions held two to six times per week in the Preprofessional Training Program. Ballet classes designed for figure skaters and gymnasts focus on balance and poise. A special summer session offers a variety of dance experiences for ages 4–18. Students get an opportunity to perform small roles (the mice, no less) in The Nutcracker.

The Cleveland San Jose Ballet performs *The Nutcracker*

Cleveland Signstage Theatre

AGES:	1½–3	3–5	5–8	8–12	12–15
RATING:	NR	★	★★	★★	★★

COST: **$–$$** PREP.: **Some**
AREA: **Near East** CITY: **Cleveland**

ADDRESS: 8500 Euclid Ave.

PHONE: (216) 229-2838 (voice), (216) 229-0341 (tty)

SEASON: Year round

HOURS: Vary

PRICES: Vary; discount available for deaf and hearing-impaired patrons.

DIRECT.: West: I-90 to Exit 172C for Carnegie Ave.; east on Carnegie; on left.

East: I-90 to Exit 175 for E. 55 St.; south on E. 55; left (east) on Euclid Ave.; on right.

South: I-77 to Exit 161 for E. 55 St.; north on E. 55; right (east) on Carnegie Ave.; on left.

WEB: www.signstage.org

✓ Strollers	✓ Groups	✓ Food Nearby
Diap Chg	Picnic	✓ Pub. Trans.
✓ Parking	Food Serv.	✓ Handicapped

This troupe mounts three main shows a year, at least one of which is geared toward the entire family. The traveling Deaf Awareness Show is available for school presentations with a question-and-answer session with the actors after the performance.

Cleveland Youth Theatre

AGES:	1½–3	3–5	5–8	8–12	12–15
RATING:	NR	★	★★	★★	★★

COST: **$–$$** PREP.: **Some–Much**
AREA: **Near West** CITY: **Cleveland**

ADDRESS: 5209 Detroit Rd.

PHONE: (216) 651-2037

SEASON: Year round

HOURS: Performances: Thu–Sat afternoons and early evenings

PRICES: Vary

DIRECT.: West: I-90 to Exit 169 for W. 44 St.; north on W. 44; left (east) on Franklin Blvd.; right (north) on W. 52 St.; left (west) on Detroit Ave.; on left.

East: I-90 to SR 2; west on SR 2 to E. 49 St.; south on W. 49; right (west) on Detroit Ave.; on left.

Strollers	✓ Groups	✓ Food Nearby
Diap Chg	Picnic	✓ Pub. Trans.
✓ Parking	✓ Food Serv.	Handicapped

This neighborhood-based theater is committed to diversity and to involving people of all ages in its three annual productions. A professionally directed full-scale musical is usually staged by the youth group (ages 13–19) in the summer. Fridays before shows are often designated Teen

Nights to allow teens to help professionals in set design, construction, and the consumption of pizza. Classes in acting and general theater skills are offered for ages 8–12.

Cudell Fine Arts Center

AGES:	1½–3	3–5	5–8	8–12	12–15
RATING:	NR	NR	★★	★★	★★

COST: **FREE–$$** PREP.: **Some**
AREA: **Near West** CITY: **Cleveland**

ADDRESS: 10013 Detroit Rd.

PHONE: (216) 664-4183; Studio: (216) 664-4103

SEASON: Year round

HOURS: Mon–Fri 12:30 p.m.–9 p.m., Sat 9:30 a.m.–6 p.m.

PRICES: Free

DIRECT.: I-90 to Exit 167 for West Blvd.; north on West Blvd.; on right before Detroit Ave.

✓ Strollers ✓ Groups ✓ Food Nearby
Diap Chg ✓ Picnic ✓ Pub. Trans.
✓ Parking Food Serv. ✓ Handicapped

Part of the City of Cleveland's Department of Recreation, this community arts group offers after-school classes for ages 7–17 in drawing, painting, ceramics, and sewing. There are also special series for parent and child, family workshops designed for younger children, and even an introductory arts program aimed at home-schooled children.

The best part is that all classes are free, with materials provided by the City of Cleveland and Cudell.

TIPS FOR TRIPS

CROWDS

For little ones, point out the correct person—by uniform or location—to ask for help if they get lost. (Not just any grown-up will do.)

Cultural Center for the Arts

Canton Museum of Art

AGES:	1½–3	3–5	5–8	8–12	12–15
RATING:	NR	★	★★	★★	★★

COST: **FREE–$** PREP.: **None–Some**
AREA: **Farther South** CITY: **Canton**

ADDRESS: 1001 Market Ave. N.

PHONE: Canton Museum of Art: (330) 453-7666
Canton Ballet box office: (330) 455-7220
Canton Symphony Orchestra: (330) 452-2094
Players Guild of Canton: (330) 453-7617

SEASON: Year round

HOURS: Tue–Sat 10 a.m.–5 p.m., Tue–Thu evenings 7–9 p.m., Sun 1–5 p.m.

PRICES: Free; fee for special programs

DIRECT.: I-77 to Exit 107 for US 62; east on US 62; south on Market Ave.; on left.

WEB: 204.210.221.2/Canton_Museum_of_Art

✓ Strollers ✓ Groups ✓ Food Nearby
Diap Chg Picnic ✓ Pub. Trans.
✓ Parking Food Serv. ✓ Handicapped

The centerpiece of the Cultural Center for the Arts, the Canton Museum of Art is a small, brightly lit two-room gallery hosting various traveling shows and a small permanent exhibit. When we visited, a collection of ceramics—pots, bowls, and assorted figures—was mounted. Classes are offered year round for families and children preschool and up and range from clay workshops to cartooning and jewelry making.

Next door, the Canton Ballet performs in the Palace Theatre October through March. Postproduction parties are regularly held for adults and children. Past performances have included *Dracula—The Ballet*, *The Nutcracker*, *Cinderella*, and the "Emerging Choreographers' Showcase."

Also performing in the facility are the Canton Symphony Orchestra (limited schedule) and the Players Guild of Canton. Family theater productions have included *The Wonderful Wizard of Oz*, *Raggedy Ann and Andy*, *Charlie and the Chocolate Factory*, and *Cinderella*. Acting classes for first-graders through adults are available and include Creative Drama, Improvisation, Scene Study, Vocal Production, and Actor's Gym.

Cuyahoga Community College Cultural Arts Program

AGES:	1½–3	3–5	5–8	8–12	12–15
RATING:	NR	NR	★	★★	★★

COST: **FREE–$$$** PREP.: **Some**
AREA: **Downtown** CITY: **Cleveland**

ADDRESS: 2900 Community College Ave.
PHONE: (216) 987-4400
SEASON: Year round
HOURS: Vary
PRICES: Vary
DIRECT.: I-77 to Exit 162A for Orange Ave./Woodland Ave.; to E. 30 St.; north on E. 30; left (west) on Community College Ave.; on left.

Strollers ✓ Groups ✓ Food Nearby
Diap Chg Picnic ✓ Pub. Trans.
✓ Parking ✓ Food Serv. ✓ Handicapped

Dance performances, drama, music, and festivals are among the range of programs presented each year by the Cultural Arts Program at Tri-C.

Cuyahoga Valley Youth Ballet

AGES:	1½–3	3–5	5–8	8–12	12–15
RATING:	NR	NR	NR	★★	★★

COST: **$–$$** PREP.: **Some–Much**
AREA: **Far South** CITY: **Cuyahoga Falls**

ADDRESS: 2315 State Rd.
PHONE: (330) 928-6479 (studio)
SEASON: Seasonal (performances Oct–May)
HOURS: Vary
PRICES: Vary
DIRECT.: I-271 to Exit 18 for SR 8; south on SR 8; east on Graham Rd.; left (south) on State Rd.; on left.

✓ Strollers ✓ Groups ✓ Food Nearby
Diap Chg Picnic ✓ Pub. Trans.
✓ Parking ✓ Food Serv. ✓ Handicapped

Since 1953, the Cuyahoga Valley Youth Ballet has been auditioning and training young dancers for performances each year at the Akron Civic Theatre. Each season it also commissions a new ballet, combining young talent with new dance interpretations. Dancers rehearse every weekend and enroll in a rigorous schedule of classes; it is no wonder alumni go on to dance professionally.

An outreach program sends the company to area schools to perform.

CWRU Department of Theater Arts

Case Western Reserve University

AGES:	1½–3	3–5	5–8	8–12	12–15
RATING:	NR	NR	★★	★★	★★

COST: **$$** PREP.: **Some**
AREA: **Near East** CITY: **Cleveland**

ADDRESS: 2070 Adelbert Rd.
PHONE: (216) 368-4868
SEASON: Seasonal (Oct–Apr)
HOURS: Vary
PRICES: $9, $7, and $5
DIRECT.: West: I-90 to Exit 173B for Chester Ave. (Eastbound: left (south) on E. 24 St.; left (east) on Chester); east on Chester; left (northeast) on Euclid Ave.; right (east) on Adelbert; on right.

East: I-271 to Exit 32 for Brainard/Cedar Rd. (Southbound: left (south) on Brainard; right (west) on Cedar); west on Cedar to University Circle; left (north) on Martin Luther King Blvd.; right (northeast) on Euclid Ave.; right (southeast) on Adelbert; on right.

Art, Music, Theater & Dance DIRECTORY

Strollers	✓ Groups	✓ Food Nearby
Diap Chg	Picnic	✓ Pub. Trans.
✓ Parking	Food Serv.	✓ Handicapped

Spotlighting both new works and old, the seasonal schedule of the theater arts department at Case Western Reserve features performances in the Eldred Theater (2070 Adelbert Rd.) and at the Mather Dance Center (11201 Bellflower Rd.) A Spotlight Series featuring the Graduate Acting Ensemble is presented at the Cleveland Play House.

Moderately priced and often experimental, it is a great place for families to experience live performances.

DANCECleveland

AGES:	1½–3	3–5	5–8	8–12	12–15
RATING:	NR	NR	★★	★★	★★

COST: **$** PREP.: **Some**
AREA: **Downtown** CITY: **Cleveland**

ADDRESS: 1148 Euclid Ave., Suite 311

PHONE: (216) 861-2213; Box office: (216) 771-4444

SEASON: Year round

HOURS: Vary

PRICES: Vary

DIRECT.: West: I-90 to Exit 171B for E. 9 St.; north on E. 9; right (east) on Euclid Ave; on right.

East: I-90 to Exit 173B for Chester Ave.; left (south) on E. 24 St.; right (west) on Chester; left (south) on E. 18 St.; right (west) on Euclid Ave.; on left.

Strollers	✓ Groups	✓ Food Nearby
Diap Chg	Picnic	✓ Pub. Trans.
✓ Parking	✓ Food Serv.	✓ Handicapped

DANCECleveland brings to Cleveland modern dance productions from across the country throughout the year. Performances are staged at the Ohio Theater and Metro Theatre at Cuyahoga Community College. Families should be on the lookout for Young People's Concerts, a matinee series for school-age children offered periodically. DANCECleveland also performs at Cain Park (see separate listing) in the summer, providing a more relaxed opportunity to see modern dance with your children.

Dobama Theatre

AGES:	1½–3	3–5	5–8	8–12	12–15
RATING:	NR	NR	★★	★★	★★

COST: **FREE–$$$** PREP.: **Some–Much**
AREA: **East** CITY: **Cleveland Hts.**

ADDRESS: 1846 Coventry Rd.

PHONE: (216) 932-6838

SEASON: Seasonal (Sept–June)

HOURS: Vary

PRICES: Vary

DIRECT.: I-271 to Exit 34 for US 322 (Mayfield Rd.); west on Mayfield; left (south) on Coventry Rd.; on right.

OR I-90 to Exit 172D for Carnegie Ave.; east on Carnegie; right (east) on Cedar Ave. to top of Cedar Hill; straight (east) on Euclid Hts. Blvd.; left (north) on Coventry Rd.; on left.

✓ Strollers	✓ Groups	✓ Food Nearby
Diap Chg	Picnic	✓ Pub. Trans.
✓ Parking	Food Serv.	Handicapped

Participation is the focus at Dobama, from the acting classes for older kids (ages 7–15) to the Marilyn Bianchi Kids' Playwriting Festival (ages 7–17). Entries in this annual playwriting festival are judged on the basis of imagination and human values as much as on playwriting skill. All festival entrants are invited to a special preview performance of the winning contestant's play.

Fairmount Fine Arts Center

AGES:	1½–3	3–5	5–8	8–12	12–15
RATING:	★	★★	★★★	★★★	★★

COST: **FREE–$$$** PREP.: **Some–Much**
AREA: **Far East** CITY: **Russell Twp.**

ADDRESS: 8400 Fairmount Rd., P.O. Box 80

PHONE: (440) 338-3171

SEASON: Year round

HOURS: Mon–Thu 9 a.m.–7 p.m.; Fri 9 a.m.–4:30 p.m.; Sat 9 a.m.–1 p.m.

PRICES: Vary

DIRECT.: I-271 to Exit 32 for Brainard/Cedar Rd.; (southbound: left (south) on Brainard; left (east) on Cedar); (northbound: right (south) on Brainard; left (east) on Cedar); right (south) on Chagrin River Rd.; left (east) on Fairmount Rd.; on left.

Strollers | ✓ Groups | ✓ Food Nearby
✓ Diap Chg | ✓ Picnic | Pub. Trans.
✓ Parking | Food Serv. | Handicapped

Concerts, youth theater, and young people's music recitals are just some of the special events scheduled here year round. But even more popular with families are the class offerings for kids, from preschool age and up. The choices are terrific: dance, music, art, and theater as well as gymnastics and karate. The Summer Arts Camp is a good way to sample them all.

Fine Arts Association

AGES:	1½–3	3–5	5–8	8–12	12–15
RATING:	★	★★★	★★★	★★	★★

COST: **$–$$$** PREP.: **Some–Much**
AREA: **East** CITY: **Willoughby**

ADDRESS: 38660 Mentor Ave.

PHONE: (440) 951-7500; Box office (440) 951-6637

SEASON: Year round

HOURS: Vary

PRICES: Vary

DIRECT.: SR 2 to Vine St.; Vine becomes Mentor Ave.; on right.

✓ Strollers | ✓ Groups | ✓ Food Nearby
Diap Chg | Picnic | Pub. Trans.
✓ Parking | Food Serv. | ✓ Handicapped

This local institution is a favorite for area families. Performances for children, by children, are included in each theater season—with moderate prices and matinees scheduled.

Classes for preschoolers and up, both during the school year and in the summer, include painting, drawing, and pottery. (This is one of few such places where children as young as age two are welcome.) For older ones, there is instruction in cartooning, calligraphy, and portrait painting.

Fine Arts Association

There's more: As part of a comprehensive program of private music lessons, children as young as age four are started in Suzuki-method violin and piano instruction. (Ages 2–3 can join Happy Fingers class with a parent.) Dance lessons are offered for the very young to adult, along with drama. A special summer drama camp is particularly popular.

Other annual special events include Discovery Day in July, an art, dance, drama, and music open house. Santa's Workshop in December features hands-on art projects, storytelling, live musical entertainment, and a visit from you-know-who. Both are open and free to the public.

Firelands Association for the Visual Arts

AGES:	1½–3	3–5	5–8	8–12	12–15
RATING:	NR	★	★★★	★★★	★★★

COST: **FREE–$$$** PREP.: **Some–Much**
AREA: **Far West** CITY: **Oberlin**

ADDRESS: 39 S. Main St., Suite 210

PHONE: (440) 774-7158

SEASON: Year round

HOURS: Office: Tue–Sat noon–5 p.m., Sun 2–4 p.m.; gallery shop: Tue–Sat 10 a.m.–5 p.m., Sun 1–5 p.m.

PRICES: Admission free for exhibitions; class fees vary

DIRECT.: I-480 to Exit 1 for SR 10 ; west on SR 10 (becomes US 20) to SR 511; west on SR 511 to campus; left (south) on SR 58 (S. Main St.); on left.

✓ Strollers ✓ Groups ✓ Food Nearby
Diap Chg ✓ Picnic Pub. Trans.
✓ Parking Food Serv. ✓ Handicapped

FAVA was founded in 1979 to provide exhibitions and art classes for kids and adults. Offerings include photography, clay sculpting, painting, drawing, theater, and music. A regular art appreciation program for preschoolers includes a free guided look at the Allen Memorial Art Museum. It is available for groups as well. Call for current schedule of classes and exhibitions. FAVA's home, the restored New Union Center for the Arts, was built in 1874 and is listed on the National Register of Historic Places.

Great Lakes Theater Festival

AGES:	1½–3	3–5	5–8	8–12	12–15
RATING:	NR	NR	★	★★★	★★★

COST: **$$$** PREP.: **Some**
AREA: **Downtown** CITY: **Cleveland**

ADDRESS: Ohio Theater, Playhouse Square

PHONE: (216) 241-5490; box office (216) 241-6000

SEASON: Seasonal (Oct–May)

HOURS: Vary

PRICES: Vary

DIRECT.: West: I-90 to Exit 172A for E. 9 St.; north on E. 9; right (east) on Euclid Ave.; on left.

East: I-90 to Exit 173A for Prospect Ave.; west on Prospect; right (north) on E. 18 St.; left (west) on Euclid Ave.; on right.

Strollers ✓ Groups ✓ Food Nearby
Diap Chg Picnic ✓ Pub. Trans.
✓ Parking ✓ Food Serv. ✓ Handicapped

The Great Lakes Theater Festival is one of the few American theater companies dedicated to classic drama, presenting Shakespeare, Molière, and the annual family favorite, *A Christmas Carol*, based on the Charles Dickens novel. Of special note to teachers: productions for schoolchildren are previewed in detailed teachers' guides.

Greenbrier Theatre

AGES:	1½–3	3–5	5–8	8–12	12–15
RATING:	NR	★	★★	★★	★★

COST: **$$** PREP.: **Some–Much**
AREA: **South** CITY: **Parma Heights**

ADDRESS: 6200 Pearl Rd.

PHONE: (440) 842-4600

SEASON: Year round

HOURS: Fri & Sat 8 p.m., Sun matinee 3 p.m.

PRICES: Adults $11, seniors & students $10; all seats $12 on Sat

DIRECT.: I-480 to Exit 12 for W. 130 St; south on W. 130; left (east) on Brookpark Rd.; right (south) on Chevrolet Blvd. (becomes Stumph Rd. after Snow Rd.); left on Pearl Rd.; on left.

Strollers | ✓ Groups | ✓ Food Nearby
Diap Chg | Picnic | ✓ Pub. Trans.
✓ Parking | ✓ Food Serv. | Handicapped

This community theater has been around for more than two decades, offering a variety of musical theater on the main stage, special-event performances, and a thriving youth theater. Drama instruction is available year round.

Heights Youth Theatre

AGES:	1½–3	3–5	5–8	8–12	12–15
RATING:	★	★★	★★	★★	★

COST: **$–$$** PREP.: **Some–Much**
AREA: **East** CITY: **University Hts.**

ADDRESS: 2155 Miramar Blvd. (Bd. of Education)

PHONE: (216) 371-7406

SEASON: Seasonal (Oct–May; winter holidays)

HOURS: Sat, Sun 2 p.m.

PRICES: Vary; group rates available

DIRECT.: I-271 to Exit 32 for Brainard/Cedar Rd. (southbound: left (south) on Brainard; right (west) on Cedar); west on Cedar; left (south) on Miramar Blvd.; Performances on right at Wiley Middle School.

✓ Strollers | ✓ Groups | ✓ Food Nearby
Diap Chg | Picnic | ✓ Pub. Trans.
✓ Parking | Food Serv. | ✓ Handicapped

Heights Youth Theatre, the oldest children's theater in this area, offers classes for children ages 4–18 in improvisation, dance, and stage production. For preschoolers there are dance and drama classes. A summer camp program culminates in an on-stage performance.

Productions for children are performed by kids in the Wiley Middle School auditorium. For birthday parties, rooms can be reserved prior to shows (bring your own cake, decorations, and party favors).

Audition schedules are often hard to find, especially for those not living in the neighborhood, so if you're interested call the office, or check with the Cleveland Heights Parks and Recreation Department.

Hugh A. Glauser School of Music

Kent State University

AGES:	1½–3	3–5	5–8	8–12	12–15
RATING:	NR	NR	★	★★	★★

COST: **FREE–$$** PREP.: **Some**
AREA: **Far South** CITY: **Kent**

ADDRESS: Kent State University

PHONE: (330) 672-3609 (24-hour info line)

SEASON: Year round

HOURS: Vary

PRICES: Concerts are free, except for special events

DIRECT.: I-271 to I-480; east on I-480 (becomes SR 14 after Frost Rd.); right (south) on SR 43; left (east) on E. Main St.; right (south) onto Horning Rd..; right (west) on Music Dr.; on left.

✓ Strollers | Groups | Food Nearby
Diap Chg | ✓ Picnic | Pub. Trans.
✓ Parking | ✓ Food Serv. | Handicapped

A comprehensive music-school program here brings a number of free and low-cost performances to the area, featuring school choirs and choruses, and chamber orchestras, as well as the Cleveland Orchestra and others. Annual music festivals are popular and well attended.

Huntington Playhouse

AGES:	1½–3	3–5	5–8	8–12	12–15
RATING:	NR	NR	★★	★★	★★

COST: **$–$$** PREP.: **Some–Much**
AREA: **West** CITY: **Bay Village**

ADDRESS: 28601 Lake Rd.

PHONE: (440) 871-8333

SEASON: Year round

HOURS: Vary; Sun matinee performances available

PRICES: Call box office; senior & student discount available for Thu & Fri performances

DIRECT.: West: I-90 to Exit 156 for Crocker Rd.; Left (north) on Crocker to Bassett Rd.; Right (east) on Lake Rd.; Playhouse on right.

East: I-90 to exit 159 for Columbia Rd.; Right (north) on Columbia; Left (west) on Lake Rd; Playhouse on left.

Strollers ✓ Groups ✓ Food Nearby
Diap Chg ✓ Picnic ✓ Pub. Trans.
✓ Parking Food Serv. ✓ Handicapped

Founded in a carriage house 40 years ago, this community troupe is known for its variety of musical theater productions as well as its year-round classes for school-age children.

Karamu Performing Arts Theater

AGES:	1½–3	3–5	5–8	8–12	12–15
RATING:	NR	★	★★	★★	★★

COST: **$–$$** PREP.: **Some–Much**
AREA: **Near East** CITY: **Cleveland**

ADDRESS: 2355 E. 89 St.

PHONE: (216) 795-7077

SEASON: Year round

HOURS: Vary

PRICES: Vary

DIRECT.: West: I-90 to Exit 172D for Carnegie Ave.; east on Carnegie; right (south) on E. 89 St.; on left.

East: I-90 to Exit 177 for Martin Luther King Blvd.; south on MLK; right (west) on Carnegie Ave. left (south) on E. 89 St.; on left.

✓ Strollers ✓ Groups ✓ Food Nearby
Diap Chg Picnic ✓ Pub. Trans.
✓ Parking Food Serv. Handicapped

There are actually two theaters here, as well as a small cabaret, exhibit galleries, and classrooms. The annual program includes theater for young audiences and classes for preschoolers and up in drama, dance, and music. A popular summer day camp offers a broad program in arts and culture for kids ages 6–12.

Founded in 1915 by graduates of Oberlin College as the Playhouse Settlement, this theater has become known nationwide for its focus on interracial theater and arts. It was renamed Karamu House in 1941 after the Swahili word for the center of the community and place of enjoyment. Karamu is especially active in the schools, and for its work the group received an award from the American Alliance of Theater in Education in 1993.

Lorain County Community College's College for Kids

AGES:	1½–3	3–5	5–8	8–12	12–15
RATING:	NR	★	★★	★★★	★★★

COST: **$–$$** PREP.: **Some–Much**
AREA: **Far West** CITY: **Elyria**

ADDRESS: Stocker Center, 1005 N. Abbe Rd.

PHONE: (800) 995-5222; College for Kids: ext. 4093; Stocker Center Box Office: ext. 4040

SEASON: Year round

HOURS: Vary

PRICES: Vary

DIRECT.: I-90 to Exit 148 for SR 254 (Detroit Rd.); east on Detroit; right (south) on SR 301 (Abbe Rd.); on left.

WEB: www.lorainccc.edu

✓ Strollers ✓ Groups ✓ Food Nearby
Diap Chg ✓ Picnic Pub. Trans.
✓ Parking ✓ Food Serv. ✓ Handicapped

Lorain County Community College's College for Kids is a growing resource for area families. For school-age children, year-round Saturday classes are offered in music, dance, karate, language, computers, visual arts, outer space, and dinosaurs. The school year is divided into three eight-week sessions; a special session during the summer allows students to mix and match coursework. Summer programs are one week long, usually in the morning.

If you are looking for performances, do not overlook the student matinee series offerings of professional performing arts (improvisation, opera, and music) especially designed for young people.

Lorain Palace Civic Theater

AGES:	1½–3	3–5	5–8	8–12	12–15
RATING:	NR	★	★	★★	★★

COST: **FREE–$$$** PREP.: **Some**
AREA: **Far West** CITY: **Lorain**

ADDRESS: 617 Broadway

PHONE: (440) 245-2323, box office

SEASON: Year round

HOURS: Vary. Box office: Mon–Fri, 10 a.m.–4 p.m.

PRICES: Vary. Ticket prices vary; movies $1.50 per person.

DIRECT.: SR 2 to Middle Ridge Rd.; north on Middle Ridge; left (north) on Broadway Ave.; on left at 6 St.

Strollers ✓ Groups ✓ Food Nearby
Diap Chg Picnic ✓ Pub. Trans.
✓ Parking ✓ Food Serv. ✓ Handicapped

Built in 1928, the Palace has long been the centerpiece in this small city's downtown. Constructed as a vaudeville showplace, it has the distinction of being the first theater in Ohio to show "talking pictures." It fell into disrepair during the 1950s and 1960s, and in 1977 a full-scale effort was begun to save the theater and rebuild an audience. These days, the Palace offers movies, musical theater, visiting performers, civic-group events, private parties, and educational programs.

Lyric Opera Cleveland

AGES:	1½–3	3–5	5–8	8–12	12–15
RATING:	NR	NR	★★	★★	★★

COST: **$–$$** PREP.: **Some**
AREA: **Near East** CITY: **Cleveland**

ADDRESS: P.O. Box 606198

PHONE: (216) 231-2484

SEASON: Seasonal (Summer festival season with year-round educational and community performances)

HOURS: Evening and matinee performances

PRICES: Vary; discounts for students, seniors, and groups

DIRECT.: East: I-90 to Exit 177 for Martin Luther King Blvd.; south on MLK; left (east) on East Blvd.; left (north) on Hazel Dr.; Cleveland Institute of Music on right.

West: I-90 to Exit 173 for Chester Ave.; east on Chester; left (east) on Euclid Ave.; left (north) on East Blvd.; right (north) on Hazel Dr.; Cleveland Institute of Music on right.

WEB: www.lyricoperacleveland.org

✓ Strollers ✓ Groups ✓ Food Nearby
Diap Chg ✓ Picnic ✓ Pub. Trans.
✓ Parking ✓ Food Serv. ✓ Handicapped

The performances of Lyric Opera are all sung in English, but some may be too serious for younger school-age children. If your older kids are interested in music and theater, however, check out the schedule. Two programs are designed specifically to tour schools each year and perform for grades K–12. Lyric Opera Cleveland regularly performs in Kulas Hall at the Cleveland Institute of Music.

Magical Theatre Company

AGES:	1½–3	3–5	5–8	8–12	12–15
RATING:	NR	★	★★	★★	★★

COST: **$–$$** PREP.: **Some–Much**
AREA: **Farther South** CITY: **Barberton**

ADDRESS: 565 W. Tuscarawas Ave.

PHONE: (330) 848-3708

SEASON: Seasonal (Oct to May)

HOURS: Office: 9 a.m.–6 p.m.; performances: times vary

PRICES: $4–$10; group discounts available

DIRECT.: I-76 to Exit 16 for Barber Rd.; south on Barber; left (east) on W. Lake Ave.; right (south) on 3 St.; right (east) on W. Tuscarawas Ave.; on left.

✓ Strollers ✓ Groups ✓ Food Nearby
Diap Chg Picnic ✓ Pub. Trans.
✓ Parking Food Serv. ✓ Handicapped

The Magical Theatre company is specifically dedicated to introducing young people and families to theater. For over 25 years it has offered professional performances, both in its resident theater and during a year-round travel schedule. Classes for ages 6–18 include basic acting, mime, creative dramatics, and makeup. The KidScripts program allows students to produce their own stories and plays.

Oberlin College Arts Dept.

AGES:	1½–3	3–5	5–8	8–12	12–15
RATING:	NR	NR	★★	★★★	★★★

COST: **$–$$** PREP.: **Some**
AREA: **Far West** CITY: **Oberlin**

ADDRESS: 173 W. Lorain St. (SR 58 & SR 511)

PHONE: (440) 775-8169 (central ticket service); (440) 774-6262 (Oberlin Chamber of Commerce)

SEASON: Year round

HOURS: Vary

PRICES: Vary

DIRECT.: I-480 to Exit 1 for SR 10 ; west on SR 10 (becomes US 20) to SR 511; west on SR 511 to campus; on left.

WEB: www.oberlin.edu

✓ Strollers ✓ Groups ✓ Food Nearby
Diap Chg ✓ Picnic ✓ Pub. Trans.
✓ Parking ✓ Food Serv. ✓ Handicapped

Oberlin College's community arts offerings include the Little Theater, Oberlin Opera, Oberlin Dance Company, Oberlin Choristers Chamber Choir, and the Artist Recital Series. Oberlin College's Little Theater's season runs through the school year; past performances have included *Gospel at Colonus*, *Women of Troy*, and *Picnic*. School-year performances by Oberlin Opera have included *The Marriage of Figaro* and *A Midsummer Night's Dream*. The Oberlin Dance Company season culminates in a spring performance.

The Oberlin Choristers Chamber Choir includes a children's choir, which performs with the Oberlin Dance Company in their annual spring performance.

The Artist Recital Series held in Finney Chapel also runs through the school year, bringing such programming as the Cleveland Orchestra, the London Brass, Hermann Prey (baritone), Grigory Sokolov (piano), and the Emerson String Quartet.

Ohio Ballet

AGES:	1½–3	3–5	5–8	8–12	12–15
RATING:	NR	NR	★★	★★	★★

COST: **$$–$$$** PREP.: **Some**
AREA: **Far South** CITY: **Akron**

ADDRESS: 354 E. Market St.

PHONE: (330) 972-7900; (216) 861-5545

SEASON: Year round

HOURS: Vary

PRICES: Vary

DIRECT.: I-271 to Exit 18 for SR 8; south on SR 8; east on Perkins St.; left (south) on Union St.; left (east) on E. Market St.; on right.

WEB: www.ohioballet.com

Strollers	✓ Groups	✓ Food Nearby
Diap Chg	Picnic	✓ Pub. Trans.
✓ Parking	Food Serv.	✓ Handicapped

Featuring a wide repertory including fairy-tale ballets, modern works, and world premieres, the Ohio Ballet's productions are a bright spot in the area's dance scene.

Of particular note, community and educational outreach has been part of the mission of the Ohio Ballet since its founding over three decades ago. Specifically for their younger audiences: KidSteps performs for area fifth-grade students, the annual summer festival brings free outdoor performances to area parks, and the Youth Interactive Program combines performance with audience participation and demonstrations. For school groups and others, a half-hour preshow Chatter program is scheduled before and after every matinee and prearranged evening show.

Ohio Chamber Orchestra

AGES:	1½–3	3–5	5–8	8–12	12–15
RATING:	NR	NR	★	★★	★★

COST: **FREE–$$$** PREP.: **Some**
AREA: **Downtown & citywide**
CITY: **Cleveland**

ADDRESS: 2026 Murray Hill Rd., Suite 210

PHONE: (216) 721-3939

SEASON: Year round

HOURS: Vary; office open Mon–Fri 10 a.m.–4:30 p.m.

PRICES: Adults $20; discount for students and children

DIRECT.: I-90 to Exit 173B for Chester Ave. (Eastbound: left (south) on E. 24 St.; left (east) on Chester); east on Chester; left northeast on Euclid Ave.; right (east) on US 322 (Mayfield Rd.); right (south) on Murray Hill; on right.

✓ Strollers	✓ Groups	✓ Food Nearby
Diap Chg	Picnic	✓ Pub. Trans.
✓ Parking	Food Serv.	✓ Handicapped

The Ohio Chamber Orchestra performs mainly at Cleveland State University's Waetgen Auditorium. A summer series brings the Orchestra to Cain Park in Cleveland Heights (see separate listing), where it offers free concerts geared toward the entire family.

Ohio Light Opera

College of Wooster

AGES:	1½–3	3–5	5–8	8–12	12–15
RATING:	NR	NR	★	★★★	★★★

COST: **$–$$$** PREP.: **Some**
AREA: **Farther South** CITY: **Wooster**

ADDRESS: College of Wooster

PHONE: (330) 263-2090

SEASON: Seasonal (Jan–Aug)

HOURS: Vary. Box office: Jan 15–May 17, Mon–Fri 10 a.m.–4:30 p.m.; May–Aug, Mon–Sat 10 a.m.–4:30 p.m.

PRICES: Vary

DIRECT.: I-71 to Exit 204 for SR 83; south on SR 83 to Wooster; right (south) on Burbank Rd. (becomes Beaver St.); left (east) on University St.; Freelander Theater on right.

WEB: www.wooster.edu/OH_LT_OPERA

Strollers	✓ Groups	✓ Food Nearby
Diap Chg	Picnic	Pub. Trans.
✓ Parking	✓ Food Serv.	✓ Handicapped

This is a great way to find out that opera can be enjoyed by anyone. All of the performances are sung in English, with a full orchestra. And they are ambitious productions (they perform the entire Gilbert and Sullivan repertoire). The Ohio Light Opera is the only professional company in the U.S. devoted entirely to producing operettas (romantic, comic operas that include dancing). With nine shows each season, there are usually several matinees to choose from that are suitable for a younger audience.

Playhouse Square Center

AGES:	1½–3	3–5	5–8	8–12	12–15
RATING:	NR	★★	★★★	★★★	★★★

COST: **$–$$$** PREP.: **Some**
AREA: **Downtown** CITY: **Cleveland**

ADDRESS: 1519 Euclid Ave.

PHONE: (216) 771-4444; Advantix: (216) 241-6000

SEASON: Year round

HOURS: Vary

PRICES: Vary

DIRECT.: West: I-90 to Exit 172A for E. 9 St.; north on E. 9; right (east) on Euclid Ave.; on left.

East: I-90 to Exit 173A for Prospect Ave.; west on Prospect; right (north) on E. 18 St.; left (west) on Euclid Ave.; on right.

Strollers ✓ Groups ✓ Food Nearby
Diap Chg Picnic ✓ Pub. Trans.
✓ Parking ✓ Food Serv. ✓ Handicapped

Closed down and boarded up by the late 1960s, theaters here have been brought back to their original splendor thanks to an ambitious renovation project. The Palace, Ohio, Allen, and State theaters, which together comprise Playhouse Square Center, were originally built in the 1920s as ornate and glamorous movie houses. With the rescue in 1998 of the Allen Theater, this complex is the largest performance arts center in the U.S. outside of New York City's Lincoln Center. Every Clevelander should visit here at least once.

The regular season brings a diverse schedule of touring theater, dance, and musical performances to Playhouse Square. Many are perfect for a special family outing (albeit an expensive one).

Younger, squirmier children will do better to attend one of the special performances offered through the Children's Theater Series. These are created especially for children ages 3 and up, and the series typically includes classic fairy tales, music, and mime, with matinee performances and lower prices (not to mention an audience of peers with the same fidgety habits).

The Playhouse Square theaters are also home to regularly scheduled performances of the Great Lakes Theater Festival, DANCECleveland, the Cleveland Opera, and the Cleveland Ballet (see separate listings for each).

For a great lesson in both Cleveland history and the arts, check out the free guided tours of the theater complex.

Riverside Academy of Music

AGES:	1½–3	3–5	5–8	8–12	12–15
RATING:	NR	★	★★★	★★★	★★★

COST: **FREE–$$** PREP.: **Some–Much**
AREA: **Near West** CITY: **Lakewood**

ADDRESS: 1414 Riverside Dr.

PHONE: (216) 228-2800

SEASON: Year round

HOURS: Office hours: Mon.–Fri. 9 a.m.–7 p.m.; Sat. 9 a.m.–1 p.m.

PRICES: Tuition fees, grants and donations

DIRECT.: I-90 to Exit 161 for SR 252 (Detroit Rd.); right (east) on Riverside Dr. after Wooster Rd.; on right.

Strollers ✓ Groups ✓ Food Nearby
Diap Chg Picnic ✓ Pub. Trans.
Parking Food Serv. Handicapped

Offering classes in instruments, voice, and Dalcroze, the Riverside Academy is a well-known treasure on the West Side. A Sunday Music Series features faculty and guest artists and is free. Student concerts are also scheduled throughout the year.

Shore Cultural Centre

City of Euclid

AGES:	1½–3	3–5	5–8	8–12	12–15
RATING:	★★	★★	★★	★★	★★

COST: **FREE–$$$** PREP.: **Some–Much**
AREA: **East** CITY: **Euclid**

ADDRESS: 291 E. 222 St.

PHONE: (216) 289-8578

SEASON: Year round

HOURS: Mon–Fri 8:30 a.m.–11 p.m.; Sat & Sun 8 a.m.–3 p.m.

PRICES: Vary

DIRECT.: I-90 to Exit 183 for E. 222 St.; north on E. 222; on right.

✓ Strollers ✓ Groups ✓ Food Nearby
Diap Chg Picnic ✓ Pub. Trans.
✓ Parking Food Serv. ✓ Handicapped

The Shore Cultural Centre, housed in a school built in 1913, offers a full and varied schedule of classes in the arts for all ages, from toddlers to seniors. For school-age children these include theater, art, pottery, and calligraphy. Special holiday workshops and hands-on classes are geared for preschoolers and their parents. Classes are offered year round; the summer program is particularly popular.

The old school's two gymnasiums are used for a variety of events (including community theater), many of them suitable for older children; instrumental and voice lessons for children are available. The building is also home to the national Cleveland-Style Polka Hall of Fame.

Trumpet in the Land

AGES:	1½–3	3–5	5–8	8–12	12–15
RATING:	NR	NR	★	★★	★★

COST: **$$** PREP.: **Much** AREA: **Farther South**
CITY: **New Philadelphia**

ADDRESS: Schoenbrunn Amphitheater

PHONE: (330) 339-1132, box office

SEASON: Seasonal (Summer)

HOURS: June–Aug nightly, except Sundays, 8:30 p.m.–11 p.m.

PRICES: Vary. Mon: Family Night; Wed: Seniors Night; Thurs: Student Night

DIRECT.: I-77 to Exit 81 for US 250; east on US 250 to SR 259; north on SR 259; on right after Schoenbrunn Village.

✓ Strollers ✓ Groups ✓ Food Nearby
Diap Chg ✓ Picnic Pub. Trans.
✓ Parking ✓ Food Serv. ✓ Handicapped

This drama reenacts the founding of Ohio's first settlement, Schoenbrunn, in 1772, on what was then the country's western frontier. It depicts the result of a struggle between Americans embroiled in the Revolutionary War and a peaceful Indian settlement. With singing, dancing, and pyrotechnics presented in an outdoor amphitheater, the production draws a large audience—buy your tickets in advance.

TIPS FOR TRIPS

AGE RANGES

When trying to accommodate different ages and interests, negotiate a trade: 15 minutes of one activity for 15 minutes of another. (This works for adults too!)

Weathervane Community Playhouse

AGES:	1½–3	3–5	5–8	8–12	12–15
RATING:	NR	NR	★★	★★	★★

COST: **$$–$$$** PREP.: **Some–Much**
AREA: **Far South** CITY: **Akron**

ADDRESS: 1301 Weathervane Ln.

PHONE: (330) 836-2626

SEASON: Year round

HOURS: Curtain times: Thu–Sat 8 p.m., Sun 2:30

PRICES: Vary; special rates for groups & seniors

DIRECT.: I-77 to Exit 138 for Ghent Rd.; south on Ghent; left (east) on Smith Rd. at Summit Mall; right (south) on Merriman Rd.; left (north) on Weathervane Ln.; on right.

Strollers ✓ Groups ✓ Food Nearby
✓ Diap Chg Picnic ✓ Pub. Trans.
✓ Parking Food Serv. ✓ Handicapped

Weathervane's main-stage productions may not always be suitable for young audiences, but there is usually something going on here for children. Classroom instruction culminates in performances, including three shows a year by youths, for youths. Separately, ProjectSTAGE brings performances to area high schools with question-and-answer sessions with performers.

Popular class offerings for ages 3–18 cover such areas as creative movement, improvisation, theater games, and advanced acting. Fall-winter sessions last for 16 weeks; spring sessions last 8 weeks. A special 2-week summer workshop includes all-around classes and a culminating performance.

Assisted Listening Devices are available for the hearing impaired at performances.

Wildwood Cultural Center

City of Mentor, Dept. of Parks, Recreation & Public Lands

AGES:	1½–3	3–5	5–8	8–12	12–15
RATING:	NR	★★	★★	★★	★★

COST: **$** PREP.: **None–Much**
AREA: **Far East** CITY: **Mentor**

ADDRESS: 7645 Little Mountain Rd.

PHONE: (440) 974-5735

SEASON: Year round

HOURS: Vary

PRICES: Vary

DIRECT.: SR 2 to SR 615 (Center St.); south on Center; left (east) on SR 84 (Johnnycake Ridge Rd.); left (north) on Little Mountain Rd.; on right.

Or, I-90 to Exit 190 for SR 306 (Chillicothe Rd.); north on SR 306; right (east) on Johnnycake Ridge Rd.; left (north) on Little Mountain Rd.; on right.

Strollers ✓ Groups ✓ Food Nearby
Diap Chg ✓ Picnic Pub. Trans.
✓ Parking Food Serv. ✓ Handicapped

Wildwood is located in a turn-of-the-century English Tudor mansion on 34 acres. (It is listed in the National Register of Historic Places.) The center offers a varied schedule of classes in arts, cooking, and music for youth and adults; changing exhibits; wellness programs; and special events, such as an annual Christmas concert and a summer arts festival. Sessions run fall, winter, spring, and summer. (The mansion is also available for private rental for events such as conferences or reunions.)

Sports and Recreation

How can parents pick the best sports activities for their children? Maturity levels, development, and age all contribute to readiness for a specific sport. Generally, T-ball, soccer, gymnastics, swimming, cycling, and skating are great for younger children. They all emphasize the development of hand-eye coordination, agility, and strength. Besides, for fun and exercise, what's better than sports?

When it comes down to signing your children up for activities, begin by taking their interests to heart. Ask them: Why do you want to play? And a reminder: don't forget to check the weekly practice and game schedule—those 5 a.m. ice-hockey practices can be hard to manage.

The following list should help narrow your search for sporting activities.

Alpine Valley

AGES:	1½–3	3–5	5–8	8–12	12–15
RATING:	NR	★★	★★	★★★	★★

COST: **$$$** PREP.: **None–Some**
AREA: **Far East** CITY: **Chesterland**

ADDRESS: 10620 Mayfield Rd.

PHONE: (440) 285-2211; ski line recording: (440) 729-9775 (during season)

SEASON: Seasonal (mid-Nov–mid-Mar)

HOURS: Mon–Fri 1–10:30 p.m.; Sat, Sun & holidays 9 a.m.–11 p.m.

PRICES: Vary; $20–34, $18–32 ages 12 & under

DIRECT.: I-271 to Exit 34 for US 322 (Mayfield Rd.); east on Mayfield; on left.

Strollers ✓ Groups ✓ Food Nearby
Diap Chg ✓ Picnic Pub. Trans.
✓ Parking ✓ Food Serv. Handicapped

The seven slopes at Alpine Valley are reached by chair lift, J-bar, and rope tow. Beginning skiers can take group lessons in the early morning and evening; each class is open to ages 4 and up. Two "Bunny" classes for ages 12 and under are held on Saturday (9 a.m.–1 p.m.) and Sunday (1–5 p.m.). Cost includes lift tickets, equipment rental, one-hour group lesson, and three hours of ski time. For even younger skiers, Uncle Bob's Preschool Ski School (ages 4-6) involves four weeks of lessons intended to help children learn the basics and to give their parents instructional tips on how to teach their kids. (An adult on skis must attend.) Private lessons are also available. Equipment rental prices are reduced for ages 6 and under. The annual WinterFest includes snow volleyball and an obstacle course.

Beachwood Municipal Pool

AGES:	1½–3	3–5	5–8	8–12	12–15
RATING:	★★	★★	★★	★★	★★

COST: **$–$$** PREP.: **None–Much**
AREA: **East** CITY: **Beachwood**

ADDRESS: 25100 Fairmount Blvd.

PHONE: (216) 292-1970

SEASON: Seasonal (Jun–Sep)

HOURS: Mon–Fri 12:15 p.m.–8 p.m.; Sat–Sun 11 a.m.–7:30 p.m.

PRICES: $4 per resident visit, $6 non-resident guests under 18, $7 adult non-resident (must be accompanied by a resident); individual family membership $15 per person, not to exceed $75; non-resident fees vary; season guest pass $70.

DIRECT.: I-271 to Exit 32 for Cedar/Brainard Rd.; west on Cedar; left (south) on Richmond Rd.; right (west) on Fairmount Blvd.; on right.

✓ Strollers	✓ Groups	✓ Food Nearby
✓ Diap Chg	✓ Picnic	✓ Pub. Trans.
✓ Parking	✓ Food Serv.	✓ Handicapped

Kiddie pool, lessons, playground.

Bexley Pool

South Euclid/Lyndhurst Recreation Dept.

AGES:	1½–3	3–5	5–8	8–12	12–15
RATING:	★★	★★	★★	★★	★★

COST: **$–$$** PREP.: **None–Much**
AREA: **East** CITY: **South Euclid**

ADDRESS: 4194 Temple Rd.

PHONE: (216) 381-0446; (216) 691-2246

SEASON: Seasonal (Jun–Sep)

HOURS: Daily 1:30 p.m.–8 p.m.

PRICES: $5 residents, $6 non-resident guests; individual family pass $30 each, maximum $90 per family

DIRECT.: I-271 to Exit 34 for Mayfield Rd.; west on Mayfield left (south) on S. Belvoir Rd.; right (west) on Wrenford Rd.; on right.

✓ Strollers	✓ Groups	Food Nearby
✓ Diap Chg	✓ Picnic	✓ Pub. Trans.
✓ Parking	✓ Food Serv.	✓ Handicapped

Kiddie pool, slides, lessons, playground.

Boston Mills and Brandywine Ski Areas

AGES:	1½–3	3–5	5–8	8–12	12–15
RATING:	NR	★★	★★	★★★	★★★

COST: **$$$** PREP.: **None–Much**
AREA: **South** CITY: **Peninsula**

ADDRESS: 7100 Riverview Rd.

PHONE: (800) 875-4241

SEASON: Seasonal (Winter—natural & artificial snow)

HOURS: Boston Mills: Mon–Thu 9:30 a.m.–10:30 p.m., Fri–Sun 9:30 a.m.–10:30 p.m.; Brandywine: Mon–Thu 3 p.m.–10:30 p.m., Fri 3 p.m.–1 a.m., Sat 8:30 a.m.–1 a.m., Sun 8:30 a.m.–10:30 p.m.

PRICES: Daily $25 (4 hrs.), $30 (8 hrs.); $5 off for ages 12 & under w/ adult

DIRECT.: I-271 to Exit 18 for SR 8 (Akron Cleveland Rd.); south on SR 8; right on E. Highland Rd.; right (north) on Olde Eighte Rd.; left (west) on W. Highland; on left.

Or, I-77 to Exit 147 for Miller Rd.; east on Miller; right (south) on SR 21 (Brecksville Rd.); left (east) on Snowville Rd.; left (north) on Riverview Rd.; right (east) on Vaughn Rd. (becomes W. Highland); on right.

WEB: www.bmbw.com

✓ Strollers	✓ Groups	✓ Food Nearby
Diap Chg	Picnic	✓ Pub. Trans.
✓ Parking	✓ Food Serv.	✓ Handicapped

Boston Mills and Brandywine ski areas

These two downhill ski areas are located three miles apart in the Cuyahoga Valley National Recreation Area. Lift tickets are good for access to both areas, and a shuttle bus operates between them, so you can ski both on the same visit.

Half the 18 slopes are for beginners. A beginner package offered for ages 8 and up includes a lift ticket, equipment rental, and a group lesson. For skiers age 3–4 there is the Tiny Tot program; for ages 5–7, Mogul Mites; and a Junior Program for ages 8–16. Classes for the younger children focus on getting kids used to the equipment and the snow, and on teaching them how to stop and turn control. (Parents without skis are asked to assist the tots.) These classes are offered every weekend morning (call for times); the price includes equipment rental, lifts, and a one-hour group lesson. Private lessons are also available. Rentals are available.

Brainard Pool

South Euclid/Lyndhurst Recreation Dept.

AGES:	1½–3	3–5	5–8	8–12	12–15
RATING:	★★	★★	★★	★★	★★

COST: **$–$$** PREP.: **None–Much**
AREA: **East** CITY: **Lyndhurst**

ADDRESS: 1840 Brainard Rd.

PHONE: (440) 442-5844

SEASON: Seasonal (Jun–Sep)

HOURS: Weekdays & Sat 1:30 p.m.–8:30 p.m. (adult swim 5:20 p.m.–6:30 p.m.), Sun 1–6 p.m.

PRICES: $5 residents, $6 non-resident guests; individual family pass $30 each, maximum $90 per family

DIRECT.: I-271 to Exit 32 for Brainard/Cedar Rd.; north on Brainard; on left.

✓ Strollers ✓ Groups Food Nearby
Diap Chg ✓ Picnic ✓ Pub. Trans.
✓ Parking Food Serv. ✓ Handicapped

Kiddie pool, slides, lessons, playground.

Brecksville Community Center

AGES:	1½–3	3–5	5–8	8–12	12–15
RATING:	★★	★★	★★	★★	★★

COST: **$$** PREP.: **None–Much**
AREA: **South** CITY: **Brecksville**

ADDRESS: One Community Dr.

PHONE: (440) 546-2300

SEASON: Year round

HOURS: Vary

PRICES: $5 (residents only). Annual memberships available for residents only ($50–$210); Available for rental

DIRECT.: I-77 to Exit 151 for Wallings Ave.; east on Wallings; right (south) on SR 21 (Brecksville Rd.); left (east) on Community Dr.; on left.

✓ Strollers ✓ Groups ✓ Food Nearby
✓ Diap Chg ✓ Picnic ✓ Pub. Trans.
✓ Parking ✓ Food Serv. ✓ Handicapped

Olympic-size pool, kiddie pool, slides, fountains, lessons. Programs open to public (residents and non-residents).

Brecksville Stables/ Emerald Riding Academy

Cleveland Metroparks

AGES:	1½–3	3–5	5–8	8–12	12–15
RATING:	NR	★★	★★	★★★	★★★

COST: **$$–$$$** PREP.: **None–Much**
AREA: **South** CITY: **Brecksville**

ADDRESS: 11921 Parkview Dr.

PHONE: (440) 526-6767

SEASON: Year round

HOURS: Vary

PRICES: Vary

DIRECT.: I-77 to Exit 149 for SR 82 (Royalton Rd.); east on SR 82; right (south) on SR 21 (Brecksville Rd.); left (east) on Parkview Dr.; left (east) on Meadows Dr., Brecksville Reservation entrance; on left.

✓ Strollers ✓ Groups ✓ Food Nearby
Diap Chg Picnic Pub. Trans.
✓ Parking Food Serv. ✓ Handicapped

The Cleveland Metroparks stables offer year-round pony rides. English saddle horseback-riding instruction includes indoor group lessons (five to a group) for ages 8 and up, and private lessons for 6- and 7-year-olds. Indoor and outdoor lessons (weather depending) are offered on weekends for all ages. A therapeutic riding program is offered on Wednesdays for the physically or mentally challenged.

A summer mini-camp is offered in one-week sessions that run every day for two hours; for younger riders (ages 4–7) there is a pony camp.

Brooklyn Recreation Center

AGES:	1½–3	3–5	5–8	8–12	12–15
RATING:	NR	★★	★★★	★★★	★★★

COST: **$** PREP.: **None–Much**
AREA: **Near West** CITY: **Brooklyn**

ADDRESS: 7600 Memphis Ave.

PHONE: (216) 351-5334 (Rec Center); (216) 351-6781 (Natatorium)

SEASON: Year round (Natatorium: year round; outdoor pool Memorial Day–Labor Day)

HOURS: Vary

PRICES: Skating: $1 adult w/ ID $4 non-resident; $.50 student w/ID, $3 non-resident; $.50 skate rental w/ID, $2 non-resident; Swimming: $1 resident w/ ID, $7 non-resident; $.50 student w/ID, $5 non-resident; $3 non-resident seniors

DIRECT.: West: I-77 to Exit 242 for Bellaire Rd.; left (northeast) on Bellaire; right (southeast) on Memphis Ave.; on left.

Or, East: I-77 to Exit 245 for Fulton Rd.; south on Fulton; right (west) on Memphis; on right.

✓ Strollers ✓ Groups ✓ Food Nearby
✓ Diap Chg ✓ Picnic ✓ Pub. Trans.
✓ Parking ✓ Food Serv. ✓ Handicapped

Open skate times are scheduled in the morning, at lunchtime, in the afternoon, and in the evening. (Slight variations do occur to accommodate hockey games.) For preschoolers, a Tot and Parent skate is offered Wednesday mornings and Thursday afternoons. Special events include an annual Skate with Santa and an ice show.

Lessons are offered for ages 3 and up in three eight-week sessions during the season. Each lesson lasts 30 minutes and includes a special one-hour practice session. Lessons are also offered through the Brooklyn Hockey Association.

Skate rental and sharpening are offered. The rink is available for rental, and birthday parties can be arranged.

The Natatorium Swim Complex offers indoor and outdoor pools, a kiddie pool, and swim lessons. The Recreation Center also offers racquetball, roller-skating, an ice-skating gymnasium, and exercise equipment.

Camp Hi Canoe Livery

AGES:	1½–3	3–5	5–8	8–12	12–15
RATING:	NR	NR	★★	★★★	★★★

COST: **$–$$** PREP.: **Some**
AREA: **Far East** CITY: **Hiram**

ADDRESS: 12274 Abbott Rd.

PHONE: (330) 569-7621

SEASON: Seasonal (Spring–Fall)

HOURS: Daily 9 a.m.–6 p.m. (reservations required: scheduled only from 9 a.m. to 3 p.m.)

PRICES: $12–15 per person, 12 & under free (children as passengers in center of canoe); 3-hr., 7-mile trip: $24 for 2; 4-hr., 10-mile trip: $30 for 2

DIRECT.: US 422 to SR 44; south on SR 44; left (east) on SR 82; left (north) Abbott Rd.; on left.

✓ Strollers ✓ Groups ✓ Food Nearby
✓ Diap Chg ✓ Picnic ✓ Pub. Trans.
✓ Parking Food Serv. ✓ Handicapped

Camp Hi offers two canoe trips: a three-hour, 7-mile excursion ($24 for two people); and a four-hour, 10-mile trip ($30 for two) on 25 miles of the upper Cuyahoga River. Primarily slow and flat, they are ideal for novices. Excursions are unguided and time slots need to be reserved between 9 a.m. and 3 p.m. Limit 10 people per group.

Chalet Recreation Area

Cleveland Metroparks

AGES:	1½–3	3–5	5–8	8–12	12–15
RATING:	NR	NR	★★	★★★	★★★

COST: **$** PREP.: **None–Some**
AREA: **Southwest** CITY: **Strongsville**

ADDRESS: 16200 Valley Pkwy. (Mill Stream Reservation)

PHONE: (440) 572-9990

SEASON: Seasonal (Sept–Feb, hayride/toboggan; Mar–Aug, reserved group picnic area)

HOURS: Vary

PRICES: Toboggan: adults $8, children $6; Hayrides: adults $6, children $4, free for children 2 and under (must ride on adult's lap)

DIRECT.: I-71 to Exit 231 for SR 82 (Royalton Rd.); east on SR 82; left (north) on Valley View Pkwy.; on left.

✓ Strollers ✓ Groups ✓ Food Nearby
Diap Chg ✓ Picnic Pub. Trans.
✓ Parking ✓ Food Serv. ✓ Handicapped

A year-round recreation spot with hayrides, square dancing, ball fields, and a playground, the chalet comes alive in the winter months for tobogganing. The 1,000-foot, refrigerated ice chutes offer a thrilling ride. (Children must be 42 inches or taller to ride.) The hike up the stairs can be chilling (gloves or mittens are required). Inside, the fireplaces are very popular indeed.

Chardon Memorial Pool

AGES:	1½–3	3–5	5–8	8–12	12–15
RATING:	★★	★★	★★	★★	★★

COST: **$** PREP.: **None–Much**
AREA: **Far East** CITY: **Chardon**

ADDRESS: 316 Maple Ave.

PHONE: (440) 286-2672

SEASON: Seasonal (Jun–Sep)

HOURS: Vary

PRICES: $3, $2 under 18, no charge under age 3; season passes avail. for residents and non-residents

DIRECT.: I-90 to Exit 200 for SR 44; south on SR 44; left (east) on Center St. through Chardon; east on N. Hambden St.; left (north) on Maple Ave; on left

✓ Strollers ✓ Groups ✓ Food Nearby
✓ Diap Chg Picnic Pub. Trans.
✓ Parking Food Serv. ✓ Handicapped

Kiddie pool, lessons, playground.

Clague Park Pool

AGES:	1½–3	3–5	5–8	8–12	12–15
RATING:	★★★	★★★	★★	★★	★★

COST: **$** PREP.: **None–Much**
AREA: **West** CITY: **Westlake**

ADDRESS: 1500 Clague Rd.

PHONE: (440) 835-6436

SEASON: Seasonal (Jun–Labor Day)

HOURS: Jun–early Aug: 1 p.m.–9 p.m.; early Aug–Labor Day: noon–8 p.m.

PRICES: Residents w/passes: $5 adults, $4.50 children (12 & under), free under age 6 with paying adult, or age 65 and older; season pass: $65 resident, $100 non-resident

DIRECT.: I-480 to Exit 7 for Clague Rd.; north on Clague; on left.

Or, I-90 to Exit 160 for Clague Rd.; south on Clague; on right.

✓ Strollers ✓ Groups ✓ Food Nearby
✓ Diap Chg ✓ Picnic ✓ Pub. Trans.
✓ Parking ✓ Food Serv. ✓ Handicapped

Kiddie pool, slides, fountain, lessons, playground.

Cleveland Heights Pavilion

Cleveland Heights Parks & Recreation

AGES:	1½–3	3–5	5–8	8–12	12–15
RATING:	NR	★★	★★★	★★★	★★★

COST: **$** PREP.: **None–Much**
AREA: **East** CITY: **Cleveland Hts.**

ADDRESS: 1 Monticello Blvd. (corner of Mayfield and Superior)

PHONE: (216) 691-7373

SEASON: Seasonal (Sep–Apr)

HOURS: Vary

PRICES: $2.25 adult residents w/ ID, $1.50 residents grades K–12, $4.50 non-residents

DIRECT.: West: I-90 to Exit 178 for Eddy Rd.; south on Eddy to Kirby Ave.; east on Kirby; right (southeast) on Coit Rd.; left (east) on Noble Rd.; left (west) on Monticello Blvd.; on left.

East: I-271 to Exit 36 for Wilson Mills Rd.; west on Wilson Mills; Wilson Mills becomes Monticello Blvd.; on left.

✓ Strollers ✓ Groups ✓ Food Nearby
✓ Diap Chg ✓ Picnic ✓ Pub. Trans.
✓ Parking ✓ Food Serv. ✓ Handicapped

The schedule of skating times changes throughout the season to accommodate lessons, hockey, and special events, such as the annual Skate with Frosty and the Halloween dress-up skate.

For preschoolers, a parent-and-tot session is held weekly. There are also Learn-to-Skate sessions for all ages.

Lessons for ages 3–adult are offered throughout the season in sessions lasting six or seven weeks.

The youth hockey league for ages 4–17 is open to residents of University Heights, Cleveland Heights, and communities that do not have ice-hockey programs. Children are placed in divisions based on their birth dates.

Skate rental, sharpening, and lockers are offered. The rink is available for rental. An annual used equipment and skate sale in the summer is a hockey league fundraiser and great way for parents to save on gear.

Cleveland Rock Gym

AGES:	1½–3	3–5	5–8	8–12	12–15
RATING:	NR	NR	NR	★★	★★★

COST: **$$–$$$** PREP.: **None–Some**
AREA: **East** CITY: **Euclid**

ADDRESS: 21200 St. Clair Ave. Bldg. B-3

PHONE: (216) 692-3300

SEASON: Year round

HOURS: Mon–Fri noon–10 p.m., Sat–Sun noon–6 p.m. (closed Mon Jun–Sep)

PRICES: $15 per person for introduction to climbing sessions Tue or Thu; $35 Sat morning or Wed eve belay class; $10 one-day pass; $5 ages 13 and under.

DIRECT.: I-90 to Exit 182 for E. 200 St.; right (south) on E. 200; left (east) on St. Clair Ave.; on right.

Strollers ✓ Groups ✓ Food Nearby
Diap Chg Picnic ✓ Pub. Trans.
✓ Parking ✓ Food Serv. ✓ Handicapped

First-timers and aficionados starved for rock-climbing experiences are both attracted to this unusual gym. The two-hour introductory class covers safety and technique and includes time on the 30-foot wall with an instructor. The wood and fake stone face covering most of the side of a former warehouse can be daunting for the novice or the faint of heart.

Cumberland Pool

Cleveland Hts. Recreation Dept.

AGES:	1½–3	3–5	5–8	8–12	12–15
RATING:	★★	★★	★★	★★	★★

COST: **$** PREP.: **None–Much**
AREA: **East** CITY: **Cleveland Hts.**

ADDRESS: 1740 Cumberland Rd.

PHONE: (216) 691-7390

SEASON: Seasonal (mid-Jun–Sep)

HOURS: Mon–Fri 1–8 p.m., Sat–Sun 1 p.m.–6 p.m.; family swim Mon–Fri 5–8 p.m.; lap swim Mon–Fri 6:45 a.m.–8 p.m.

PRICES: $2 adult residents w/ ID, $1.50 student resident w/ ID, $3 non-resident guests

DIRECT.: West: I-90 to Exit 173B for Chester Ave. (Eastbound: left (south) on E. 24 St.; left (east) on Chester); east on Chester; left (northeast) on Euclid Ave.; right (east) on US 322 (Mayfield Rd.); right (south) on Cumberland Dr.; on right.

East: I-271 to Exit 34 for US 322 (Mayfield Rd.); west on Mayfield; after Lee Rd., left (south) on Cumberland Dr.; on right.

✓ Strollers	✓ Groups	✓ Food Nearby
✓ Diap Chg	✓ Picnic	✓ Pub. Trans.
✓ Parking	✓ Food Serv.	✓ Handicapped

Kiddie pool, lessons.

Dan Kostel Recreation Center

Garfield Hts. Recreation Dept.

AGES:	1½–3	3–5	5–8	8–12	12–15
RATING:	★★	★★	★★	★★	★★

COST: **$–$$** PREP.: **None–Much**
AREA: **South** CITY: **Garfield Hts.**

ADDRESS: 5411 Turney Rd.

PHONE: (216) 475-7272

SEASON: Seasonal (pool: mid-Jun–Labor Day; skating: mid-Sep–mid-Mar)

HOURS: Vary

PRICES: Resident ID card $4; admission with ID—$2 adult, $1.50 students/children, ages 4 and under free with paying adult. Non-resident ID card can be purchased if enrolling in skating or swimming class.

DIRECT.: I-480 to Exit 21 for Transportation Blvd.; north on Transportation; right (east) on Granger Rd.; right (south) on Turney Rd.; left at Civic Center; on right.

Strollers	✓ Groups	✓ Food Nearby
Diap Chg	✓ Picnic	✓ Pub. Trans.
✓ Parking	✓ Food Serv.	✓ Handicapped

The daily ice schedule changes to accommodate lessons, hockey, and special events, including a Halloween skate and a skate with Santa.

Skating lessons for ages 3 and up, including a preschooler with parent lesson, are held throughout the season in three sessions. Hockey also starts at preschool age, with season-long play. Skate rentals and skate sharpening are available. Private parties can be arranged.

Kiddie pool and lessons are also offered.

Denison Pool

Cleveland Hts. Recreation Board

AGES:	1½–3	3–5	5–8	8–12	12–15
RATING:	★★	★★	★★	★★	★★

COST: **$** PREP.: **None–Much**
AREA: **East** CITY: **Cleveland Hts.**

ADDRESS: 1015 Quarry Rd.

PHONE: (216) 691-7393

SEASON: Seasonal (mid-Jun–Sep)

HOURS: Mon–Fri 1–8 p.m., Sat–Sun 1–6 p.m.; family swim Mon–Fri 5–8 p.m.

PRICES: $2 adult residents w/ ID, $1.50 student resident w/ ID, $3 non-resident guests

DIRECT.: I-271 to Exit 36 for Wilson Mills Rd.; west on Wilson Mills; Wilson Mills becomes Monticello Blvd.; left (southeast) on Quarry Rd.; on right.

✓ Strollers	✓ Groups	✓ Food Nearby
✓ Diap Chg	✓ Picnic	✓ Pub. Trans.
✓ Parking	✓ Food Serv.	✓ Handicapped

Kiddie pool, slides, lessons.

Dudley Pool

Willowick Recreation Dept.

AGES:	1½–3	3–5	5–8	8–12	12–15
RATING:	★★	★★	★★	★★	★★

COST: **$** PREP.: **None**
AREA: **East** CITY: **Willowick**

ADDRESS: 31500 Willowick Dr.

PHONE: (440) 943-3970

SEASON: Seasonal (Jun–Sep)

HOURS: Mon–Fri 11 a.m.–8 p.m., Sat–Sun 11 a.m.–5 p.m.

PRICES: $3 residents/non-residents

DIRECT.: SR 2 to E. 305 St.; north on E. 305; right (east) on Willowick Dr.; on left.

✓ Strollers ✓ Groups ✓ Food Nearby
✓ Diap Chg ✓ Picnic Pub. Trans.
✓ Parking Food Serv. ✓ Handicapped

Water slides and playground equipment.

Dunham Recreation Center

Maple Heights Recreation Dept.

AGES:	1½–3	3–5	5–8	8–12	12–15
RATING:	★★	★★	★★	★★	★★

COST: **$** PREP.: **None–Much**
AREA: **Southeast** CITY: **Maple Hts.**

ADDRESS: 15005 Schreiber Rd.

PHONE: (216) 475-1811; (216) 663-0552 (office)

SEASON: Seasonal (Mid-Jun–Aug)

HOURS: Vary

PRICES: Residents: $.50, $.25 under age 18; non-residents: $4, $3 under age 18

DIRECT.: I-480 to Exit 22 for Granger Rd.; west on Granger; left (south) on Turney Rd.; right (south) on Dunham Rd.; right (west) on Schreiber Rd.; on right.

Strollers Groups ✓ Food Nearby
✓ Diap Chg ✓ Picnic ✓ Pub. Trans.
✓ Parking ✓ Food Serv. ✓ Handicapped

Olympic-size pool, kiddie pool, slides, fountains, lessons.

Euclid Orr Ice Rink

Euclid Park and Recreation Dept.

AGES:	1½–3	3–5	5–8	8–12	12–15
RATING:	NR	★	★★★	★★★	★★

COST: **$** PREP.: **None–Much**
AREA: **East** CITY: **Euclid**

ADDRESS: 22550 Milton Dr.

PHONE: (216) 289-8649; Recording: (216) 289-8630

SEASON: Seasonal (Sep–early May)

HOURS: Vary

PRICES: $3 adult residents w/ID, $2.50 under 18 w/ID, $3.50 non-residents, $2 seniors, $1.50 skate rental

DIRECT.: I-90 to Exit 184A/B for Babbitt Rd.; north on Babbitt; left (west) on Milton Ave.; on left.

✓ Strollers ✓ Groups ✓ Food Nearby
Diap Chg ✓ Picnic ✓ Pub. Trans.
✓ Parking ✓ Food Serv. ✓ Handicapped

Open skating sessions vary to accommodate lessons and hockey games. Annual events include a Halloween Costume Skate and a Skate with Santa, as well as hockey tournaments.

Skating lessons are offered for ages 3 and up in four six-week sessions. Lessons are also available through the youth hockey program. Skate rental, skate sharpening, and lockers are available. Birthday parties can be arranged.

Foster Pool

Lakewood Recreation Dept.

AGES:	1½–3	3–5	5–8	8–12	12–15
RATING:	★★	★★	★★	★★	★★

COST: **$** PREP.: **None–Much**
AREA: **Near West** CITY: **Lakewood**

ADDRESS: 14532 Lake Ave. (at Belle and Lake)

PHONE: (216) 529-4121

SEASON: Seasonal (Jun–Sep)

HOURS: Open swims: Mon–Fri 1–4 p.m. & 6–8 p.m., Sat & Sun 1 p.m.–8 p.m.

PRICES: Residents: adults $2.50, students $2, children 6 and under & seniors free; Nonresidents: adults $3.50, students $3, children 6 and under & seniors $2

DIRECT.: I-90 to Warren Rd.; north on Warren; right (east) on Clifton Blvd.; left (north) on Belle Ave.

✓ Strollers ✓ Groups ✓ Food Nearby
✓ Diap Chg ✓ Picnic ✓ Pub. Trans.
✓ Parking ✓ Food Serv. ✓ Handicapped

Kiddie pool, lessons, playground. Located adjacent to the lakefront in Lakewood Park.

Grand River Canoe Livery

AGES:	1½–3	3–5	5–8	8–12	12–15
RATING:	NR	★	★	★★★	★★★

COST: **$$–$$$** PREP.: **None–Some**
AREA: **Far East** CITY: **Rock Creek**

ADDRESS: 3825 Fobes Rd.

PHONE: (800) ME-CANOE

SEASON: Seasonal (Daily in summer; weekends spring & fall)

HOURS: 9 a.m.–dusk

PRICES: $19–27.50 per canoe, depending on number of passengers

DIRECT.: I-90 to Exit 223 for SR 45; south on SR 45; right (west) on Fobes Rd.

Strollers	✓ Groups	✓ Food Nearby
Diap Chg	✓ Picnic	Pub. Trans.
✓ Parking	Food Serv.	Handicapped

Canoe trips from two to five hours in length (with the longest ones in the fall) start from this small livery on the Grand River, a state-designated scenic waterway which runs through woods and farmland in Ashtabula and Lake counties. Tours are not guided. Four to seven canoes are available for large groups.

Great Lakes Gymnastics

AGES:	1½–3	3–5	5–8	8–12	12–15
RATING:	★★	★★	★★	★★	★★

COST: **$$$** PREP.: **Much**
AREA: **Far West** CITY: **Avon Lake**

ADDRESS: 33600 Pin Oak Pkwy. P.O. Box 12

PHONE: (440) 933-2674

SEASON: Year round

HOURS: Office hours weekdays 9 a.m.–1 p.m.

PRICES: Vary

DIRECT.: I-90 to Exit for SR 611; northwest on SR 611; right (east) on Chester Rd.; left (north) on Moore Rd.; right (east) on Pin Oak Pkwy.; on right.

Strollers	✓ Groups	✓ Food Nearby
Diap Chg	Picnic	Pub. Trans.
✓ Parking	Food Serv.	✓ Handicapped

Gymnastics classes for boys and girls in this 15,000-square-foot gymnasium feature an exercise or warm-up period to develop strength and flexibility. Classes are subdivided so that students are working on skills appropriate for their abilities.

Preschoolers as young as 2 work with their parents to acquire basic gymnastic and movement-coordination skills. Kindergarten classes are divided into boys' and girls' groups and equipment is adapted to the interests and capabilities of the age group.

Greenbrier Ice Rink

Parma Heights Recreation Center

AGES:	1½–3	3–5	5–8	8–12	12–15
RATING:	NR	★★	★★	★★★	★★

COST: **$** PREP.: **None–Much**
AREA: **South** CITY: **Parma Hts.**

ADDRESS: 6200 Pearl Rd.

PHONE: (440) 842-5005

SEASON: Seasonal (Sep–May, special programs during the summer)

HOURS: Vary

PRICES: Residents: $3.50 adult, $2.50 student; non-residents: $4 adult, $3 student; Skate rental: $2

DIRECT.: West: I-480 to Exit 12 for Brookpark Rd.; left (east) on Brookpark; right (south) on Chevrolet Blvd. (becomes Stumph Rd. after Snow Rd.); left (north) on Pearl Rd.; on left.

East: I-480 to Exit 16 for SR 94 (State Rd.); south on State; right (west) on SR 17 (Brookpark Rd.); left (south) on Pearl Rd.; on right.

✓ Strollers	✓ Groups	✓ Food Nearby
Diap Chg	✓ Picnic	✓ Pub. Trans.
✓ Parking	✓ Food Serv.	✓ Handicapped

Open skating sessions include an after-school session for families. Lessons are offered for ages 3 and up throughout the season, primarily on weekends. Lessons are also available through the youth hockey program. Skate rentals and lockers are available. Birthday parties can be arranged.

Gymboree Play and Music, Beachwood

AGES:	1½–3	3–5	5–8	8–12	12–15
RATING:	★★★	★★	NR	NR	NR

COST: **$$$** PREP.: **None–Much**
AREA: **East** CITY: **Beachwood**

ADDRESS: 1980 S. Green Rd.

PHONE: (216) 291-9969

SEASON: Year round

HOURS: Vary

PRICES: $125 for 14-week courses

DIRECT.: Beachwood: I-271 to Exit 32 for Brainard/Cedar Rd.; left (south) on Brainard; right (west) on Cedar; right (north) on S. Green Rd.; on left.

✓ Strollers · Groups · ✓ Food Nearby
✓ Diap Chg · Picnic · ✓ Pub. Trans.
✓ Parking · Food Serv. · Handicapped

Music, movement, fun, and games are offered here in a colorful room created for playful interaction by parents and their 3-month- to 5-year-old children. Kindermusik creative music classes for children 1½–5 years are also offered.

Gymboree Play and Music, Strongsville

AGES:	1½–3	3–5	5–8	8–12	12–15
RATING:	★★★	★★	NR	NR	NR

COST: **$$$** PREP.: **None–Much**
AREA: **East** CITY: **Strongsville**

ADDRESS: 18100 Royalton Rd.

PHONE: (440) 878-6000

SEASON: Year round

HOURS: Vary

PRICES: $125 for 14-week courses

DIRECT.: Strongsville: I-71 to Exit 231 for SR 82 (Royalton Rd.); west on Royalton; on right in Target shopping center at Strongsville Recreation Center.

✓ Strollers · Groups · ✓ Food Nearby
✓ Diap Chg · Picnic · ✓ Pub. Trans.
✓ Parking · Food Serv. · Handicapped

(See previous listing.)

Houston-Fisher Pool

AGES:	1½–3	3–5	5–8	8–12	12–15
RATING:	★★	★★	★★	★★	★★

COST: **$** PREP.: **None–Much**
AREA: **East** CITY: **Eastlake**

ADDRESS: Jakse Dr.

PHONE: (440) 975-4269

SEASON: Seasonal (Jun–Sep)

HOURS: Daily 1–5 p.m., 6–9 p.m. (closes at 8 p.m. on Tue, Thu, Fri)

PRICES: $2 per person; $55 family season pass, $25 individual season pass

DIRECT.: SR 2 to SR 91; north on SR 91; left (west) on Stevens Blvd.; left (south) on Jakse Dr.

✓ Strollers · ✓ Groups · ✓ Food Nearby
Diap Chg · ✓ Picnic · Pub. Trans.
✓ Parking · Food Serv. · ✓ Handicapped

Kiddie pool, lessons, playground.

Jewish Community Center
Mandel Campus

AGES:	1½–3	3–5	5–8	8–12	12–15
RATING:	★★	★★	★★	★★	★★

COST: **FREE–$$** PREP.: **Much**
AREA: **East** CITY: **Beachwood**

ADDRESS: 26001 S. Woodland Rd.

PHONE: (216) 831-0700

SEASON: Year round

HOURS: Mon–Thu 6 a.m.–10:30 p.m., Fri 6 a.m.–5:30 p.m., Sat noon–6:30 p.m., Sun 8 a.m.–6 p.m.

PRICES: Vary

DIRECT.: I-271 to Exit 29 for Chagrin Blvd.; west on Chagrin; right (north) on Richmond Rd.; right (east) on S. Woodland Rd.; on left.

✓ Strollers ✓ Groups ✓ Food Nearby
✓ Diap Chg ✓ Picnic Pub. Trans.
✓ Parking ✓ Food Serv. ✓ Handicapped

This neighborhood institution offers a flurry of activities for younger children and their parents. Class offerings are extensive. For children ages 4 months and up there is infant massage, music therapy, tumbling, arts and crafts, and storytelling. Through the preschool department (ages 2½–5) there are classes in dance, cooking, swimming, drama, and pottery.

For adults, parenting classes cover nutrition, separation anxiety, and infant care. Each year there are special workshops and discussions.

In summer months, there are a number of camps designed around age groups and special activities.

Of special interest to parents is Family Place. Specifically designed for parents with children up to age 3½, it provides a drop-in center with parent-child activities and support from other parents and staff.

Special events here are also popular, with a concentration on traditional Jewish holidays. Chanukah is celebrated with a program including music, arts, crafts, and food for the entire family. A new meeting and catering facility holds up to 500 people for large gatherings.

Jewish Community Center
Mayfield Campus

AGES:	1½–3	3–5	5–8	8–12	12–15
RATING:	★★	★★	★★	★★	★★

COST: **FREE–$$** PREP.: **Much**
AREA: **East** CITY: **Cleveland Hts.**

ADDRESS: 3505 Mayfield Rd.
PHONE: (216) 382-4000
SEASON: Year round
HOURS: Mon–Thu 6 a.m.–10 p.m., Fri 6 a.m.–5 p.m., Sat Closed, Sun 8 a.m.–5 p.m.
PRICES: Vary
DIRECT.: West: I-90 to Exit 178 for Eddy Rd.; south on Eddy to Kirby Ave.; east on Kirby; right (southeast) on Coit Rd.; left (east) on Noble Rd.; left (west) on Mayfield Rd.; on right.
East: I-271 to Exit 34 for Mayfield Rd.; west on Mayfield; on right.

✓ Strollers ✓ Groups ✓ Food Nearby
✓ Diap Chg ✓ Picnic ✓ Pub. Trans.
✓ Parking ✓ Food Serv. ✓ Handicapped

See previous listing for Jewish Community Center, Beachwood for details.

Extended day care (all day preschool program) and After-school Kid Center classes available.

Lake Erie Gymnastics School

AGES:	1½–3	3–5	5–8	8–12	12–15
RATING:	★★	★★	★★★	★★★	★★★

COST: **$$–$$$** PREP.: **Much**
AREA: **Far East** CITY: **Mentor**

ADDRESS: 9373 Hamilton Dr.
PHONE: (440) 358-1284
SEASON: Year round
HOURS: Vary
PRICES: Vary
DIRECT.: SR 2 to Heisley Rd.; south on Heisley; left (east) on Hamilton Dr.; on left.

✓ Strollers ✓ Groups ✓ Food Nearby
Diap Chg Picnic Pub. Trans.
✓ Parking Food Serv. ✓ Handicapped

This gymnastics school includes team-level instruction for boys and girls through their high-school years. Special classes are designed for preschoolers ages 2–5, including a parent-and-child tumbling class. Also available: recreational gymnastic instruction for first grade through high school; evening classes in high-school cheerleading and tumbling (combined).

Lakeland Community College/College for Kids

AGES:	1½–3	3–5	5–8	8–12	12–15
RATING:	★★	★★	★★	★★★	★★★

COST: **$$$** PREP.: **Some–Much**
AREA: **Far East** CITY: **Kirtland**

ADDRESS: 7700 Clocktower Dr.

PHONE: (440) 953-7116

SEASON: Year round

HOURS: Vary

PRICES: Vary

DIRECT.: I-90 to Exit 190 for SR 306; south on SR 306; left (east) on Clocktower Dr.

WEB: www.lakeland.cc.oh.us

Strollers | Groups | ✓ Food Nearby
Diap Chg | ✓ Picnic | ✓ Pub. Trans.
✓ Parking | ✓ Food Serv. | ✓ Handicapped

Lakeland's College for Kids lists extensive course offerings in creative arts, ballet, aikido, and computers. Quarterly sessions typically run for 8 to 12 weeks, depending on the type of class. Also offered are 8 weeks of summer camps and a week-long mini-camp in early spring, designed around recreational and educational activities, arts, and crafts.

College for Kids, Lakeland Community College

Lakeland's College for Teens programs offer a variety of educational and leisure activities for junior and senior high school students, including Computer-Aided Design, Criminalistics, Theater, Video Production, Hands-On Science, and more. All classes are offered quarterly; some are held in neighborhood locations. There are also spring and summer camps. For younger kids there is a First Steps body awareness and coordination program and gymnastics.

An annual two-day jazz festival showcases area high-school bands.

Little Gym, North Olmsted

AGES:	1½–3	3–5	5–8	8–12	12–15
RATING:	★★★	★★★	★★★	★	NR

COST: **$$** PREP.: **Some–Much**
AREA: **West** CITY: **North Olmsted**

ADDRESS: 24140 Lorain Rd. (Lauren Hill Plaza)

PHONE: (440) 734-4900

SEASON: Year round

HOURS: Mon–Fri 9 a.m.–7:30 p.m.; Sat 9 a.m.–1 p.m.; class times vary by age; birthday parties on Fri evenings, Sat & Sun afternoons

PRICES: Vary

DIRECT.: I-90 to Exit 159 for SR 252 (Columbia Rd.); south on Columbia; left (east) on SR 10 (Lorain Rd.); on right.

Or, I-480 to Exit 6 for Great Northern Blvd.; north on Great Northern; right (east) on SR 10 (Lorain Rd.); on right.

Strollers | ✓ Groups | ✓ Food Nearby
Diap Chg | Picnic | ✓ Pub. Trans.
✓ Parking | Food Serv. | Handicapped

This child-friendly fitness and development center offers age-appropriate instruction in gymnastics, sports skills, karate, and fitness. Programs are designed to build self-confidence and self-esteem. Weekend birthday parties are available.

Sports & Recreation DIRECTORY

✓ Strollers	✓ Groups	Food Nearby
Diap Chg	✓ Picnic	✓ Pub. Trans.
✓ Parking	Food Serv.	✓ Handicapped

Kiddie pool, lessons, playground.

Little Gym, Twinsburg

AGES:	1½–3	3–5	5–8	8–12	12–15
RATING:	★★★	★★★	★★★	★	NR

COST: **$$** PREP.: **Much**
AREA: **East** CITY: **Twinsburg**

ADDRESS: 8922 Darrow Rd.

PHONE: (330) 405-9640

SEASON: Year round

HOURS: Mon–Fri 9 a.m.–7:30 p.m.; Sat 9 a.m.–1 p.m.; class times vary by age; birthday parties on Fri evenings, Sat & Sun afternoons

PRICES: Vary

DIRECT.: I-480 to Exit 37 for SR 91; north on SR 91; on left.

Strollers	✓ Groups	✓ Food Nearby
Diap Chg	Picnic	✓ Pub. Trans.
✓ Parking	Food Serv.	Handicapped

This child-friendly fitness and development center offers age-appropriate instruction in gymnastics, sports skills, karate, and fitness. Programs are designed to build self-confidence and self-esteem. Weekend birthday parties are available.

Lyndhurst Pool

South Euclid/Lyndhurst Recreation Dept.

AGES:	1½–3	3–5	5–8	8–12	12–15
RATING:	★★	★★	★★	★★	★★

COST: **$–$$** PREP.: **None–Much**
AREA: **East** CITY: **Lyndhurst**

ADDRESS: 1331 Parkview Rd.

PHONE: (440) 442-8469

SEASON: Seasonal (Jun–Sep)

HOURS: Mon–Sat 1:30–8:30 p.m., Sun 1–6 p.m.

PRICES: $5 residents, $6 non-resident guests; individual family pass $30 each, maximum $90 per family

DIRECT.: I-271 to Exit 34 for Mayfield Rd.; west on Mayfield; right (north) on Parkview Rd.; on right.

Madison Pool

AGES:	1½–3	3–5	5–8	8–12	12–15
RATING:	★★	★★	★★	★★	★★

COST: **$** PREP.: **None–Much**
AREA: **Near West** CITY: **Lakewood**

ADDRESS: 13029 Madison Ave.

PHONE: (216) 529-4120

SEASON: Seasonal (Jun–Sep)

HOURS: Weekdays 1–7 p.m., weekends 1–8 p.m.

PRICES: Residents: adults $2.50, students $2, children 6 and under & seniors free; non-residents: adults $3.50, students $3, children 6 and under & seniors $2. Season passes: residents: adults $25, students $20; non-residents: adults $50, students $40, seniors $40

DIRECT.: East: I-90 to Exit 166 for W. 117 St.; north on W. 117; left (west) on Madison Ave.; Madison Park on left.

West: I-90 to Exit 165 for W. 140/Bunts Rd.; north on Bunts; right (east) on Madison Ave.; Madison Park on right.

✓ Strollers	✓ Groups	✓ Food Nearby
✓ Diap Chg	✓ Picnic	✓ Pub. Trans.
✓ Parking	✓ Food Serv.	✓ Handicapped

Kiddie pool, fountain, slide, lessons, playground.

Manry Pool

Willowick Recreation Dept.

AGES:	1½–3	3–5	5–8	8–12	12–15
RATING:	★★	★★	★★	★★	★★

COST: **$** PREP.: **None–Much**
AREA: **East** CITY: **Willowick**

ADDRESS: 30100 Arnold Dr.

PHONE: (440) 944-1575

SEASON: Seasonal (Jun–Sep)

HOURS: Mon–Fri 1 p.m.–8 p.m.; Sat–Sun 11 a.m.–6 p.m.

Mentor Civic Arena and Waterpark

PRICES: $3 residents & non-residents; kiddie pool free; family swim free Mon & Wed 8–10 p.m.

DIRECT.: SR 2 to E. 305 St.; north on E. 305; left (east) on Arnold St.

✓ Strollers ✓ Groups ✓ Food Nearby
✓ Diap Chg ✓ Picnic ✓ Pub. Trans.
✓ Parking ✓ Food Serv. Handicapped

Kiddie pool (FREE to the public), swim lessons, playground.

Mentor Civic Arena and Waterpark

AGES:	1½–3	3–5	5–8	8–12	12–15
RATING:	★★	★★	★★	★★	★★

COST: **$** PREP.: **None–Much**
AREA: **Far East** CITY: **Mentor**

ADDRESS: 8600 Munson Rd.

PHONE: (440) 974-5730; (440) 974-8260 (pool)

SEASON: Year round (pool: Memorial Day–Labor Day; skating: year round)

HOURS: Vary

PRICES: Pool: $3.50, $3 ages 4–17, no charge under age 3; Rink: adults $3.75, ages 4–17 $3.25; locker rental available; pool rental available.

DIRECT.: SR 2 to SR 615; north on SR 615; right (east) on Civic Center Blvd.; right (south) on Munson Rd.; on left.

✓ Strollers ✓ Groups ✓ Food Nearby
✓ Diap Chg ✓ Picnic ✓ Pub. Trans.
✓ Parking ✓ Food Serv. ✓ Handicapped

Open skating sessions include after-school skates Monday through Thursday, luncheon skates, and evening skates on weekends, with special hours during the winter holidays. Skating lessons for ages 3 and up are offered in several sessions through the season, including a mini-session during the winter holidays. Skate rentals, sharpening, and lockers are available; the rink can be rented for private parties.

The pool also has a kiddie pool, slides, and lessons. The recreation center gym is used for gymnastics, tumbling, and indoor activities.

North Coast Gymnastics Center

AGES:	1½–3	3–5	5–8	8–12	12–15
RATING:	★★	★★	★★	★★	★★

COST: **$$–$$$** PREP.: **Much**
AREA: **East** CITY: **Cleveland**

ADDRESS: 4505 Northfield Rd.

PHONE: (216) 663-6993

SEASON: Year round

HOURS: Vary

PRICES: Vary

DIRECT.: West: I-480 to Exit 25C for SR 8 (Northfield Rd.); left (north) on Northfield; on right.

East: I-271 to Exit 27 for Miles Rd.; right (north) on Miles; right (north) on Northfield Rd.; on right.

South: I-480 to Exit 25 for Aurora Rd.; left (northwest) on Aurora; right (north) on Northfield Rd.; on right.

Strollers	Groups	✓ Food Nearby
Diap Chg	Picnic	✓ Pub. Trans.
✓ Parking	Food Serv.	✓ Handicapped

Olympic-style instruction for boys and girls starts from age 10 months. Classes for 7–9 and 10–teen include power tumbling and competitive teams. Parent and tot classes begin with Tiny Tumblers for ages 1–2.

North Olmsted Recreation Center

AGES:	1½–3	3–5	5–8	8–12	12–15
RATING:	★★	★★	★★	★★	★★

COST: **$** PREP.: **None–Much**
AREA: **West** CITY: **North Olmsted**

ADDRESS: 26000 Lorain Rd.

PHONE: (440) 734-8200

SEASON: Year round

HOURS: Vary

PRICES: $3–$5 depending on activity

DIRECT.: I-480 to Exit 6 for Great Northern Blvd.; north on Great Northern; left (west) on Lorain Rd.; on right.

✓ Strollers	✓ Groups	✓ Food Nearby
✓ Diap Chg	Picnic	✓ Pub. Trans.
✓ Parking	✓ Food Serv.	✓ Handicapped

The ice-skating schedule here varies; open sessions are held most afternoons and weekend evenings (October to mid-April). Special events include a Halloween skate and a Skate with Frosty and Santa. A hockey minicamp is also offered in late December.

Skating lessons for ages 3 and up are offered in five sessions during the season. Hockey lessons for ages 4–8 are also offered through the Hockey Club's Mighty Mite program. Skate rentals, skate sharpening, and lockers are available. Birthday parties can be arranged.

Other activities here include swimming and a playground. The indoor gym is used for gymnastics, volleyball, basketball, and karate. Holiday craft classes are also offered.

Public Square Ice-Skating Rink

AGES:	1½–3	3–5	5–8	8–12	12–15
RATING:	NR	★	★★	★★	★★

COST: **$** PREP.: **None**
AREA: **Downtown** CITY: **Cleveland**

ADDRESS: 200 Tower City Center, 50 Public Square

PHONE: (216) 621-3300

SEASON: Seasonal (Fri after Thanksgiving–mid-Jan)

HOURS: Vary

PRICES: Vary

DIRECT.: West: I-90 to Exit 171B for Ontario St.; north on Ontario; on left.

East: SR 2 to East 9 St.; south on E. 9; left (west) on Lakeside Ave.; left (south) on Ontario St.; on right.

Strollers	Groups	✓ Food Nearby
Diap Chg	Picnic	✓ Pub. Trans.
Parking	Food Serv.	✓ Handicapped

Aside from open skating, this small rink hosts a variety of special events, such as figure-skating exhibitions and ice-carving competitions, all arranged by the Greater Cleveland Growth Association. Skate rentals are offered; the rink is available for private parties.

Note: The ice rink plans to reopen in 1999 with changes in hours and prices. For a complete schedule (which varies from year to year) send a self-addressed, stamped envelope to

Holiday Activity Schedule, Greater Cleveland Growth Association, 50 Public Square, Cleveland, 44113.

Public Square Ice-Skating Rink

Quarry Pool

South Euclid/Lyndhurst Recreation Dept.

AGES:	1½–3	3–5	5–8	8–12	12–15
RATING:	★★	★★	★★	★★	★★

COST: **$–$$** PREP.: **None**
AREA: **East** CITY: **South Euclid**

ADDRESS: 711 S. Belvoir Blvd.

PHONE: (216) 381-7674

SEASON: Seasonal (Jun–Sep)

HOURS: Daily 1:30 p.m.–8 p.m.

PRICES: $5 residents, $6 non-resident guests; individual family pass $30 each, maximum $90 per family

DIRECT.: I-271 to Exit 36 for Wilson Mills Rd.; west on Wilson Mills; Wilson Mills becomes Monticello Blvd.; left (southeast) on S. Belvoir Blvd.; on left.

✓ Strollers ✓ Groups Food Nearby
Diap Chg ✓ Picnic ✓ Pub. Trans.
✓ Parking ✓ Food Serv. ✓ Handicapped

This pool is equipped with a water slide, a baby wading pool, and a "mushroom" with sprinklers; there is no diving board.

Rocky River Recreation Center

AGES:	1½–3	3–5	5–8	8–12	12–15
RATING:	★★	★★	★★	★★	★★

COST: **$–$$** PREP.: **None–Much**
AREA: **West** CITY: **Rocky River**

ADDRESS: 21018 Hilliard Blvd.

PHONE: (440) 356-5657

SEASON: Seasonal (pool: June–Labor Day; skating: Sep–Mar; indoor soccer: Apr–Aug)

HOURS: Vary

PRICES: Vary (call for programs & prices)

DIRECT.: East: I-90 to Exit 162 for Hilliard Rd.; west on Hilliard; on right after Wagar Rd.

West: I-90 to Exit 161 for SR 254 (Detroit Rd.); east on Detroit; right (south) on Wagar Rd.; right (west) on Hilliard Blvd.; on right.

✓ Strollers ✓ Groups ✓ Food Nearby
Diap Chg ✓ Picnic ✓ Pub. Trans.
✓ Parking ✓ Food Serv. ✓ Handicapped

Open skating at the Hamilton Ice Arena is scheduled for afternoons and evenings; hours vary to accommodate special events such as the annual Skate with Santa. For preschoolers, there is a Parent and Tot session scheduled for Wednesday afternoons.

Skating lessons are offered for ages 3 and up with several six-week sessions through the season; classes last 30–45 minutes. Smaller group instruction is offered for tots; there is a special Parent and Tot Learn to Skate which includes lessons for both parent and child along with time to skate together. Youth hockey is also offered through the local league. Indoor soccer is offered during non-skating season.

Skate rental, skate sharpening, and lockers are available. Birthday parties can be arranged.

The municipal pool also has a kiddie pool, slides, a fountain, and lessons.

Rocky River Stables

Cleveland Metroparks

AGES:	1½–3	3–5	5–8	8–12	12–15
RATING:	NR	NR	★★	★★	★★

COST: **$$** PREP.: **Some–Much**
AREA: **West** CITY: **Cleveland**

ADDRESS: 19901 Puritas Ave.

PHONE: (216) 267-2525

SEASON: Year round (seasonal pony rides)

HOURS: Vary

PRICES: Vary

DIRECT.: I-480 to Exit 9 for Grayton Rd.; north on Grayton; left (west) on Puritas Ave.; on left.

✓ Strollers ✓ Groups ✓ Food Nearby
Diap Chg ✓ Picnic ✓ Pub. Trans.
✓ Parking Food Serv. ✓ Handicapped

Cleveland Metroparks stables offer year-round pony camps and English saddle riding lessons. There is an indoor arena and two outdoor rings for individual lessons and mini-camps for small groups. Ages 8 to 12 can attend a week-long horse camp; pony camp is available for ages 4 to 7. All lessons stress riding safety and grooming. An annual Christmas pony ride features dressed ponies just for three-year-olds.

Rocky River Stables

Rollerworld

AGES:	1½–3	3–5	5–8	8–12	12–15
RATING:	NR	NR	★	★★	★★★

COST: **$–$$** PREP.: **None**
AREA: **South** CITY: **Parma**

ADDRESS: 5310 Hauserman Rd.

PHONE: (440) 843-7490

SEASON: Year round

HOURS: Vary

PRICES: $5–$8

DIRECT.: I-480 to Exit 13 for Tiedeman Rd.; south on Tiedeman (becomes Hauserman Rd. after Brookpark Rd.); on right.

Strollers ✓ Groups ✓ Food Nearby
Diap Chg Picnic ✓ Pub. Trans.
✓ Parking ✓ Food Serv. Handicapped

This in-line skating arena boasts youth and adult roller hockey leagues, open skate nights every Friday and Saturday, a video arcade, and skate rental.

Skate Station

AGES:	1½–3	3–5	5–8	8–12	12–15
RATING:	NR	★	★★	★★	★★

COST: **$–$$** PREP.: **None–Some**
AREA: **Far South** CITY: **Brunswick**

ADDRESS: 1261 North Industrial Pkwy.

PHONE: (330) 273-5750, schedule information: (330) 225-9842

SEASON: Year round

HOURS: Vary

PRICES: Skate rental $1.50, inlines $3, all sessions

DIRECT.: I-71 to Exit 226 for Center Rd.; east on Center; left (north) on Industrial Pkwy.; on right.

Strollers ✓ Groups ✓ Food Nearby
Diap Chg Picnic ✓ Pub. Trans.
✓ Parking ✓ Food Serv. Handicapped

Open skate sessions at the Skate Station can really be wild—the arena is open to both traditional roller skaters as well as the newer, in-line variety. (Both types are available for rental.) Live organ music accompanies adult-only skates, and the Christian Music Night with WZLE-AM is very popular. Children as young as three can learn to skate in the Saturday classes.

Solon Municipal Pool

AGES:	1½–3	3–5	5–8	8–12	12–15
RATING:	★★	★★	★★	★★	★★

COST: **$** PREP.: **None–Much**
AREA: **Southeast** CITY: **Solon**

ADDRESS: 33355 Arthur Rd.

PHONE: (440) 248-0650

SEASON: Seasonal (Memorial Day–Labor Day)

HOURS: Mon–Fri 1 p.m.–8:45 p.m., Sat–Sun 11 a.m.–8:45 p.m.

PRICES: $3 without pass; season passes: $30 individual, $70 family (Solon residents only unless accompanied by a Solon resident); seniors and children under 7 free

DIRECT.: US 422 to SR 91 (SOM Center Rd.); south on SR 91; right (west) on Arthur Rd.

✓ Strollers	✓ Groups	✓ Food Nearby
✓ Diap Chg	✓ Picnic	✓ Pub. Trans.
✓ Parking	✓ Food Serv.	✓ Handicapped

Kiddie pool, lessons (outdoor only during summer months). Also in the summertime, a 50-meter outdoor pool and 1- and 3-meter diving boards are available. During the school year, an indoor 25-yard-high school pool and 1-meter diving board are available. Open swim Saturdays 2–5 p.m., Sundays 1–4 p.m. All swim lessons and recreational swim teams for Solon residents only.

Stafford Recreation Center

Maple Hts. Recreation Dept.

AGES:	1½–3	3–5	5–8	8–12	12–15
RATING:	★★	★★	★★	★★	★★

COST: **$** PREP.: **None–Much**
AREA: **East** CITY: **Maple Hts.**

ADDRESS: 5400 Mayville Rd.

PHONE: (216) 663-8738

SEASON: Seasonal (Memorial Day–late Aug)

HOURS: Weekdays and Sat 1–8 p.m., Sun 1–6 p.m.

PRICES: Residents: $1, $.25 under age 18; non-residents: $4; $3 under age 18 (fees w/ ID card, $1 for residents, $5 non-residents, good all season)

DIRECT.: West: I-480 to Exit 25 for Warrensville Center Rd.; south on Warrensville Center; right (southwest) on Maple Hts. Blvd.; left (south) on Mayville Ave.; on right.

East: I-271/I-480 to Exit 27 for Miles Rd.; west on Miles; left (south) on Northfield Rd.; right (west) on Libby Rd.; right (north) on Mayville Ave.; on left.

South: I-480 to Exit 25 for Aurora Rd.; northwest on Aurora; left (south) on Northfield Rd.; right (west) on Libby Rd.; right (north) on Mayville Ave.; on left.

Strollers	✓ Groups	✓ Food Nearby
✓ Diap Chg	✓ Picnic	✓ Pub. Trans.
✓ Parking	✓ Food Serv.	✓ Handicapped

Kiddie pool, slides, lessons. Pool rental available only during off-hours.

Thornton Park

Shaker Hts. Recreation Dept.

AGES:	1½–3	3–5	5–8	8–12	12–15
RATING:	★★	★★	★★	★★	★★

COST: **$–$$** PREP.: **None–Much**
AREA: **East** CITY: **Shaker Hts.**

ADDRESS: 20701 Farnsleigh Rd.

PHONE: (216) 491-1290

SEASON: Year round (pool Memorial Day–Labor Day)

HOURS: Summer season: Mon–Fri noon–9 p.m., Sat & Sun 10 a.m.–9 p.m.; call for hours outside of summer season

PRICES: Pool: resident: adults $5, ages 6–18 $4, under 6 free; non-resident: adults $5.50, children $4.50: Skating rink: resident: adult $3.25, ages 6-18 $2.50, under 6 free; non-resident $4

DIRECT.: I-271 to Exit 29 for Chagrin Blvd; west on Chagrin; right (north) on Warrensville Center Rd.; right (east) on Farnsleigh Rd.; on left.

✓ Strollers ✓ Groups ✓ Food Nearby
✓ Diap Chg ✓ Picnic ✓ Pub. Trans.
✓ Parking ✓ Food Serv. ✓ Handicapped

Open skating is typically scheduled for weekdays, with morning, afternoon, and evening sessions; weekend afternoons; and a Sunday-evening family skate. Hours vary for special events, such as the annual hockey tournament and ice show.

Skating classes are offered for ages 3 and up with several sessions through the year. Youth Hockey is also offered through the Shaker Youth Hockey Association. Skate rental, skate sharpening, and lockers are offered. The rink is available for private rental, and birthday parties can be arranged.

The swimming pool also has a kiddie pool, slides, fountain, and lessons.

Victory Pool

South Euclid/Lyndhurst Recreation Dept.

AGES:	1½–3	3–5	5–8	8–12	12–15
RATING:	★★	★★	★★	★★	★★

COST: **$–$$** PREP.: **None–Much**
AREA: **East** CITY: **South Euclid**

ADDRESS: 1352 Victory Dr.

PHONE: (216) 381-0435

SEASON: Seasonal (Jun–Sep)

HOURS: Daily 1:30–8 p.m.

PRICES: $5 residents, $6 non-resident guests; individual family pass $30 each, maximum $90 per family

DIRECT.: I-271 to Exit 34 for Mayfield Rd.; west on Mayfield; right (north) on Victory Dr.; on left.

✓ Strollers ✓ Groups ✓ Food Nearby
Diap Chg ✓ Picnic ✓ Pub. Trans.
✓ Parking Food Serv. ✓ Handicapped

Kiddie pool, slides, lessons.

Westlake Recreation Department

AGES:	1½–3	3–5	5–8	8–12	12–15
RATING:	★★★	★★★	★★★	★★★	★★★

COST: **$–$$** PREP.: **None–Much**
AREA: **West** CITY: **Westlake**

ADDRESS: 28955 Hilliard Blvd.

PHONE: (440) 808-5700

SEASON: Year round

HOURS: Mon–Fri 6 a.m.–10 p.m., Sat 8 a.m.–8 p.m., Sun noon–5 p.m. (closing times vary with seasons)

PRICES: Vary; guests $8/day, youth $5/day; Memberships by the year or quarter-year for residents

DIRECT.: I-90 to Exit 156 for Crocker/Bassett Rd.; south on Crocker; left (east) on Hilliard Blvd.; on right.

✓ Strollers Groups ✓ Food Nearby
✓ Diap Chg ✓ Picnic ✓ Pub. Trans.
✓ Parking ✓ Food Serv. ✓ Handicapped

Open to Westlake residents (and their guests) only, this multimillion-dollar community center opened in mid-1998 features five indoor swimming pools, an elevated indoor jogging track, gymnasiums, and a supervised toddler area. On an 86-acre, fully landscaped lot with a 1.5-mile multipurpose trail,a five-acre lake, and tennis courts, it is an impressive recreation area.

Winterhurst Municipal Ice Rink

Lakewood Recreation Dept.

AGES:	1½–3	3–5	5–8	8–12	12–15
RATING:	NR	★★	★★	★★	★★

COST: **$** PREP.: **None–Much**
AREA: **Near West** CITY: **Lakewood**

ADDRESS: 14740 Lakewood Hts. Blvd.

PHONE: (216) 529-4400

SEASON: Year round

HOURS: Vary

PRICES: Vary

DIRECT.: I-90 to Exit 165 for Warren Rd.; north on Warren; right (east) on Lakewood Hts. Blvd.; on left.

✓ Strollers ✓ Groups ✓ Food Nearby
Diap Chg ✓ Picnic ✓ Pub. Trans.
✓ Parking ✓ Food Serv. ✓ Handicapped

Sports & Recreation DIRECTORY

This indoor rink is among the largest in the country. Open skating sessions vary widely to accommodate special events, which include hockey tournaments, figure-skating competitions, speed skating, and skating derbies. For families, each year there is a Halloween Costume Skate, pizza skates, Skate with Santa, and a Skate with the Easter Bunny. For preschoolers, a parent and tot session is offered Tuesday mornings.

Skating lessons are offered for ages 3 and up in seven-week sessions four times a year. Lessons are also available through the Winterhurst Ice Hockey Association. Skate rentals, skate sharpening, and lockers are available. The rink is available for private rental. Birthday parties can be arranged.

YMCA, Broadway Branch

AGES:	1½–3	3–5	5–8	8–12	12–15
RATING:	★★	★★	★★	★★	★★

COST: **$$** PREP.: **None–Much**
AREA: **Near East** CITY: **Cleveland**

ADDRESS: 11300 Miles Ave.

PHONE: (216) 341-1860

SEASON: Year round

HOURS: Mon–Fri 7 a.m.–9 p.m.; Sat. 8 a.m.–4 p.m.

PRICES: Vary

✓ Strollers ✓ Groups ✓ Food Nearby
✓ Diap Chg Picnic ✓ Pub. Trans.
✓ Parking Food Serv. ✓ Handicapped

For swimming lessons, a summer day camp, a T-ball league, or karate classes for your kids, check out the neighborhood YMCA. While the facilities vary, general offerings are similar (most have indoor pools, large gyms, and fitness centers). YMCA members and non-members alike can sign up for classes that are offered year round.

The parent-child Indian Guides program forms new tribes each September with groups of five or more from ages 5–15. Holidays generally bring special events and family parties.

The Broadway branch has a swimming pool, gym, fitness room, racquetball, and summer day camp.

YMCA, Brooklyn Branch

AGES:	1½–3	3–5	5–8	8–12	12–15
RATING:	★★	★★	★★	★★	★★

COST: **$$** PREP.: **None–Much**
AREA: **Near West** CITY: **Cleveland**

ADDRESS: 3881 Pearl Rd.

PHONE: (216) 749-2355

SEASON: Year round

HOURS: Mon–Fri 6 a.m.–10 p.m.; Sat 8 a.m.–5 p.m.; Sun noon–5 p.m.

PRICES: Vary

✓ Strollers ✓ Groups ✓ Food Nearby
Diap Chg Picnic ✓ Pub. Trans.
✓ Parking ✓ Food Serv. ✓ Handicapped

(See Broadway branch listing for general YMCA information.)

Swimming (including youth swim), gym, fitness room, handball and racquetball courts, day camp, game rooms. Also available: all-day preschool care and other preschool programs.

YMCA, Central Branch

AGES:	1½–3	3–5	5–8	8–12	12–15
RATING:	★★	★★	★★	★★	★★

COST: **$$** PREP.: **None–Much**
AREA: **Far East** CITY: **Painesville**

ADDRESS: 933 Mentor Ave.

PHONE: (440) 352-3303

SEASON: Year round

HOURS: Oct–Apr: Mon–Fri 5 a.m.–11 p.m., Sat 5 a.m.–9 p.m., Sun 1–5 p.m.; Summer: Mon–Fri 5 a.m.–10 P.M., Sat 5 a.m.– 4 p.m.., Sun closed

PRICES: Annual pass: family $666, youth $181

✓ Strollers ✓ Groups ✓ Food Nearby
✓ Diap Chg ✓ Picnic ✓ Pub. Trans.
✓ Parking ✓ Food Serv. ✓ Handicapped

(See Broadway branch listing for general YMCA information.)

Swimming pool, gym, fitness room, track, racquetball and handball courts, day camp. Other special facilities include the Family Adventure Center, day care center, game room, and a whirlpool with sauna/steam room.

YMCA, East End Branch

AGES:	1½–3	3–5	5–8	8–12	12–15
RATING:	★★	★★	★★	★★	★★

COST: **$$** PREP.: **None–Much**
AREA: **Far East** CITY: **Madison**

ADDRESS: 730 N. Lake St.

PHONE: (440) 428-5125

SEASON: Year round

HOURS: Summer: Mon–Fri 5:30 a.m.–9:30 p.m., Sat 8 a.m.–noon, Sun closed;
Winter: Mon–Fri 5:30 a.m.–10 p.m., Sat 8 a.m.–2:30 p.m., Sun closed

PRICES: Annual passes: family $682, individual $397

✓ Strollers ✓ Groups ✓ Food Nearby
✓ Diap Chg Picnic ✓ Pub. Trans.
✓ Parking ✓ Food Serv. ✓ Handicapped

(See Broadway branch listing for general YMCA information.)

Swimming pool, gym, fitness and weight room, preschool center, babysitting room, outdoor recreational area, summer day camp.

YMCA, Elyria Family

AGES:	1½–3	3–5	5–8	8–12	12–15
RATING:	★★	★★	★★	★★	★★

COST: **$$** PREP.: **None–Much**
AREA: **Far West** CITY: **Elyria**

ADDRESS: 265 Washington Ave.

PHONE: (440) 323-5500

SEASON: Year round

HOURS: Mon–Thu 5:45 a.m.–10 p.m.; Fri 5:45 a.m.– 9 p.m.; Sat 8 a.m.–8 p.m., Sun 2 p.m.–6 p.m. (closed Sundays during summer months)

PRICES: Season passes: guest $8; family $404, adult $290, youth (18 and under) $114, seniors $168

✓ Strollers ✓ Groups ✓ Food Nearby
✓ Diap Chg Picnic ✓ Pub. Trans.
✓ Parking Food Serv. ✓ Handicapped

(See Broadway branch listing for general YMCA information.)

Swimming, gymnastics, fitness room, day camp, preschool, and child care.

YMCA, Euclid Family Branch

AGES:	1½–3	3–5	5–8	8–12	12–15
RATING:	★★	★★	★★	★★	★★

COST: **$$** PREP.: **None–Much**
AREA: **East** CITY: **Euclid**

ADDRESS: 631 Babbitt Rd.
PHONE: (216) 731-7454
SEASON: Year round
HOURS: Mon–Fri 6 a.m.–10 p.m.; Sat 8:30 a.m.–5 p.m.; Sun 1–4 p.m.
PRICES: Vary; 1-day pass $7; adult and family packages available

Strollers ✓ Groups ✓ Food Nearby
✓ Diap Chg ✓ Picnic ✓ Pub. Trans.
✓ Parking ✓ Food Serv. ✓ Handicapped

(See Broadway branch listing for general YMCA information.)

Swimming, gymnastics, day camp, school-age day care, youth sports, martial arts, fitness center, and weight room.

TIPS FOR TRIPS

NEW EXPERIENCES

One way to encourage your family to try new things is to let your kids take the lead. Create a new-activity jar and take turns drawing different activities to try.

YMCA, Geauga County

AGES:	1½–3	3–5	5–8	8–12	12–15
RATING:	★★	★★	★★	★★	★★

COST: **$–$$** PREP.: **None–Much**
AREA: **Far East** CITY: **Newbury**

ADDRESS: 12121 Kinsman Rd.
PHONE: (440) 564-7158
SEASON: Year round
HOURS: Mon–Fri 6:30 a.m.–6:30 p.m.
PRICES: Vary; youth membership $25

✓ Strollers Groups Food Nearby
Diap Chg Picnic ✓ Pub. Trans.
✓ Parking Food Serv. Handicapped

(See Broadway branch listing for general YMCA information.)

Most of the programs here are held outside or at other locations in Geauga County. There is a basketball court and workout programs, a child-care center, Indian Guides, and a summer day camp

YMCA, Glenville Branch

AGES:	1½–3	3–5	5–8	8–12	12–15
RATING:	★★	★★	★★	★★	★★

COST: **$** PREP.: **None–Much**
AREA: **Near East** CITY: **Cleveland**

ADDRESS: 11111 St. Clair Ave.
PHONE: (216) 851-4700
SEASON: Year round
HOURS: Mon–Fri 6 a.m.–8 p.m.; Sat 9 a.m.–1 p.m.
PRICES: Vary; 1-day $5

Strollers ✓ Groups ✓ Food Nearby
Diap Chg Picnic ✓ Pub. Trans.
✓ Parking Food Serv. ✓ Handicapped

(See Broadway branch listing for general YMCA information.)

Swimming pool, gym, fitness room, summer day camp.

YMCA, Heights Family Branch

AGES: 1½–3 3–5 5–8 8–12 12–15
RATING: ★★ ★★ ★★ ★★ ★★

COST: **$–$$** PREP.: **None–Much**
AREA: **East** CITY: **Cleveland Hts.**

ADDRESS: 2340 Lee Rd.

PHONE: (216) 371-2323

SEASON: Year round

HOURS: Mon–Fri 6:30 a.m.–8:30 p.m., Sat 8 a.m.–5 p.m., Sun 1–4 p.m.

PRICES: Vary

Strollers	✓ Groups	✓ Food Nearby
Diap Chg	Picnic	✓ Pub. Trans.
✓ Parking	✓ Food Serv.	✓ Handicapped

(See Broadway branch listing for general YMCA information.)

Swimming, gymnastics, fitness & weight-lifting room, day camp. Aerobics classes also available.

YMCA, Hillcrest Family Branch

AGES: 1½–3 3–5 5–8 8–12 12–15
RATING: ★★ ★★ ★★ ★★ ★★

COST: **$–$$** PREP.: **None–Much**
AREA: **East** CITY: **Lyndhurst**

ADDRESS: 5000 Mayfield Rd.

PHONE: (216) 382-4300

SEASON: Year round

HOURS: Mon–Fri 6 a.m.–10 p.m., Sat 8 a.m.–6 p.m., Sun 1–4 p.m. (summer hours vary, call ahead)

PRICES: Annual passes: Adult $312, family $555, senior $282, youth $108 (plus sales tax; also add $60 initiation fee for adult, family, and seniors passes)

Strollers	✓ Groups	✓ Food Nearby
Diap Chg	Picnic	✓ Pub. Trans.
✓ Parking	Food Serv.	✓ Handicapped

(See Broadway branch listing for general YMCA information.)

Swimming pool, gym, fitness areas, day camp, child care and babysitting, youth and adult programming, martial arts.

YMCA, Lake County Outdoor Family Center

AGES: 1½–3 3–5 5–8 8–12 12–15
RATING: ★★ ★★ ★★ ★★ ★★

COST: **$–$$** PREP.: **None–Much**
AREA: **Far East** CITY: **Perry Twp.**

ADDRESS: 4540 River Rd.

PHONE: (440) 259-2724

SEASON: Year round (lodge: year round; cross-country ski trails: winter)

HOURS: Lodge Mon–Fri 9 a.m.–dusk, Sat 10 a.m.–dusk, Sun noon–dusk (hours vary by season, please call ahead)

PRICES: Vary; Annual passes: youth $68, adult $110, family $195, senior $82 (age 65 and up); Summer passes: youth $57, adult $93, family $167, seniors $70; Daily passes (aquatic center only): youth $6, adult $8, family $20, seniors $6

✓ Strollers	✓ Groups	✓ Food Nearby
✓ Diap Chg	✓ Picnic	Pub. Trans.
✓ Parking	✓ Food Serv.	✓ Handicapped

(See Broadway branch listing for general YMCA information.)

In winter, cross-country ski trails here cover nearly 5 miles over 180 acres of woods, fields, and scenic river valley. Overlooking the river from atop a scenic bluff is a stone-and-timber lodge with a large fireplace—a popular gathering spot. Winter activities feature sledding, moonlight ski outings, skating, and hiking. In the warmer months there is outdoor tennis, racquetball, sand volleyball, and basketball. An outdoor pool complex includes a kiddie pool and water slide. A special-events calendar includes youth sports, family nights, and monthly preschool programs. Five picnic pavilions are available, and there's a rock-climbing gym inside.

YMCA, Lakewood Branch

AGES: 1½–3 3–5 5–8 8–12 12–15
RATING: ★★ ★★ ★★ ★★ ★★

COST: $–$$ PREP.: None–Much
AREA: Near West CITY: Lakewood

ADDRESS: 16915 Detroit Rd.

PHONE: (216) 521-8400

SEASON: Year round

HOURS: Mon–Fri 6 a.m.–10:30 p.m.; Sat 7 a.m.–9 p.m.; Sun noon–9 p.m.

PRICES: Vary; monthly memberships available, adult $28.89, family $50.29

✓ Strollers ✓ Groups ✓ Food Nearby
✓ Diap Chg Picnic ✓ Pub. Trans.
✓ Parking ✓ Food Serv. ✓ Handicapped

(See Broadway branch listing for general YMCA information.)

Swimming pool, gymnasium, fitness room, day camp, stroller aerobics, and water classes. Sports programs for home-schooled children available.

YMCA, Lorain Family

AGES: 1½–3 3–5 5–8 8–12 12–15
RATING: ★★ ★★ ★★ ★★ ★★

COST: $–$$ PREP.: None–Much
AREA: Far West CITY: Lorain

ADDRESS: 1121 Tower Blvd.

PHONE: (440) 282-4144

SEASON: Year round

HOURS: Mon–Fri 6 a.m.–10:30 p.m.; Sat 8 a.m.–5 p.m.

PRICES: Guest fees: child $2, high school $4, adult $6; Annual memberships: youth $73, adult $231, family $352

✓ Strollers ✓ Groups ✓ Food Nearby
✓ Diap Chg ✓ Picnic ✓ Pub. Trans.
✓ Parking Food Serv. ✓ Handicapped

(See Broadway branch listing for general YMCA information.)

Swimming pool, gym, racquetball, summer day camp, free weight room, track, school-age and all-day child care, Toddler Center.

Other branches:

Longfellow Park YMCA, 300 Longfellow Pkwy., Lorain (440) 282-4144

North Coast YMCA (see separate listing)

YMCA, North Coast

AGES: 1½–3 3–5 5–8 8–12 12–15
RATING: ★★ ★★ ★★ ★★ ★★

COST: $ PREP.: None–Much
AREA: Far West CITY: Avon Lake

ADDRESS: 216 Miller Rd. (inside the Aqua Marine Resort)

PHONE: (440) 933-9100

SEASON: Year round

HOURS: Mon–Thu 5:30 a.m.–9 p.m., Fri 5:30 a.m.–10 p.m. Sat–Sun 8 a.m.–10 p.m.

PRICES: Guest fee: youth/high school $3, adult $5; Annual membership: youth $76, adult $454, family $627

Strollers Groups ✓ Food Nearby
Diap Chg Picnic Pub. Trans.
✓ Parking ✓ Food Serv. ✓ Handicapped

(See Broadway branch listing for general YMCA information.)

Child care and preschool programs, including athletic exercise; adult fitness programs; weights and exercise equipment; racquetball courts with league competition; sauna and fully equipped locker rooms.

YMCA, Ridgewood Branch

AGES: 1½–3 3–5 5–8 8–12 12–15
RATING: ★★ ★★ ★★ ★★ ★★

COST: $–$$ PREP.: None–Much
AREA: South CITY: Parma

ADDRESS: 6840 Ridge Rd.

PHONE: (440) 842-5200

SEASON: Year round

HOURS: Mon–Fri 5:45 a.m.–9:30 p.m., Sat 8 a.m.–6 p.m., Sun 10 a.m.–4 p.m.

PRICES: Vary; $60 enrollment fee; annual membership: adult $346, family $577

Strollers ✓ Groups ✓ Food Nearby
✓ Diap Chg Picnic ✓ Pub. Trans.
✓ Parking Food Serv. ✓ Handicapped

(See Broadway branch listing for general YMCA information.)

Swimming, gymnasium, fitness room, preschool enrichment classes, day camp.

YMCA, Southeast Branch

AGES: 1½–3 3–5 5–8 8–12 12–15
RATING: ★★ ★★ ★★ ★★ ★★

COST: $–$$ PREP.: None–Much
AREA: South CITY: Bedford

ADDRESS: 460 Northfield Rd.

PHONE: (216) 663-7522

SEASON: Year round

HOURS: Mon–Fri 6 a.m.–10 p.m., Sat 7:30 a.m.–4 p.m., Sun 1 p.m.–4 p.m.

PRICES: Vary

✓ Strollers ✓ Groups ✓ Food Nearby
Diap Chg Picnic ✓ Pub. Trans.
✓ Parking Food Serv. ✓ Handicapped

(See Broadway branch listing for general YMCA information.)

Swimming pool, gym, fitness room, day camp, child care programs, child and adult physical fitness programs/leagues.

YMCA, Southwest Branch

AGES: 1½–3 3–5 5–8 8–12 12–15
RATING: ★★ ★★ ★★ ★★ ★★

COST: $$ PREP.: None–Much
AREA: Southwest CITY: Strongsville

ADDRESS: 15290 Pearl Rd.

PHONE: (440) 238-8600

SEASON: Year round

HOURS: Mon–Fri 8:30 a.m.–5 p.m.; Sat 9 a.m.–noon

PRICES: Vary

Strollers Groups ✓ Food Nearby
Diap Chg Picnic ✓ Pub. Trans.
✓ Parking Food Serv. ✓ Handicapped

(See Broadway branch listing for general YMCA information.)

Summer day camp, gymnastics, soccer and sports leagues; after-school child care available.

YMCA, West End Branch

AGES: 1½–3 3–5 5–8 8–12 12–15
RATING: ★★ ★★ ★★ ★★ ★★

COST: $–$$ PREP.: None–Much
AREA: East CITY: Willoughby

ADDRESS: 37100 Euclid Ave.

PHONE: (440) 946-1160

SEASON: Year round

HOURS: Mon–Fri 5:30 a.m.–10:30 p.m., Sat 7 a.m.–9 p.m., Sun noon–6 p.m. (closed Sundays during summer)

PRICES: Vary; monthly memberships: family $48, individual $27; initiation fee: individual $79, family $127

✓ Strollers ✓ Groups ✓ Food Nearby
✓ Diap Chg ✓ Picnic ✓ Pub. Trans.
✓ Parking Food Serv. ✓ Handicapped

(See Broadway branch listing for general YMCA information.)

Swimming pool, gym, fitness room, summer day camp. Babysitting free for members. Many different programs for preschoolers to seniors. A 10,000-foot addition has added racquetball and volleyball courts.

YMCA, West Park-Fairview Branch

AGES:	1½–3	3–5	5–8	8–12	12–15
RATING:	★★	★★	★★	★★	★★

COST: **$–$$** PREP.: **None–Much**
AREA: **Near West** CITY: **Cleveland**

ADDRESS: 15501 Lorain Ave.

PHONE: (216) 941-5410

SEASON: Year round

HOURS: Mon–Fri 6 a.m.–9:30 p.m.; Sat 8 a.m.–4 p.m.; Sun 12:30 p.m.–5 p.m.

PRICES: Vary, call for annual rates; 1-day pass available $3–$6

✓ Strollers ✓ Groups ✓ Food Nearby
Diap Chg Picnic ✓ Pub. Trans.
✓ Parking Food Serv. ✓ Handicapped

(See Broadway branch listing for general YMCA information.)

Swimming pool, gym, fitness room, yoga, aerobics, summer day camp. Day care available.

YMCA, West Shore Family Branch

AGES:	1½–3	3–5	5–8	8–12	12–15
RATING:	★★	★★	★★	★★	★★

COST: **$–$$** PREP.: **None–Much**
AREA: **West** CITY: **Westlake**

ADDRESS: 1575 Columbia Rd.

PHONE: (440) 871-6885

SEASON: Year round

HOURS: Mon–Fri 5:30 a.m.–10 p.m.; Sat 7 a.m.–6 p.m.; Sun noon–6 p.m.

PRICES: Vary; 1-day pass $7, $5 with membership (call for rates)

✓ Strollers ✓ Groups ✓ Food Nearby
✓ Diap Chg ✓ Picnic ✓ Pub. Trans.
✓ Parking ✓ Food Serv. ✓ Handicapped

(See Broadway branch listing for general YMCA information.)

Swimming pool, gymnasium, fitness room, day camp.

YMCA, West Side Branch

AGES:	1½–3	3–5	5–8	8–12	12–15
RATING:	★★	★★	★★	★★	★★

COST: **$–$$** PREP.: **None–Much**
AREA: **Near West** CITY: **Cleveland**

ADDRESS: 3200 Franklin Blvd.

PHONE: (216) 961-3277

SEASON: Year round

HOURS: Mon–Fri 5:30 a.m.–9 p.m.; Sat 5 a.m.–4:30 p.m.; Sun 8:30 a.m.–4:30 p.m.

PRICES: Vary; 1-day pass $6; annual membership: adult $308, family $510

✓ Strollers ✓ Groups Food Nearby
✓ Diap Chg Picnic ✓ Pub. Trans.
✓ Parking Food Serv. ✓ Handicapped

(See Broadway branch listing for general YMCA information.)

Swimming pool, gym, fitness room, racquetball, day camp.

YWCA of Lorain

AGES:	1½–3	3–5	5–8	8–12	12–15
RATING:	★★	★★	★★	★★	★★

COST: **$–$$** PREP.: **None–Much**
AREA: **Far West** CITY: **Lorain**

ADDRESS: 200 9th St.

PHONE: (440) 244-1919

SEASON: Year round

HOURS: Mon–Fri 8 a.m.–4 p.m.

PRICES: Vary

✓ Strollers	✓ Groups	✓ Food Nearby
✓ Diap Chg	Picnic	Pub. Trans.
✓ Parking	✓ Food Serv.	Handicapped

After-school programs, summer day camp.

Spectator Sports

Clevelanders love sports. Their waistlines may not always show it, but their wallets do. In 1931, residents laid out $2.5 million to build Municipal Stadium in hopes of wooing the Olympics. The Games never came, but the city got the cavernous 78,189-seat stadium anyway. In 1990, mobilized by the threat of losing the Cleveland Indians baseball team to another city, Cleveland-area residents dipped into their wallets to provide most of the funds for the $400-million Gateway sports complex including Jacobs Field and Gund Arena. Since moving to their new home, the Indians have been among the winningest teams in baseball. New digs have also given a boost to other area teams, including the Lumberjacks (minor-league hockey) at Gund Arena, and the Crunch (indoor soccer) at the Cleveland State University Convocation Center. In 1995, area residents voted to help foot the bill for a new multimillion-dollar stadium for the NFL's new Cleveland Browns.

Akron Aeros

AGES:	1½–3	3–5	5–8	8–12	12–15
RATING:	NR	★	★★	★★★	★★

COST: **$$** PREP.: **Some**
AREA: **Far South** CITY: **Akron**

ADDRESS: Canal Park Stadium
300 South Main St.
PHONE: (800) 97-AEROS
SEASON: Seasonal (Apr–Sep)
HOURS: Vary
PRICES: Adults $8; seniors, juniors (12 & under) $6
DIRECT.: I-77/I-76 to SR 59; north on SR 59; east on E. Exchange St.; left on S. Main St.; Canal Park Stadium on left.
Or, I-77/I-76 to Exit 22 for S. Main St.; north on S. Main; on left after E. Exchange St.

Strollers | Groups | ✓ Food Nearby
Diap Chg | Picnic | ✓ Pub. Trans.
✓ Parking | ✓ Food Serv. | Handicapped

A new stadium at Canal Park, inexpensive tickets, and rising talent headed for the Cleveland Indians still haven't helped fill the seats here. Still, this is a good place to introduce young fans to the game, and if you leave in the middle you won't feel so bad.

Baldwin-Wallace College

AGES:	1½–3	3–5	5–8	8–12	12–15
RATING:	NR	★	★	★★	★★

COST: **$–$$** PREP.: **Some**
AREA: **Southwest** CITY: **Berea**

ADDRESS: 275 Eastland Rr.
PHONE: (440) 826-2184
SEASON: Year round
HOURS: Vary
PRICES: Vary
DIRECT.: I-77 to Exit 235 for Bagley Rd.; west on Bagley to campus.
WEB: www.bw.edu

✓ Strollers | Groups | ✓ Food Nearby
✓ Diap Chg | Picnic | ✓ Pub. Trans.
✓ Parking | ✓ Food Serv. | ✓ Handicapped

Spectator sports on campus here include men's football; men and women's soccer; men and women's cross country; men and women's basketball; men and women's indoor and outdoor track; men's swimming; men's wrestling; women's softball; men's baseball; men and women's tennis; men and women's golf.

Case Western Reserve University

AGES:	1½–3	3–5	5–8	8–12	12–15
RATING:	NR	★	★	★★	★★

COST: **$–$$** PREP.: **Some**
AREA: **Near East** CITY: **Cleveland**

ADDRESS: 10900 Euclid Ave.

PHONE: (216) 368-2867

SEASON: Year round

HOURS: Vary

PRICES: Vary

DIRECT.: East: I-90 to Exit 177 for Martin Luther King Blvd.; south on MLK; left (east) on Euclid Ave. to CWRU campus.

West: I-90 to Exit 173 for Chester Ave.; east on Chester; left (east) on Euclid Ave. to CWRU.

✓ Strollers Groups ✓ Food Nearby
✓ Diap Chg ✓ Picnic ✓ Pub. Trans.
✓ Parking ✓ Food Serv. ✓ Handicapped

Sports here include: Men's baseball; men and women's basketball; men and women's cross country; men and women's fencing; men's football; men's golf; men and women's soccer; women's softball; men and women's swimming; men and women's tennis; men and women's indoor and outdoor track; women's volleyball; and men's wrestling.

Cleveland Browns

AGES:	1½–3	3–5	5–8	8–12	12–15
RATING:	NR	NR	★★	★★★	★★★

COST: **$$$** PREP.: **Much**
AREA: **Downtown** CITY: **Cleveland**

ADDRESS: Browns Stadium

PHONE: (216) 891-5050; (216) 891-5000; (888) 891-1999

SEASON: Seasonal (Aug–Dec)

HOURS: Vary

PRICES: Vary

DIRECT.: SR 2 to E. 9 St.; north on E. 9; left (west) on Erieside Ave; on left.

Or, from SR 2, take exit for W. 3 St.; north on W. 3; on right.

WEB: www.clevelandbrowns.com

Strollers ✓ Groups ✓ Food Nearby
Diap Chg Picnic ✓ Pub. Trans.
✓ Parking ✓ Food Serv. ✓ Handicapped

With a new team and a new stadium, Cleveland fans in 1999 are in a football frenzy. After years of complaining, the bathroom situation has definitely been solved, according to stadium literature. There are not only more restrooms, but a number of them are unisex, solving the problem of escorting your children. Another complaint resolved: there are no obstructed views for the 72,000-plus seats. And tailgate partiers now have their own space. Watch for year-round family promotions: the NFL Flag Teams are for ages 6 to 14 (1-800-NFL-SNAP).

Cleveland Cavaliers

AGES:	1½–3	3–5	5–8	8–12	12–15
RATING:	NR	NR	★★	★★★	★★★

COST: **$$$** PREP.: **Some**
AREA: **Downtown** CITY: **Cleveland**

ADDRESS: Gund Arena, Huron Rd. & Ontario St.

PHONE: (800) 332-2287

SEASON: Seasonal (Nov–Apr)

HOURS: Vary. Usually 7:30 p.m. weeknights; some weekends

PRICES: Ticket prices: $10–$58; discounts available for groups of 20 or more

DIRECT.: West: I-90 to Exit 171B for Ontario St; north on Ontario; on right.

East: I-90 to Exit 173A for Prospect Ave.; west on Prospect; left (west) on Huron Rd.; on left.

WEB: www.cavs.com

Strollers	✓ Groups	✓ Food Nearby
✓ Diap Chg	Picnic	✓ Pub. Trans.
✓ Parking	✓ Food Serv.	✓ Handicapped

The Cavs' home at Gund Arena is as nice as any in the NBA. Although the seating is steep, sight lines are good. In addition to professional basketball action, Gund Arena includes a team store, two restaurants, and a food court area. With non-nosebleed seats starting at $35 apiece, many in the crowd are corporate types, who are usually pretty sedate. The same cannot be said of the arena's state-of-the-art sound system, which can be painfully loud.

Gund Arena, home of the Cleveland Cavaliers

Cleveland Crunch

AGES:	1½–3	3–5	5–8	8–12	12–15
RATING:	NR	NR	★	★★★	★★★

COST: **$$** PREP.: **Some–Much**
AREA: **Downtown** CITY: **Cleveland**

ADDRESS: 2000 Prospect Ave.

PHONE: Main office: (440) 349-2090; Cleveland SportsPlex: (216) 587-STAR

SEASON: Seasonal (Oct–Apr)

HOURS: Home games at CSU Convocation Center, Fri 7:30 p.m, Sat 7:05 p.m., Sun 3:05 p.m.

PRICES: Tickets: $11–$18, no charge under age 2, discounts available for groups of 25 or more

DIRECT.: West: I-90 to Exit 173A for Prospect Ave.; west on Prospect; on left.

East: I-90 to Exit 172A for E. 9 St.; north on E. 9; left (east) on Carnegie Ave.; on right.

✓ Strollers	✓ Groups	✓ Food Nearby
✓ Diap Chg	Picnic	✓ Pub. Trans.
✓ Parking	✓ Food Serv.	✓ Handicapped

The Cleveland Crunch offers championship-caliber indoor soccer at CSU's Convocation Center and sports training and advice from players and coaches, a nice change of pace for a professional sports team. Many special promotional nights throughout the season feature such giveaways as hats, posters, and tickets.

For young soccer players, summertime brings five-day Crunch soccer camps offered at various sites throughout the metro area for boys and girls ages 6–14. (A special session is also offered in December.) Fine points of the game such as ball control, shooting, and passing are taught by Crunch players. The price includes instruction, a tee-shirt, and tickets to a Camper Night home game.

Cleveland Indians

AGES:	1½–3	3–5	5–8	8–12	12–15
RATING:	NR	NR	★★	★★★	★★★

COST: **$$–$$$** PREP.: **Much**
AREA: **Downtown** CITY: **Cleveland**

ADDRESS: 2401 Ontario St.

PHONE: Tickets: (216) 241-8888; fan info line: (216) 420-4636; office: (216) 420-4200; groups: (216) 420-4487

SEASON: Seasonal (Apr–Oct)

HOURS: Games Mon–Fri usually 7:05 p.m.; Sat, Sun usually 1:05 p.m.; consult schedule

PRICES: $8 (bleachers)–$30 (field box), group rates available

DIRECT.: West: I-90 to Exit 171B for Ontario St; north on Ontario; on right.

East: I-90 to Exit 173A for Prospect Ave.; west on Prospect; left (south) on E. 18 St.; right (west) on Carnegie Ave.; on right.

WEB: www.indians.com

A Cleveland Indians player greets fans

Strollers	✓ Groups	✓ Food Nearby
✓ Diap Chg	✓ Picnic	✓ Pub. Trans.
✓ Parking	✓ Food Serv.	✓ Handicapped

We're hard-pressed to think of a nicer place to watch a baseball game. Inspired by intimate, old-fashioned ballparks like Chicago's Wrigley Field and Boston's Fenway Park, Jacobs Field has nary a bad seat. Unlike those older parks, however, this one has amenities galore, from a white-linen-tablecloth restaurant to a kids' area behind right field, complete with climbing gyms and a sandbox. There are bars, TVs in the women's washroom, and seatside food and drink service.

Getting a ticket is another story. After spending more than 40 years as major league baseball's doormat, the Indians have become one of the American League's hottest teams, sweeping the city (and the region) with Tribe fever. Now, tickets for the season are usually sold out before Opening Day. And as long as the team continues to win, that is not likely to change.

Cleveland Lumberjacks

AGES:	1½–3	3–5	5–8	8–12	12–15
RATING:	NR	★	★★★	★★★	★★★

COST: **$$–$$$** PREP.: **Some**
AREA: **Downtown** CITY: **Cleveland**

ADDRESS: 200 Huron Rd.

PHONE: (216) 420-0000

SEASON: Seasonal (Sep–Apr)

HOURS: Home games Sat, Sun 7:30 p.m.; some weeknights & afternoons (consult schedule)

PRICES: $10, $15, $18, $23 group discounts available; coupon books offer lower prices

DIRECT.: West: I-90 to Exit 171B for Ontario St; north on Ontario St.; on right.

East: I-90 to Exit 173A for Prospect Ave.; west on Prospect Ave.; left (west) on Huron Rd.; on left.

WEB: www.jackshockey.com

✓ Strollers	✓ Groups	✓ Food Nearby
✓ Diap Chg	✓ Picnic	✓ Pub. Trans.
✓ Parking	✓ Food Serv.	✓ Handicapped

What the city's minor-league hockey team (affiliated with the International Hockey League) may lack in stick-handling skill they more than make up for in enthusiasm. They check hard and their slapshots reverberate off the Plexiglas. And when they score, a foghorn kicks in, followed by blaring rock music.

In-between-period activities include tot-hockey championships and interactive events for the fans. This franchise works very hard getting families to show up—giveaways are frequent, and kids can also join the on-ice action with after-game skates on Friday evenings.

Cleveland Rockers

AGES:	1½–3	3–5	5–8	8–12	12–15
RATING:	NR	NR	★★	★★★	★★★

COST: **$$$** PREP.: **Some**
AREA: **Downtown** CITY: **Cleveland**

ADDRESS: Gund Arena, Huron Rd. & Ontario Ave.

PHONE: (800) 332-2287

SEASON: Seasonal (Jun–Aug)

HOURS: Games usually begin at 7 p.m.

PRICES: Floor seats $27–$60; Arena seats $7-$18; discounts available for groups of 20 or more

DIRECT.: West: I-90 to Exit 171B for Ontario St.; north on Ontario; on right.

East: I-90 to Exit 173A for Prospect Ave.; west on Prospect; left (west) on Huron Rd.; on left.

WEB: www.clevelandrockers.com

Strollers	✓ Groups	✓ Food Nearby
Diap Chg	Picnic	✓ Pub. Trans.
✓ Parking	✓ Food Serv.	Handicapped

Women's basketball has a rather erratic record—several versions of a national league have been started and have failed. The two-year-old Women's National Basketball Association hopes to change that reputation. For their part, in the second season of play, the Rockers took home the Eastern Conference Title—the first pro basketball team to snag a conference banner for Cleveland, the team is eager to point out. And, surprising many critics, the summer season games have been pulling in the crowds—some 10,000 fans per game. With very accessible prices, the same stand-out arena that the Cavs use, and very aggressive play, it's no wonder. A summer camp program for boys and girls offers budding players a chance to learn from the pros.

Cleveland Rockers Jam Center for kids

Cleveland State University

AGES:	1½–3	3–5	5–8	8–12	12–15
RATING:	NR	★	★	★★	★★

COST: **$$** PREP.: **Some**
AREA: **Downtown** CITY: **Cleveland**

ADDRESS: Convocation Center 2000 Prospect Ave.; Campus 1983 E. 24 St.

PHONE: Convocation Center (216) 687-5119; Campus (216) 687-4800; Ticket office (216) 687-4848

SEASON: Year round

HOURS: Vary

PRICES: Vary

DIRECT.: West: I-90 to Exit 172B for E. 22 St.; left (north) on E. 22; left (west) on Carnegie; Convocation Center on right.

East: I-90 to Exit 173A for Prospect; right (west) on Prospect; Convocation Center on left.

WEB: www.csuohio.edu/athletics/

Strollers	✓ Groups	✓ Food Nearby
Diap Chg	Picnic	✓ Pub. Trans.
✓ Parking	✓ Food Serv.	✓ Handicapped

The CSU Vikings men's and women's basketball teams can show

off their talents to 13,000-plus fans in the state-of-the-art Convocation Center. Both teams consistently rank well in the Midwestern Collegiate Conference of the NCAA. Other sports on campus here: men's baseball; women's softball; men's wrestling; men and women's fencing; men and women's swimming; men and women's soccer; women's volleyball.

High-School Sports

AGES:	1½–3	3–5	5–8	8–12	12–15
RATING:	NR	★	★★	★★	★

COST: **FREE–$** PREP.: **Some**

One way to introduce your kids to team sports is at nearby high-school games. Not only are they inexpensive, it's a great place to teach the rules of the game through illustration. In our neighborhood, there are plenty of fouls, flags and incomplete plays.

John Carroll University

AGES:	1½–3	3–5	5–8	8–12	12–15
RATING:	NR	★	★	★★	★★

COST: **$–$$** PREP.: **Some**
AREA: **East** CITY: **University Heights**

ADDRESS: 20700 N. Park Blvd.
PHONE: (216) 397-4416
SEASON: Year round
HOURS: Vary
PRICES: Vary
DIRECT.: I-271 to Exit 32 for Cedar Rd./Brainard Rd.; west on Cedar; left (south) on Richmond Rd.; right (west) on Fairmount Blvd.; right (north) on Hadleigh Rd. to campus.

✓ Strollers | Groups | ✓ Food Nearby
✓ Diap Chg | Picnic | ✓ Pub. Trans.
✓ Parking | ✓ Food Serv. | ✓ Handicapped

Sports on campus here: men and women's cross country; men's football; men and women's golf; men and women's soccer; men and women's tennis; women's volleyball; men and women's basketball; men and women's swimming and diving; men and women's indoor and outdoor track; men's wrestling; men's baseball; women's softball.

Kent State University

AGES:	1½–3	3–5	5–8	8–12	12–15
RATING:	NR	★	★	★★	★★

COST: **$–$$** PREP.: **Some**
AREA: **Far South** CITY: **Kent**

ADDRESS: E. Main & Lincoln Sts.
PHONE: (330) 672-2244
SEASON: Year round
HOURS: Vary
PRICES: Vary
DIRECT.: I-271 to I-480; east on I-480 (becomes SR 14 after Frost Rd.); right (south) on SR 43; left (east) on E. Main St.; right (south) onto Lincoln St. left (east) on Summit St. to KSU campus.

✓ Strollers | ✓ Groups | ✓ Food Nearby
Diap Chg | Picnic | ✓ Pub. Trans.
✓ Parking | ✓ Food Serv. | ✓ Handicapped

Sports here: men's baseball; men and women's basketball; women's field hockey; men's football; men and women's golf; women's gymnastics; women's soccer; women's softball; men and women's track; women's volleyball; men's wrestling.

Northfield Park

AGES:	1½–3	3–5	5–8	8–12	12–15
RATING:	NR	NR	★	★★	★★

COST: **$** PREP.: **None**
AREA: **South** CITY: **Northfield**

ADDRESS: 10705 Northfield Rd.
PHONE: (330) 467-4101
SEASON: Year round

Spectator Sports DIRECTORY

HOURS: Vary; live racing Mon, Wed, Fri, Sat evenings (also Sun evening Sept 26–Dec 19)

PRICES: $1.50 (grandstand), $3 (clubhouse)

DIRECT.: I-271/I-480 to Exit 23 for Forbes Rd.; west on Forbes; left (south) on SR 8 (Northfield Rd.)

✓ Strollers	✓ Groups	✓ Food Nearby
Diap Chg	Picnic	Pub. Trans.
✓ Parking	✓ Food Serv.	✓ Handicapped

Publicity schemes here include Saturday-night barbeques, the sale of ownership stakes in harness horses for as little as the price of admission, and busing in elementary-school students for stable tours. (A Kids Korner provides games and babysitting so that grown-ups can place bets.) Kitschy fun.

Oberlin College

AGES:	1½–3	3–5	5–8	8–12	12–15
RATING:	NR	★	★	★★	★★

COST: **$–$$** PREP.: **Some**
AREA: **Far West** CITY: **Oberlin**

ADDRESS: 200 Woodland

PHONE: (440) 775-8500

SEASON: Year round

HOURS: Vary

PRICES: Vary

DIRECT.: I-480 to Exit 1 for SR 10 ; west on SR 10 (becomes US 20) to SR 511; west on SR 511 to campus

WEB: www.oberlin.edu

✓ Strollers	Groups	✓ Food Nearby
Diap Chg	Picnic	Pub. Trans.
✓ Parking	✓ Food Serv.	✓ Handicapped

Men's football; men and women's cross country; men and women's soccer; men and women's indoor and outdoor track; men and women's tennis; men and women's lacrosse; men and women's basketball; men and women's swimming; men's baseball; women's field hockey; women's volleyball.

Thistledown Racing Club

AGES:	1½–3	3–5	5–8	8–12	12–15
RATING:	NR	NR	★	★★	★★

COST: **$–$$** PREP.: **None**
AREA: **Southeast** CITY: **North Randall**

ADDRESS: SR 8

PHONE: (216) 662-8600

SEASON: Year round (live racing Mar–Nov)

HOURS: Noon–9 p.m.

PRICES: $1, 12 & under free, Sunday brunch $15.95 per person

DIRECT.: West: I-480 to Exit 25 for Warrensville Center Rd.; north on Warrensville Center; right (east) on Emery Rd.; on left.

East: I-271 to I-480; west on I-480 to Exit 27 for Miles Rd.; north on Miles.; right (north) on Northfield Rd.; left (west) on Emery Rd.; on right.

WEB: www.thistledown.com

✓ Strollers	✓ Groups	✓ Food Nearby
Diap Chg	Picnic	✓ Pub. Trans.
✓ Parking	✓ Food Serv.	✓ Handicapped

Shopping mall developer Edward J. DeBartolo liked horse racing so much that he built a track near his Youngstown home (he would fly a private plane to the track, land it on the infield, and take his seat in the grandstand complex to watch the races). In the late 1980s, he plowed $26 million into renovating the aging facility to keep railbirds warmer in the winter and cooler in the summer (the live racing season starts March 1 and ends November 30). Simulcast betting is available January through November. Thoroughbreds run only during daylight hours. We took advantage of the Sunday brunch and found it an easy way to organize a family outing and lose money at the same time.

Group Tours

Ever wonder how crayons are made or chocolate molded? Curious to explore the stables of the mounted police or behind the scenes of a theater? When choosing tours for young children, keep in mind their interests. And, know the length of the tour beforehand, because children at young ages have short attention spans. Thirty minutes in one place can be much too long; a tour should keep moving. Listed here are a number of tours in the area that are both fun and educational. While some welcome walk-ins, most require at least a few weeks' notice and are open only to organized groups.

African-American Heritage Tour

AGES:	1½–3	3–5	5–8	8–12	12–15
RATING:	NR	NR	★	★★	★★★

COST: **$$** PREP.: **None–Some**
AREA: **Farther West** CITY: **Oberlin**

ADDRESS: Oberlin College Campus & city of Oberlin

PHONE: Ohio Heritage Center: (440) 774-1700; Lorain County Visitors Bureau: (440) 245-5282

SEASON: Year round

HOURS: Tue, Thu, Sat 10:30 a.m. & 1:30 p.m. (special appointments by request)

PRICES: $4 per person

DIRECT.: I-480 to Exit 1 for SR 10 ; west on SR 10 (becomes US 20) to SR 511; west on SR 511 to campus

Strollers	✓ Groups	✓ Food Nearby
Diap Chg	Picnic	Pub. Trans.
✓ Parking	Food Serv.	Handicapped

Oberlin became nationally known in the pre–Civil War era as a safe haven for fugitive slaves following the Underground Railroad toward freedom in Canada. A walking tour, lasting just over an hour, is narrated by local history buffs/volunteers who relate the story of this small city since its founding in 1833. Included are three preserved historic buildings—the Monroe House, home to two noted abolitionists; the Little Red Schoolhouse Museum, a one-room schoolhouse; and Jewett House, listed on the National Register of Historic Places.

Other buildings and monuments, such as the memorial to the Underground Railroad on the Oberlin College campus, may also be visited on foot but are not on the formal tour. A map to the grave sites of a number of those who were a part of making history is available from the Westwood Cemetery.

Though the content and sites here are aimed at older, school-age kids, a Children's Activity Guide to the sites is in the works to make the city's history more accessible. Special events are hosted throughout the year, including HiStorytelling hours designed for children and a gingerbread house baking and decorating contest.

Cleveland Department of Water—Filtration Plants

AGES:	1½–3	3–5	5–8	8–12	12–15
RATING:	NR	NR	★★	★★	★

COST: **FREE** PREP.: **Some**
AREA: **various** CITY: **Cleveland**

ADDRESS: Several locations (see description)

PHONE: (216) 664-2444 ext. 5663

SEASON: Year round

HOURS: Open during National Drinking Water Week (early May); other times by appt. (required); minimum group size: 12.

PRICES: Free

Strollers	✓ Groups	✓ Food Nearby
Diap Chg	✓ Picnic	✓ Pub. Trans.
✓ Parking	Food Serv.	Handicapped

Have you ever driven by one of Cleveland's impressive-looking filtration plants and wondered what was inside? Wonder no more. The plants are open to anyone wanting to know how our water is cleansed, processed, and sent on its way to our faucets. The one-hour tour includes a walk through the plant and an 11-minute video on the history of the Cleveland Water Dept., covering the early 1900s to the present. About 30 to 40 tours are given each year. Reservations are required, except during National Drinking Water Week (early May); the minimum group size is 12.

Locations:

Baldwin Plant, 11216 Stokes Blvd., Cleveland
Crown Plant, 955 Clague Rd., Westlake
Garrett A. Morgan Plant, 1245 W. 45 St., Cleveland
Nottingham Plant, 1230 Chardon Rd., Euclid

Cleveland Mounted Police Stables

AGES:	1½–3	3–5	5–8	8–12	12–15
RATING:	NR	★	★★★	★★	★

COST: **FREE** PREP.: **Some**
AREA: **Near East** CITY: **Cleveland**

ADDRESS: 1150 E. 38 St.

PHONE: (216) 623-5653

SEASON: Year round

HOURS: Mon–Sat 10 a.m.–4 p.m. (by appointment only)

PRICES: Free

DIRECT.: I-90 to Exit 175 for E. 55 St.; south on E. 55; right (west) on S. Marginal St.; left (south) on E. 38 St.; on right.

Strollers	✓ Groups	✓ Food Nearby
Diap Chg	✓ Picnic	✓ Pub. Trans.
✓ Parking	Food Serv.	✓ Handicapped

The Cleveland Mounted Police have been patrolling the city's streets on horseback since 1905. Their horses (typically numbering about 16) are donated from area stables. The tour lasts 45 minutes and includes a walk through the stables to learn how the horses are fed, groomed, and cared for; the blacksmith shows how they are shod.

Reservations for tours are required and can accommodate no fewer than 10 and no more than 40 people (adult supervision is a must). The barns are open for self-guided walking tours from 10 a.m. through 4 p.m.

Cleveland Postal Business Center

AGES:	1½–3	3–5	5–8	8–12	12–15
RATING:	NR	NR	NR	★★	★★

COST: **FREE** PREP.: **Some**
AREA: **Downtown** CITY: **Cleveland**

ADDRESS: Main Post Office, 2400 Orange Ave.

PHONE: (216) 443-4401

SEASON: Year round

HOURS: Daily 9 a.m.–12 p.m. (Mon–Thu mornings preferred)

PRICES: Free (Reservations required—no children under 10)

DIRECT.: West: I-90 to 171A for Orange Ave.; east on Orange; on right.

East: I-90 to Exit 173A for Prospect Ave.; left (south) on E. 22 St.; right (east) on Orange Ave; on right.

Strollers	✓ Groups	✓ Food Nearby
Diap Chg	Picnic	✓ Pub. Trans.
✓ Parking	✓ Food Serv.	✓ Handicapped

Want to show your kids how letters get from the mailbox to their proper destination? Visit the main post office on Orange Avenue. A tour, guided by postal employees, lasts an hour and includes a 15-minute movie and a walk through the mailroom floor to see the behind-the-scenes activities, such as sorting and preparation, as well as the machinery involved in the mail service. Reservations are required and limited to groups of up to 45 people.

Cuyahoga County Airport

AGES:	1½–3	3–5	5–8	8–12	12–15
RATING:	NR	NR	★	★★	★★

COST: **FREE** PREP.: **Some**
AREA: **East** CITY: **Richmond Hts.**

ADDRESS: 26300 Curtiss Wright Pkwy.

PHONE: (216) 289-4111

SEASON: Year round

HOURS: Weekdays only, by appointment (tour is 1½ hours)

PRICES: Free (reservations required)

DIRECT.: West: I-90 to Exit 187 for Bishop Rd.; south on Bishop; right (west) on Curtiss Wright Pkwy; on left.

East: I-271 to Exit 36 for Wilson Mills Rd.; west on Wilson Mills; right (north) on Richmond Rd.; right (west) on Curtiss Wright Pkwy; on right.

Strollers ✓ Groups ✓ Food Nearby
Diap Chg Picnic ✓ Pub. Trans.
✓ Parking Food Serv. Handicapped

A tour here includes a look at the Aircraft Rescue Firefighting Station and the hangar facilities with an emphasis on what makes airplanes fly safely. Limited to ages five and older, this is a popular destination for East Side school groups.

Dixon Ticonderoga Crayon Factory

AGES:	1½–3	3–5	5–8	8–12	12–15
RATING:	NR	NR	★★	★★★	★★

COST: **FREE** PREP.: **Much**
AREA: **Farther West** CITY: **Sandusky**

ADDRESS: 1706 Hayes Ave.

PHONE: (419) 625-9545

SEASON: Seasonal (Sep–May)

HOURS: Tue, Wed, Thu 10 a.m.

PRICES: Free; no one under age 5 admitted; reservation required for groups (no more than 30 people)

DIRECT.: SR 2 to SR 4 (Hayes Ave.); north on Hayes; on right.

WEB: www.dixonticonderoga.com

Strollers ✓ Groups ✓ Food Nearby
Diap Chg Picnic Pub. Trans.
✓ Parking Food Serv. ✓ Handicapped

This century-old business merged in 1984 with the American Crayon Company but continues to delight children with free samples and an up-close look at crayon manufacturing. Tours last one hour and include a walk through the factory to see how crayons are mixed, molded, labeled, and packaged. Reservations are required and are typically booked up to a year in advance. Tour group size ranges from 10 to 30; tours are open only to schools, scout troops, and other organized groups.

Federal Reserve Bank

AGES:	1½–3	3–5	5–8	8–12	12–15
RATING:	NR	NR	NR	NR	★★★

COST: **FREE** PREP.: **None**
AREA: **Downtown** CITY: **Cleveland**

ADDRESS: E. 6 St. at Superior

PHONE: (216) 579-2125

SEASON: Year round

HOURS: Weekdays by appointment

PRICES: Free

DIRECT.: West: I-90 to Exit 172A for E. 9 St.; north on E. 9; left (west) on Superior Ave.; on right.

WEB: www.clev.frb.org

Strollers	✓ Groups	✓ Food Nearby
Diap Chg	Picnic	✓ Pub. Trans.
✓ Parking	Food Serv.	Handicapped

After a $117-million renovation, it ought to be impressive. And the marble lobby of the Federal Reserve Bank of Cleveland, with its gold-ornamented, vaulted ceilings, is just that. The 12-story structure was built in 1923 in the Italian Renaissance style and modeled after the fortress/home of the Medici, the great bankers of Florence. An architectural gem, it is a National Historic Building.

Next door, in the modern operations center, a three-story vault with a 100-ton steel door is accessed by robotic vehicles that move huge bins of currency to and from the loading docks.

Tours here include a look at U.S. money through the ages (dating from the Civil War) and a cash-handling system with machines that can process 90,000 checks an hour. The one-hour group tour is very popular—school groups are limited to ages 14 and older.

Goodtime III

AGES:	1½–3	3–5	5–8	8–12	12–15
RATING:	NR	★	★★	★★★	★★

COST: **$$** PREP.: **Some**
AREA: **Downtown** CITY: **Cleveland**

ADDRESS: 825 E. 9 St. Pier

PHONE: (216) 861-5110

SEASON: Seasonal (Jun 15–Labor Day; weekends Memorial Day–Jun 15)

HOURS: Mon–Sat 12 p.m. & 3 p.m.; Sun 12 p.m., 3 p.m., & 6 p.m.

PRICES: $12.50 adults, $11.50 seniors, $7.50 ages 2–11, no charge under age 2

DIRECT.: East: SR 2 to E. 9 St.; north on E. 9. West: I-90 to Exit 172A for E. 9 St.; north on E. 9.

✓ Strollers	✓ Groups	✓ Food Nearby
✓ Diap Chg	Picnic	✓ Pub. Trans.
✓ Parking	✓ Food Serv.	✓ Handicapped

Goodtime sightseeing boats have been cruising the Cuyahoga River since 1958. The current boat, the *Goodtime III*, tours the Cleveland lakefront and 6½ miles of the 100-mile-long Cuyahoga in two hours. A highlight for most kids is seeing the 21 different bridges that span the crooked river. A tour guide accompanies the trip, armed with little-known historical facts—about the river's hand-dug mouth, its original entrance (by Edgewater Park), and the early inhabitants of its shorelines. The *Goodtime III* sails rain or shine, but the route changes daily depending on lake and river traffic.

No food or beverages may be brought on board. Reservations are not required; there is no minimum group size. Cheap parking is available at Burke Lakefront Airport.

The *Goodtime III* on the Cuyahoga River

Goodyear World of Rubber Museum

AGES:	1½–3	3–5	5–8	8–12	12–15
RATING:	NR	NR	★	★★	★★

COST: **FREE** PREP.: **None–Much**
AREA: **Far South** CITY: **Akron**

ADDRESS: 1144 E. Market St. Dept. 799

PHONE: (330) 796-7117

SEASON: Year round

HOURS: Mon–Fri 8 a.m.–4:30 p.m.; closed holidays; reservations required for groups of 10 or more

PRICES: Free

DIRECT.: I-76 to Exit 24 for Kelly Ave.; north on Kelly; right (east) on 3 Ave.; left (north) on Martha Ave.; left (west) on E. Market St.; on right.

WEB: www.goodyear.com

✓ Strollers ✓ Groups ✓ Food Nearby
Diap Chg Picnic ✓ Pub. Trans.
✓ Parking Food Serv. ✓ Handicapped

As company museums go, this is way above the norm. For starters, there is a replica of Charles Goodyear's kitchen gum workshop where he discovered how to vulcanize rubber, giving birth to the tire industry (not to mention Akron's former moniker, the "Rubber City").

As manufacturing history, it is packed with good stuff: enter the museum through a small grove of rubber trees and see how tires got their start. (These days, of course, tires come from petroleum products and modern chemistry; for details to satisfy the most inquisitive of six-year-old minds there is an entire exhibit devoted to how tires are now made.) In addition to tires, Goodyear has gotten a lot of mileage out of its blimps, to which the museum also devotes a large amount of attention with pictures and entire sections of dirigible frames.

Also on display are Indianapolis 500 race cars, an artificial heart, a moon-rover tire, and a short history of the beginnings of the interstate trucking industry. Film segments accompany many exhibits.

Fighter jocks (both young and old) will like the open cockpit of a World War II–era Corsair, also made by Goodyear.

The small gift shop is worth checking out for its mini-blimps and logo-adorned items.

Reservation are required for groups of 20 or more. Special tours can be arranged with 30-day advance notice.

Guggisberg Cheese Factory

AGES:	1½–3	3–5	5–8	8–12	12–15
RATING:	NR	★	★★	★★	★

COST: **FREE** PREP.: **Some–Much**
AREA: **Far South** CITY: **Millersburg**

ADDRESS: 5060 SR 557

PHONE: (330) 893-2500

SEASON: Year round

HOURS: Mon–Sat 8 a.m.–5 p.m.; also open Sundays 11 a.m.–4 p.m. April–Dec; one-week advance reservation requested

PRICES: Free

DIRECT.: I-77 to Exit 83 for SR 39; west on SR 39; left (south) on SR 557; on right.

Strollers ✓ Groups ✓ Food Nearby
Diap Chg Picnic Pub. Trans.
✓ Parking ✓ Food Serv. ✓ Handicapped

This small factory specializes in Baby Swiss (in fact, they claim to have originated the recipe here). A tour includes watching the cheese being made through the large glass viewing windows. Milk is first brought from neighboring Amish farms, cultures and enzymes are added, and the curd is pressed into molds. If you happen upon the factory in the afternoon when the cheese has already been made for the day, a short video details the process. Tastes are also offered.

Cheese is typically made from 8 a.m. to 2 p.m. on weekdays.

Harry London Candies

AGES:	1½–3	3–5	5–8	8–12	12–15
RATING:	NR	NR	★	★★	★★

COST: **$** PREP.: **Some**
AREA: **Farther South** CITY: **North Canton**

ADDRESS: 5353 Lauby Rd.

PHONE: (800) 321-0444

SEASON: Year round

HOURS: Mon–Sat 9 a.m.–4 p.m., Sun noon–3:30 p.m. (reservations required)

PRICES: Adults $2, children & teens 6–18 $1, under 6 free

DIRECT.: I-77 to Exit 113 for Akron Canton Airport; right (north) on Lauby Rd.; on right.

✓ Strollers ✓ Groups ✓ Food Nearby
✓ Diap Chg Picnic Pub. Trans.
✓ Parking Food Serv. ✓ Handicapped

Guided tours of this large (80,000 square feet) chocolate factory include a short video on how candy is made, views of the candy kitchen, and a sample of chocolates as they're being made. A fudge-making demonstration is typically ongoing in the store. The 1½-hour tour includes ample time at the end for shopping.

Heinen's

AGES:	1½–3	3–5	5–8	8–12	12–15
RATING:	NR	NR	★	★	★

COST: **FREE** PREP.: **Some**
AREA: **East** CITY: **Warrensville Hts.**

ADDRESS: 20601 Aurora Rd.

PHONE: (216) 475-2300

SEASON: Year round

HOURS: By arrangement

PRICES: Free

DIRECT.: West: I-480 to Exit 25B for Warrensville Center Rd.; north on Warrensville Center; right (east) on Aurora Rd.; on left.

East: I-271/I-480 to Exit 27 for Miles Rd.; west on Miles; left (south) on Warrensville Center Rd.; left (west) on Aurora Rd.; on left.

South: I-480 to Exit 25 for Aurora Rd.; northwest on Aurora; on right.

Strollers ✓ Groups ✓ Food Nearby
Diap Chg Picnic ✓ Pub. Trans.
✓ Parking ✓ Food Serv. Handicapped

This locally owned grocery-store chain regularly schedules children's cooking classes at the Pepper Pike Cooking School location—especially around the holidays for candy making and gingerbread house decorating. For school groups, tours of the market can be arranged by the store managers at each location. Groups are walked through each department for an explanation of the food groups as well as the tastings.

Hoover Historical Center

AGES:	1½–3	3–5	5–8	8–12	12–15
RATING:	NR	★	★	★★	★

COST: **FREE** PREP.: **None–Some**
AREA: **Farther South** CITY: **North Canton**

ADDRESS: 1875 Easton N.W.

PHONE: (330) 499-0287

SEASON: Year round

HOURS: Tue–Sun 1–5 p.m.

PRICES: Free

DIRECT.: I-77 to Exit 111 for North Canton/Canal Fulton; east on Portage Rd.; right (south) on Wise St.; left (east) on Maple Ave. (becomes Easton St.); on left across from Walsh College.

Strollers ✓ Groups ✓ Food Nearby
Diap Chg ✓ Picnic ✓ Pub. Trans.
✓ Parking Food Serv. ✓ Handicapped

This small museum is among the most specialized collections in Ohio: it lays claim to being the only vacuum-cleaner museum in the world. What makes the Hoover Historical Center an attraction for families is its schedule of annual events. They include shadow-puppet performances, a program of storytelling for children geared to ages 4–7 (held outside in the herb garden during the summer with a snack provided), and holiday festivals. Most events are free. Also worth mentioning are the elaborate herb gardens maintained by the Center's Herb Society.

Inside the completely restored, Victorian-era farmhouse—the boyhood home of William H. Hoover, founder of the Hoover Company—is the world's most extensive collection of antique vacuum cleaners. They range from 1800s sweepers to early electric models—some weighing nearly 100 pounds. Tours include a short video depicting Hoover's start in industry, and a walk through the tannery and barn. The farm's three buildings were moved to the park in 1997 to create a center for special events.

Jacobs Field

AGES:	1½–3	3–5	5–8	8–12	12–15
RATING:	NR	NR	★★	★★★	★★★

COST: **$–$$** PREP.: **Some**
AREA: **Downtown** CITY: **Cleveland**

ADDRESS: 2401 Ontario St.

PHONE: (216) 420-4487

SEASON: Seasonal (May–Sept)

HOURS: Mon–Sat 10 a.m.–2 p.m. on the half hour

PRICES: $6 adults, $4 children and seniors

DIRECT.: West: I-90 to Exit 171B for Ontario St; north on Ontario; on right.

East: I-90 to Exit 173A for Prospect Ave.; west on Prospect; left (south) on E. 18 St.; right (west) on Carnegie Ave.; on right.

WEB: www.indians.com

Strollers ✓ Groups ✓ Food Nearby
✓ Diap Chg ✓ Picnic ✓ Pub. Trans.
✓ Parking ✓ Food Serv. ✓ Handicapped

Tours of Jacobs Field are offered by arrangement Monday through Saturday from May to September and include visits to the press box, dugout, and club lounge.

Malley's Chocolates

AGES:	1½–3	3–5	5–8	8–12	12–15
RATING:	NR	★	★★	★	★

COST: **$** PREP.: **Some**
AREA: **South** CITY: **Cleveland**

ADDRESS: 13400 Brookpark Rd.

PHONE: (800) 835-5684

SEASON: Year round

HOURS: Mon–Fri 10 a.m.–3 p.m. by appointment (open Sat Oct–Apr)

PRICES: $2, $1 ages 12 and up, $1 ages 3–11, no charge age 2 and under

DIRECT.: I-480 to Exit 12B for W. 130 St.; south on W. 130; right (west) on Brookpark Rd.; on right.

WEB: www.malleys.com

✓ Strollers ✓ Groups ✓ Food Nearby
Diap Chg Picnic ✓ Pub. Trans.
✓ Parking Food Serv. ✓ Handicapped

The Malley family has been producing sweets in the Cleveland area since 1935. Their Brookpark plant was designed specifically with factory tours in mind. The tour lasts 30 to 45 minutes and includes a look at nut roasting, chocolate making, filling preparation, coating, designing, and packaging, all in the order of production. Guides' commentaries are tailored to the ages and interests of the group. In theory, three chocolate samples are given: one to get kids going at the beginning, one to move them out at the finish, and a candy bar to take home. (Our son, however, managed to consume seven.) Reservations are required; group size is limited to 15–45, and individuals are required to join a scheduled group.

Malley's Chocolates

Municipal Court of Cleveland

AGES:	1½–3	3–5	5–8	8–12	12–15
RATING:	NR	NR	NR	★	★★

COST: **FREE** PREP.: **Some**
AREA: **Downtown** CITY: **Cleveland**

ADDRESS: 1200 Ontario St.

PHONE: (216) 664-4757

SEASON: Year round

HOURS: By appointment (Fridays preferred)

PRICES: Free

DIRECT.: West: I-90 to Exit 171B for Ontario St.; north on Ontario; on left.

East: SR 2 to E. 9 St.; south on E. 9; right (west) on Lakeside Ave.; left (south) on Ontario St.; on right.

Strollers ✓ Groups ✓ Food Nearby
Diap Chg Picnic ✓ Pub. Trans.
✓ Parking Food Serv. Handicapped

While this tour is not for everyone—the court deals with an array of crimes from traffic violations to felony convictions—it is designed to be a look at the court system and law-enforcement procedures. School groups are welcome but need to make arrangements well in advance.

Old Stone Church

First Presbyterian Society of Cleveland

AGES:	1½–3	3–5	5–8	8–12	12–15
RATING:	NR	NR	★	★★	★★

COST: **FREE** PREP.: **None–Some**
AREA: **Downtown** CITY: **Cleveland**

ADDRESS: 91 Public Square

PHONE: (216) 241-6145

SEASON: Year round

HOURS: Mon–Fri 9:30 a.m.–4:30 p.m. (self-guided); by reservation for guided tours

PRICES: Free

DIRECT.: West: I-90 to Exit 171B for Ontario St.; north on Ontario; on left.

East: SR 2 to East 9 St.; south on E. 9; left (west) on Lakeside Ave.; left (south) on Ontario St.; on right.

✓ Strollers ✓ Groups ✓ Food Nearby
Diap Chg Picnic ✓ Pub. Trans.
Parking Food Serv. ✓ Handicapped

A downtown tour of Cleveland's history should include the Old Stone Church, a venerable institution on Public Square for more than 175 years. It is the oldest building on the Square. (It even survived fire damage in 1857 and 1884.) With its Tiffany stained-glass windows, frescoed walls, and stunning vaulted wooden ceiling, the church is very much worth visiting. Tours and regular musical events offer a glimpse of the historic interior of this "spiritual lighthouse of Cleveland."

Old Stone Church

Patterson's Farm

AGES:	1½–3	3–5	5–8	8–12	12–15
RATING:	★★	★★	★★★	★	★

COST: **$–$$** PREP.: **None–Some**
AREA: **Far East** CITY: **Chesterland**

ADDRESS: 8765 Mulberry Rd. (Market: 11414 Caves Rd.)

PHONE: (800) 48-FRUIT

SEASON: Seasonal (Mid-Sept–Oct, apples; June, strawberries)

HOURS: Weekdays: 2 p.m.–6 p.m; weekends: 10 a.m.–5 p.m.

PRICES: $2-$3 per person (extra fee for hayrides)

DIRECT.: Farm: I-271 to Exit 34 for US 322 (Mayfield Rd.); east on US 322; left (north) on Caves Rd.; right (east) on Mulberry Rd.; on left.

Market: I-271 to Exit 34 for US 322 (Mayfield Rd.); east on US 322; left (north) on Caves Rd.; on left.

WEB: www.pattersonfarm.com

✓ Strollers ✓ Groups Food Nearby
Diap Chg ✓ Picnic Pub.Trans.
✓ Parking ✓ Food Serv. Handicapped

With apples, strawberries, sweet corn, and other vegetables, this local farm and farm market is a popular picking spot for local families. Most tours begin at the Caves Road Market location and include a tractor-pulled or horse-drawn hayride (or sleigh ride, if there is snow) through the farm and orchards. Shelters can also be reserved for picnics in front of a bonfire.

Each fall a Family Fun Fest combines apple picking, hiking, hay mazes and crafts—it is popular among area preschools. If you are looking for a group outing, be sure to reserve early.

Plain Dealer Production and Distribution Center

AGES:	1½–3	3–5	5–8	8–12	12–15
RATING:	NR	NR	NR	NR	★★★

COST: **FREE** PREP.: **Some**
AREA: **Near West** CITY: **Brooklyn**

ADDRESS: 4800 Tiedeman Rd.

PHONE: (216) 999-5665

SEASON: Year round

HOURS: Private tours: Thu & Fri 9 a.m., 11 a.m., 1 p.m., and 3 p.m.; Tues & Sat 9 a.m., 11 a.m., and 3 p.m.; Public tours Tues & Sat 1 p.m.; registration required.

PRICES: Free (15 or more considered as a private group)

DIRECT.: I-480 to Exit 13 for Tiedeman Rd.; north on Tiedeman; on left.

✓ Strollers ✓ Groups ✓ Food Nearby
Diap Chg Picnic ✓ Pub. Trans.
✓ Parking Food Serv. ✓ Handicapped

Want to know what $220 million buys these days? For *The Plain Dealer*, it bought a state-of-the-art printing and distribution center. Inside the Brooklyn compound, trains pull up to drop off huge rolls of newsprint. From there, robots take the rolls to the presses and entire sections of the paper wait in adjoining rooms before being put together. There, they are moved into tractor trailers that spill out onto I-480. Because production for *The Plain Dealer* occurs late at night, call first to see if you'll find the place humming with activity. Regardless, it's an impressive factory tour.

Plidco Pipeline Museum

AGES:	1½–3	3–5	5–8	8–12	12–15
RATING:	NR	NR	★	★★	★★

COST: **FREE** PREP.: **Some**
AREA: **Near West** CITY: **Cleveland**

ADDRESS: 1841 Columbus Rd.

PHONE: (440) 871-5700

SEASON: Year round

HOURS: Mon–Fri, visiting hours by appointment

PRICES: Free

DIRECT.: West: I-90 to Exit 245 for US 42 (W. 25 St.); north on W. 25; right (north) on Columbus Rd.; on right.

East: I-90 to Exit 171 for Abbey Ave.; west on Abbey; right (north) on Columbus Rd.; on right.

WEB: www.plidco.com

Strollers	✓ Groups	✓ Food Nearby
Diap Chg	Picnic	Pub. Trans.
✓ Parking	Food Serv.	Handicapped

Pipelines from different eras provide a perspective on Cleveland's industrial past. Exhibits include pipe samples as old as the Roman Empire and as recent as the Alaskan oil pipeline. There are no real kids' programs or hands-on activities here, so this museum is better suited for elementary- school children or school groups especially interested in the subject matter.

Rockin' R Ranch

AGES:	1½–3	3–5	5–8	8–12	12–15
RATING:	NR	★	★★	★★	★

COST: **$$** PREP.: **Some–Much**

AREA: **Far West** CITY: **Columbia Station**

ADDRESS: 19066 E. River Rd.

PHONE: (440) 236-5454

SEASON: Seasonal (May–Nov)

HOURS: Fall Family Fun Fest: Sat & Sun 11 a.m.–5 p.m.; group outings by appointment

PRICES: Fall Family Fun Fest: $6.50 per person; Birthdays $8 per child

DIRECT.: I-480 to Exit 6 for Great Northern Blvd./SR 252 (Columbia Rd.); south on Columbia; on right after SR 82.

Strollers	✓ Groups	Food Nearby
Diap Chg	✓ Picnic	Pub. Trans.
✓ Parking	✓ Food Serv.	Handicapped

The folks at the Ranch attempt to re-create the West right here in Northeast Ohio, with 22 acres of woods and fields, a tractor-drawn hayride, a visit with some animals in a small petting farmyard, hay mazes, and a bonfire. To top it off, each participant leaves with a cowboy hat!

Schrock's Amish Farm and Home

AGES:	1½–3	3–5	5–8	8–12	12–15
RATING:	NR	★	★★	★★	★

COST: **$** PREP.: **Some**

AREA: **Farther South** CITY: **Berlin**

ADDRESS: 4363 SR 39

PHONE: (330) 893-3232

SEASON: Seasonal (Apr–Oct)

HOURS: Mon–Fri 10 a.m.–5 p.m.; Sat 10 a.m.–6 p.m.; closed Sun

PRICES: $2–$6; group rates for groups of 20 or more. Tour of Main House and Grampa's House includes video, buggy rides, and animal petting area

DIRECT.: I-77 to Exit 83 for Dover/Sugarcreek; right (west) on SR 39; on right.

✓ Strollers	✓ Groups	✓ Food Nearby
Diap Chg	✓ Picnic	Pub. Trans.
✓ Parking	✓ Food Serv.	Handicapped

This privately owned farm, opened to the public in 1989, is still an actual residence. Tours begin with a 20-minute slide show covering the lifestyle of the Amish, followed by a guided walk through the home. They last from 45 minutes to two hours and can be tailored to your group. Visitors can also take a 10-minute buggy ride around the farm grounds to see the barn animals (sheep, calves, geese, and ponies) and visit the petting area. Reservations are not required, and there is no minimum group size.

Schwebel's Baking Co.

AGES:	1½–3	3–5	5–8	8–12	12–15
RATING:	NR	NR	NR	★★	★★

COST: **FREE** PREP.: **Some**
AREA: **Far South** CITY: **Cuyahoga Falls**

ADDRESS: 1950 Newberry St.

PHONE: (330) 929-9822

SEASON: Seasonal (Closed in summer—too hot!)

HOURS: By appointment only

PRICES: Free

DIRECT.: I-271 to Exit 18 for SR 8; south on SR 8; east on Tallmadge Rd.; right (south) on Newberry St.; on right.

Strollers ✓ Groups ✓ Food Nearby
Diap Chg Picnic ✓ Pub. Trans.
✓ Parking Food Serv. Handicapped

On a 30-minute tour of this bakery, visitors see all phases of production from mixing to packaging, while more than 100,000 loaves a day are baked for stores all over the region.

Older school groups may be impressed with the process. Everyone is required to wear hair nets and safety glasses,and as it is very loud, earphones are needed in order to hear the tour guide's explanations.

Temple Museum of Religious Art

AGES:	1½–3	3–5	5–8	8–12	12–15
RATING:	NR	NR	NR	★★	★★

COST: **FREE** PREP.: **Some**
AREA: **Near East** CITY: **Cleveland**

ADDRESS: The Temple-Tifereth Israel, 1855 Ansel Rd.

PHONE: (216) 791-7755

SEASON: Year round

HOURS: Museum open by appointment (please call ahead)

PRICES: Free

DIRECT.: East: I-90 to Exit 177 for Martin Luther King Blvd.; south on MLK; right (west) on Wade Park Ave.; left (south) on Ansel Rd. on left.

West: I-90 to Exit for 173B for Chester Ave.; east on Chester; on left after E. 101 St.

Strollers ✓ Groups ✓ Food Nearby
Diap Chg Picnic ✓ Pub. Trans.
✓ Parking Food Serv. Handicapped

One of the most prominent and comprehensive collections of Judaic art is housed at The Temple Museum, the fourth-oldest museum of Judaica in the United States.

As there are no real kids' programs or hands-on activities here, this museum is better suited for elementary-school children or school groups especially interested in the subject matter.

Terminal Tower Observation Deck

AGES:	1½–3	3–5	5–8	8–12	12–15
RATING:	★	★	★★	★★	★★

COST: **$** PREP.: **None**
AREA: **Downtown** CITY: **Cleveland**

ADDRESS: Terminal Tower, 42nd floor, 50 Public Square

PHONE: (216) 621-7981; Convention and Visitors Bureau: (216) 621-4110

SEASON: Year round

HOURS: (Sat, Sun) Oct–Apr 11 a.m.–3:30 p.m.; May–Sep 11 a.m.–4:30 p.m.

PRICES: $2 adults, $1 ages 6–16, free age 5 & under

DIRECT.: West: I-90 to Exit 171B for Ontario Ave.; north on Ontario to Public Square; on left.

East: SR 2 to E. 9 St.; south on E. 9; right (west) on Superior Ave. to Public Square.

✓ Strollers ✓ Groups ✓ Food Nearby
Diap Chg Picnic ✓ Pub. Trans.
✓ Parking Food Serv. ✓ Handicapped

The observation deck offers a fine 360-degree view of the city (on clear days). It also has some displays with historical information about the Terminal Tower (completed in 1930) and the downtown area.

Terminal Tower observation deck

Thistledown Race Track

AGES:	1½–3	3–5	5–8	8–12	12–15
RATING:	NR	NR	★	★★	★★

COST: **FREE** PREP.: **Some**
AREA: **Southeast** CITY: **North Randall**

ADDRESS: SR 8

PHONE: (216) 662-8600

SEASON: Year round (live racing Mar–Nov)

HOURS: In the morning, racing days; reservations required

PRICES: Free

DIRECT.: West: I-480 to Exit 25 for Warrensville Center Rd.; north on Warrensville Center; right (east) on Emery Rd.; on left.

East: I-271 to I-480; west on I-480 to Exit 27 for Miles Rd.; north on Miles; right (north) on Northfield Rd.; left (west) on Emery Rd.; on right.

WEB: www.thistledown.com

✓ Strollers ✓ Groups ✓ Food Nearby
Diap Chg Picnic ✓ Pub. Trans.
✓ Parking ✓ Food Serv. ✓ Handicapped

Satisfy a budding interest in horses with a Barn Tour, held in the morning on racing days (reservations are a must). A trainer guides you through the stables and answers questions.

Trolley Tours of Cleveland

AGES:	1½–3	3–5	5–8	8–12	12–15
RATING:	NR	NR	★	★★	★★

COST: **$$** PREP.: **Some**
AREA: **Downtown** CITY: **Cleveland**

ADDRESS: 1831 Columbus Rd.

PHONE: (800) 848-0173

SEASON: Year round

HOURS: Memorial Day to Labor Day: 1-hour tour: Mon–Sat 12:30 p.m., Sun 3:30 p.m. (Fri–Sat 6 p.m. tours available); 2-hour tour: Mon–Sat 9:30 a.m. & 2 p.m., Sun 1 p.m.; Winter schedule: Fri & Sat 12:30 p.m. (1-hour tour) and 2 p.m. (2-hour tour).

PRICES: 1-hour tour: adult $8, senior $7, children 12 & under $5, under 2 free; 2-hour tour: adult $12, senior $11, children (5 to 12) $8.

DIRECT.: East: I-90 to SR 2; west on SR 2 to W. 28 St.; north on W. 28; right (east) on Washington Ave.; right (south) on W. 25 St.; left (east) on Washington; left (north) on Winslow Ave. to Nautica parking lot.

West: I-90 to Exit 170 for W. 25 St.; north on W. 25; right (east) on Washington Ave.; left (north) on Winslow Ave. to Nautica parking lot.

WEB: www.lollytrolley.com

Strollers ✓ Groups ✓ Food Nearby
Diap Chg Picnic ✓ Pub. Trans.
✓ Parking Food Serv. ✓ Handicapped

"Lolly the Trolley" and her siblings carry riders on a variety of tours, including a one-hour city sights tour of Cleveland's North Coast Harbor and the Rock and Roll Hall of Fame and Museum, downtown Cleveland, the Flats and the Warehouse District, Ohio City, and the West Side Market. The two-hour tour also includes Playhouse Square, University Circle, and a drive along the Lake Erie shore. Children under age five are not permitted on the two-hour tour.

Lolly the Trolley, Trolley Tours of Cleveland

United States Coast Guard Station

AGES:	1½–3	3–5	5–8	8–12	12–15
RATING:	NR	★	★★	★★★	★★

COST: **FREE** PREP.: **Some**
AREA: **Downtown** CITY: **Cleveland**

ADDRESS: 1055 E. 9 St.

PHONE: (216) 522-4412

SEASON: Year round (Best time for tours: mid-May–mid-September)

HOURS: Open 24 hours/day; call ahead to schedule tours

PRICES: Free

DIRECT.: SR 2 to E. 9 St.; north on E. 9; on right.

Strollers ✓ Groups ✓ Food Nearby
Diap Chg Picnic ✓ Pub. Trans.
✓ Parking Food Serv. ✓ Handicapped

At the Coast Guard Station you can take either a 20-minute tour (station only) or a tour that's about an hour long (station and boat). In the station you will see the emergency room and living quarters of the Coast Guard. Down on the water are the ice breaker *Neah Bay*, which is the most popular feature here (when it is docked), and the emergency rescue boats. Reservations are required (ask if the boat will be in). There is no limit on group size.

West Side Market

AGES:	1½–3	3–5	5–8	8–12	12–15
RATING:	NR	★	★★	★★	★

COST: **FREE** PREP.: **None**
AREA: **Near West** CITY: **Cleveland**

ADDRESS: 1979 W. 25 St. (at Lorain Rd.)

PHONE: (216) 664-3386

SEASON: Year round

HOURS: Mon, Wed 7 a.m.–4 p.m.; Fri–Sat 7 a.m.–6 p.m.

PRICES: Free

DIRECT.: East: I-90 to SR 2; west on SR 2 to W. 28 St.; north on W. 28; right (east) on Washington Ave.; right (south) on W. 25 St.; on left.

West: I-90 to Exit 170 for W. 25 St.; north on W. 25; on right.

WEB: www.westsidemarket.com

✓ Strollers ✓ Groups ✓ Food Nearby
Diap Chg Picnic ✓ Pub. Trans.
✓ Parking ✓ Food Serv. ✓ Handicapped

The West Side Market is the bustling home to dozens of produce vendors representing the wide array of ethnic groups that have helped shape Cleveland. The building, designated a National Historic Landmark, was constructed in 1912 in the European market-hall tradition with a dramatic 44-foot-high vaulted ceiling. It is also filled with a delicious and exotic assortment of foods.

There is no guided tour here, but the possibilities are terrific for sampling ethnic flavors and getting a feel for shopping in an open-air market. No reservations are required, but be prepared for a packed house on the weekends and before holidays. (Although parents do bring kids in strollers and backpacks, be aware that this really is a crowded place, especially outside in the produce arcades.)

Restrooms are not handicapped accessible.

Jan Ormerod
WHEN WE WENT TO THE
ZOO

Neighborhood Resources

It can be easy to overlook the places that are right in your own neighborhood. But don't, because they offer lots of useful resources for families. (For example, these days most libraries are equipped with computers that allow access to the internet; software can be sampled and previewed; video and CD collections are varied, and the offerings of computer classes extend way beyond the children's room.)

Here is a list of neighborhood organizations with programming of particular interest to families.

Akron-Summit County Public Library

AGES:	1½–3	3–5	5–8	8–12	12–15
RATING:	★★	★★★	★★★	★★	★★

COST: **FREE** PREP.: **None–Some**
AREA: **Far South** CITY: **Akron**

ADDRESS: 55 S. Main St.

PHONE: (330) 643-9000; Bookmobile (330) 643-9055; delivery (330) 643-9060

SEASON: Year round

HOURS: Main Library: Mon–Thu 9 a.m.–9 p.m., Fri 9 a.m.–6 p.m., Sat 9 a.m.–5 p.m., Sun 1–5 p.m.; Branches: Mon & Wed 10 a.m.–8:30 p.m., Tue & Thu noon–8:30 p.m., Fri noon–6 p.m., Sat 10 a.m.–5 p.m., closed Sun

PRICES: Free

✓ Strollers ✓ Groups ✓ Food Nearby
Diap Chg Picnic ✓ Pub. Trans.
✓ Parking Food Serv. ✓ Handicapped

Each branch offers storytimes for children ages 6 months and up, after-school activities, and holiday events. They often host Saturday films for children, too. Science Corner activity kits, available on request, offering hands-on project ideas.

Branches:

Ayres: 1765 W. Market St., (330) 836-1081
Chamberlain: 760 E. Archwood Ave., (330) 724-2126
East: 60 Goodyear Blvd., (330) 784-7522
Ellet: 485 Canton Rd., (330) 784-2019
Green: 4759 Massillon Rd., (330) 896-9074
Kenmore: 2200 14th St., SW, (330) 745-6126
McDowell: 3101 Smith Rd., (330) 666-4888
Main Library: 55 S. Main St., (330) 643-9000
Maple Valley: 1293 Copley Rd., (330) 864-5721
Mogadore: 1 S. Cleveland Ave., (330) 628-9228
Nordonia Hills: 9458 Olde Eight Rd., (440) 467-8595
North: 183 E. Cuyahoga Falls Ave., (330) 535-9423
Norton: 3930 S. Cleve-Mass Rd., (330) 825-7800
Portage Lakes: 4261 Manchester Rd., (330) 644-7050
Richfield: 4400 W. Streetsboro Rd., (440) 659-4343
Tallmadge: 32 South Ave., (330) 633-4345
West Hill: 807 W. Market St., (330) 376-2927
Wooster: 600 Wooster Ave., (330) 434-8726

Avon Lake Pub. Library

AGES:	1½–3	3–5	5–8	8–12	12–15
RATING:	★★★	★★★	★★	★★	★★

COST: **FREE** PREP.: **None–Some**
AREA: **West** CITY: **Avon Lake**

ADDRESS: 32649 Electric Blvd.

PHONE: (440) 933-8128

SEASON: Year round

HOURS: Mon–Thu 9 a.m.–9 p.m., Fri–Sat 9 a.m.–5 p.m., Sun 1–5 p.m. (Sep–May); Discovery Works Tue, Wed, Thu 10 a.m.–noon, 3 p.m.–5 p.m.; Sat noon–4 p.m.; Sept–May also Sun 2 p.m.–4 p.m

PRICES: Free

WEB: www.kellnet.com/allib/alpl.htm

✓ Strollers ✓ Groups ✓ Food Nearby
✓ Diap Chg ✓ Picnic ✓ Pub. Trans.
✓ Parking ✓ Food Serv. ✓ Handicapped

Preschool storytimes (ages 3–5) run in 10-week sessions in fall, winter, and spring. A summer reading program is open to all readers. Three children's groups, the Explorers Club (grades K–2), the Adventure Club (grade 3 and up), and the Junior Friends Group (grade 3 and up), offer stories, crafts, and other activities throughout the year. Computer education workshops are also offered.

Programs are scheduled occasionally, but most kids just like to come play. Favorites are the floor-to-ceiling bubble-maker and the small appliance take-apart area. Budding Mr. and Ms. Fix-its have a field day.

This is a true community center. Performances, lectures, and discussions regularly include programs for families.

Cleve. Heights-University Heights Public Library

AGES:	1½–3	3–5	5–8	8–12	12–15
RATING:	★★	★★★	★★★	★★★	★★

COST: **FREE–$$** PREP.: **None–Some**
AREA: **East** CITY: **Cleveland Hts.**

ADDRESS: 2345 Lee Rd. (Main Library)

PHONE: (216) 932-3600

SEASON: Year round

HOURS: Mon–Fri 9 a.m.–9 p.m.; Sat 9 a.m.–5:30 p.m.; Sun 1–5 p.m. (branch hrs. vary)

PRICES: Free

WEB: www.chuhpl.lib.oh.us

Strollers	✓ Groups	✓ Food Nearby
✓ Diap Chg	Picnic	✓ Pub. Trans.
✓ Parking	Food Serv.	✓ Handicapped

Each branch holds storytimes and programs for toddlers (30–36 months with parent) and preschool-age children (3–5), as well as for school-age kids (6 and up). Programs run from one day to 10 weeks. Computer classes for kids begin at age 3. Events are scheduled throughout the year include holiday storytelling, games, and crafts. (Most programs require preregistration.) A guide to events is published four times a year.

Branches:

Coventry Village: 1925 Coventry Rd., (216) 321-3400 (no parking); (216) 321-0739 (tty)

Noble Neighborhood: 2800 Noble Rd., (216) 291-5665

University Heights: 13866 Cedar Rd., (216) 321-4700

Cleveland Public Library

AGES:	1½–3	3–5	5–8	8–12	12–15
RATING:	★★★	★★★	★★★	★★★	★★★

COST: **FREE–$$** PREP.: **None–Some**
AREA: **Various** CITY: **Cleveland**

ADDRESS: 325 Superior Ave. (Admin. office)

PHONE: (216) 623-2800; Children's Services: (216) 623-2834

SEASON: Year round

HOURS: Mon–Sat 9 a.m.–6 p.m.; Sun 1–5 p.m. (branch hrs. vary)

PRICES: Free; fee for some classes

WEB: www.cpl.org

✓ Strollers	✓ Groups	✓ Food Nearby
✓ Diap Chg	Picnic	✓ Pub. Trans.
✓ Parking	Food Serv.	✓ Handicapped

The CPL's Main Library is a world-class resource—so extensive that a scheduled tour is not a bad idea. Each branch of the library system offers preschool storytimes and after-school activities such as crafts and movies. All branches have a summer reading club from mid-June to August. Throughout the year the library system works with the Cleveland Indians and Cleveland Lumberjacks to provide inspiration and incentives (such as game tickets) to keep reading. Homebound delivery is available.

Branches:

Addison: 6901 Superior Ave., (216) 623-6906

Broadway: 5417 Broadway, (216) 623-6913
Brooklyn: 3706 Pearl Rd., (216) 623-6920
Carnegie West: 1900 Fulton Rd., (216) 623-6927
Collinwood: 856 E. 152 St., (216) 623-6934
East 131: 3830 E. 131 St., (216) 623-6941
Eastman: 11602 Lorain Rd., (216) 623-6955
Fleet: 7224 Broadway, (216) 623-6962
Fulton: 3545 Fulton Rd., (216) 623-6969
Garden Valley: 7100 Kinsman Rd., (216) 623-6976
Glenville: 11900 St. Clair Ave., (216) 623-6983
Harvard-Lee: 16918 Harvard Ave., (216) 623-6990
Hough: 1566 Crawford Ave., (216) 623-6997
Jefferson: 850 Jefferson Ave., (216) 623-7004
Lorain: 8216 Lorain Ave., (216) 623-7011
Martin Luther King Jr.: 1962 E. 107 St. (Stokes Blvd.), (216) 623-7018
Memorial: 17109 Lake Shore Blvd., (216) 623-7039
Mt. Pleasant: 14000 Kinsman Rd., (216) 623-7032
Rice: 2820 E. 116 St., (216) 623-7046
Rockport: 4421 W. 140 St., (216) 623-7053
South: 3096 Scranton Rd., (216) 623-7060
South Brooklyn: 4303 Pearl Rd., (216) 623-7067
Sterling: 2200 E. 30 St., (216) 623-7074
Union: 3463 E. 93 St., (216) 623-7088
Walz: 7910 Detroit Ave., (216) 623-7095
West Park: 3805 W. 157 St., (216) 623-7102
Woodland: 5806 Woodland Ave., (216) 623-7109

Cuyahoga County Public Libraries

AGES:	1½–3	3–5	5–8	8–12	12–15
RATING:	★★	★★	★★	★★	★★

COST: **FREE–$$** PREP.: **None–Some**
AREA: **Various** CITY: **Parma (Admin. office)**

ADDRESS: 2111 Snow Rd.

PHONE: (216) 398-1800; Children's Services: (216) 749-9353

SEASON: Year round

HOURS: Vary

PRICES: Free; fee for some classes

WEB: www.clio1.cuyahoga.lib.oh.us

✓ Strollers ✓ Groups ✓ Food Nearby
✓ Diap Chg Picnic ✓ Pub. Trans.
✓ Parking Food Serv. ✓ Handicapped

Each branch offers activities, such as storytimes, crafts, shows, and after-school events. They also participates in Project LEAP, which provides story-time book kits and puppet shows based on a theme of your choice and designed specifically for preschool teachers, care providers, and parents. Of special interest to parents, the Brooklyn branch has a toy lending library. With a library card, patrons can borrow blocks, puzzles, puppets, and items to encourage learning about science, nature, the arts, and language. For specific information and a schedule for all programs, request a copy of *The Corridor*, which is published quarterly.

Branches:

Bay Village: 502 Cahoon Rd., (440) 871-6392
Beachwood: 25501 Shaker Blvd., (216) 831-6868
Berea: 7 Berea Commons, (440) 234-5475
Brecksville: 9089 Brecksville Rd., (440) 526-1102
Brook Park: 6155 Engle Rd., (216) 267-5250
Brooklyn: 4480 Ridge Rd., (216) 398-4600
Chagrin Falls: 100 E. Orange., (440) 247-3556
Fairview Park: 21255 Lorain Rd., (440) 333-4700
Garfield Heights: 5409 Turney Rd., (216) 475-8178
Gates Mills: 7580 Old Mill Rd., (440) 423-4808
Independence: 6361 Selig Dr., (216) 447-0160
Maple Heights: 5225 Library Lane, (216) 475-5000
Mayfield: 6080 Wilson Mills Rd., (440) 473-0350
Middleburg Heights: 15600 E. Bagley Rd., (440) 234-3600
North Olmsted: 27425 Butternut Ridge Rd., (440) 777-6211
North Royalton: 14600 State Rd., (440) 237-3800
Olmsted Falls: 7850 Main St., (440) 235-1150
Orange: 31300 Chagrin Blvd., (216) 831-4282
Parma Heights: 6206 Pearl Rd., (440) 884-2313
Parma: 7335 Ridge Rd., (440) 885-5362
Parma-Ridge: 5850 Ridge Rd., (440) 888-4300
Parma-Snow: 2121 Snow Rd., (216) 661-4240
Richmond Mall: 691 Richmond Rd., (440) 449-2666
Solon: 34125 Portz Pkwy., (440) 248-8777
South Euclid-Lyndhurst: 4645 Mayfield Rd., (216) 382-4880
Southeast: 70 Columbus Rd., (440) 439-4997
Strongsville: 13213 Pearl Rd., (440) 238-5530
Warrensville: 22035 Clarkwood Pkwy., (216) 464-5280

East Cleveland Public Libraries

AGES:	1½–3	3–5	5–8	8–12	12–15
RATING:	★★★	★★★	★★★	★★★	★★★

COST: **FREE** PREP.: **None–Much**
AREA: **Near East** CITY: **Cleveland**

ADDRESS: 14101 Euclid Ave. (Main Branch)
PHONE: (216) 541-4128
SEASON: Year round
HOURS: Vary by season
PRICES: Free

✓ Strollers	✓ Groups	✓ Food Nearby
Diap Chg	Picnic	✓ Pub. Trans.
✓ Parking	Food Serv.	✓ Handicapped

There are storytimes for toddlers (ages 2–5) at the Main and North branches and for preschoolers (ages 3–5) at the Caledonia branch. Sessions run for 10 weeks. There are also activities and workshops for school-age children throughout the year. Most require preregistration. Project Nia provides library services (including book kits and story programs) to child-care centers.

A computer resource center at the main branch is equipped with both IBM and Macintosh computers. Reservations are required. A Math and Science Enrichment Center is open after school and on special family nights. Printed program lists are available at the branches, and homebound delivery of books is available.

Branches:
Caledonia: 960 Caledonia Ave., (216) 268-6280 (no stroller access)
North: 1425 Hayden Ave., (216) 268-6283

Euclid Public Library

AGES:	1½–3	3–5	5–8	8–12	12–15
RATING:	★★	★★	★★	★★	★★

COST: **FREE** PREP.: **None–Some**
AREA: **East** CITY: **Euclid**

ADDRESS: 631 E. 222 St.
PHONE: (216) 261-5300
SEASON: Year round
HOURS: Main Branch: Mon–Thu 9 a.m.–9 p.m.; Fri, Sat 9 a.m.–5 p.m.; Sun 1–5 p.m. (during school year)
PRICES: Free
WEB: www.euclid.lib.oh.us

✓ Strollers	✓ Groups	✓ Food Nearby
✓ Diap Chg	Picnic	✓ Pub. Trans.
✓ Parking	Food Serv.	✓ Handicapped

Storytime sessions start young, with "Lap Sit" sessions for newborns and new walkers accompanied by an adult; there are also sessions for toddlers (ages 2½–3½) and preschoolers (ages 3½–5). For school-age children there is a summer reading program. Registration is required for storytimes and other library activities.

Homebound delivery is available.

Geauga Co. Pub. Library

AGES:	1½–3	3–5	5–8	8–12	12–15
RATING:	★	★★	★★	★★	★★

COST: **FREE–$$** PREP.: **None–Much**
AREA: **Far East** CITY: **Chardon (Admin. office)**

ADDRESS: 12701 Ravenwood Dr.
PHONE: (440) 286-6811
SEASON: Year round
HOURS: Mon–Thu 9 a.m.–9 p.m., Fri–Sat 9 a.m.–5 p.m.; branches vary
PRICES: Free; fee for some classes

✓ Strollers	✓ Groups	✓ Food Nearby
✓ Diap Chg	✓ Picnic	Pub. Trans.
✓ Parking	Food Serv.	✓ Handicapped

Storytimes for infants, toddlers

(ages 2–3), and preschoolers (ages 3–5). Length of the sessions varies throughout the year. A summer reading program includes activities for school-age children, teenagers (middle school–high school), and adults. Registration is preferred. Special events and programs are prepared seasonally by the individual branches, so call to see if a printed list of activities is available.

Branches:

Bainbridge: 17222 Snyder Rd., (440) 543-5611
Chardon: 110 E. Park, (440) 285-7601
Geauga West: 13455 Chillicothe Rd., (440) 729-4250
Middlefield: 15982 E. High, (440) 632-1961
Newbury: 14775 Auburn, (440) 564-7552
Thompson: 16700 Thompson Rd., (440) 298-3831

Heights Parent Center

AGES:	1½–3	3–5	5–8	8–12	12–15
RATING:	★★★	★★★	★★	★	NR

COST: **FREE–$** PREP.: **None**
AREA: **East** CITY: **Cleveland Hts.**

ADDRESS: 1700 Crest Rd.
PHONE: (216) 321-0079
SEASON: Year round
HOURS: Program hours vary
PRICES: Vary for special events and classes; some programs free

✓ Strollers ✓ Groups ✓ Food Nearby
✓ Diap Chg Picnic ✓ Pub. Trans.
✓ Parking Food Serv. ✓ Handicapped

The mission here is to provide education, support, and activities for families with children from birth to age 10. It's especially helpful to new families in need of assistance or those that have just moved to the area. Drop-in sessions and regular discussion groups involve parents and kids in hands-on activities, songs, stories, and games. There is a toy lending library for infants to school-age kids. A parenting resource library offers books and tapes.

Lakewood Family Room, Toyland & Library

Lakewood Dept. of Human Services

AGES:	1½–3	3–5	5–8	8–12	12–15
RATING:	★★★	★★	★	NR	NR

COST: **FREE** PREP.: **None**
AREA: **Near West** CITY: **Lakewood**

ADDRESS: 17400 Northwood Ave.
PHONE: (216) 521-0001
SEASON: Year round
HOURS: Sat 9 a.m.–11 a.m.; alternate Wed. 6 p.m.–8 p.m.
PRICES: Free

✓ Strollers Groups ✓ Food Nearby
Diap Chg Picnic ✓ Pub. Trans.
✓ Parking Food Serv. Handicapped

New parents can pick up information about parenting, child development, nutrition, and health care—most of it free for the asking. Anyone with young kids should check out the Toy Lending Library where you can borrow and sample a variety of age-appropriate toys—a great service to parents confused about all of the gadgets on the market.

Lakewood Pub. Libraries

AGES:	1½–3	3–5	5–8	8–12	12–15
RATING:	★★	★★★	★★★	★★★	★★

COST: **FREE–$$** PREP.: **None–Much**
AREA: **Near West** CITY: **Lakewood**

ADDRESS: 15425 Detroit Ave. (Main Branch)
PHONE: (216) 226-8275
SEASON: Year round
HOURS: Main: Mon–Fri 9 a.m.–9 p.m., Sat 9 a.m.–6 p.m., Sun 1 p.m.–9 p.m.
PRICES: Free
WEB: www.lkwdpl.org

✓ Strollers ✓ Groups ✓ Food Nearby
✓ Diap Chg Picnic ✓ Pub. Trans.
✓ Parking Food Serv. ✓ Handicapped

There are storytimes for toddlers (ages 2½–3 with parents), preschoolers (ages 3–5), and kindergartners in six-week sessions. Also for younger prereaders, Weekend Wonders programs are scheduled every weekend year round at both branches; these include stories and make-and-take projects that are perfect for creating enthusiasm about the library and reading.

For school-age children, After-School Sensations are offered daily during the school year and Summer Sensations in the summertime. Activities are organized by weekly topics, with each day offering something new. For example, during the World Geography focus, South of the Equator week featured a trip down the Congo on Monday and a day in Cairo on Tuesday. After-School Sensations and Weekend Wonders programs are free, and there is no need to register in advance. Registration is required for children's storytimes.

New-media programs are available for children of all ages, including seasonal computer camps (offered for seniors as well) and weekday computer use, which complements other library reading and learning programs. In addition, the Madison branch recently opened the KidKiosk, a kiosk display featuring samples of educational and entertainment software that promote kindergarten reading readiness skills.

Branches:

Madison Branch: 13229 Madison Ave., (216) 228-7428. (Sunday hours: 1–5 p.m.)

Mentor Public Library

AGES:	1½–3	3–5	5–8	8–12	12–15
RATING:	★	★★	★★	★★	★★

COST: **FREE** PREP.: **None–Much**
AREA: **Far East** CITY: **Mentor**

ADDRESS: 8215 Mentor Ave. (Main Library)

PHONE: (440) 255-8811

SEASON: Year round

HOURS: Mon–Fri 9 a.m.–9 p.m., Sat 9 a.m.–5 p.m., Sun noon–4 p.m. (branches vary)

PRICES: Free

WEB: www.mentor.lib.oh.us

✓ Strollers ✓ Groups ✓ Food Nearby
Diap Chg Picnic ✓ Pub. Trans.
✓ Parking Food Serv. ✓ Handicapped

There are storytimes for toddlers (age 2 with adult) and preschoolers (ages 3–5). Sessions run six to eight weeks. The All-Aboard Express storytime runs every Thursday at 1:30 p.m. and is designed for children 3 and up with an adult. Mother Goose Time, an infant story hour, requires advance registration. For ages 6 and up, there is the after-school Book Break program. Call for information.

For school-age children, the summer reading program begins the Monday after school lets out and runs until the end of July.

Watch for seasonal specials and make-and-take activities in the winter months. Ask for the seasonal schedule.

Branches:

Headlands: 4669 Corduroy Rd., (440) 257-2000
Lake: 5642 Andrews Rd., (440) 257-2512

Polaris Career Center

AGES:	1½–3	3–5	5–8	8–12	12–15
RATING:	★	★★	★★	NR	NR

COST: **$–$$** PREP.: **Some–Much**
AREA: **West** CITY: **Middleburg Hts.**

ADDRESS: 7285 Old Oak Blvd.

PHONE: (440) 891-7750

SEASON: Year round

HOURS: Sep–May: Mon–Thu 8:30 a.m.–9 p.m., Fri 8:30 p.m.–3:30 p.m.; Jun–Aug: Mon–Fri 8:30 a.m.–3:30 p.m.

PRICES: Vary

WEB: www.polaris.edu

✓ Strollers	Groups	✓ Food Nearby
✓ Diap Chg	Picnic	✓ Pub. Trans.
✓ Parking	✓ Food Serv.	✓ Handicapped

Designed as an adult education/community center, Polaris is also known for its parent education and support. What many folks don't realize is that there are creative playtime programs and craft classes scheduled throughout the year.

Rocky River Pub. Library

AGES:	1½–3	3–5	5–8	8–12	12–15
RATING:	★★	★★	★★★	★★★	★★★

COST: **FREE** PREP.: **None–Much**
AREA: **West** CITY: **Rocky River**

ADDRESS: 1600 Hampton Rd.

PHONE: (440) 333-7610; (440) 333-3219 (tty); online access (440) 333-5098

SEASON: Year round

HOURS: Mon–Thu 9 a.m.–9 p.m.; Fri, Sat 9 a.m.–6 p.m.; Sun (during school year) 1–5 p.m.

PRICES: Free

WEB: www.rrpl.org

✓ Strollers	✓ Groups	✓ Food Nearby
✓ Diap Chg	Picnic	✓ Pub. Trans.
✓ Parking	Food Serv.	✓ Handicapped

There are storytimes for infants (up to 12 months), toddlers (ages 2 to 3), preschoolers (ages 4–5) and school-age groups. Registration is required. Computer classes begin at the first-grade level.

The newsletter *Ex Libris*, which contains class and special event information, is sent to Rocky River residents three times a year.

Also, the Cowan Pottery Collection is on display throughout the library.

Shaker Family Center

AGES:	1½–3	3–5	5–8	8–12	12–15
RATING:	★★★	NR	NR	NR	NR

COST: **FREE–$$** PREP.: **None–Some**
AREA: **East** CITY: **Shaker Hts.**

ADDRESS: 19824 Sussex Rd.

PHONE: (216) 921-2023

SEASON: Year round

HOURS: Vary

PRICES: Vary

✓ Strollers	✓ Groups	✓ Food Nearby
✓ Diap Chg	Picnic	✓ Pub. Trans.
✓ Parking	Food Serv.	✓ Handicapped

This playroom is a perfect spot to beat back the winter blues, or even that new mom or dad feeling, with other youngsters and parents. A nominal membership fee includes gym time and special presentations.

Shaker Hts. Pub. Library

AGES:	1½–3	3–5	5–8	8–12	12–15
RATING:	★★	★★★	★★★	★★★	★★★

COST: **FREE–$$** PREP.: **None–Much**
AREA: **East** CITY: **Shaker Hts.**

ADDRESS: 16500 Van Aken Blvd. (Main Branch)

PHONE: (216) 991-2030

SEASON: Year round

HOURS: Mon–Thu 9 a.m.–9 p.m.; Fri 9 a.m.–6 p.m.; Sat 9 a.m.–5:30 p.m.; Sun 1–5 p.m. (Sep–Jun, Main only); branch hours same but closed Sun

PRICES: Free; fees for some programs

✓ Strollers ✓ Groups ✓ Food Nearby
✓ Diap Chg Picnic ✓ Pub. Trans.
✓ Parking Food Serv. ✓ Handicapped

There are storytimes for infants (12 months and up with parent), toddlers (age 2), preschoolers (ages 3–5), and Book Bugs (grades K–3) throughout the school year. Computer instruction begins at age 8.

After School Specials for school-age children feature a book-related activity and sometimes a craft. A summer reading club is open to readers of any age and runs from mid-June through early August. Preteen (ages 9–12), teenage, and family programs are offered. The library also features large-print books and books on tape for children and adults. The second floor, renovated in 1998, includes a new Technology Center and Teen Resource Center.

Registration is requested for most of the activities. Call either branch for listings.

Branch:

Bertram Woods: 20600 Fayette Rd. (216) 991-2421 (no Sunday hours; no diaper-changing facility.)

Shaker Heights Youth and Family Center

AGES:	1½–3	3–5	5–8	8–12	12–15
RATING:	★★	★★	★★	★★	★★

COST: **$–$$** PREP.: **Some–Much**
AREA: **East** CITY: **Shaker Hts.**

ADDRESS: 16700 Van Aken Blvd.

PHONE: (216) 752-9292

SEASON: Year round

HOURS: Mon–Fri 9 a.m.–5 p.m.; evenings by appointment

PRICES: Counseling Center will work with insurance carriers to cover services at discounted price for residents of Shaker Hts.

Strollers Groups ✓ Food Nearby
Diap Chg Picnic ✓ Pub. Trans.
✓ Parking Food Serv. ✓ Handicapped

Most of the center's programs are focused on the problems that seem to hit families during the preteen and teenage years. Education programs and parenting workshops address issues such as drug abuse, school problems, and emotional difficulties. Counseling sessions for parents and children are also offered.

Westlake Porter Public Library

AGES:	1½–3	3–5	5–8	8–12	12–15
RATING:	★	★★	★★	★★	★★

COST: **FREE–$$** PREP.: **None–Much**
AREA: **West** CITY: **Westlake**

ADDRESS: 24350 Center Ridge Rd.

PHONE: (440) 871-2600

SEASON: Year round

HOURS: Mon–Thu 9 a.m.–9 p.m.; Fri, Sat 9 a.m.–5 p.m.; Sun (during school year) 1–5 p.m.

PRICES: Free; fees for some classes

WEB: www.westlakelibrary.org

✓ Strollers ✓ Groups ✓ Food Nearby
Diap Chg Picnic ✓ Pub. Trans.
✓ Parking Food Serv. ✓ Handicapped

Storytimes are offered for preschoolers (ages 3–5) in 10-week sessions each fall and winter. Family summer reading programs run June through August. A special Summer Reading Team recruits volunteers to help beginning readers.

Look for arts-and-crafts instruction, theater presentations, special programs, and other activities throughout the year.

Wickliffe Public Library

AGES: 1½–3 3–5 5–8 8–12 12–15
RATING: ★★ ★★★ ★★★ ★★ ★★

COST: **FREE** PREP.: **None–Some**
AREA: **East** CITY: **Wickliffe**

ADDRESS: 1713 Lincoln Ave. (Main Branch)

PHONE: (440) 944-6010

SEASON: Year round

HOURS: Mon–Thu 9 a.m.–9 p.m.; Fri 9 a.m.–6 p.m.; Sat 9 a.m.–5 p.m.; Sun 1–5 p.m.

PRICES: Free

✓ Strollers ✓ Groups ✓ Food Nearby
✓ Diap Chg Picnic ✓ Pub. Trans.
✓ Parking Food Serv. ✓ Handicapped

After a $2-million renovation, Wickliffe Library's main branch reopened in 1998 with double its previous space. New to the children's area are the "Secret Garden," an aquarium, and "Discovery Rock." Seasonal storytimes (fall, winter, and spring) are held for toddlers (ages 2½–3½) and preschoolers (ages 3½–5). A Summer Reading Program is offered to all readers and nonreading preschoolers. Special craft events usually take place around the holidays. Preregistration is required for storytimes and special events.

A schedule of events can be picked up at the library.

Branch:

Wickliffe Civic Branch: 900 Warden Rd., (440) 944-6010

Willoughby-Eastlake Public Libraries

AGES: 1½–3 3–5 5–8 8–12 12–15
RATING: ★ ★★ ★★ ★★ ★★

COST: **FREE** PREP.: **None–Much**
AREA: **East** CITY: **Willowick**

ADDRESS: 263 E. 305 St.

PHONE: (440) 943-4151

SEASON: Year round

HOURS: Eastlake: Mon–Wed 9 a.m.–9 p.m., Thu 9 a.m.–5:30 p.m., Fri & Sat 9 a.m.–5 p.m.; Willoughby & Willowick Mon, Tues & Thu 9 a.m.–9 p.m., Wed 9 a.m.–5:30 p.m., Fri & Sat 9 a.m.–5 p.m.

PRICES: Free

WEB: www.wepl.lib.oh.us

✓ Strollers ✓ Groups Food Nearby
✓ Diap Chg Picnic ✓ Pub. Trans.
✓ Parking Food Serv. ✓ Handicapped

Seasonal (fall, winter, and spring) storytimes run in eight-week sessions for preschoolers (ages 3–5), toddlers (ages 2–3), and babies (up to 24 months). Preregistration is required. Reading Buddies (on Wednesdays) and Twilight Tales (on Thursdays) are offered for school-age children. Special storytimes are scheduled around holidays. Summer Reading programs for children, young adults, and adults begin in June.

Each library releases a schedule three times a year (Jan–May, Jun–Aug, and Sep–Dec).

Branches:

Eastlake Public Library: 36706 Lake Shore Blvd., Eastlake, (440) 942-7880

Willoughby Public Library: 30 Public Square, Willoughby, (440) 942-3200

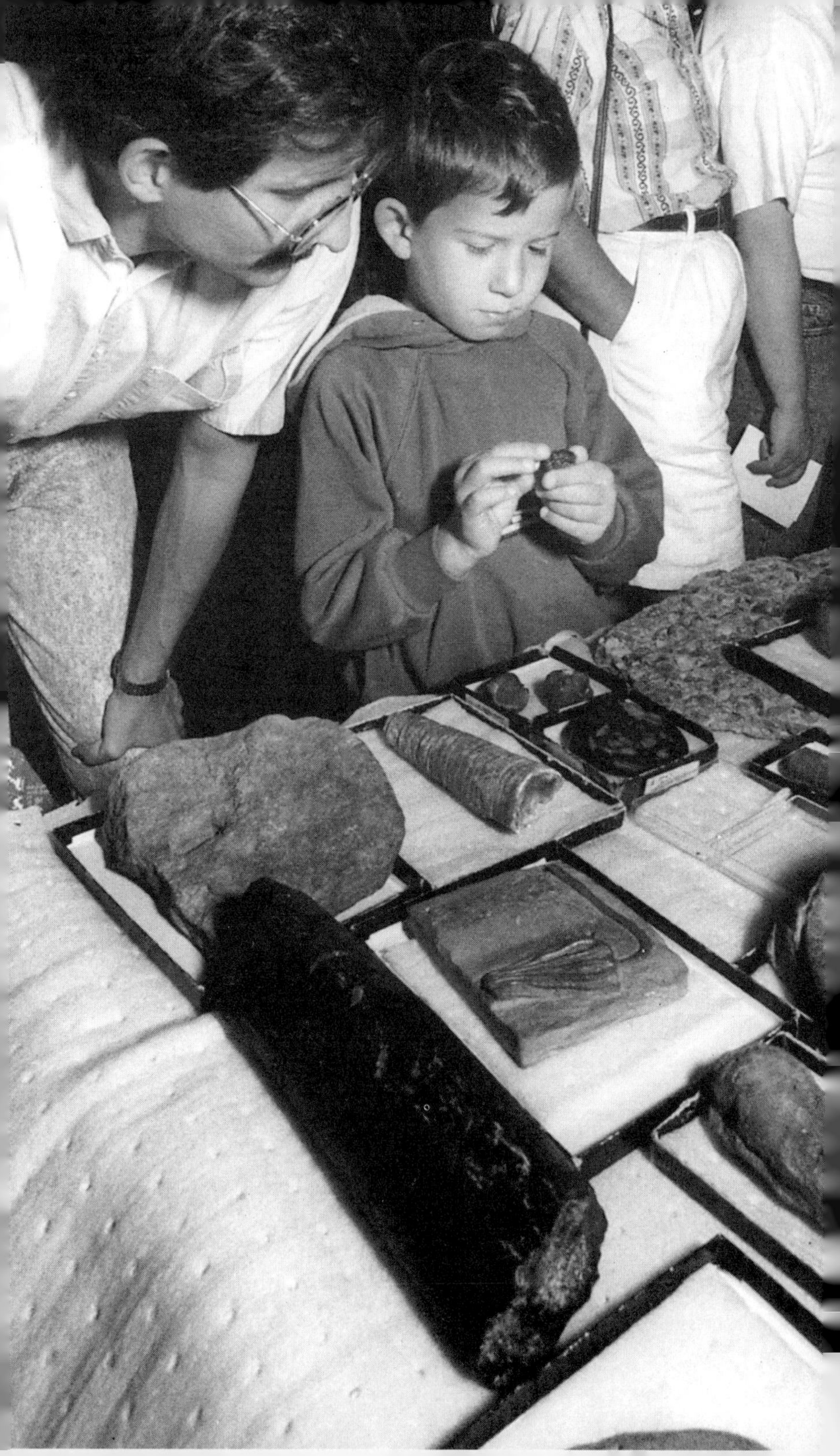

Family Festivals and Annual Events

Does this ever happen to you? Someone tells you about a great family festival, and how much fun it was, and how you should be sure to go with your family. But of course you'll have to wait until *next* year, because the event is already over. Well, it needn't happen again. Here are some of the best annual local events that every family should try at least once.

▼ JANUARY ▼

Buckeye Classic Sled Dog Race

AGES:	1½–3	3–5	5–8	8–12	12–15
RATING:	NR	★	★★	★★	★★

COST: PREP.: **Some**
AREA: **Far East** CITY: **Newbury**

ADDRESS: Punderson State Park, 11755 Kinsman Rd. (SR 87)

PHONE: (440) 888-9585

SEASON: Seasonal January

HOURS: n/a

PRICES: n/a

DIRECT.: US 422 to SR 44 (Ravenna Rd.); north on SR 44; left (east) on SR 87 (Kinsman Rd.); on left.

Or, I-271 to Exit 29 for Chagrin Blvd.; east on Chagrin; at Lander Circle, east on SR 87 (Pinetree Rd.); Pinetree becomes S. Woodland Rd., then Kinsman Rd.; on right.

WEB: www.dnr.state.oh.us/odnr/parks

✓ Strollers Groups Food Nearby
✓ Diap Chg Picnic Pub. Trans.
✓ Parking ✓ Food Serv. Handicapped

The Classic Sled Dog Race at Punderson State Park pits a variety of mushers against one another in the race to cover 2-, 3-, and 5-mile courses. Over the course of the weekend, other winter festivities include ice carving and children's races.

Hand-feed Chickadees

Brecksville Nature Center

AGES:	1½–3	3–5	5–8	8–12	12–15
RATING:	NR	★★	★★★	★★	★★

COST: **FREE** PREP.: **Some**
AREA: **South** CITY: **Brecksville**

ADDRESS: Chippewa Creek Dr.

PHONE: (440) 526-1012

SEASON: Seasonal January

HOURS: Weekends

PRICES: Free

DIRECT.: I-77 to Exit 149 for SR 82 (Royalton Rd.); east on Royalton; right (south) on Chippewa Creek Dr.; on right.

WEB: www.clemetparks.com

✓ Strollers ✓ Groups ✓ Food Nearby
✓ Diap Chg Picnic ✓ Pub. Trans.
✓ Parking Food Serv. ✓ Handicapped

This annual tradition dates back to the 1930s. If you stand still, the birds will land right on your hand. Metroparks staff provide the birdseed.

Martin Luther King Jr. Program

Western Reserve Historical Society

AGES:	1½–3	3–5	5–8	8–12	12–15
RATING:	NR	★	★	★★	★★

COST: **FREE–$** PREP.: **Some**
AREA: **Near East** CITY: **Cleveland**

ADDRESS: 10825 East Blvd.

PHONE: (216) 721-5722

SEASON: Seasonal January

HOURS: Vary

PRICES: Vary

DIRECT.: East: I-90 to Exit 177 for Martin Luther King Blvd.; south on MLK; right (east) on East Blvd.; on left.

West: I-90 to Exit 173B for Chester Ave.; east on Chester; left (east) on Euclid Ave.; left (north) on East Blvd.; on right after Hazel Dr.

WEB: www.whrs.org

✓ Strollers ✓ Groups ✓ Food Nearby
Diap Chg ✓ Picnic ✓ Pub. Trans.
✓ Parking ✓ Food Serv. ✓ Handicapped

Martin Luther King Jr. is remembered with a special program.

Winter Carnival

Mill Stream Run Reservation

AGES:	1½–3	3–5	5–8	8–12	12–15
RATING:	NR	NR	★	★★	★★

COST: **FREE–$$** PREP.: **Some**
AREA: **Southwest** CITY: **Strongsville**

ADDRESS: Valley Pkwy. (S. of Bagley Rd., N. of Drake Rd.)

PHONE: (440) 572-9990

SEASON: Seasonal January

HOURS: Sat–Sun noon–5 p.m.

PRICES: Free, fee for tobogganing

DIRECT.: I-71 to Exit 231 for SR 82 (Royalton Rd.); east on Royalton; right (south) on Valley Pkwy.; on right.

WEB: www.clemetparks.com

✓ Strollers ✓ Groups ✓ Food Nearby
Diap Chg ✓ Picnic Pub. Trans.
✓ Parking ✓ Food Serv. ✓ Handicapped

Winter Expo at The Chalet in the Cleveland Metroparks Mill Stream Run Reservation Chalet Recreation Area traditionally includes dogsled and cross-country ski demonstrations and ice sculpture. The toboggan run is also open, and there is a warm-up fire inside the Chalet.

Winter Flower Displays

Rockefeller Greenhouse

AGES:	1½–3	3–5	5–8	8–12	12–15
RATING:	★	★★	★★	★★	★

COST: **FREE** PREP.: **Some**
AREA: **Near East** CITY: **Cleveland**

ADDRESS: 750 E. 88 St.

PHONE: (216) 664-3103

SEASON: Seasonal January

HOURS: Daily 10 a.m.–4 p.m.

PRICES: Free

DIRECT.: I-90 to Exit 177 for Martin Luther King Blvd.; south on MLK to E. 88 St.; left (north) on E. 88; on left.

✓ Strollers ✓ Groups ✓ Food Nearby
✓ Diap Chg ✓ Picnic ✓ Pub. Trans.
✓ Parking Food Serv. ✓ Handicapped

If you're craving colors other than gray, check out the annual winter flower displays at the city greenhouse. Traditionally, poinsettias are out until mid-January, followed by a lush display of primroses.

▼ MARCH ▼

Buzzard Day

Hinckley Reservation

AGES:	1½–3	3–5	5–8	8–12	12–15
RATING:	NR	★	★★	★★	★★

COST: **FREE** PREP.: **Some**
AREA: **South** CITY: **Hinckley**

ADDRESS: off Bellus and State Rds.

PHONE: (216) 351-6300

SEASON: Seasonal March

HOURS: Sun

PRICES: Free

DIRECT.: I-71 to Exit 145 for Brecksville Rd.; south on Brecksville; right (west) on SR 303 (Streetsboro Rd.); left (south) on SR 94 (State Rd.); after Bellus Rd.

WEB: www.clemetparks.com

✓ Strollers	✓ Groups	✓ Food Nearby
Diap Chg	✓ Picnic	✓ Pub. Trans.
✓ Parking	✓ Food Serv.	✓ Handicapped

Buzzard Day celebrates the annual migration of the turkey vulture. These large, garish birds perch on the rock ledges of this reservation. The event features a pancake breakfast, exhibits, and activities, but be forewarned: participants rarely see a bird.

Maple Sugaring Weekends

Rocky River Reservation

AGES:	1½–3	3–5	5–8	8–12	12–15
RATING:	NR	★	★★★	★★★	★

COST: **FREE** PREP.: **Some**
AREA: **West** CITY: **Rocky River**

ADDRESS: 24000 Valley Pkwy.

PHONE: (440) 734-6660

SEASON: Seasonal March

HOURS: Sat–Sun 10 a.m.–4:30 p.m.

PRICES: Free

DIRECT.: I-480 to Exit 6 for Great Northern Blvd.; south on Great Northern; left (east) on Butternut Ridge Rd.; left (north) on Columbia Rd.; right (east) on Cedar Point Rd.; left on Valley Pkwy.; on left.

WEB: www.clemetparks.com

✓ Strollers	✓ Groups	✓ Food Nearby
Diap Chg	✓ Picnic	Pub. Trans.
✓ Parking	Food Serv.	✓ Handicapped

Stirring, tapping, guided hikes, and pancake tasting are part of the tradition on Maple Sugaring Weekends, held at the Cleveland Metroparks Maple Grove Picnic Area in the Rocky River Reservation. Drilling and tapping are also a part of the demonstrations at the Lorain County Metroparks annual events.

Sap's-A-Risin' Day

Swine Creek Reservation

AGES:	1½–3	3–5	5–8	8–12	12–15
RATING:	NR	★	★★	★★	★★

COST: **FREE** PREP.: **Some**
AREA: **Far East** CITY: **Middlefield Twp.**

ADDRESS: 16004 Hayes Rd.

PHONE: (440) 286-9504

SEASON: Seasonal March

HOURS: Sat

PRICES: Free

DIRECT.: US 422 to SR 528 (Madison Rd.) at Parkman; north on SR 528; at SR 608, right (east) on Swine Creek Rd.; left on Hayes Rd.; on left.

WEB: www.tourgeauga.com

✓ Strollers	✓ Groups	✓ Food Nearby
✓ Diap Chg	✓ Picnic	Pub. Trans.
✓ Parking	Food Serv.	✓ Handicapped

Folk music, sugarhouse tours, and crafts are part of Sap's-A-Risin' Day at Geauga Park District's Swine Creek Reservation. (Remember to dress in warm clothing and add some boots—trekking to maple trees often includes some muddy trails.) Also this month, the Geauga County Maple Festival features syrup making, contests and carnival rides.

St. Patrick's Day Parade

AGES:	1½–3	3–5	5–8	8–12	12–15
RATING:	NR	★	★	★	★

COST: **FREE** PREP.: **Some**
AREA: **Downtown** CITY: **Cleveland**

ADDRESS: Euclid Ave., downtown

PHONE: (216) 621-4110

SEASON: Seasonal March 17 (St. Patrick's Day)

HOURS: Vary

PRICES: Free

DIRECT.: I-90 to Exit 173B for Chester Ave.; west on Chester; left (south) on E. 21 St. to Euclid Ave.

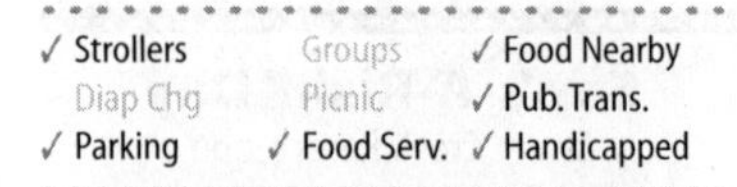

✓ Strollers | Groups | ✓ Food Nearby
Diap Chg | Picnic | ✓ Pub. Trans.
✓ Parking | ✓ Food Serv. | ✓ Handicapped

Like parades? Check out the St. Patrick's Day Parade, held downtown each year along Euclid Avenue.

▼ APRIL ▼

Blessing of the Fleet

AGES:	1½–3	3–5	5–8	8–12	12–15
RATING:	NR	★	★	★★	★★

COST: **FREE** PREP.: **Some**
AREA: **Various** CITY: **Marblehead, Put-in Bay, Ashtabula**

ADDRESS: various locations
PHONE:
SEASON: Seasonal April
HOURS: Vary
PRICES: Free
DIRECT.: I-90 to SR 2; west on SR 2;

Strollers | Groups | ✓ Food Nearby
Diap Chg | Picnic | Pub. Trans.
✓ Parking | ✓ Food Serv. | Handicapped

Northeast Ohio's fishing fleets continue the tradition of celebrating a new season with the annual Blessing of the Fleet. Festivities include food, music, and boat parades in such fishing holes as Marblehead, Put-in-Bay, and Ashtabula.

Cleveland International Film Festival

AGES:	1½–3	3–5	5–8	8–12	12–15
RATING:	NR	NR	★	★★	★★

COST: **\$–\$\$** PREP.: **Some**
AREA: **Downtown** CITY: **Cleveland**

ADDRESS: Tower City Cinemas, 50 Public Square
PHONE: (440) 349-FILM
SEASON: Seasonal April
HOURS: Week-long
PRICES: Vary
DIRECT.: West: I-90 to Exit 171B for Ontario St.; north on Ontario St.; Tower City parking on left.
East: I-90 to SR 2; west on SR 2 to E. 9 St.; south on E. 9 St.; right (west) on Superior Ave.; left (south) on Ontario St.; Tower City parking on right.

✓ Strollers | ✓ Groups | ✓ Food Nearby
✓ Diap Chg | Picnic | ✓ Pub. Trans.
✓ Parking | ✓ Food Serv. | ✓ Handicapped

The Cleveland International Film Festival typically devotes a portion of its schedule to family films, usually a bit off-beat and guaranteed to prompt some discussion.

Earth Day Festival
Cleveland Metroparks Zoo

AGES:	1½–3	3–5	5–8	8–12	12–15
RATING:	NR	★	★	★	★

COST: **\$** PREP.: **Some**
AREA: **South** CITY: **Cleveland**

ADDRESS: 3900 Wildlife Way
PHONE: (216) 661-7511
SEASON: Seasonal April
HOURS: Sun
PRICES: \$5 adults, \$3 children
DIRECT.: I-71 to Exit 245 for Fulton Rd.; south on Fulton; right (east) on Brookside Park Dr.; on left.
Or, I-480 to Exit 16 for SR 94 (State Rd.); north on State; right (north) on Pearl Rd.; left (west) on Brookside Park Dr.; on right.
WEB: www.clemetzoo.com

✓ Strollers | ✓ Groups | ✓ Food Nearby
✓ Diap Chg | ✓ Picnic | ✓ Pub. Trans.
✓ Parking | ✓ Food Serv. | ✓ Handicapped

Each year, the Earth Day Coalition sponsors an Earth Day festival, a day of environmentally oriented education, information, activities, and performances. The Cleveland Metroparks Zoo is usually the place to be for the area's largest Earth Day celebration, but festivities are also held at Lake Metroparks and Mentor Marsh.

Tri-C Jazz Fest

Cuyahoga Community College
Metro Campus

AGES:	1½–3	3–5	5–8	8–12	12–15
RATING:	★	★	★★	★★★	★★★

COST: PREP.: **Some**
AREA: **Downtown** CITY: **Cleveland**

ADDRESS: 2900 Community College Ave.
PHONE: (216) 987-4400
SEASON: Seasonal April
HOURS: Vary
PRICES: Vary
DIRECT.: I-77 to Exit 162A for Orange Ave.; east on Orange Ave.; left (north) on E. 30 St.; left (west) on Community College Ave.; on left.

Strollers | ✓ Groups | ✓ Food Nearby
Diap Chg | Picnic | ✓ Pub. Trans.
✓ Parking | ✓ Food Serv. | ✓ Handicapped

The Tri-C Jazz Fest showcases national jazz talent as well as young performers in concerts at Cuyahoga Community College's Metro campus and at other area locations, such as Playhouse Square, Severence Hall, and community centers. A Road Shows program takes music to area schools. Annual Family Jazz Day includes instrument demos and student performances.

▼ MAY ▼

Familyland Fair

Mandel Jewish Community Center

AGES:	1½–3	3–5	5–8	8–12	12–15
RATING:	★	★★	★★	★★	★

COST: **FREE** PREP.: **Some**
AREA: **East** CITY: **Beachwood**

ADDRESS: 26001 S. Woodland Rd.
PHONE: (216) 831-0700
SEASON: Seasonal May
HOURS: Sun
PRICES: Free
DIRECT.: I-271 to Exit 29 for Chagrin Blvd.; west on Chagrin; right (north) on Richmond Rd.; right (east) on S. Woodland Rd.; on left.

✓ Strollers | ✓ Groups | ✓ Food Nearby
✓ Diap Chg | Picnic | ✓ Pub. Trans.
✓ Parking | Food Serv. | ✓ Handicapped

A day filled with entertainment, arts and crafts, and exhibits from the zoo and nature centers, specifically for children.

International Migratory Bird Day

Magee Marsh Nature Preserve

AGES:	1½–3	3–5	5–8	8–12	12–15
RATING:	NR	★	★★	★★	★★

COST: **FREE** PREP.: **Some**
AREA: **Far West** CITY: **Oak Harbor**

ADDRESS: 13229 West State Rt. 2
PHONE: (419) 898-0960
SEASON: Seasonal May
HOURS: 8 a.m.–5 p.m.
PRICES: Free
DIRECT.: SR 2 through Port Clinton; on right.

✓ Strollers | Groups | Food Nearby
Diap Chg | ✓ Picnic | Pub. Trans.
✓ Parking | ✓ Food Serv. | Handicapped

Honor the return of the birds from parts south at the annual International Migratory Bird Day at Magee Marsh Nature Preserve with wagon rides, food, and raptor displays along with bird banding.

May Day Festival

Cuyahoga Valley National Recreation Area

AGES:	1½–3	3–5	5–8	8–12	12–15
RATING:	★	★★	★★	★★	★★

COST: **FREE** PREP.: **Some**
AREA: **South** CITY: **Brecksville**

ADDRESS: 15610 Vaughn Rd.

PHONE: (800) 433-1986
SEASON: Seasonal May
HOURS: Sat
PRICES: Free
DIRECT.: I-77 to Exit 149 for SR 82 (Royalton Rd.); east on Royalton; right (south) on Riverview Rd.; left (east) on Vaughn Rd.; on right.
WEB: www.nps.gov/cuva/

✓ Strollers	✓ Groups	✓ Food Nearby
Diap Chg	✓ Picnic	Pub. Trans.
✓ Parking	Food Serv.	✓ Handicapped

May Day Festival at the Cuyahoga Valley National Recreation Area features music, crafts, traditional May Pole dancing, and old-fashioned games such as lawn bowling and croquet.

Marilyn Bianchi Kids' Playwriting Festival

AGES:	1½–3	3–5	5–8	8–12	12–15
RATING:	NR	NR	★★	★★★	★★★

COST: **FREE** PREP.: **Some**
AREA: **East** CITY: **Cleveland Hts.**

ADDRESS: Dobama Theatre, 1846 Coventry Rd.
PHONE: (216) 932-6838
SEASON: Seasonal June
HOURS: Vary
PRICES: Free
DIRECT.: I-90 to Exit 172D for Carnegie Ave.; east on Carnegie; right (east) on Cedar Ave. to top of Cedar Hill; straight (east) on Euclid Hts. Blvd.; left (north) on Coventry Rd.; on left.
WEB: www.nitekich@multiverse.com

✓ Strollers	✓ Groups	✓ Food Nearby
Diap Chg	Picnic	✓ Pub. Trans.
✓ Parking	Food Serv.	Handicapped

Budding playwrights are encouraged to submit entries to the Marilyn Bianchi Kids' Playwriting Festival, a contest sponsored by Dobama Theatre each year for Cuyahoga County students in the 1st through 12th grades. In June, the plays are staged free for the public.

Murray Hill Summer Art Walk

AGES:	1½–3	3–5	5–8	8–12	12–15
RATING:	NR	NR	★★	★★★	★★★

COST: **FREE** PREP.: **Some**
AREA: **Near East** CITY: **Cleveland**

ADDRESS: Murray Hill Rd. and Mayfield Rd.
PHONE: (216) 721-4100
SEASON: Seasonal June
HOURS: Vary
PRICES: Free
DIRECT.: I-90 to Exit 177 for Martin Luther King Dr.; south on MLK; left (east) on Euclid Ave.; right (east) on US 322 (Mayfield Rd.) to Murray Hill.

Strollers	Groups	✓ Food Nearby
Diap Chg	Picnic	✓ Pub. Trans.
✓ Parking	✓ Food Serv.	✓ Handicapped

For older kids and anyone interested in modern art, check out the Summer Art Walk in Little Italy. During this public walking tour, more than 30 private galleries exhibit many works of art and crafts, including some works in progress.

Parade the Circle Celebration

AGES:	1½–3	3–5	5–8	8–12	12–15
RATING:	★★	★★★	★★★	★★	★★

COST: **FREE** PREP.: **Some**
AREA: **Near East** CITY: **Cleveland**

ADDRESS: University Circle
PHONE: (216) 421-7340
SEASON: Seasonal June
HOURS: Sat 10 a.m.–5 p.m. with parade at noon
PRICES: Free
DIRECT.: I-90 to Exit 177 for Martin Luther King Dr.; south on MLK Dr. to University Circle
WEB: www.clemusart.com

✓ Strollers	✓ Groups	✓ Food Nearby
✓ Diap Chg	✓ Picnic	✓ Pub. Trans.
✓ Parking	✓ Food Serv.	✓ Handicapped

Parade the Circle Celebration presented by University Circle, Inc. features a wildly nontraditional parade organized by the Cleveland Museum of Art that is filled with handmade, people-powered floats. The rest of the day includes continuous entertainment, puppet shows, and craft activities. Workshops for parade participants are held throughout May.

▼ JULY ▼

Cain Park Arts Festival

AGES:	1½–3	3–5	5–8	8–12	12–15
RATING:	★	★	★★	★★	★★

COST: **FREE** PREP.: **Some**
AREA: **East** CITY: **Cleveland Hts.**

ADDRESS: Superior Rd. between Lee and S. Taylor

PHONE: (216) 291-2828

SEASON: Seasonal July

HOURS: Fri 3 p.m–8 p.m.; Sat–Sun noon–8 p.m.

PRICES: Free

DIRECT.: West: I-90 to Exit 173B for Chester Ave. (Eastbound: left (south) on E. 24 St.; left (east) on Chester); east on Chester; left northeast on Euclid Ave.; right (east) on US 322 (Mayfield Rd.); right (south) on Superior Rd., on left.

East: I-271 to Exit 32 for Cedar/Brainard Rd. (Southbound: left (south) on Brainard; right (west) on Cedar); west on Cedar; right (north) on S. Taylor; left (west) on Superior Rd.; on right.

✓ Strollers	✓ Groups	✓ Food Nearby
Diap Chg	✓ Picnic	✓ Pub. Trans.
✓ Parking	✓ Food Serv.	✓ Handicapped

This annual festival brings music, art demonstrations, and arts and crafts projects for children.

Cleveland Kidsfest

AGES:	1½–3	3–5	5–8	8–12	12–15
RATING:	★	★	★	★	NR

COST: **$$** PREP.: **Some**
AREA: **West** CITY: **Cleveland**

ADDRESS: Nautica Entertainment Complex, west bank of Flats

PHONE: (440) 247-2722

SEASON: Seasonal July

HOURS: Sat–Sun 10 a.m.–6 p.m.

PRICES: $7 adults, $5 kids

DIRECT.: East: SR 2 to E. 28 St.; left (east) on Detroit Ave.; left (north) on W. 25 St.; right (east) on Washington Ave. (left) north on Winslow Ave. to parking.

West: I-90 to Exit 170 for US 42 (W. 25 St.); north on US 42 (W. 25); right (east) on Washington Ave. (left) north on Winslow Ave. to parking.

✓ Strollers	✓ Groups	✓ Food Nearby
✓ Diap Chg	✓ Picnic	✓ Pub. Trans.
✓ Parking	✓ Food Serv.	✓ Handicapped

Cleveland Kidsfest, organized by Belkin Entertainment, combines a lineup of nationally known children's entertainers such as Parachute Express and Thomas the Tank Engine with a slew of local exhibitors, a Fun Run, sandcastle building, and a scavenger hunt.

E. 185th Street Festival

AGES:	1½–3	3–5	5–8	8–12	12–15
RATING:	NR	NR	★	★	★

COST: **FREE** PREP.: **Some**
AREA: **East** CITY: **Euclid**

ADDRESS: E. 185 between Pawnee and Chickasaw

PHONE: (216) 692-8981

SEASON: Seasonal July

HOURS: Wed–Sun

PRICES: Free

DIRECT.: I-90 to Exit 182A for E. 185 St.; north on E. 185 past Chickasaw Ave.

✓ Strollers | Groups | ✓ Food Nearby
Diap Chg | ✓ Picnic | ✓ Pub. Trans.
Parking | ✓ Food Serv. | ✓ Handicapped

The E. 185th Street Festival on E. 185th between Pawnee and Chickasaw has celebrated Euclid's ethnic heritage since 1977 with German, Italian, Croatian, and Lithuanian food; three bandstands; a parade; rides; and dancing.

Festival of the Fish

AGES:	1½–3	3–5	5–8	8–12	12–15
RATING:	★	★★	★★	★★	★★

COST: **FREE** PREP.: **Some**
AREA: **Far West** CITY: **Vermilion**

ADDRESS: Victory Park, Main St.
PHONE: (440) 967-4477
SEASON: Seasonal July
HOURS: Fri–Sat noon–11 p.m.; Sun noon–6 p.m.
PRICES: Free
DIRECT.: I-90 to SR 2; west on SR 2; north on SR 60 (Savannah Vermilion Rd.); right (east) on South Rd.; left (north) on Main St.
WEB: www.lcvb.org

✓ Strollers | Groups | ✓ Food Nearby
Diap Chg | ✓ Picnic | Pub. Trans.
✓ Parking | ✓ Food Serv. | ✓ Handicapped

A boat parade, music, carnival rides, and sand-castle building are part of the lakeside fun at Vermilion's Festival of the Fish.

Great Mohican Indian Pow-Wow

AGES:	1½–3	3–5	5–8	8–12	12–15
RATING:	NR	★	★	★★	★★

COST: **$** PREP.: **Some**
AREA: **Farther South** CITY: **Loudonville**

ADDRESS: Call for location.
PHONE: (800) 722-7588
SEASON: Seasonal July and September
HOURS: Vary
PRICES: $6 adults, $2.50 children
DIRECT.: I-71 to Exit 169 for SR 13; south on SR 13; east on SR 97; north on SR 3 to Loudonville.

Strollers | Groups | ✓ Food Nearby
Diap Chg | ✓ Picnic | Pub. Trans.
✓ Parking | ✓ Food Serv. | Handicapped

Tribes are here from around the country for performances, food, crafts, and demonstrations.

Little Mountain Folk Festival

Lake Co. Historical Society & History Ctr.

AGES:	1½–3	3–5	5–8	8–12	12–15
RATING:	NR	★	★★	★★	★★

COST: **FREE–$** PREP.: **Some**
AREA: **Far East** CITY: **Kirtland Hills**

ADDRESS: 8610 King Memorial Rd.
PHONE: (440) 255-8979
SEASON: Seasonal late July
HOURS: Sat 10 a.m.–7 p.m.; Sun 11 a.m.–6 p.m.
PRICES: $5 adults, kids free
DIRECT.: I-90 to Exit 190 for SR 306; north on SR 306; right (east) on SR 84; right (south) on Little Mountain Rd.; right (south) on Mentor Rd.; on right.

✓ Strollers | ✓ Groups | ✓ Food Nearby
✓ Diap Chg | ✓ Picnic | Pub. Trans.
✓ Parking | ✓ Food Serv. | ✓ Handicapped

Look for this event in late July. It features craft demonstrations, music, and living history exhibits and performances.

Tour du Corridor

AGES:	1½–3	3–5	5–8	8–12	12–15
RATING:	NR	NR	NR	★★	★★★

COST: **$$$** PREP.: **Some**
AREA: **South** CITY: **Valley View**

ADDRESS: Rockside and Canal Rd. Towpath Trailhead
PHONE: (216) 348-1825

SEASON: Seasonal July

HOURS: Sat starts at 7:30 a.m.

PRICES: $30–$60

DIRECT.: I-77 to Exit 155 for Rockside Rd.; east on Rockside Rd.; left (north) on Canal Rd.; right (east) on Sweet Valley Dr.; left (north) on Towpath Dr.

WEB: www.ohiocanal.org

Strollers	✓ Groups	Food Nearby
Diap Chg	✓ Picnic	Pub. Trans.
✓ Parking	✓ Food Serv.	Handicapped

The annual Tour du Corridor is a group bicycle ride along the Ohio & Erie Canal that can be great fun in the 40-mile segment or a bit grueling at 120 miles.

All-American Soap Box Derby

AGES:	1½–3	3–5	5–8	8–12	12–15
RATING:	NR	★	★★	★★	★★

COST: **$** PREP.: **Some**
AREA: **Far South** CITY: **Akron**

ADDRESS: 79 Derby Downs Dr.

PHONE: (330) 733-8723

SEASON: Seasonal July–August

HOURS: Daily 10 a.m.–5 p.m.

PRICES: $5

DIRECT.: I-77 to Exit 122 for US 224; east on US 224 to George Washington Blvd.; north on George Washington Blvd.; on left.

✓ Strollers	Groups	✓ Food Nearby
Diap Chg	✓ Picnic	✓ Pub. Trans.
✓ Parking	✓ Food Serv.	✓ Handicapped

Run the same way since 1934, the Soap Box Derby event at Derby Downs in Akron features youths from over 100 local competitions. Three racing divisions include stock, kit cars, and a masters' division.

▼ AUGUST ▼

Feast of the Assumption

AGES:	1½–3	3–5	5–8	8–12	12–15
RATING:	NR	★	★	★	★

COST: **FREE** PREP.: **Some**
AREA: **Near East** CITY: **Cleveland**

ADDRESS: Mayfield Rd. and Murray Hill Rd.

PHONE: (216) 421-2995

SEASON: Seasonal August

HOURS: Vary

PRICES: Admission free, fee for food

DIRECT.: I-90 to Exit 177 for Martin Luther King Blvd.; south on MLK; left (east) on Euclid Ave.; right (east) on US 322 (Mayfield Rd.) to Murray Hill.

Strollers	Groups	✓ Food Nearby
Diap Chg	Picnic	✓ Pub. Trans.
Parking	✓ Food Serv.	✓ Handicapped

Celebrations of the Feast of the Assumption in mid-August include food, rides, music, fireworks, and a parade in Little Italy at Mayfield Rd. and Murray Hill Rd.

Glenville Neighborhood Fest

AGES:	1½–3	3–5	5–8	8–12	12–15
RATING:	★	★	★	★	★

COST: **FREE** PREP.: **Some**
AREA: **Downtown** CITY: **Cleveland**

ADDRESS: at E. 110 and St. Clair Ave.

PHONE: (216) 268-FEST

SEASON: Seasonal August

HOURS: Fri–Sun

PRICES: Free

DIRECT.: East: I-90 to Exit 178 for Bratenahl Pl.; south on Bratenahl Pl.; right (west) on St. Clair Ave to E. 110 St.

West: I-90 to Exit 177 for Martin Luther King Dr.; south on MLK ; east on St. Clair Ave to E. 110th St.

	Groups	✓ Food Nearby
...p Chg	✓ Picnic	✓ Pub. Trans.
✓ Parking	✓ Food Serv.	✓ Handicapped

The Glenville Neighborhood Fest brings families to a park on St. Clair Ave. for food, games, and local talent featuring African-American & Puerto Rican dancing and singing.

Slavic Village Heritage Festival

AGES:	1½–3	3–5	5–8	8–12	12–15
RATING:	NR	★	★	★	★

COST: **FREE** PREP.: **Some**
AREA: **Near West** CITY: **Cleveland**

ADDRESS: Fleet Ave.
PHONE: (216) 271-5591
SEASON: Seasonal August
HOURS: Sat–Sun
PRICES: Free
DIRECT.: I-77 to Exit 159 for Fleet Ave.

✓ Strollers	Groups	✓ Food Nearby
Diap Chg	✓ Picnic	✓ Pub. Trans.
✓ Parking	✓ Food Serv.	✓ Handicapped

The Slavic Village Heritage Festival runs along 10 blocks of Fleet Ave. in a historic Polish neighborhood. This street fair has ethnic food, crafts, a Kielbasa Cook-Off, dancing, games, and rides.

Twins Day Festival

AGES:	1½–3	3–5	5–8	8–12	12–15
RATING:	NR	★	★★	★★	★★

COST: **$** PREP.: **Some**
AREA: **East** CITY: **Twinsburg**

ADDRESS: Glenn Chamberlain Park
PHONE: (330) 425-3652
SEASON: Seasonal August
HOURS: Fri–Sun
PRICES: Registration fee for twins; $1 non-twins ages 4 and up.
DIRECT.: I-480 to Exit 36 for Aurora Rd.; east on SR 82 (Aurora Rd.); left (north) on SR 91 (Darrow Rd.); left (west) on Ravenna Rd.; on left.

✓ Strollers	✓ Groups	✓ Food Nearby
✓ Diap Chg	✓ Picnic	Pub. Trans.
✓ Parking	✓ Food Serv.	✓ Handicapped

The Twins Day Festival is the nation's largest gathering of twins, with contests and entertainment including a parade and fireworks.

▼ SEPTEMBER ▼

Annual Bug Day
Penitentiary Glen Reservation

AGES:	1½–3	3–5	5–8	8–12	12–15
RATING:	★★★	★★★	★★★	★★	★★

COST: **FREE** PREP.: **Some**
AREA: **Far East** CITY: **Kirtland**

ADDRESS: 8668 Kirtland-Chardon Rd.
PHONE: (440) 256-1404
SEASON: Seasonal September
HOURS: Vary
PRICES: Free
DIRECT.: I-90 to Exit 190 for SR 306; south on SR 306; left (east) on Kirtland-Chardon Rd.; on left.
WEB: www.lakemetroparks.com

✓ Strollers	Groups	Food Nearby
✓ Diap Chg	✓ Picnic	Pub. Trans.
✓ Parking	Food Serv.	✓ Handicapped

The annual Bug Day is a popular, all-ages, family event with a bug show, exhibits, bug bingo, and other buggy games.

Cleveland National Air Show

AGES:	1½–3	3–5	5–8	8–12	12–15
RATING:	NR	NR	★★	★★	★★

COST: **$$** PREP.: **Some**
AREA: **Downtown** CITY: **Cleveland**

ADDRESS: Burke Lakefront Airport

PHONE: (216) 781-0747

SEASON: Seasonal September (Labor Day Weekend)

HOURS: Sat–Mon

PRICES: $8–17; 5 & under free

DIRECT.: I-90 to SR 2; west on SR 2 to E. 9 St.; north on E. 9; right (east) on N. Marginal Dr.; on left.

WEB: www.clevelandairshow.com

✓ Strollers	✓ Groups	✓ Food Nearby
Diap Chg	✓ Picnic	✓ Pub. Trans.
✓ Parking	✓ Food Serv.	Handicapped

The National Air Show at Burke Lakefront Airport has five-hour shows each day featuring precision-flying displays by groups such as the Blue Angels, Thunderbirds, or Golden Knights, and fly-bys of unusual and vintage aircraft. Many aircraft are parked and open to view, touch, and sometimes even sit in.

Elyria Apple Festival

AGES:	1½–3	3–5	5–8	8–12	12–15
RATING:	★	★★	★★	★	★

COST: **FREE** PREP.: **Some**
AREA: **Far West** CITY: **Elyria**

ADDRESS: Elyria Park, Elyria Square

PHONE: (440) 324-2000

SEASON: Seasonal September

HOURS: Fri 11 a.m.–9 p.m.; Sat–Sun 10 a.m.–9 p.m.

PRICES: Free

DIRECT.: I-90 to Exit 145 for SR 57 (Lorain Blvd.); south on SR 57 (Lorain Blvd.); left (east) on Lake Ave. to Broad St.; west on Broad St.; on left.

✓ Strollers	Groups	✓ Food Nearby
Diap Chg	✓ Picnic	Pub. Trans.
✓ Parking	✓ Food Serv.	Handicapped

Hay mazes, hayrides, food, two stages with live entertainment, and a crafts fair are part of the fun at the annual Apple Butter Festival in Elyria.

Geauga County Fair

AGES:	1½–3	3–5	5–8	8–12	12–15
RATING:	★	★★	★★	★★	★★

COST: **$–$$** PREP.: **Some**
AREA: **Far East** CITY: **Burton**

ADDRESS: Geauga County Fairgrounds, 14373 N. Cheshire St.

PHONE: (440) 834-1846

SEASON: Seasonal September (Labor Day Weekend)

HOURS: Vary

PRICES: Vary

DIRECT.: I-271 to Exit 29 for SR 87 (Chagrin Blvd); east on SR 87 to Burton; right (south) on Park Ave. (around the square) to N. Cheshire St.; on right.

WEB: www.tourgeauga.com

✓ Strollers	✓ Groups	✓ Food Nearby
✓ Diap Chg	✓ Picnic	Pub. Trans.
✓ Parking	✓ Food Serv.	✓ Handicapped

With the distinction of being the area's largest, the Geauga County Fair in Burton includes a heritage village of craft demonstrations, country music, a frog-jumping contest, and hot air balloons.

Other fairs this month:

Cuyahoga Co. Fair, Berea (440) 243-0090
Ashtabula Co. Fair, Jefferson (440) 576-7626
Lorain Co. Fair, Wellington (440) 647-2781
Lake Co. Fair, Painesville (440) 354-3339
Medina Co. Fair, Medina (330) 723-9633
Summit Co. Fair, Tallmadge (330) 633-6200

Geneva Area Grape Jamboree

AGES:	1½–3	3–5	5–8	8–12	12–15
RATING:	NR	★	★	★	★

COST: **FREE** PREP.: **Some**
AREA: **Farther East** CITY: **Geneva**

ADDRESS: Downtown Geneva

PHONE: (440) 466-JAMB

SEASON: Seasonal September

HOURS: Sat 10 a.m.–9 p.m.; Sun 11 a.m.–8 p.m.

PRICES: Free

DIRECT.: I-90 to SR 534; north on SR 534 to Geneva.

WEB: www.ashtabula.net/accvb

✓ Strollers | Groups | ✓ Food Nearby | Diap Chg | ✓ Picnic | Pub. Trans. | ✓ Parking | ✓ Food Serv. | ✓ Handicapped

The Geneva Area Grape Jamboree in downtown Geneva celebrates the grape harvest with grape tasting, grape-juice making, parades, food, and rides.

Melon Festival

AGES:	1½–3	3–5	5–8	8–12	12–15
RATING:	★	★★	★★	★★	★

COST: **FREE** PREP.: **Some**
AREA: **Far West** CITY: **Milan**

ADDRESS: Village Square

PHONE: (419) 499-2766

SEASON: Seasonal September

HOURS: Sat 10 a.m.–11 p.m.; Sun noon–11 p.m.; Mon 10 a.m.–10 p.m.

PRICES: Free

DIRECT.: I-80/I-90 to Exit 7 for US 250; south on US 250 to Milan; left (east) on Church St. to Village Square.

✓ Strollers | Groups | ✓ Food Nearby | Diap Chg | ✓ Picnic | Pub. Trans. | ✓ Parking | ✓ Food Serv. | ✓ Handicapped

If you've never had melon ice cream before, check out the annual Melon Festival in Milan. This harvest celebration includes entertainment, a parade, and ice cream, of course!

Pioneer Days Festival

Vermilion River Reservation

AGES:	1½–3	3–5	5–8	8–12	12–15
RATING:	NR	★★	★★	★	★

COST: **FREE** PREP.: **Some**
AREA: **Far West** CITY: **Brownhelm Twp.**

ADDRESS: N. Ridge and Vermilion Rds.

PHONE: (440) 458-5121

SEASON: Seasonal September

HOURS: Fri–Sun

PRICES: Free

DIRECT.: I-90 to SR 2; west on SR 2 to Baumhart Rd.; south on Baumhart Rd.; right (west) on North Ridge Rd.; Reservation at Vermilion Rd.

✓ Strollers | ✓ Groups | ✓ Food Nearby | ✓ Diap Chg | ✓ Picnic | Pub. Trans. | ✓ Parking | ✓ Food Serv. | ✓ Handicapped

The Pioneer Days Festival at Lorain County Metroparks' Vermilion River Reservation celebrates our past with crafts, music, and hands-on activities for children.

Renaissance Fayre and Giant Puppet Parade

Baycrafters

AGES:	1½–3	3–5	5–8	8–12	12–15
RATING:	★★	★★	★★★	★★★	★★

COST: **$** PREP.: **Some**
AREA: **West** CITY: **Bay Village**

ADDRESS: 28795 Lake Rd.

PHONE: (440) 871-5678

SEASON: Seasonal September (Labor Day Weekend)

HOURS: Sat–Mon

PRICES: $5

DIRECT.: I-90 to Exit 156 for Crocker Rd./Bassett Rd.; north on Crocker (becomes Bassett); right on Lake Rd.; on right.

Strollers | ✓ Groups | ✓ Food Nearby | Diap Chg | ✓ Picnic | ✓ Pub. Trans. | ✓ Parking | ✓ Food Serv. | ✓ Handicapped

This annual festival at Baycrafters in the Cleveland Metroparks Huntington Reservation features arts, music, jesters, jugglers, and puppets.

Festivals & Events DIRECTORY

▼ OCTOBER ▼

Apple Butter Festival

Century Village

AGES:	1½–3	3–5	5–8	8–12	12–15
RATING:	NR	★★	★★	★★	★

COST: **FREE** PREP.: **Some**
AREA: **Far East** CITY: **Burton**

ADDRESS: 14653 E. Park St.

PHONE: (440) 834-4012

SEASON: Seasonal October

HOURS: Fri–Sun 10 a.m.–5 p.m.

PRICES: Free

DIRECT.: I-271 to Exit 29 for Chagrin Blvd.; east on Chagrin; east on SR 87.

Or, US 422 to SR 700; north on SR 700; left (northeast) on SR 168 (Tavern Rd.).

✓ Strollers ✓ Groups ✓ Food Nearby
✓ Diap Chg ✓ Picnic ✓ Pub. Trans.
✓ Parking ✓ Food Serv. ✓ Handicapped

The Apple Butter Festival includes apple butter simmering in kettles over an outside fire, fritters to eat, and cider to drink.

Boo at the Zoo

Cleveland Metroparks Zoo

AGES:	1½–3	3–5	5–8	8–12	12–15
RATING:	NR	★	★★	★★	★

COST: **$** PREP.: **Some**
AREA: **South** CITY: **Cleveland**

ADDRESS: 3900 Wildlife Way

PHONE: (216) 661-6500

SEASON: Seasonal October

HOURS: Week-long 5:30 p.m.–9 p.m.

PRICES: $2

DIRECT.: I-71 to Exit 245 for Fulton Rd.; south on Fulton; right (east) on Brookside Park Dr.; on left.

Or, I-480 to Exit 16 for SR 94 (State Rd.); north on State; right (north) on Pearl Rd.; left (west) on Brookside Park Dr.; on right.

WEB: www.clemetzoo.com

✓ Strollers ✓ Groups ✓ Food Nearby
✓ Diap Chg ✓ Picnic ✓ Pub. Trans.
✓ Parking ✓ Food Serv. ✓ Handicapped

For Halloween fun, check out the annual Boo at the Zoo at the Cleveland Metroparks Zoo, with costume parades, treats, clowns, and face painting with safe and scary fun. The Akron Zoo holds a similar event.

Civil War Reenactment

Lake Co. Historical Society & History Ctr.

AGES:	1½–3	3–5	5–8	8–12	12–15
RATING:	NR	★	★★	★★	★★

COST: **$** PREP.: **Some**
AREA: **Far East** CITY: **Kirtland Hills**

ADDRESS: 8610 King Memorial Rd.

PHONE: (440) 255-8979

SEASON: Seasonal October

HOURS: Sat–Sun

PRICES: $5

DIRECT.: I-90 to Exit 190 for SR 306; north on SR 306; right (east) on SR 84; right (south) on Little Mountain Rd.; right (south) on Mentor Rd.; on right.

WEB: www.lakevisit.com

✓ Strollers ✓ Groups ✓ Food Nearby
✓ Diap Chg ✓ Picnic Pub. Trans.
✓ Parking Food Serv. ✓ Handicapped

In September hundreds of Civil War reenactors gather for the largest Civil War encampment and battle reenactment in Northeast Ohio.

Covered Bridge Festival

AGES:	1½–3	3–5	5–8	8–12	12–15
RATING:	NR	★★	★★	★★	★★

COST: **$** PREP.: **Some**
AREA: **Farther East** CITY: **Ashtabula**

ADDRESS: 25 W. Jefferson St.

PHONE: (440) 576-3769

SEASON: Seasonal October

HOURS: 8 a.m.–6 p.m.

PRICES: $2 adults, 12 and under free

DIRECT.: I-90 to SR 11; south on SR 11 to SR 46; south on SR 46; right on W. Jefferson St.

WEB: www.ashtabula.net/accvb

Strollers	Groups	✓ Food Nearby
Diap Chg	✓ Picnic	Pub. Trans.
✓ Parking	✓ Food Serv.	Handicapped

Did you know there are more covered bridges in Ashtabula County than in any other county in Ohio? Check out all 15 of them at the Annual Ashtabula Covered Bridge Festival. With the tour as an excuse, the county fairgrounds hosts a craft show, farmer's market, and parade. If it's just the bridges you're looking for, tour maps are available at 25 West Jefferson St.

Fall Festival Family Fun Day

Lake Erie Nature and Science Center

AGES:	1½–3	3–5	5–8	8–12	12–15
RATING:	★	★★★	★★★	★★	★

COST: **FREE** PREP.: **Some**
AREA: **West** CITY: **Bay Village**

ADDRESS: 28728 Wolf Rd.

PHONE: (440) 871-2900

SEASON: Seasonal October

HOURS: Sat

PRICES: Free

DIRECT.: I-90 to Exit 159 for SR 252 (Columbia Rd); north on Columbia; left (west) on Wolf Rd., on right.

WEB: www.bbs2.rmrc.net/~/lensc/

✓ Strollers	✓ Groups	✓ Food Nearby
Diap Chg	✓ Picnic	✓ Pub. Trans.
✓ Parking	Food Serv.	✓ Handicapped

This Fun Day at the Lake Erie Nature and Science Center offers a hands-on afternoon filled with crafts, pumpkin decorating, and games.

Harvest Fest

Hale Farm and Village

AGES:	1½–3	3–5	5–8	8–12	12–15
RATING:	★	★★	★★	★★	★★

COST: **$–$$** PREP.: **Some**
AREA: **Far South** CITY: **Bath**

ADDRESS: 2686 Oak Hill Rd.

PHONE: (800) 589-9703

SEASON: Seasonal October

HOURS: Sat–Sun

PRICES: $9 adult, $5.50 child, 5 and under free

DIRECT.: I-77 to Exit 143 for Richfield; west on Wheatley Rd.; left (south) on Brecksville Rd.(becomes Cleveland-Massillon Rd.); left (east) on Ira Rd.; left (north) on Oak Hill Rd.; on left.

WEB: www.whrs.org

✓ Strollers	✓ Groups	Food Nearby
✓ Diap Chg	✓ Picnic	Pub. Trans.
✓ Parking	✓ Food Serv.	Handicapped

Demonstrations of butter churning, cider pressing, soap making and cooking with hands-on participation and sampling are part of this annual festival. Square dancing and hay rides are also part of the fun.

Woolly Bear Festival

AGES:	1½–3	3–5	5–8	8–12	12–15
RATING:	★★	★★	★★	★	★

COST: **FREE–$$** PREP.: **Some**
AREA: **Far West** CITY: **Vermilion**

ADDRESS: Downtown Vermilion

PHONE: (440) 967-4477

SEASON: Seasonal October

HOURS: Sat 9 a.m.–6 p.m.

PRICES: Free; fees for some activities

DIRECT.: I-90 to SR 2; west on SR 2 to SR 60 (Savannah Vermilion Rd.; north on SR 60 to downtown Vermilion.

✓ Strollers	Groups	✓ Food Nearby
Diap Chg	✓ Picnic	Pub. Trans.
✓ Parking	✓ Food Serv.	✓ Handicapped

The city of Vermilion traditionally hosts the Woolly Bear Fest to forecast the length of the coming winter. It features a parade, a woolly bear (fat caterpillar) costume contest, food, games, rides, and entertainment.

▼ NOVEMBER ▼

Family Day

Western Reserve Historical Society

AGES:	1½–3	3–5	5–8	8–12	12–15
RATING:	★	★	★★	★★	★★

COST: **$** PREP.: **Some**
AREA: **Near East** CITY: **Cleveland**

ADDRESS: 10825 East Blvd.
PHONE: (216) 751-5722
SEASON: Seasonal November
HOURS: Fri–Sun
PRICES: Vary
DIRECT.: East: I-90 to Exit 177 for Martin Luther King Blvd.; south on MLK; right (east) on East Blvd.; on left.
West: I-90 to Exit 173B for Chester Ave.; east on Chester; left (east) on Euclid Ave.; left (north) on East Blvd.; on right after Hazel Dr.
WEB: www.whrs.org

✓ Strollers ✓ Groups ✓ Food Nearby
Diap Chg ✓ Picnic ✓ Pub. Trans.
✓ Parking ✓ Food Serv. ✓ Handicapped

Family Day at the Western Reserve Historical Society, held Thanksgiving Weekend, showcases the Society's exhibits with craft demonstrations, entertainment, workshops, and children's activities.

Thanksgiving Day Parade

AGES:	1½–3	3–5	5–8	8–12	12–15
RATING:	NR	★	★	★	★

COST: **FREE** PREP.: **Some**
AREA: **Downtown** CITY: **Cleveland**

ADDRESS: Downtown Cleveland
PHONE: (216) 621-3300
SEASON: Seasonal November
HOURS: Sat
PRICES: Free
DIRECT.: East: I-90 to SR 2; west on SR 2 to E. 9 St.; south on E. 9 St.; right (west) on Superior Ave.
West: I-90 to Exit 171 for Ontario St.; right (east) on Superior Ave.

✓ Strollers Groups ✓ Food Nearby
Diap Chg Picnic ✓ Pub. Trans.
✓ Parking Food Serv. ✓ Handicapped

The annual Thanksgiving Day Parade downtown is followed by the official holiday lighting of Public Square.

▼ DECEMBER ▼

Christmas on the Western Reserve

Lake Co. Historical Society & History Ctr.

AGES:	1½–3	3–5	5–8	8–12	12–15
RATING:	NR	★	★★	★★	★★

COST: **$** PREP.: **Some**
AREA: **Far East** CITY: **Kirtland Hills**

ADDRESS: 8610 King Memorial Rd.
PHONE: (440) 255-8979
SEASON: Seasonal December
HOURS: Vary
PRICES: Vary
DIRECT.: I-90 to Exit 190 for SR 306; north on SR 306; right (east) on SR 84; right (south) on Little Mountain Rd.; right (south) on Mentor Rd.; on right.

✓ Strollers ✓ Groups ✓ Food Nearby
✓ Diap Chg ✓ Picnic Pub. Trans.
✓ Parking Food Serv. ✓ Handicapped

Christmas on the Western Reserve, with the staff aided by high-school volunteers, offers a day of crafts and cookies for ages 5–12.

Family New Year's Eve Party

Cuyahoga Valley National Recreation Area

AGES:	1½–3	3–5	5–8	8–12	12–15
RATING:	NR	★	★★	★★	★★

COST: $ PREP.: Some
AREA: South CITY: Peninsula

ADDRESS: Happy Days Visitor Center, SR 303
PHONE: (330) 650-4636
SEASON: Seasonal December
HOURS: New Year's Eve, 8:30 p.m.–midnight
PRICES: $5; $1 children 12 and under.
DIRECT.: I-90 to Exit 189 for SR 91 (SOM Center Rd.); south on SR 91; left (east) on US 6 (Chardon Rd.); left (north) on SR 174 (Chagrin River Rd.); right (east) on Skyline Dr.
WEB: www.nps.gov/cvnra

✓ Strollers ✓ Groups ✓ Food Nearby
Diap Chg ✓ Picnic Pub.Trans.
✓ Parking Food Serv. ✓ Handicapped

A quiet celebration for families, this alternative New Year's Eve includes storytelling, music, dancing, and star-gazing.

First Night, Akron

AGES:	1½–3	3–5	5–8	8–12	12–15
RATING:	NR	NR	★	★★	★★

COST: $$ PREP.: Some
AREA: Far South CITY: Akron

ADDRESS: Downtown Akron
PHONE: 330-762-9550
SEASON: Seasonal December
HOURS: New Year's Eve 5 p.m.–midnight
PRICES: $10
DIRECT.: I-77 to Exit 22 for Broadway; north on Broadway; right (east) on Bowery St. to Quaker Square.

Strollers Groups ✓ Food Nearby
Diap Chg Picnic ✓ Pub.Trans.
✓ Parking ✓ Food Serv. ✓ Handicapped

A New Year's Eve party for all ages with activities beginning at 5 p.m. and ending (with fireworks) at midnight. The first, held in 1996, took place in several locations around downtown. It brought together short performances by the Akron Symphony Orchestra and the Ohio Ballet, and included mimes, jugglers, and ice-carving. Tickets required (one price includes the entire evening).

First Night, North Ridgeville

AGES:	1½–3	3–5	5–8	8–12	12–15
RATING:	NR	NR	★	★★	★★

COST: $ PREP.: Some
AREA: West CITY: North Ridgeville

ADDRESS: Downtown North Ridgeville
PHONE: (440) 327-3737
SEASON: Seasonal December
HOURS: New Year's Eve, 7 p.m.–midnight
PRICES: $5
DIRECT.: I-90 to Exit 153 for SR 83 (Avon Center Rd.); south on SR 83 (Avon Center Rd.) to North Ridgeville.

Strollers Groups ✓ Food Nearby
Diap Chg Picnic Pub.Trans.
✓ Parking ✓ Food Serv. Handicapped

First Night, an annual celebration of New Year's Eve for families, is celebrated in North Ridgeville with music, dance, fireworks, and comedy along Center Ridge Rd.

Holiday Circlefest

AGES:	1½–3	3–5	5–8	8–12	12–15
RATING:	★	★★	★★	★★★	★★

COST: FREE PREP.: Some
AREA: East CITY: Cleveland

ADDRESS: University Circle
PHONE: (216) 791-3900
SEASON: Seasonal December
HOURS: Wed. 5 p.m.–9 p.m.

PRICES: Free

DIRECT.: I-90 to Exit 177 for Martin Luther King Blvd.; south on MLK to University Circle.

✓ Strollers	Groups	✓ Food Nearby
✓ Diap Chg	Picnic	✓ Pub. Trans.
✓ Parking	✓ Food Serv.	✓ Handicapped

Annual Holiday Open House including a number of the institutions in the Circle. Sidewalks are candle-lit; activities, music and treats are all offered free—including admission to the museums.

Nela Park Holiday Lights Display

GE Lighting

AGES:	1½–3	3–5	5–8	8–12	12–15
RATING:	★★★	★★★	★★★	★★	★★

COST: **FREE** PREP.: **Some**
AREA: **Near East** CITY: **Cleveland**

ADDRESS: GE Lighting, Nela Park, 1975 Noble Rd.

PHONE: (216) 266-2121

SEASON: Seasonal December

HOURS: Dusk–dawn

PRICES: Free

DIRECT.: I-90 to Exit 178 for Eddy Rd.; south on Eddy Rd. to Kirby Ave.; east on Kirby Ave.; right (south) on Coit Rd.; left (east) on Noble Rd.; on left.

Strollers	Groups	✓ Food Nearby
Diap Chg	Picnic	Pub. Trans.
Parking	Food Serv.	Handicapped

GE's lighting display at its Nela Park world headquarters is turned on at the 1975 Noble Road property. For seven decades this display has been the area's largest, featuring thousands of lights over several acres, with a replica of the National Christmas Tree as its centerpiece.

Winter Solstice Celebration

Swine Creek Reservation

AGES:	1½–3	3–5	5–8	8–12	12–15
RATING:	NR	★	★	★★	★★

COST: **FREE** PREP.: **Some**
AREA: **Far East** CITY: **Middlefield Twp.**

ADDRESS: 16004 Hayes Rd.

PHONE: (440) 286-9504

SEASON: Seasonal December

HOURS: Dawn

PRICES: Free

DIRECT.: US 422 to SR 528 (Madison Rd.) at Parkman; north on SR 528; at SR 608, right (east) on Swine Creek Rd.; left on Hayes Rd.; on left.

✓ Strollers	✓ Groups	✓ Food Nearby
✓ Diap Chg	✓ Picnic	Pub. Trans.
✓ Parking	Food Serv.	✓ Handicapped

A formal winter solstice celebration at the Swine Creek Reservation of the Geauga Park District includes a candlelight evening walk. Other parks that celebrate the annual event include Cleveland Metroparks and the Nature Center at Shaker Lakes.

Section 3

Indexes

Alphabetical Index

Alphabetical Index (continued)

INDEXES

Alphabetical Index (continued)

Geographical Index

Farther East

Near West

West

Far West

Geographical Index (continued)

Geographical Index (continued)

INDEXES

Activity Index

INDEXES

Activity Index (continued)

INDEXES

Activity Index (continued)

Activity Index (continued)

INDEXES

Activity Index (continued)

Age Index

The attractions in this index are rated in the Directory section as **Good** or **Ideal** for the age range under which they are listed here. I have sorted them by type of interest and also included the **Area** in which they are located and the estimated **Cost** range.

D	Downtown	*NrW*	Near West	*FS*	Far South	Cost is rated on a per-person basis
NrE	Near East	*W*	West	*FrS*	Farther South	**$** = under $6
E	East	*FW*	Far West	*SE*	Southeast	**$$** = under $12
FE	Far East	*FrW*	Farther West	*SW*	Southwest	**$$$** = over $12
FrE	Farther East	*S*	South			

Ages 1½–3

INDEXES

Sports & Recreation

Group Tours

Neighborhood Resources

Festivals & Events

Ages 3–5

Fun & Games

History, Science, Technology

Nature & Outdoors

INDEXES

Age Index (continued)

Art, Music, Theater, Dance

Sports & Recreation

INDEXES

Age Index (continued)

Ages 5-8

INDEXES

Age Index (continued)

Art, Music, Theater, Dance

Sports & Recreation

INDEXES

Age Index (continued)

Spectator Sports

Group Tours

Neighborhood Resources

Festivals & Events

Ages 8–11

Fun & Games

History, Science, Technology

INDEXES

Age Index (continued)

Nature & Outdoors

INDEXES

Age Index (continued)

Art, Music, Theater, Dance

Sports & Recreation

Age Index (continued)

INDEXES

Age Index (continued)

Ages 11–13

Fun & Games

History, Science, Technology

Nature & Outdoors

Age Index (continued)

Art, Music, Theater, Dance

Sports & Recreation

Age Index (continued)

Spectator Sports

Group Tours

Neighborhood Resources

Festivals & Events

INDEXES

Map Index

(See next page for start of listing)

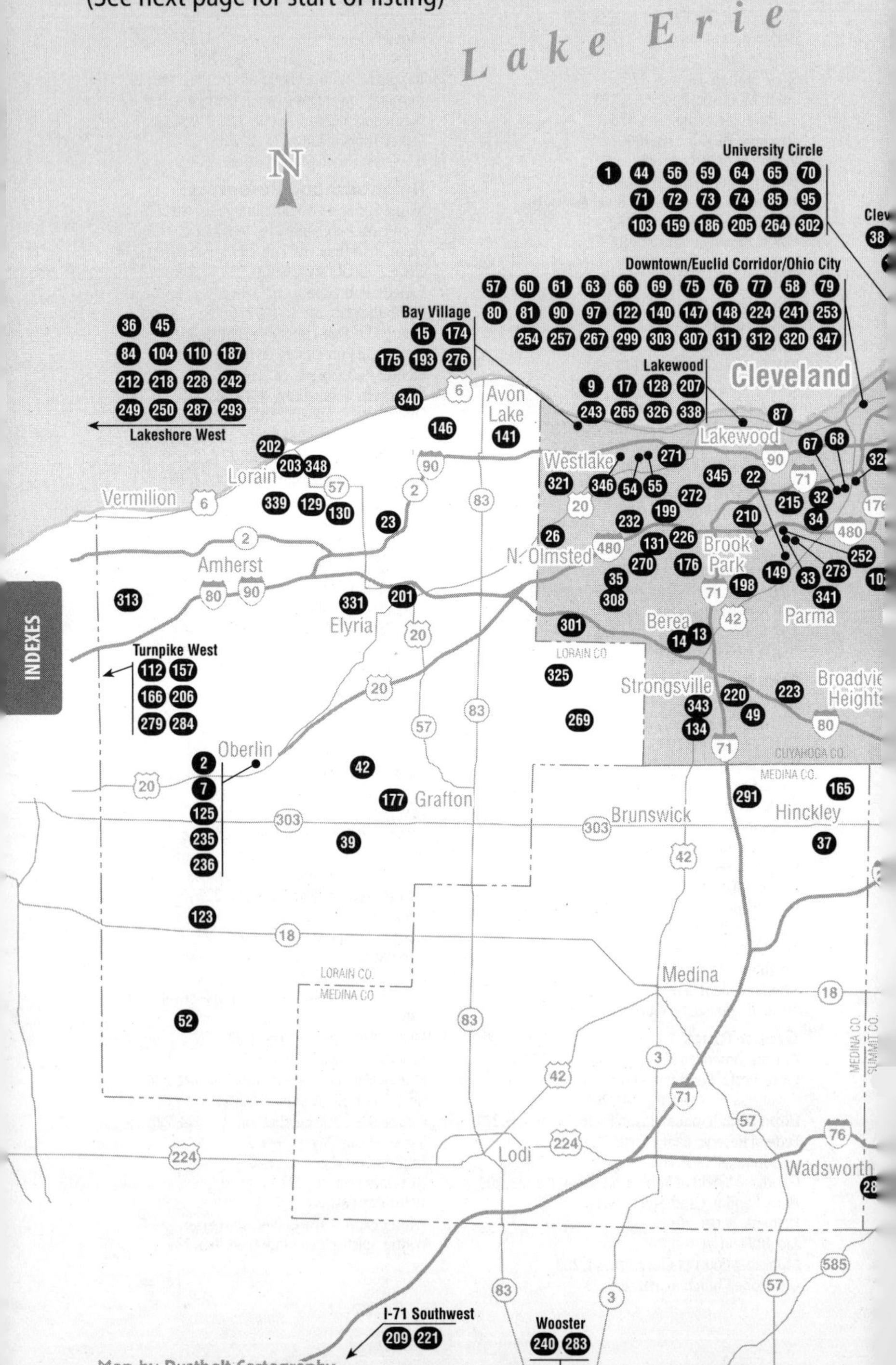

Lake Erie

N

University Circle
1 44 56 59 64 65 70
71 72 73 74 85 95
103 159 186 205 264 302

Downtown/Euclid Corridor/Ohio City
57 60 61 63 66 69 75 76 77 58 79
80 81 90 97 122 140 147 148 224 241 253
254 257 267 299 303 307 311 312 320 347

Bay Village
15 174
175 193 276

Lakewood
9 17 128 207
243 265 326 338

Lakeshore West
36 45
84 104 110 187
212 218 228 242
249 250 287 293

Turnpike West
112 157
166 206
279 284

I-71 Southwest
209 221

Wooster
240 283

Cleveland
Lakewood
Westlake
Avon Lake
Lorain
Vermilion
Amherst
Elyria
N. Olmsted
Brook Park
Parma
Berea
Strongsville
Broadview Heights
Oberlin
Grafton
Brunswick
Hinckley
Medina
Lodi
Wadsworth

LORAIN CO.
CUYAHOGA CO.
MEDINA CO.
SUMMIT CO.

340 146 141 202 203 348 339 129 130 23 313 331 201 2 7 125 235 236 123 52 42 177 39 301 325 269 26 321 346 54 55 271 345 22 272 199 232 131 226 270 176 35 308 210 215 32 34 67 68 87 149 33 273 252 341 198 14 13 343 134 220 49 223 291 165 37 38

Map by Rustbelt Cartography

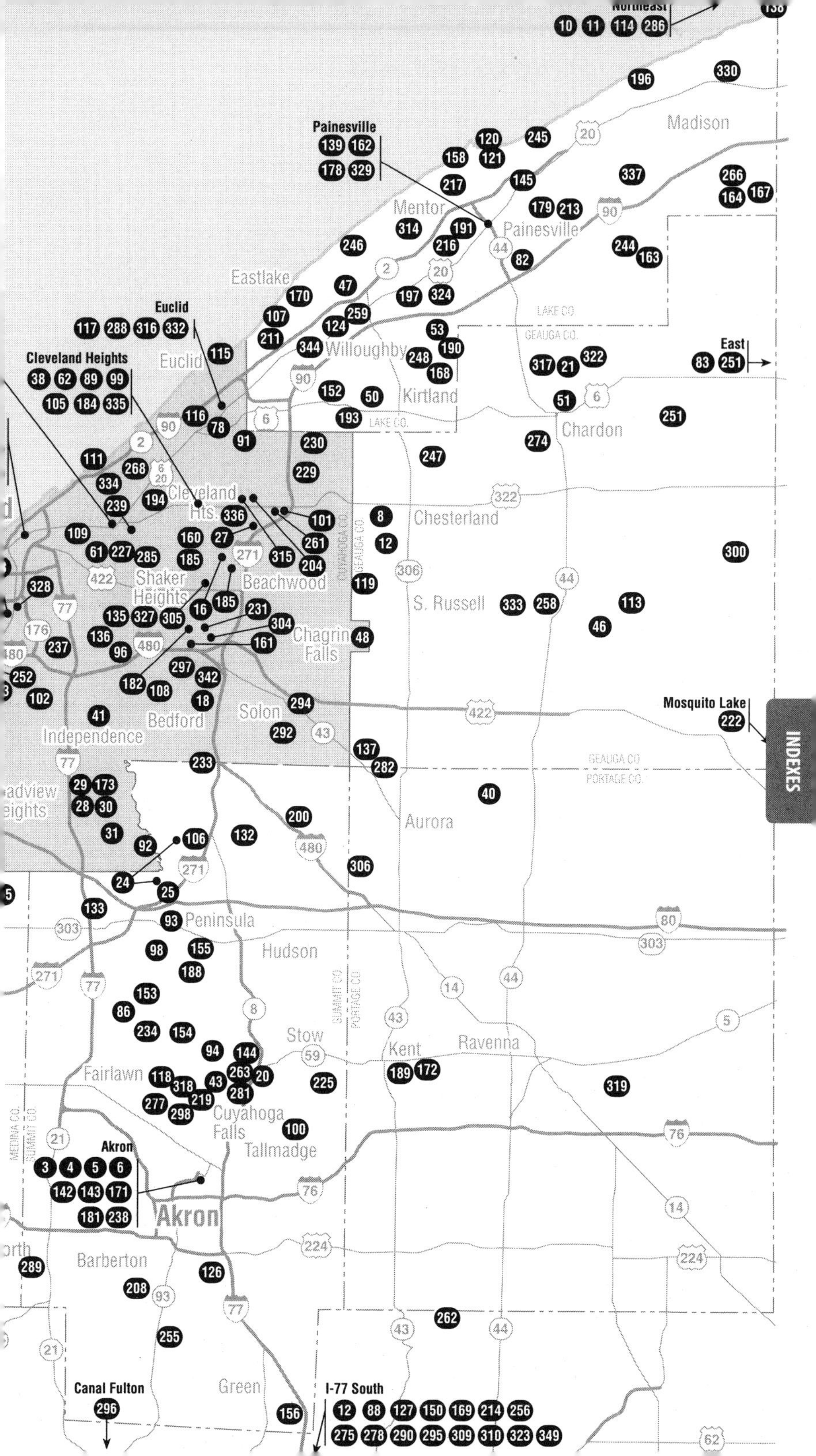

Northeast
10 11 114 286
Painesville
139 162 178 329
Euclid
117 288 316 332
Cleveland Heights
38 62 89 99 105 184 335
East
83 251
Mosquito Lake
222
Akron
3 4 5 6 142 143 171 181 238
Canal Fulton
296
I-77 South
12 88 127 150 169 214 256 275 278 290 295 309 310 323 349
Madison
Mentor
Painesville
Eastlake
Willoughby
Kirtland
Euclid
Chardon
Cleveland Hts.
Chesterland
Shaker Heights
Beachwood
S. Russell
Chagrin Falls
Solon
Bedford
Independence
Aurora
Peninsula
Hudson
Stow
Kent
Ravenna
Fairlawn
Cuyahoga Falls
Tallmadge
Akron
Barberton
Green
LAKE CO
GEAUGA CO.
CUYAHOGA CO.
PORTAGE CO.
SUMMIT CO.
MEDINA CO.
INDEXES

Map Index (continued)

INDEXES

Map Index (continued)

Map Index (continued)

Notes

- Young's Dairy Farm
  Yellow Springs, OH
  www.youngsdairy.com
- Freshwater Farms of Ohio Urbana, OH 43078
  www.fwfarms.com
- www.HockingHillspark.com
  caves, falls, streams, cliffs
- www.OhioTraveler.com
- www.visitamish-country.com 1-866-ohio-866
  www.holmescountychamber.com
- www.fpubs.com/oac/index.html
- Jungle Jim's International Farmers Market
  Fairfield, OH 45014 www.junglejims.com
- www.middlefieldcheese.com
- www.rossipasta.com Marietta, OH
- www.ransbottompottery.com
  Roseville, 43777
- Quaker oats Akron
  www.quakersquare.com
- Popcorn Gallery Lima, OH
  419-227-2676 call ahead